Internal Communication and Employee Engagement

This book aims to explore the connection between internal communication and employee engagement in both educational and business settings. Through the collection of chapters contributed by leading public relations, communication, and management scholars as well as seasoned practitioners, readers will gain new insights into current issues in internal communication and employee engagement through a series of real-world case studies analyzing current issues and offering the best practices in internal communication and employee engagement in specific industry and organization settings.

Learning outcomes and discussion questions for both classroom use and business strategizing round out each chapter, providing a springboard to further inquiry, research, and initiative development in these intricately intertwined areas so crucial to employee satisfaction and organizational success. This makes *Internal Communication and Employee Engagement* an ideal resource for the intended audience of Business and Management scholars and students, internal communication managers, and organizational leaders.

Nance McCown (Ph.D., University of Maryland) is a professor of communication at Messiah University. Her research focuses on the confluence of internal public relations/employee communication, workplace culture, and leadership style and its effects on employee engagement. She also conducts research related to narrative and internal public relations. McCown has presented at numerous conferences, garnering several top paper awards from the Public Relations Society of America's Educators Academy. She has published in leading refereed journals, including the *Journal of Public Relations Research*, *PRism Journal*, and the *Journal of Communication and Religion*, and also contributed a book chapter to *Social Media and Crisis Communication* (Austin & Jin, Eds.,

2017, Routledge). McCown is the recipient of both the Messiah University Robert & Marilyn Smith Outstanding Teaching Award and the Pennsylvania Public Relations Society's Ernest R. McDowell Award for Excellence in Public Relations.

Linjuan Rita Men (Ph.D., University of Miami; APR) is a professor of public relations at the University of Florida. Her research interests include internal communication, leadership communication, social media, and entrepreneurial communication. Men has published over 80 articles in leading refereed journals, such as *Communication Research, New Media and Society, Journal of Public Relations Research, Management Communication Quarterly*, among others, and as book chapters. She is the lead author/editor of three books, *Excellence in Internal Communication Management* published by Business Expert Press in 2017, *Strategic Communication for Startups and Entrepreneurs in China* by Routledge in 2020, and *Current Trends and Issues in Internal Communication: Theory and Practice* by Palgrave Macmillan in 2021. Men is the 2022 recipient of the Krieghbaum Under-40 Award from the Association for Education in Journalism and Mass Communication.

Hua Jiang (Ph.D., University of Maryland) is an associate professor in the public relations department of the Newhouse School, Syracuse University. Jiang's research expertise focuses on corporate communication practices and statistics consulting. Her primary research interests include employee communication, social media engagement, corporate social responsibility/corporate social/political advocacy, relationship/reputation management, and mental health campaigns. Jiang's work has appeared in leading refereed journals, such as *Journal of Public Relations Research, Communication Research, Public Relations Review, Journal of Applied Communication Research, Journal of Health Communication, Telematics and Informatics, Journal of Communication Management*, and *International Journal of Strategic Communication*, among others. Jiang was also a 2014 fellow of the Plank Center for Leadership in Public Relations and a 2017–2018 Arthur W. Page Center Legacy Scholar.

Hongmei Shen (Ph.D., University of Maryland; APR) is a professor and public relations emphasis head in the School of Journalism & Media Studies at the San Diego State University. She has published book chapters and articles on relationship management, conflict management, crisis communication, and health communication in a variety of top journals, such as *Journal of Public Relations Research, Journalism & Mass Communication Quarterly, Public Relations Review, Health Communication*, and *Journal of Health Communication*. Shen was the 2016 Associate Editor for the *Journal of Public Relations Research*.

Internal Communication and Employee Engagement

A Case Study Approach

Edited by
Nance McCown
Linjuan Rita Men
Hua Jiang
Hongmei Shen

LONDON AND NEW YORK

Designed cover image: © Getty Images

First published 2023
by Routledge
4 Park Square, Milton Park, Abingdon, Oxon OX14 4RN

and by Routledge
605 Third Avenue, New York, NY 10158

Routledge is an imprint of the Taylor & Francis Group, an informa business

British Library Cataloguing-in-Publication Data
A catalogue record for this book is available from the British Library

ISBN: 9781032050058 (hbk)
ISBN: 9781032050041 (pbk)
ISBN: 9781003195580 (ebk)

DOI: 10.4324/9781003195580

Typeset in Univers LT Std
by KnowledgeWorks Global Ltd.

Contents

Contributors

Callie Burnette (North Carolina State University) is a second-year master's of communication student and teaching assistant at North Carolina State University. She uses her work expertise in delivering high-impact communications and marketing as a global marketing intern for industrial automation at Schneider Electric. Her current research and studies are focused on crisis communication, public relations, and public administration.

Alfonsa Butera (Università IULM) is adjunct professor of Corporate Communication and head of Coordination and Researcher of the Centre for Employee Relations and Communication, operating at the department of business, law, economics and consumer behaviour "Carlo A. Ricciardi." She is a freelance consultant in the field of corporate communication, dealing with the communication activities of B2B and B2C customers. Her main research interests are employee communication and engagement; internal crisis communication; organizational voice, silence, and dissent; and media relations.

Yi-Ru Regina Chen (Ph.D., University of Maryland) is an associate professor and department co-chair at Hong Kong Baptist University. Her research areas include strategic communication, social media engagement and gamification, CSR, and creating shared values. She received the Hong Kong General Research Grant and the ICA Public Relation Division's Robert Heath Award.

Yang Cheng (Ph.D., Missouri School of Journalism, University of Missouri-Columbia) is an associate professor in the department of communication at North Carolina State University. She has published more than 70 journal articles and book chapters on social media and crisis communication.

Sara Conti (Università IULM) is a Ph.D. candidate in the communication, markets and society program at the Università IULM Doctoral School. She is also research assistant at the Centre for Employee Relations and Communication, operating at the department of business, law, economics and consumer behaviour "Carlo A. Ricciardi." Her main research interests are organizational voice, silence, and dissent; whistleblowing; and newcomers onboarding in hybrid working contexts.

Chuqing Dong (Ph.D., University of Minnesota—Twin Cities) is an assistant professor of advertising and public relations at Michigan State University. Her research focuses on public relations, corporate social responsibility, ethics of care, and digital media. Chuqing's work has been published in flagship journals in the field of public relations, and she was selected as a Page/Johnson Legacy Scholar in 2021.

Cheng Hong (Ph.D., University of Miami) is an assistant professor of public relations in the department of communication studies at California State University Sacramento. Her research areas include corporate social advocacy, brand activism, consumer boycott and buycott behavior, and DEI communication. She has published in several journals including *Journalism & Mass Communication Quarterly, Journal of Public Relations Research, Public Relations Review, Journal of Advertising,* and *Mass Communication and Society,* among others.

Chun-Ju Flora Hung-Baesecke (Ph.D., University of Maryland) is senior lecturer in the School of Communication at University of Technology Sydney, Australia. Her research interests focus on corporate social responsibility, stakeholder engagement, social media, and relationship management. She has published in peer-reviewed journals and won several faculty top paper awards at international conferences, such as the International Communication Association.

Jie Jin (University of Florida) is a Ph.D. student in the department of public relations at the University of Florida. She is also a research editor at the Institute for Public Relations' Organizational Communication Research Center. Her main research interests focus on activism, employee communication, and leadership communication. Her publications have appeared in *Journalism and Mass Communication Quarterly, Public Relations Review,* and *International Journal of Business Communication.*

Conilyn Poulsen Judge (Ph.D., Grand Canyon University) is the managing director and principal consultant of Eden communication strategies. A performance psychologist, she is internationally known for her work in change/internal communication, organizational culture, and executive presence, working primarily in the United States, Europe/U.K., and the Middle East. Her research areas include leader extraversion/introversion and the use of behavioral economics in organizational change initiatives.

Minjeong Kang (Ph.D. Syracuse University) is an associate professor and teaches strategic communication courses at the Media School, Indiana University. Her research interests primarily focus on understanding the concept of engagement in various stakeholder contexts such as member, employee, and volunteer relations and its positive impacts in eliciting supportive communication and behavioral outcomes. Dr. Kang's research has received several national and international recognitions.

Solyee Kim (Ph.D., University of Georgia) is a visiting lecturer at the University of Georgia. Her research focuses on identity, representation, and culture in public relations including DEI issues and experiences of marginalized communities. She has presented her research at national and international conferences including those hosted by AEJMC, EUPRERA, and ICA, and won several top paper awards from AEJMC.

Young Kim (Ph.D., Louisiana State University) is an associate professor of strategic communication at the J. William and Mary Diederich College of Communication at Marquette University. His research focuses on relationship and reputation management, especially crisis management and communication in the external and internal context of organizations. Dr. Kim has been a recipient of "the 2016 Most Downloaded Article" and "Top Cited Article 2020–2021" in *Journal of Public Relations Research*, "the 2019 Emerald Literati Awards (the 2019 Outstanding Paper)" in *Journal of Communication Management*, and more than ten top paper awards at national and international conferences.

Raymond L. Kotcher (M.Sci., Boston University) served as professor of the practice of public relations at Boston University's (BU) College of Communication (COM) from 2017 to 2022. Prior to that, he spent more than 30 years at Ketchum and, from 2000 to 2016, served as the agency's CEO and then chairman. In 2019, Ketchum was awarded Best Agency of the Past 20 Years by PRWeek. Ray is a recipient of the PRSA Gold Anvil, is a member of the Page Society Hall of Fame and is a distinguished alum of both Boston University and its College of Communication.

Arunima Krishna (Ph.D., Purdue University) is an assistant professor of public relations at Boston University's College of Communication. Her research focuses on understanding publics' perceptions of controversial social issues including anti-vaccine activism, climate change, and workplace gender discrimination. Her work has been published in premier communication journals such as *Communication Research*, *Journal of Applied Communication Research*, *Public Relations Review*, and the *Journal of Public Relations Research*. She serves on the editorial board for the *Journal of Public Relations Research* and *Health Communication*, and on the advisory committee for the International Public Relations Research Conference.

Jeonghyun Janice Lee (M.A., Ph.D. candidate, University of Georgia) is a graduate research assistant and instructor of the department of advertising & public relations at the University of Georgia. Her research focuses on leadership in communication and organizational crisis communication, as well as the affordances of new technologies for strategic communication practices. Recently, she published Readiness for Industry 4.0

in public relations: A conceptual framework of competencies for communication professionals in the workplace in *Journal of Communication Management* and co-authored a book chapter titled, *Vaccine Support and Hesitancy on Twitter: Opposing Views, Similar Strategies, and the Mixed Impact of Conspiracy Theories.*

Laura L. Lemon (Ph.D., University of Tennessee) is an assistant professor of public relations at The University of Alabama. Her award-winning research program focuses on theory building in internal public relations, with an emphasis on internal communication and employee engagement. Dr. Lemon specializes in qualitative methods to capture the lived experience of organizational members. Her work can be found in the top public relations journals including *Journal of Public Relations Research, Public Relations Review, Public Relations Inquiry,* and the *Public Relations Journal.*

Hyunji (Dana) Lim (Ph.D., University of Florida) is an assistant professor of critical corporate communication in the department of communication at the University of Wisconsin at Parkside. She is interested in researching crisis communication, reputation management, and international strategic communication. Her work is published in scholarly journals including *Journal of Contingencies and Crisis Management, Public Relations Review,* and *Asian Journal of Public Relations.* She has also taught a variety of conceptual and applied public relations courses, such as Principles of Public Relations, PR Strategy Development, PR Research, PR Writing, PR Campaigns, and International Public Relations and Crisis Communication Management.

Peiyao Liu (North Carolina State University) is a master's student in the department of communication at North Carolina State University. Her research interests focus on social media, crisis communication, and computer-mediated communication. She has worked as a public relations specialist and has rich experience in public relations and crisis communications.

Yi Luo (Ph.D., University of Maryland) is an associate professor and the graduate program coordinator in the School of Communication and Media at Montclair State University. Her research interests focus on organizational change, internal communication, employee engagement, communication leadership, social media management, crisis communication, and corporate social responsibility. Dr. Luo would like to thank Sharon Scalora, Assistant Vice President of Internal Communications at RWJBarnabas Health, and her team for their assistance and support to this research project.

Minqin Ma (Hong Kong Baptist University) is a Ph.D. candidate at Hong Kong Baptist University. Her research interests include corporate volunteering, internal communication, employee behavior, co-worker relationships, and employee-organization relationships. She has presented conference papers at the International Communication Association (ICA) and The International Association for Media and Communication Research (IAMCR).

Vibeke Thøis Madsen (Ph.D., Aarhus University) is a senior associate professor in strategic communication at DMJX, Danish School of Media and Journalism. Her research interests are focused on participatory communication on internal social media and how it influences internal communication, leadership, employee engagement, and organizational listening. Furthermore, she is interested in employees as strategic communicators and the many communication roles they enact. She has written articles about self-censorship, spirals of voice, and how employees construct organizational identity on internal social media.

Alessandra Mazzei (Università IULM) is associate professor of management and director of the Centre for Employee Relations and Communication. She is also deputy director of the department of business, law, economics and consumer behaviour "Carlo A. Ricciardi" and coordinator of the bachelor program in Corporate Communication and Public Relations. Her main research interests are corporate communication; employee communication and engagement; organizational voice, silence, and dissent; whistleblowing; diversity & inclusion; and internal crisis communication.

Nance McCown (Ph.D., University of Maryland) is a professor of communication at Messiah University. Her research focuses on the confluence of internal public relations/employee communication, workplace culture, and leadership style and its effects on employee engagement. She also conducts research related to narrative and internal public relations. McCown has presented at numerous conferences, garnering several top paper awards from the Public Relations Society of America's Educators Academy. She has published in leading refereed journals, including the *Journal of Public Relations Research, PRism Journal*, and the *Journal of Communication and Religion*, and also contributed a book chapter to *Social Media and Crisis Communication* (Austin & Jin, Eds., 2017, Routledge).

Feihong Pan (City University of Hong Kong) is a Ph.D. student in the media and communication department at City University of Hong Kong. Her research interests are in the public relations, management and human resources, and journalism fields. She has published two journal articles (one in SSCI and one in SCI) and a conference paper. Her work has also garnered the City University of Hong Kong's Top Research Case Award on Chinese Good Stories.

Keonyoung Park (Ph.D., Syracuse University) is an assistant professor in public relations in the Department of Communication Studies at Hong Kong Baptist University. Her research has explored diverse topics under the umbrella of corporate communications and advocacy communications in the era of new media; specific topics include corporate social responsibility (CSR), corporate social advocacy (CSA), technology application in activism, and social media advocacy ethics. Dr. Park's work has been published in the *International Journal of Business Communication, Journal of Marketing Communications, Journal of Promotion Management, Telematics & Informatics, Social Media and Society, International Journal of Nonprofit and Voluntary Sector Marketing,* and *Journal of Korean Society for Journalism & Communication Studies.*

Luca Quaratino (Università IULM) is an assistant professor of organization theory and behaviors. He is director of the master in communication & human resources and a member of the scientific committee and senior project leader of the Centre for Employee Relations and Communication, operating at the department of business, law, economics and consumer behaviour "Carlo A. Ricciardi." His main research interests are employee communication and engagement, organizational culture, people management and psychological contract, generation mix management, and adult learning.

Kevin Ruck (Ph.D., University of Central Lancashire, U.K.) is the co-founder of the PR Academy, the U.K.'s largest Chartered Institute of Public Relations (CIPR) accredited teaching center. His research is focused on the associations between internal communication and employee engagement, internal communication measurement and evaluation, leadership communication, and listening to employees.

Masamichi Shimizu is a corporate communication consultant in Tokyo, Japan, with extensive experience as both a practitioner and educator. After working for 25 years as a corporate PR professional, he joined Shukutoku University as a professor in corporate communication and environmental communication. Since he left the university in 2014, he has been actively advising various organizations while leading internal communication initiatives for the Japan Society for Corporate Communication Studies.

Baobao Song (Ph.D., University of Florida) is an assistant professor of public relations at Virginia Commonwealth University. Her research interests include corporate social responsibility communication, strategic stakeholder relationship management, and crisis communication. A three-time Arthur W. Page Legacy Scholar, her work has been published in leading peer-reviewed journals such as *Corporate Social Responsibility and Environmental Management, Public Relations Review,* and *Journal of Consumer Research.* She currently serves on the editorial board of the *Journal of Public Relations Research.*

Chase Spears (Ph.D. student, Kansas State University) spent a career in military public affairs with the U.S. Army. His coaching work focuses on communication as a function of organizational leadership and strategic enabler. As a researcher, Spears specializes in how institutions use discourse to shape identities and expectations of members. In addition to holding three master's degrees, he is the recipient of multiple awards for his published work on communication ethics and strategy.

Ward van Zoonen (Ph.D., University of Amsterdam) is an associate professor of organizational dynamics at Erasmus University and visiting professor of organizational communication at the University of Jyväskylä. His work focuses on the rapid transition into the new era of data-intensive and technology-supported work. He specifically focuses on questions related to the use and challenges associated with new technologies and the management of visibilities in organizations.

Joost Verhoeven (Ph.D., University of Twente) is an assistant professor of employee communication at Tilburg University. He specializes in strategic communication, communication roles, brand advocacy, motivation, and work engagement.

Marc Vielledent (Ph.D., University of Florida) is the chief of strategy at U.S. Special Operations Command. As a U.S. Army officer and Goodpaster Scholar, Vielledent's research interests include leadership communication, social media, strategic planning and policy, and risk articulation. His publications have appeared in Oxford University Press, *Computers and Human Behavior, Telematics and Information, Leadership Communication Quarterly*, and *Mass Communication Quarterly*.

Donald K. Wright (Ph.D., University of Minnesota) is the Harold Burson professor of public relations and chair of the department of mass communication, advertising & public relations in the College of Communication at Boston University. The bulk of his widely published research focuses on communication ethics, employee communication, and the use of new technologies in public relations practice. He worked full-time in corporate, agency, and professional sports public relations, served 24 years on the board of trustees of the Arthur W. Page Society and has served more than 30 years on the board of the Institute for Public Relations (IPR). He's a past president of the International Public Relations Association (IPRA), a past chair of the IPR measurement commission and a former head of both the public relations division of the Association for Education in Journalism and Mass Communication (AEJMC) and the educator's academy of the Public Relations Society of America (PRSA). His awards include the Pathfinder Award for research excellence from the IPR, the PRSA Educator of the Year Award, the Page

Society distinguished service award, and the Jackson, Jackson & Jackson Behavioral Science Prize from PRSA.

Koichi Yamamura (Ph.D., University of Miami) is a communication consultant with extensive experience in corporate communication, crisis management, and global public relations. He is a member of the International Public Relations Research Conference Advisory Committee and serves as an AMEC Award judge for the International Association for Measurement and Evaluation of Communication, and he has written several case studies and book chapters, including "Public Relations in Japan: Evolution in a Culture of Lifetime Employment" that he co-edited. While he serves clients including a bio-startup and environmental NPO, he teaches global public relations at Akita International University in winter.

Leping You (Ph.D., University of Florida) is an assistant professor of strategic communication at Miami University. You's research interests focus on corporate political advocacy, civic engagement on social media, and value advocacy in corporate-consumer relationship management. You's research has appeared in peer-reviewed journals including *Public Relations Review, Telematics and Informatics*, and *Journal of Communication Management*, among others. As a Co-PI, You has been awarded the Arthur W. Page Center Research Grant from Penn State University and the Insight Development Grant from the Social Sciences and Humanities Research Council of Canada.

Acknowledgments

Nance would like to thank her cherished family: husband Jon McCown, children and spouses Steve McCown and Courtney Potteiger, Kate and Nathan Gale, and Christie McCown and Ryan Huggins, as well as extended family, dear friends, and "alpaca" small group members for their support, encouragement, prayers, and nudges throughout this project's conception and birthing. She would also like to thank her gifted and incredibly hard-working co-editors and "sisters," Drs. Linjuan Rita Men, Hua Jiang, and Hongmei Shen for stepping out together in faith on this venture and for ensuring the process remained stimulating, encouraging, and fun. Our contributing chapter authors have truly outdone themselves in applying their expertise to a wide range of organizational contexts and in revealing valuable insights from both theoretical and practical standpoints, and we thank them for entrusting their work to this project. Finally, Nance would like to thank her former Messiah University student Miriam Thurber (2019) for her diligent assistance in initial literature review research for the nonprofit chapter, Messiah University colleagues for their dedicated support and camaraderie, and her Lord and Savior Jesus for providing the vision, life experiences, and learning opportunities that prompted her career-long exploration of internal communication and employee engagement. *Soli deo gloria.*

Rita would like to thank her beloved family members, husband Andrew Hu, daughter Aria Hu, son Aaron Hu, mother Li Men, and mother-in-law Li Jiang for their unconditional support in the completion of this important undertaking. She would also like to thank her amazing co-editors Drs. Nance McCown, Hua Jiang, and Hongmei Shen for their friendship and inspiration and for making it such a pleasant, enjoyable, and rewarding journey. It was a genuine passion for internal communication and love for research that bound everyone together. This book cannot be successful without the dedication and contributions from our chapter authors, each of whom are respected experts and thought leaders in our field. Lastly, she would like to extend her thanks to the College of Journalism and Communications at the University of Florida for granting her the research sabbatical leave to have this important work done.

Hua wants to thank her husband Yongjing Zhang, daughter Adalyn Zhang, mom Xingsheng Yang, and dad Haiping Jiang for their incredible support and unconditional love during the process of finishing the book project. She is also highly appreciative of her outstanding co-editors Drs. Nance McCown, Rita Men, and Hongmei Shen, and all the authors who have contributed to the completion of the book significantly with their commitment, dedication, enthusiasm, hard work, and support. Hua feels so blessed to be surrounded by those family members, friends, and colleagues. Without them, such an accomplishment—an edited book of inspiring works on internal communication and employee engagement—would not have been possible.

Hongmei hopes to express her gratitude first and foremost to her family members: husband Shi, daughter Olivia, and families in China for supporting this important project. She is equally grateful to her co-editors Drs. Nance McCown, Rita Men, and Hua Jiang, as well as our contributing authors, who have shown such strong work ethic, unwavering support for one another, and dedication to the research and practice of internal communication and employee engagement. One of her favorite authors Rabindranath Tagore once said, "You cannot cross the sea merely by standing and staring at the water." These loving family members, friends, and colleagues have made "crossing the sea" a less daunting task.

Introduction

Linjuan Rita Men, Nance McCown, Hua Jiang, and Hongmei Shen

Organizational leaders and scholars agree: employees are an organization's greatest asset. Their loyalty, motivation, engagement, and productivity profoundly affect their organization's reputation and bottom line (Men & Bowen, 2017). Employee engagement has been defined in a variety of ways but comprehensively includes aspects of employees' dedication to their job roles, willingness to give their best at work, and emotional commitment to the organization and its mission (Ewing et al., 2019; Shen & Jiang, 2019). Research has documented significant benefits of employee engagement for organizations, including its contribution to profitability, customer satisfaction, customer loyalty, and overall competitive advantage of the organization (Harter et al., 2002; Saks, 2006). It has also been linked to employees' individual benefits, such as energy, mental resilience, and self-significance (Schaufeli & Bakker, 2004). Despite this plethora of beneficial outcomes, Gallup's latest Employee Engagement Survey (Harter, 2022) revealed that only 32% of employees are engaged, meaning "highly involved in, enthusiastic about and committed to their work and workplace" (p. 1). The COVID-19 pandemic has further compounded the issue. The decline in the percentage of engaged employees in the U.S. in the past two years was evident across remote, hybrid, and on-site work groups (Harter, 2022).

Scholars and consultants alike have never ceased to identify the sundry factors that drive employee engagement: leadership, organizational culture, work environment, and communication, to name a few (Men & Bowen, 2017). Among these factors, internal communication arguably plays a central role, given its innate connection to other engagement drivers such as leadership and culture. Defined as "the strategic management of interactions and relationships between stakeholders within organizations" (Welch & Jackson, 2007, p. 184), internal communication is argued as both a management and communication function that serves various roles, including to inform, listen, connect, acculturate, motivate and engage (Men, 2021). Recent research has demonstrated the contribution of symmetrical, transparent, authentic communication, two-way communication that emphasizes listening and voice, effective use of communication channels, and social media from both the organization and leaders' perspectives to employee engagement (e.g., Karanges et al., 2015; McCown, 2014; Men et al., 2020; Ruck et al., 2017; Shen & Jiang, 2019). While empirical evidence on the role of internal communication in

DOI: 10.4324/9781003195580-1

rendering employee engagement has accumulated, contextualized case studies that provide in-depth and nuanced understanding of this process are in need.

This book builds upon recent theoretical development in internal communication and employee engagement and explores their applications in a variety of related organizational issues and domains, including internal branding/culture cultivation, internal social media, internal corporate social responsibility, change communication, internal issues and crises, leadership communication, employee activism, work-life integration, global/cross-cultural communication, corporate social advocacy, trust, and diversity, equity, and inclusion.

Organization of the Book

Divided into nine sections, this book provides students, scholars, internal communication managers, and organizational leaders with new insights into current issues in internal communication and employee engagement through a series of case studies featuring best practices in a wide range of organization and industry settings. Each chapter within the sections consists of a case study, learning outcomes, discussion questions, suggestions for further reading, and a full set of references.

Section I: Leadership and Trust

The external roles of CEOs as corporate spokespersons are widely recognized. Internally, CEOs and executives set the company vision and direction, define the DNA of the organization, and shape the organization's culture, character, and internal and external communication processes. Supervisors or line managers interact with employees on a day-to-day basis and are regarded as role models and go-to persons for information and concerns. Executive and supervisory leadership communication is essential to achieve the best results of employee communication. In addition, trust between leaders and employees, as well as throughout the organization, is paramount for corporations and nonprofit organizations to survive and thrive. Research has shown transparent and symmetrical internal communication can build trust among employees and foster employee engagement, which ultimately helps organizations retain their pool of talent. With the availability of newer organizational internal communication tools and applications, how organizations can best communicate with their employees to maintain trusting relationships and continue engaging employees is an important question, both theoretically and practically.

Dr. Nance McCown's chapter examines the way international communication, leadership style, and workplace environment/culture converge to result in high employee engagement in a U.S.-based Christian, international, nonprofit organization–HOPE International. Using in-depth interviews, participant observation, and content analysis, the study identifies the way HOPE's leadership style, faith-based workplace environment/culture, employee participation, empowerment, and transparent, dialogic, and responsive internal communication intersect to cultivate employee engagement based off of long-term trust and shared values.

Dr. Laura L. Lemon's chapter examines how dialogic internal communication and informal exchanges build trust among government contractor employees. This case study demonstrates that the company's intranet and email were ineffective in building trust due to a lack of tailoring, while genuine dialogic communication and active listening ultimately lead to greater employee engagement.

The chapter by Dr. Marc Vielledent and Chase Spears examines leadership communication during change. Through a case study of the recent U.S. Army overhaul of a long-standing physical fitness exam in use for over 40 years, their chapter showcases how effective, consistent leader and institutional messaging maintains trust and mitigates dissent in the public space via social engagement.

Section II: Organizational Change

Organizations seek change for many reasons, such as downsizing, mergers and acquisitions, disasters, expansion, and the adoption of new technology. An important prerequisite for modern organizations to grow and succeed in a dynamic and competitive global market is to scan and monitor their environment constantly, make necessary adjustments, and embrace change. Many changes fail due to ineffective communication.

The chapter by Dr. Conilyn Poulsen Judge presents a qualitative case study on the effects of interdisciplinary approaches to internal change communication. Through the theoretical lens of agile project management and neuroeconomics, her case study of a 55,000-employee National Oil Company based in the middle east demonstrates the critical role of internal communication in the company's COVID-induced change management.

Dr. Yi Luo's case study explores how RWJBarnabas Health, New Jersey's largest integrated healthcare delivery system, managed its internal communication programs during COVID-19. It underlines the strategic value of transparent internal communication and various employees and community-centered campaigns aiming to reinforce the organization's core and sustaining identities during an unplanned change.

Section III: Internal Issues and Crises

Crises happen on a daily basis for organizations, bringing ambiguities, uncertainties, and challenges for organizational control. Internal crisis communication is composed of situations in which the employees interpret and make sense of the organizational management's crisis communication. When an organizational crisis happens, communications can flow in multiple ways: management communicating to employees; employees communicating to managers and one another; and employees communicating to external publics. These chapters consider effective crisis communication strategies with internal stakeholders and/or how organizational contextual factors such as leadership and culture influence internal crisis communication.

Using simulated time-lagged research in a survey of nearly 400 employees, Dr. Minjeong Kang's study explores how employee crisis communication during the first lockdown brought on by COVID-19 contributed to work intentions in the U.S. Hospitality industry. Findings highlight the importance of employee communication that focuses on employees' informational and emotional needs to reduce the stress that may negatively impact employee engagement and loyalty.

Dr. Hyunji (Dana) Lim and Dr. Young Kim examine a racial discrimination case filed against Facebook by its employees. Applying the public segmentation approach centered on the concepts of employee resilience and situational perceptions, they conducted a national survey of 871 full-time employees. The findings of the study suggest that situational perceptions and resilience should be considered when crisis managers deal with employee voice and silence regarding their leadership's decision-making in crisis communication.

The chapter by Dr. Yang Cheng, Ms. Peiyao Liu, and Ms. Callie Burnette applies the concept of contingent organization-public relationships (COPR) to examine internal relationships and employee engagement during Activision Blizzard's crisis. Using a qualitative content analysis, they present a glimpse into the dynamic relationships between organizations and their employees during a crisis, highlighting the importance of internal communication and employee engagement.

Section IV: Employee Activism

A recent report released by Weber Shandwick showed that workers today, especially millennials, are more empowered to be employee activists (Weber Shandwick, 2019). Many employees believe they are entitled to speak up for or against their organization when it comes to issues that impact the society. Employee activism can be seen as an extended form of employee voice behavior, but it can also be a constructive or disruptive force for the organization, with the potential leading to positive change or an internal crisis. An examination of employee activism and the role of internal communication in engaging companies and leaders in dialogue with employee activists to address their needs and concerns and achieve a win-win solution will help to answer important questions.

Using qualitative data from a survey of public relations and communication professionals, Dr. Arunima Krishna, Raymond L. Kotcher, and Dr. Donald K. Wright examine the use of internal communication and employee engagement strategies to address, encourage, and manage employee activism. Applying their findings to the Netflix/Dave Chapelle case, they unpack best both practices and tensions experienced by public relations professionals in addressing employee activism.

Diving into the realm of artificial intelligence, Ms. Jie Jin and Dr. Leping You examine Google's interactions with its employees in the context of the #MakeAIEthical campaign. Their case study demonstrates that a lack of organizational listening and effective internal communication could alienate employees and turn them into internal activists.

Section V: Internal Communication and Emerging Technologies

The landscape of organizational communication has significantly changed with the evolution of new technology. As social media and other emerging technologies such as cybersecurity) continue to penetrate the workplace and reshape internal communication strategies, several key questions arise in this transformative process: What are the benefits or challenges in adopting internal social media? How can communication leaders leverage the advantages of different channels to fully realize the potential of social tools for employee communication and engagement? How can internal communication and employee engagement prevent or mitigate the effects of cybersecurity threats?

The chapter by Dr. Vibeke Thøis Madsen explores the emergence of employee engagement as they solve problems and co-create knowledge on internal social media. Her case study of Jyske Bank, the third largest bank in Denmark, demonstrates how the communication arena enabled by internal social media empowers employee voice.

Dr. Joost Verhoeven and Dr. Ward van Zoonen's chapter examines role expectations on enterprise social media in the aviation industry. Through a case study of employees' use of Yammer at a large European airline company, they demonstrate the communicative dynamics and the contribution of enterprise social media to organizational functioning and performance.

Based on a survey on perceptions about cybersecurity with 1,046 communication professionals in the United States and Canada, Dr. Solyee Kim and Dr. Jeonghyun Janice Lee's chapter examines communication professionals' organizational experiences about cyberattacks and discusses the implications of internal information management for cybersecurity. This chapter generates great insights for organizations' internal communication, employee engagement, and management of emerging threats to cybersecurity.

Section VI: Internal CSR/CSA

Employee participation in corporate social responsibility (CSR) can reflect a company's culture or values associated with giving back to the community or doing good for society. It can also help establish trust among external stakeholders that a company's CSR efforts are genuine and rooted in its fundamental value systems instead of cosmetic work. As publics are putting more demand for private sectors in solving societal issues, employees are expecting their employers to do better in balancing their financial and social goals. Developing best practices to take CSR communication to the next level of authentic, purposeful engagement has become a new challenge for business leaders and communication professionals. Relatedly, publics today are placing increasing expectations on organizations to play a part in social change. We see more and more corporations pressured by their employees or consumers to take a stance on controversial socio-political issues. An increasing amount of empirical research on corporate social advocacy (CSA) has demonstrated that CSA is connected to corporate purpose and important outcomes such as positive organization-public relationships and customer brand loyalty. However, most of the discussions have been centered around the impact of CSA on consumer attitudes and perceptions and less is known on how the impact of internal communication in CSA affects employee perceptual, psychological, and behavioral outcomes such as trust and engagement.

In their chapter, Drs. Yi-Ru Regina Chen, Minqin Ma, and Chun-Ju Flora Hung-Baesecke propose a framework integrating social influence theory, motivation-based theory of volunteerism, and levels of internal communication. They then validate that framework through a case study of Tencent, a 2020 Fortune 200 company based in mainland China, using interviewing and content analysis of internal communication to explore corporate volunteering (CV) by Tencent's employees.

Dr. Chuqing Dong and Dr. Baobao Song's case study examines Home Depot's internal CSR communication strategies targeting employees. Based on interviews with Home Depot Foundation managers and a content analysis of Home Depot's annual CSR reports, this chapter discovered how Home Depot applies CSR communication strategies and promotes employee CSR engagement. The study provides implications for internal CSR communication and employee engagement.

Using an online survey, Dr. Keonyoung Park explores how CSA can help improve organization-employee relationships and, in turn, employee engagement. The extent to which organizations express support for the #StopAsianHate movement contributes to employees' organization-based self-esteem and organizational identification. Such employees also report higher engagement at work.

Section VII: Diversity, Equity, and Inclusion

The workforce in the 21st century is characterized by an increasing number of women, minorities, people with disabilities, international workers, and employees from other under-represented groups. To ensure recruitment and retention of talent from those groups, many organizations have incorporated DEI initiatives in their long-term organizational vision through (a) establishing recruitment and retention goals, (b) tracking workplace characteristics, (c) linking DEI to goals and objectives of its strategic plan (the eradication of discrimination, promotion of DEI at all levels, and opportunities for participation), (d) developing action plans, and (e) integrating DEI in leadership training programs. This case study will analyze best DEI practices in internal communication and suggest ways to remove barriers, motivate all employees to develop and use a full range of skills and competencies, encourage participation, boost morale, and facilitate community building within organizations. It is pivotal for organizations to cultivate an organizational environment with a high level of responsiveness to diverse voices of employees and inclusiveness of all individual differences.

Dr. Cheng Hong uses a thematic analysis of university strategic plans and chief diversity officers at 23 California State University system institutions to explore the engagement of employees in DE&I issues within the workplace, identifying common themes and practices.

Section VIII: Remote Work, Flexible Work, and Work-Life Integration

Research has long associated employee wellbeing and work-life balance with important employee and organizational outcomes such as employee engagement, work commitment, retention, and job performance. The COVID-19 pandemic has pushed more organizations to open to remote work and flexible schedules. While employee work-life balance and integration has become an increasingly salient issue for employers, most discussions have happened among human resources (HR) practitioners.

In their chapter, Drs. Alessandra Mazzei, Luca Quaratino, Alfonsa Butera, and Sara Conti propose three pillars for building a hybrid workplace able to support sustainable engagement over time. They then present mini case studies of three Italy-based corporations—the Campari Group, the Sella Group, and the Unipol Group—to examine the use of these pillars in organizational settings.

Building on the work-life border theory, Ms. Feihong Pan investigates the impact of Chinese employees' after-hour smartphone use on their work-family conflict via a survey of 396 employees who have worked remotely during the COVID-19 pandemic. She further identifies best practices to enhance employee engagement in the remote-work context.

Section IX: Internal Branding and Engagement in a Global Context

Recent research has shown a clear link between employee engagement, consistent internal communication, and strong workplace internal branding and culture cultivation. Organizational efforts to engage employees through effective internal branding communication, employee incentive and recognition programs, and activities promoting employee relationship building have increased loyalty and productivity. Within the global context, many companies have stretched across borders to a point where they have larger operations and more employees in other parts of the world than in their home countries. At the same time, skilled and well-educated workers from developing countries seek higher wages and better opportunities across borders, thereby shaping a globalized, diverse, and multicultural workforce. How to engage and integrate a global and multicultural workforce is a new puzzle for modern organizations.

Dr. Kevin Ruck's chapter applied the Alignment-Voice-Identification-Dialogue (AVID) framework to analyze strengths and weaknesses of internal communication at a fire and

Rescue Service in the U.K. His case study showcased the importance of listening and voice in fostering genuine dialogue in the workplace.

In their chapter, Masamichi Shimizu and Dr. Koichi Yamamura examine efforts by Yamaha Motors Co.'s president to implant Japanese style operations management in overseas operations. This case study unpacks various internal communication philosophies and tools used, noting that respect for local culture and employee participation were keys to achieving hard-won success.

Concluding Thoughts

As illustrated in the chapter descriptions, this work includes a wide range of perspectives from authors based in countries spanning the globe. As such, the case studies have wide application in a variety of cultures and workplace types. Moreover, their broad theoretical underpinnings highlight the unique challenges and advantages of conducting effective internal communication and garnering increased employee engagement across many organizational contexts. We hope this book will appeal to public relations and corporate/internal communication scholars and educators as well as graduate students studying our focus areas. We also believe its practical insights and application will invite public relations, strategic communication, and human resource practitioners, as well as business leaders and management team members, to further explore and implement improvements in their organizations' internal communication and engagement strategies. Finally, we hope this work will prompt scholars and practitioners to collaborate on further research, ultimately resulting in new theories and innovations to promote stronger internal communication, greater engagement, and more valued, satisfied, and productive employees.

References

Ewing, M., Men, L. R., & O'Neil, J. (2019). Using social media to engage employees: Insights from internal communication managers. *International Journal of Strategic Communication, 13*, 110–132. https://doi.org/10.1080/1553118X.2019.1575830

Harter, J. (2022). U.S. employee engagement slump continues. Retrieved from https://www.gallup.com/workplace/391922/employee-engagement-slump-continues.aspx

Harter, J. K., Schmidt, F. L., & Hayes, T. L. (2002). Business-unit-level relationship between employee satisfaction, employee engagement, and business outcomes: A meta-analysis. *Journal of Applied Psychology, 87*, 268–279. https://doi.org/10.1037/0021-9010.87.2.268

Karanges, E., Johnston, K. A., Beatson, A. T., & Lings, I. (2015). The influence of internal communication on employee engagement: A pilot study. *Public Relations Review, 41*(1), 129–131.

McCown, N. (2014). Building leader-employee relationships and dialog through internal public relations, leadership style, and workplace spirituality. *PRism Journal*, (11). Retrieved from: http://www.prismjournal.org/homepage.html.

Men, L. R. (2021). Evolving research and practices in internal communication. In L. R. Men & A. Tkalac Vercic (Eds.), *Current trends and issues in internal communication: Theory and practice* (1–18). London: Palgrave Macmillan.

Men, L. R., & Bowen, S. (2017). *Excellence in internal communication management.* New York: Business Expert Press.

Men, L. R., O'Neil, J., & Ewing, M. (2020). Examining the effects of internal social media usage on employee engagement. *Public Relations Review, 46*(2). https://doi.org/10.1016/j.pubrev.2020.101880

Ruck, K., Welch, M., & Menara, B. (2017). Employee voice: An antecedent to organizational engagement? *Public Relations Review, 43*(5), 904–914.

Saks, A. M. (2006). Antecedents and consequences of employee engagement. *Journal of Managerial Psychology, 21*(7), 600–619.

Schaufeli, W. B., & Bakker, A. B. (2004). Job demands, job resources, and their relationship with burnout and engagement: A multi-sample study. *Journal of Organizational Behavior, 25*(3), 293–315. https://doi.org/10.1002/job.248

Shen, H., & Jiang, H. (2019). Engaged at work? An employee engagement model in public relations. *Journal of Public Relations Research, 31*(1–2), 32–49.

Weber Shandwick (May 29, 2019). Employee activism in the age of purpose: Employees (up) rising. Retrieved from: https://www.webershandwick.com/news/employee-activism-age-of-purpose/

Welch, M., & Jackson, P. R. (2007). Rethinking internal communication: A stakeholder approach. *Corporate Communications: An International Journal, 12*, 177–198. https://doi.org/10.1108/13563280710744847

Section I

Leadership and Trust

Chapter One

Hope International: A Case Study in Nonprofit Employee Engagement through Internal Communication, Leadership, and Culture

Nance McCown

Introduction

Successful organizations know employees are their greatest assets. Yet for multiple years running, Gallup reports have consistently identified two-thirds of U.S. employees as disengaged or actively disengaged, costing billions of dollars in lost productivity annually (e.g., Harter, 2019). With this understanding, both professionals and scholars have spotlighted increasing engagement as a primary concern.

How can companies promote employee engagement? Berger (2014) noted the "crucial importance" of organizational culture and leadership for strong internal communication that leads to greater engagement (p. 3). More recently, scholars have explored how these elements can combine to positively influence employee engagement and relationship-building within organizations (McCown, 2010, 2014, 2017, 2019; Men, 2014a, 2014b; Men & Bowen, 2017; Men & Jiang, 2016; Men & Stacks, 2013, 2014; Shen & Jiang, 2019).

Men and Bowen's (2017) integrated, normative employee engagement model provides the foundation for this qualitative organizational case study to explore the confluence of internal communication, leadership style, and work environment/workplace culture in fostering an engaged employee base at HOPE International, a U.S.-based Christian, international, nonprofit organization specializing in microfinance (https://www.hopeinternational.org/). In 20 years, HOPE has expanded from serving one Eastern European location to providing loans to underserved populations in 16 countries on 4 continents. Its employee base has grown to more than 120, with approximately 65 working out of the U.S. headquarters, another 30+ working remotely in North America, and about 12–15 working globally in the field. The organization features empowering leadership styles; transparent, highly relational internal communication; and a work environment/culture known for its openly spiritual foundations and participative practices.

DOI: 10.4324/9781003195580-3

Literature Review

Several theoretical streams provide context to this research problem: internal communication, leadership style, workplace culture, and employee engagement.

Internal Communication

According to Berger (2008), internal communication brings organizational value through helping "individuals and groups coordinate activities to achieve goals, and [is] vital in socialization, decision-making, problem-solving, and change-management processes" (p. 2). Historically, research shows that decentralized, less formal, and often more complex communication processes, as well as two-way symmetrical internal communication (Grunig, 2001), foster a participative, organic culture affording employees significant decision-making input. These practices relay messages and help give voice to all parties, building leader-employee relationships and leading to employee job satisfaction/increased productivity (i.e., Grunig et al., 2002). "Openness, two-way dialogues, collaboration, and concern with employees' welfare and voices" can strengthen organization-employee relationship quality (Men, 2014b, p. 271). Also, symmetry's resulting transparency fosters "mutual understanding, collaboration, and reciprocity," producing "substantial, complete, timely, accurate, balanced, and unequivocal information" that leads to employees' positive organizational associations (Men & Stacks, 2014, pp. 315–316; also Jiang & Men, 2015).

Depending on the communication's purpose, employees exhibit preferences for internal face-to-face and email for promoting community and communication among project team members (Stein, 2006; White et al., 2010). CEOs most often use email and face-to-face communication with employees, and employees more positively view CEOs with responsive communication styles/who use social media (Men, 2015).

Finally, the complexity of international NGOs and nonprofits, with staff at home and abroad, calls for strengthened internal communication (Anheier, 2005). Also, strategic internal communication helps "build cohesion and commitment" among employees (Hume & Leonard, 2014, p. 303).

Leadership Style

Organizational leaders use internal communication for building key stakeholder relationships (employees included), determining direction, casting vision, establishing collective purpose, and managing culture (Fanelli & Misangyi, 2006; McCown, 2010,

2014, 2017, 2019). In short, "leadership is enacted through communication" (Men & Bowen, 2017, p. 122).

Recent research supports transformational, ethical or principle-centered, servant, and authentic leadership styles as best able to foster strategic internal communication (McCown, 2010, 2014, 2017, 2019; Men & Stacks, 2013, 2014). First, transformational leaders (Yukl, 2006) empower followers to reach their highest potential and exercise individualized consideration (Musser, 1997) through friendly, close behavior and treating followers as equals. Transformational leader outcomes include enhanced relationship-building, leader-employee trust, high organizational commitment, control mutuality, and employee satisfaction (i.e., McCown, 2006, 2010, 2014, 2017, 2019; Men, 2014a).

Next, ethical or principle-centered leaders employ ethics, character, and personal principles to "an emotional bank account" that fosters employee empowerment and trust (Covey, 1992, p. 155). They also treat others fairly, share power, clarify roles, adopt a people-oriented approach, display integrity, demonstrate sustainability, and offer ethical guidance (Kalshoven et al., 2001). In particular, the servant leader (Greenleaf, 1998) displays listening and empathy (Spears, 1998) and encourages an empowered team and vision supported by hope/faith and undergirded with workplace spirituality (Fry, 2003). Established as an organization's foundation, servant leaders serve others and promote their success (Bowen et al., 2010; Men & Bowen, 2017), fostering high levels of organizational commitment and productivity (McCown, 2010, 2014, 2017, 2019).

Finally, authentic leaders exhibit consistency between ideas and behaviors (Terry, 1993), portraying confidence, optimism, resilience, and high moral character (Avolio et al., 2004) and actions based on values, convictions, and purpose (Shamir & Eilam, 2005). They empower followers to become leaders themselves (Luthans & Avolio, 2003) and possess "self-transcendent values and positive, other-directed emotions" (Michie & Gooty, 2005, p. 441). Employees value authentic leadership because it "conveys trustworthiness"; "authentic leaders appear to be true to themselves, without pretense or barriers, and tend to display an amazing consistency across multiple types of situations" (Men & Bowen, 2017, p. 53). This leadership style fosters symmetrical and transparent communication (McCown, 2010, 2014, 2017, 2019; Men, 2014b; Men & Stacks, 2014); openness to alternative viewpoints (Men & Bowen, 2017); increased leader-follower intimacy/trust and engagement; and greater workplace performance (Wong & Cummings, 2009).

Workplace Culture

Schein (1985) defined workplace culture as a set of assumptions developed through group consensus and shared experiences, "valid" enough to teach new group members (p. 9); key elements include a consensual mission statement and shared economic/esoteric purposes. Workplace culture is "central to all aspects of organizational life" (Alvesson, 2002, p. 1) and emerges as shared values and group behaviors prompted through top management's organizational philosophy and vision casting (Kotter & Heskett, 1992).

Research also connects workplace culture and communication. Participative, decentralized workplace cultures promote transparent, symmetrical communication; welcome diversity; and foster control mutuality/shared decision-making (Grunig et al., 2002); multiple studies confirm that these cultures increase employee satisfaction, loyalty, and productivity (i.e., McCown 2010, 2014, 2017, 2019).

Some workplace cultures include a spiritual dimension, where employees often exhibit a sense of vocational calling, connecting with cultural values that facilitate their "experience of transcendence through the work process" and foster "feelings of compassion and joy" (Giacalone & Jurkiewicz, 2003, p. 13). McCormick (1994) identified several spiritual workplace traits: compassion, right livelihood (the Buddhist principle of work choice that avoids human or animal suffering), selfless service (Christian and Hindu principles); and work as meditative. Employees also use spirituality to process difficult work situations (Schein, 1985).

Achieving a spiritually based organizational culture requires specific leader behaviors and actions: honesty; promotion of the company's spiritual foundations/philosophy; fostering trust, integrity, and dedication to quality/service; maintaining commitment to employees; and hiring for "fit" with organizational values (Wagner-Marsh & Conley, 1999). Clearly defined spirituality in the organization's written mission statement also helps avoid employee confusion and frustration (Konz & Ryan, 1999). When leaders encourage widespread commitment to spiritual foundations, employees move from mere conformity to ethical code internalization (Conley & Wagner-Marsh, 1998).

Employee Engagement

Recently, scholars have explored various facets of workplace engagement (see literature review by Jelen-Sanchez, 2017). Ensuring appropriate internal information flow/adequacy while providing ongoing feedback for job performance and organizational issues helps to increase engagement (Walden et al., 2017). Also, face-to-face leader-employee communication fosters engagement (Mishra et al., 2014). In addition, higher employee satisfaction with internal communication leads to higher engagement levels (Verčič & Vokić, 2017). Finally, Shen and Jiang's (2019) structural model of employee engagement supports specific organizational engagement strategies: adequate information sharing to encourage employee self-disclosure regarding their organizations, partnerships with professional networks to enhance career growth, and genuine care about employee concerns.

Men and Bowen (2017) fully fleshed out multiple descriptions of employee engagement, with three notable standouts relevant to this study. First, engaged employees are "all in," connecting actively with their work; disengaged employees are detached from work roles (Kahn, 1990). Second, engagement is "a positive, fulfilling, work-related state of mind … characterized by vigor, dedication, and absorption" (Schaufeli et al., 2002, p. 74). Last, engagement is best viewed over time, not as "one off" actions/emotional responses; engaged employees invest in work with their entire being—physically, intellectually, and emotionally (Christian et al., 2011).

Positing engagement drivers, Men and Bowen's (2017) ten-point, normative, integrated model combines leadership style, internal communication, and environment/workplace culture:

1) Establish a suitable, safe, positive, and supportive work environment with adequate physical resources, facilities, and conditions.
2) Provide coaching, offer employees personal growth and development opportunities and programs, and stress employees' work-life balance and enhancement needs in organizational initiatives and communications.
3) Place employees in job positions that fit their strengths, capabilities, and skill sets and pay attention to the effect of job characteristics (e.g., complexity, variety, and significance) to minimize its negative consequences.
4) Establish a fair reward and compensation system to recognize achievements and outstanding performance.
5) Hire individuals with high psychological capital factors, such as optimism, resilience, self-efficacy, positivity, and hope.
6) Encourage organizational leaders, including executives, managers, and supervisors across levels, to implement transformational, transactional, authentic, and ethical leadership styles.

7) Provide communication training to senior management and develop an authentic and engaging communication style that is characterized by warmth, friendliness, empathy, responsiveness, and genuineness.
8) Use emerging technology and social media channels to build internal communities; foster conversations between leaders and employees, as well as employers and employees; promote openness, transparency, and dialogues; and incubate creativity.
9) Establish a two-way, empowering, participative, and stakeholder-centered symmetrical and transparent communication system; wholeheartedly listen to what employees have to say and make adjustments accordingly for their best interests.
10) Cultivate an engaging culture that values ethics, integrity, trust, employee participation, innovation, sharing and learning, fairness, diversity, social responsibility, equality, collaboration, and employee happiness (pp. 125–127).

Research Questions and Organization Contextualization

Drawing from previous engagement research with a particular focus on Men and Bowen's (2017) model, this study explores two specific research questions:

RQ1: How do the organization's leadership style (CEO and other leaders) and work environment/workplace culture influence internal communication practices?

RQ2: How does the interplay of this organization's leadership style, internal communication practices, and work environment/workplace culture influence employee engagement?

Method

Blurred lines between context and phenomenon support a qualitative case study (Yin, 2003) for exploring this study's research questions. Data collection occurred through a three-pronged, iterative process. Purposive sampling involved in-depth interviews (Lindlof & Taylor, 2002; Rubin & Rubin, 2005) with 12 employees (6 females, 6 males) across all organizational levels, from entry-level employees through middle management, the executive team, and the president and CEO. Time of employment ranged from 6 months to nearly 20 years. Lasting from 50 to 75 minutes, interviews followed a pre-tested, semi-structured, 25-question protocol and occurred primarily in person, with 3 via Skype or phone due to remote participants. Six hours of participant observation in small- and large-group meetings yielded contextual "witnessing evidence" (Lindlof & Taylor, 2002, pp. 135, 139). Document analysis of key internal materials (an employee manual and samples of organization-wide emails from the top leader and several departments) provided "confirmatory evidence" (Potter, 1996, p. 96). Data analysis used constant comparative strategies (Strauss & Corbin, 1998) to categorize recurring themes. In addition to triangulation (Kvale, 1995), the month-long fieldwork duration increased validity, resulting in "thick description" (Geertz, 1973) and saturation (Glaser & Strauss, 1967). Frequent reflexive memo writing helped bracket potential researcher bias (Lindlof & Taylor, 2002). Appropriate Institutional Review Board approvals and ethical participant treatment (Lindlof & Taylor, 2002; Rubin & Rubin, 2005) respected and empowered participants in the research process.

Results

As gathered from previous research (McCown, 2017), HOPE International's CEO and other top leaders generally exhibited transformational, ethical/principled, servant, and authentic leadership style traits. All of them espoused Christian principles and lived those out in leading others. Participants described leaders as consistent, full of integrity, Christ-centered, passionate, kind, caring (beyond job performance), empowering, investing, competent, respectful, listening, responsive, servant-like, humble, and willing to learn. In short, leaders demonstrated genuineness and authenticity while empowering/respecting employees. Further, HOPE's work environment and culture, deeply rooted in Christian spiritual foundations, fostered a mission-driven, participatory, relational culture where employees reported feeling "cared for" in a "fun," family-like atmosphere. Leaders provided appropriate resourcing and workspace to foster employee productivity and satisfaction and organically involved employees in strategic planning and decision-making, demonstrating trust and respect for employee competence, knowledge, and insight. Leaders also facilitated employee growth through professional development funding, niche-finding "lateral learning assignments," and "stretch assignments" beyond typical responsibilities. Finally, the organization's culture and leadership intentionally fostered and strategically supported employee work-life balance.

The current case study's two research questions present a framework for specific emerging themes related to internal communication and employee engagement. To give contextual understanding and preserve confidentiality, participants are identified by general position levels.

RQ1: Internal Communication

International complexity requires HOPE International to communicate with 120+ employees in global locations. Interviews and observations revealed internal communication characterized by responsiveness, transparency, openness, symmetry, dialogue, timeliness, and accuracy.

Electronic communication (emails, updates, announcements, and online intranet and project management systems) facilitated timely, accurate communication to local and remote employees, with ample opportunity for response and dialogue. The CEO noted that erring toward over-communication while recognizing necessary privacy for some sensitive issues is key, at a frequency that ensures timeliness while avoiding annoyance or distraction from work. Participants especially appreciated the CEO's monthly employee update emails—basically, Board report recaps. One staff member stated, "We feel like we're in the loop of what [the CEO and the Board] are discussing. I feel like that builds trust."

The organization also highly values face-to-face communication for comprehension, clarity, and relationship-building. Besides frequent one-on-ones, HOPE holds required biweekly staff meetings as well as optional weekly devotionals and prayer gatherings (which most employees choose to attend); local staff join in one large meeting space, with remote employees joining virtually. Staff unable to attend may access the recordings and written summaries of all organization-wide meetings. In addition to "lightning round" department updates and more in-depth, "special topic" presentations, staff meetings feature awards recognizing employees "caught" living out the organization's mission/culture in tangible ways. Finally, a weeklong annual summit gathers all local and global employees to reflect on the past year's work, celebrate together, build relationships, and establish future direction.

During meeting observations, the researcher noted leaders consistently "stepping back," empowering staff to initiate ideas, voice opinions, and offer feedback. Both staff and managers led meetings, depending on the topic. Respect, teamwork, encouragement, and a sense of equality seasoned the discussions and peppered with friendliness and fun. During every observed meeting, leaders invited employees to give feedback and raise concerns, questions, or differing viewpoints; whenever someone did, they were heard and valued. As one staff member shared,

> I have the confidence I can go to my supervisor or even [the CEO] and tell him anything, whether it's ... personally related or tension points in my job .... [The leaders are] invested in me as a person and as a brother in Christ. That creates so much trust.

Although every participant expressed comfort in approaching managers, senior leadership, and even the CEO about nearly any topic, and although leadership clearly encouraged personal as opposed to anonymous communication, HOPE International recognizes that some topics may be more difficult to broach. The organization allows for confidential feedback via the annual Best Christian Workplace survey, which asks questions about mission buy-in, communication, culture, productivity, job satisfaction, and more. Despite its consistently ultra-high survey rankings, HOPE takes the results seriously and demonstrates transparency by sharing them with all staff. Participants noted communication/decision-making process changes brought about by those results; in fact, one observed post-survey meeting empowered employees to brainstorm solutions to streamline and improve organizational decision-making.

Social media also plays a role in internal communication. Departments, teams, and other employee groups participate regularly in Skype chats, online forums, and Facebook groups for discussions, practical assistance (i.e., ride-sharing for traveling employees), or mutual support and enjoyment. Participants did not mention the organization's active external social media sites.

Many participants did not view HOPE's internal communication as particularly formalized. As evidence, several years ago, a communication sequencing issue about a critical decision meant that the affected department heard about it simultaneously with all other employees. Since then, employees and leaders have reviewed internal communication intentionality and processes to clarify the information dissemination sequence.

RQ2: Employee Engagement Outcomes

Participants described engagement through a variety of overlapping themes rooted in the interplay of leadership style, internal communication, and work environment/workplace culture. One manager stated, "We have really high levels of commitment to the mission, and people don't leave [HOPE International] easily." A staff member added, "People are really on board here." Reasons cited for high engagement include hiring well-qualified people with mission fit, "calling," organizational investment in employees, opportunities for growth and advancement, communication transparency, long-term trust, appropriate handling of dissent or problems, and strong relationships with employees at all levels who share similar values.

> First, according to a supervisor, HOPE International hires people with ...the right heart, and has poured into them, trained them and given them stretch assignments. I feel like I am only where I am because they were willing to invest in me, and when you see that happening, that makes you want to stay.

A staff member added, "I'm impressed with the caliber of people working here and the dedication they have. They could be working elsewhere but they choose to be HERE because they believe in the calling that God has for them and the mission."

Also, all participants expressed high, long-term trust in the organization and its leaders, in part due to communication transparency. Even occasional frustration did not diminish trust. One staff member noted, "I am probably one of the most 'angsty' people here – it's just my nature to want to change and improve things. But I trust individual leaders. Trust here is insanely high and there's a lot of good will."

Many participants noted that HOPE International leaders appropriately handle issues with respect and humility. A staff member stated, "There are things we struggle through, but the tension points are dealt with so well that it's seen as an opportunity for growth." Another shared,

> There is so much freedom here to ask questions, to do things differently as a team without changing organizational foundation and direction. And with that, I think there is joy to do my role in a way that I am pursuing the gifts that God has given me.

Relationally, all participants expressed shared values/strong bonds with others across the organization, including leadership. "All of us are invested in each other's lives, which builds trust," stated one staff member. Another added, "It's really good to be part of a group that holds similar values."

Several leaders shared struggles with keeping remote/international employees engaged. The CEO mused that according to the Best Christian Workplace survey, employee engagement was "not perfect, but high. I think the reality is, the more that you increase geographic distance, the more difficult it becomes to really make sure that you are staying on track with unified direction and culture." To increase global employee engagement, HOPE International initiated a global branding project, ensuring consistency not just with facilities décor and the "look" of online/printed materials, but also with core elements of culture.

Finally, one participant shared struggles with disengagement, citing frustrations over a large project that "seemed pointless." After discussing the situation with his manager, though, the employee shifted teams and projects and is now "beginning to feel more engaged again." Leadership responsiveness to his concerns, clear processes for internal communication, and an agile workplace environment and culture enabled the employee to state concerns and make needed changes to increase his engagement.

Discussion

This study confirmed previous engagement research findings, as well as every aspect of Men and Bowen's (2017) normative employee engagement model as influenced through internal communication, leadership style, and work environment/culture. It also added a spiritual dimension to culture, enhancing the model.

Public Relations Theory Implications

As found in previous research (McCown, 2017), HOPE International's CEO and leaders effectively enacted several empowering leadership styles: transformational, principle-centered, ethical, servant, and authentic. In addition, HOPE's pleasant, well-resourced work environment, fully permeating and healthy workplace culture, and participative, decentralized culture fostered control mutuality/shared decision-making increased employee satisfaction, loyalty, and productivity. Spiritual foundations informed every aspect of workplace culture—including decision-making and personal/professional interactions.

Together, HOPE International's combination of enacted leadership style and established workplace culture (particularly spiritually based) fostered strategic, symmetrical, transparent communication (Grunig, 2001; Grunig et al., 2002) for timely and substantial information dissemination and feedback, relationship-building, goal alignment, and collaboration (Berger, 2008; Men, 2014b), leading to employees' positive workplace associations (Men & Stacks, 2014). Face-to-face (with remote and international access) meeting structures, chances for individual feedback, appropriately frequent CEO/department email updates, and online project management/communication systems confirmed research on employee/CEO communication preferences and employees' positive views of leaders' communication found in previous research (Men, 2015; Stein, 2006; White et al., 2010). The study did not confirm CEO social media usage (Men, 2015), although employees used some social channels internally. Also, HOPE's intentional, strategic internal communication, particularly through Skype use and other online access for remote employees, effectively addressed communication concerns regarding global nonprofits and international non-governmental organizations (INGOs) (Anheier, 2005; Hume & Leonard, 2014). Although data collection occurred just prior to the global COVID-19 pandemic, having strong virtual communication methods already in place with frequent usage likely enabled the organization to pivot successfully from primarily face-to-face communication.

Lastly, the confluence of HOPE International's internal communication practices, leadership style enactment, and strong, shared culture steeped in spiritual foundations produced extremely high levels of employee engagement, confirming previously proposed strategies (Mishra et al., 2014; Shen & Jiang, 2019; Verčič & Vokić, 2017; Walden et al., 2017). Most importantly, this combination of practices both confirmed and added a new dimension, that of a spiritual culture foundation, to Men and Bowen's (2017) normative model. Employee attitudes at all levels indicated job satisfaction, loyalty/commitment to the organization and its mission/values; and "perceived" empowerment. Regarding employee behaviors, the organizational mission and personal spiritual beliefs drove employees to high performance and productivity, caring and compassionate interactions, and workplace longevity or a desire for the same. As for organizational outcomes, although "profitability" did not apply in this case, the organization's growth over its 20-year history, dependent on donor funding as well as client interest/satisfaction, inferentially has come at least in part as a result of high employee engagement (Men & Bowen, 2017, p. 126). Employee willingness to take lower salaries than those in for-profit, corporate jobs lends further support for high engagement.

Practical Implications

This study's findings have implications for nonprofit organizations, as well as organizations of all types, to more effectively engage employees. Internal communication practices matter greatly, and transparency, symmetry, and dialogue strengthen relationships as well as shared vision. Leaders whose style demonstrates value for employees, a willingness to learn, and a desire to facilitate employee growth/empowerment foster more satisfied, productive employees. Also, purposefully cultivated, participatory, relational, caring workplace cultures and environments that effectively resource employees and provide pleasant, comfortable, productivity-enhancing workspaces also add to engagement. Finally, spirituality can play a vital role in internal communication, leadership, and culture as it is consistently "lived out" in both work practices/policies and interactions. Intentionality is key to both fostering and maintaining successful employee engagement.

Study Limitations and Future Research

Common to many organizational case studies, necessary reliance on HOPE International leadership to provide potential interviewee names may have been a limiting factor. In addition, Skype and telephone settings for several interviews may have affected the researcher's ability to fully note nonverbal and context clues, another potential study limitation.

Future research could include exploration of the convergence of internal communication, leadership, and workplace environment/workplace culture in secular nonprofits as well as in NGOs and INGOs. In addition, repeating the study with HOPE International to ascertain the effects of the COVID-19 global pandemic would also enrich understanding and test the organization's ability to maintain consistently high levels of employee engagement under extreme duress.

Conclusion

This qualitative study's theoretical, descriptive, and practical richness adds to the understanding of employee engagement as affected by internal communication, leadership styles, and workplace culture. Its unique contribution to the knowledge body surrounding nonprofits, as well as workplace spirituality, also provides new insights and value. Ultimately, working to engage employees strengthens them both as individuals and as organizational assets and helps them derive greater meaning from the work to which they devote such a significant portion of their lives.

Learning Outcomes

1) Explore the influence of various leadership styles and workplace cultures on internal communication.
2) Examine the confluence of particular leadership styles, workplace cultures, and internal communication practices and their impact on employee engagement.
3) Understand factors leading to effective internal communication and increased employee engagement as applied in a specific nonprofit organization with spiritual foundations.

Discussion Questions

1) How did HOPE International's leadership style and workplace culture influence the organization's internal communication practices? In particular, what did the culture's spiritual foundations add to the mix?
2) Which characteristics of leadership style, workplace culture, and internal communication do you think are most important in fostering increased employee engagement at HOPE International?
3) If any aspects of leadership style, workplace culture, or internal communication practices were removed, how do you think that would affect Hope International's level of employee engagement?
4) Which characteristics of leadership style, workplace culture, and internal communication practices gleaned from this reading do you think have affected employee engagement in organizations where you have worked?
5) What keys to fostering effective internal communication and increasing employee engagement will you take away from this reading and apply in your current or future workplace?

Further Readings

Jelen-Sanchez, A. (2017). Engagement in public relations discipline: Themes, theoretical perspectives and methodological approaches. *Public Relations Review, 43*(5), 934–944. https://doi.org/10.1016/j.pubrev.2017.04.002

Men, R. L., & Bowen, S. A. (2017). *Excellence in internal communication management.* New York: Business Expert Press.

Men, R. L, & Verčič, A. T. (2021). *Current trends and issues in internal communication: Theory and practice.* London: Palgrave MacMillan.

References

Alvesson, M. (2002). *Understanding organizational culture.* London: Sage.

Anheier, H. K. (2005). *Nonprofit organisations: Theory, management, policy.* London: Routledge.

Avolio, B. J., Luthans, F., & Walumbwa, F. O. (2004). *Authentic leadership: Theory building for veritable sustained performance.* Working paper: Gallup Leadership Institute, University of Nebraska-Lincoln, Omaha, NE, USA.

Berger, B. K. (2008). *Employee/organizational communications.* Gainesville, FL: Institute for Public Relations. Retrieved from: http://www.instituteforpr.org/topics/employee-organizational-communications/

Berger, B. K. (2014). *READ MY LIPS: Leaders, supervisors and culture are the foundations of strategic employee communication.* Gainesville, FL: Institute for Public Relations. Retrieved from http://www.instituteforpr.org/read-lips-leaders-supervisors-culture-foundations-strategic-employee-communications/

Bowen, S. A., Rawlins, B. L., & Martin, T. M. (2010). *An overview of the public relations function.* New York: Business Expert Press.

Christian, M. S., Garza, A. S., & Slaughter, J. E. (2011). Work engagement: A quantitative review and test of its relations with task and contextual performance. *Personnel Psychology, 64*(1), 89–136. https://doi.org/10.1111/j.1744-6570.2010.01203.x

Covey, S. R. (1992). *Principle-centered leadership.* New York: Fireside.

Conley, J., & Wagner-Marsh, F. (1998). The integration of business ethics and spirituality in the workplace. In L. C. Spears, (Ed.), *Insights on leadership: Service, stewardship, spirit, and servant-leadership* (251–257). New York: John Wiley & Sons.

Fanelli, A., & Misangyi, V. F. (2006). Bringing out charisma: CEO charisma and external stakeholders. *Academy of Management Review, 31,* 1049–1061. https://doi.org/10.5465/AMR.2006.22528170

Fry, L. W. (2003). Toward a theory of spiritual leadership. *Leadership Quarterly, 14,* 693–727. https://doi.org/10.1016/j.leaqua.2003.09.001

Geertz, C. (1973). Thick description: Toward an interpretive theory of culture. In C. Geertz (Ed.), *The interpretation of cultures: Selected essays* (3–30). New York: Basic Books.

Giacalone, R. A., & C. L. Jurkiewicz, (Eds.) (2003). *Handbook of workplace spirituality and organizational performance* (3–28). New York: M. E. Sharp.

Glaser, B. G., & Strauss, A. L. (1967). *The discovery of grounded theory: Strategies for qualitative research.* Chicago: Aldine.

Greenleaf, R. K. (1998). Servant-leadership. In L. C. Spears (Ed.), *Insights on leadership: Service, stewardship, spirit, and servant-leadership* (15–20). New York: John Wiley & Sons.

Grunig, J. E. (2001). Two-way symmetrical public relations: Past, present, and future. In R. Heath (Ed.), *Handbook of public relations* (11–30). Thousand Oaks, CA: Sage.

Grunig, L. A., Grunig, J. E., & Dozier, D. M. (2002). *Excellent public relations and effective organizations: A study of communication management in three countries.* Mahwah, NJ: Lawrence Erlbaum.

Harter, J. (2019). 4 Factors driving record high employee engagement in U.S. Retrieved from https://www.gallup.com/workplace/284180/factors-driving-record-high-employee-engagement.aspx

Hume, J., & Leonard, A. (2014). Exploring the strategic potential of internal communication in international non-governmental organisations. *Public Relations Review, 40,* 294–304. https://doi.org/10.1016/j.pubrev.2013.10.011

Jelen-Sanchez, A. (2017). Engagement in public relations discipline: Themes, theoretical perspectives and methodological approaches. *Public Relations Review, 43*(5), 934–944. https://doi.org/10.1016/j.pubrev.2017.04.002

Jiang, H., & Men, R. L. (2015). Creating an engaged workforce: The impact of authentic leadership, transparent organizational communication, and work-life enrichment. *Communication Research*. https://doi.org/10.1177/0093650215613137

Kahn, W. A. (1990). Psychological conditions of personal engagement and disengagement at work. *Academy of Management Journal 33*, 692–724. https://doi.org/10.2307/256287

Kalshoven, K., Den Hartog, D. N., & De Hoogh, A. H. B. (2001). Ethical leadership at work questionnaire (ELW): Development and validation of a multidimensional measure. *The Leadership Quarterly*, *22*(1), 51–69. https://doi.org/10.1016/j.leaqua.2010.12.007

Konz, G. N. P., & Ryan, F. X. (1999). Maintaining an organizational spirituality: No easy task. *Journal of Organizational Change Management*, *12*(3), 200–210. https://doi.org/10.1108/09534819910273865

Kotter, J. P., & Heskett, J. L. (1992). *Corporate culture and performance*. New York: The Press.

Kvale, S. (1995). The social construction of validity. *Qualitative Inquiry*, *1*(1), 19–40. https://doi.org/10.1177/107780049500100103

Lindlof, T. R., & Taylor, B. C. (2002). *Qualitative communication research methods* (2nd ed.). Thousand Oaks, CA: Sage.

Luthans, F., & Avolio, B. J. (2003). Authentic leadership: A positive developmental approach. In K. S. Cameron, J. E. Dutton, & R. E. Quinn (Eds.), *Positive organizational scholarship* (241–261). San Francisco: Berrett-Koehler.

McCormick, D. W. (1994). Spirituality and management. *Journal of Managerial Psychology*, *9*(6), 5–8. https://doi.org/10.1108/02683949410070142

McCown, N. (2006, November). *Internal public relations and relationship-building through individualized considerations: A transformational leader exemplar*. Paper presented to the annual conference of the Public Relations Society of America Educators Academy, Salt Lake City, UT.

McCown, N. (2010). *Intersections and overlaps: Building leader-employee relationships through internal public relations, leadership style, and workplace spirituality*. Paper presented to the annual conference of the Public Relations Society of America Educators Academy, Washington, DC.

McCown, N. (2014). Building leader-employee dialogue and relationships through internal public relations, leadership style, and workplace spirituality. *PRism Journal*, *11*(2). https://www.prismjournal.org/v11-no2.html

McCown, N. (2017). *Nonprofit employee engagement through internal communication, leadership, and culture*. Paper presented to the annual conference of the Public Relations Society of America Educators Academy, Boston, MA.

McCown, N. (2019). *Emerging brand employee engagement through internal communication, leadership and culture*. Paper presented to the annual conference of the Public Relations Society of America Educators Academy, San Diego.

Men, L. R. (2014a). Why leadership matters to internal communication: Linking transformational leadership, symmetrical communication, and employee outcomes. *Journal of Public Relations Research*, *26*, 256–279. https://doi.org/10.1080/1062726X.2014.908719

Men, L. R. (2014b). Internal reputation management: The impact of authentic leadership and transparent communication. *Corporate Reputation Review, 17*(4), 254–272. https://doi.org/10.1057/crr.2014.14

Men, L. R. (2015). The internal communication role of the chief executive officer: Communication channels, style, and effectiveness. *Public Relations Review, 41*(4), 461–471. https://doi.org/10.1016/j.pubrev.2015.06.021

Men, R. L., & Bowen, S. A. (2017). *Excellence in internal communication management*. New York: Business Expert Press.

Men, L. R., & Jiang, H. (2016). Cultivating quality employee-organization relationships: The interplay among organizational leadership, culture, and communication. *Journal of Strategic Communication, 10*(5), 462–479. https://doi.org/10.1080/1553118X.2016.1226172

Men, L. R., & Stacks, D. W. (2013). The impact of leadership style and employee empowerment on perceived organizational reputation. *Journal of Communication Management 17*(2), 171–192. https://doi.org/10.1108/13632541311318765

Men, L. R., & Stacks, D. W. (2014). The effects of authentic leadership on strategic internal communication and employee-organization relationships. *Journal of Public Relations Research, 26*, 301–324. https://doi.org/10.1080/1062726X.2014.908720

Mishra, K., Boynton, L, and Mishra, A. (2014). Driving employee engagement: The expanded role of internal communications. *International Journal of Business Communication, 51*(2), 183–202. https://doi.org/10.1177/2329488414525399

Michie, S., & Gooty, J. (2005). Values, emotions, and authenticity: Will the real leader please stand up? *Leadership Quarterly, 16*, 441–457. https://doi.org/10.1016/j.leaqua.2005.03.006

Musser, S. J. (1997). A study of the impact of religious conversion on the giving of individualized consideration by leaders. *Proceedings of the Annual Meeting of the Institute of Behavioral and Applied Management, 5*, 102–108.

Potter, W. J. (1996). *An analysis of thinking and research about qualitative methods*. Mahwah, NJ: Lawrence Erlbaum Associates.

Rubin, H. J., & Rubin, I. S. (2005). *Qualitative interviewing: The art of hearing data*. Thousand Oaks, CA: Sage.

Schaufeli, W. B., Salanova, M., Gonzalez-Roma, V., & Bakker, A. B. (2002). The measurement of engagement and burnout: A two sample confirmatory factor analytic approach. *Journal of Happiness Studies, 3*(1), 71–92. https://doi.org/10.1023/A:1015630930326

Schein, E. H. (1985). *Organizational culture and leadership*. San Francisco: Jossey-Bass.

Shamir, B., & Eilam, G. (2005). "What's your story?" A life-stories approach to authentic leadership development. *Leadership Quarterly, 16*, 395–417. https://doi.org/10.1016/j.leaqua.2005.03.005

Shen, H., & Jiang, H. (2019). Engaged at work? An employee engagement model in public relations. *Journal of Public Relations Research, 31*(1/2), 32–49. https://doi.org/10.1080/1062726X.2019.1585855

Spears, L. C. (1998). Servant-leadership and the Greenleaf legacy. In C. Spears (Ed.), *Insights on leadership: Service, stewardship, spirit, and servant-leadership* (1–14). New York: John Wiley & Sons.

Stein, A. (2006). Employee communications and community: An exploratory study. *Journal of Public Relations Research, 18*(3), 249–264. https://doi.org/10.1207/s1532754xjprr1803_3

Strauss, A., & Corbin, J. (1998). *Basics of qualitative research: Techniques and procedures for developing grounded theory* (2nd ed.). Thousand Oaks, CA: Sage.

Terry, R. W. (1993). *Authentic leadership: Courage in action.* San Francisco, CA: Jossey-Bass.

Verčič, A. T., & Vokić, N. P. (2017). Engaging employees through internal communication. *Public Relations Review, 43*, 885–893. https://doi.org/10.1016/j.pubrev.2017.04.005

Wagner-Marsh, F., & Conley, J. (1999). The fourth wave: The spiritually-based firm. *Journal of Organizational Change Management, 12*(4), 292–301. https://doi.org/10.1108/09534819910282135

Walden, J., Jung, E. H., & Westerman, K. (2017). Employee communication, job engagement, and organizational commitment: A study of members of the Millennial Generation. *Journal of Public Relations Research.* https://doi.org/10.1080/1062726X.2017.1329737

White, C., Vanc, A., & Stafford, G. (2010). Internal communication, information satisfaction and sense of community: The effect of personal influence. *Journal of Public Relations Research, 22*(1), 65–84. https://doi.org/10.1080/10627260903170985

Wong, C. A., & Cummings, G. G. (2009). The influence of authentic leadership behaviors on trust and work outcomes of health care staff. *Journal of Leadership Studies, 3*, 6–23. https://doi.org/10.1002/jls.20104

Yin, R. K. (2003). *Case study research: Design and methods* (3rd ed.). Thousand Oaks, CA: Sage.

Yukl, G. (2006). *Leadership in organizations* (6th ed.). Upper Saddle River, NJ: Prentice Hall.

Chapter Two

Exploring Internal Communication, Employee Engagement and Trust within a Government Contractor: A Case Study

Laura L. Lemon

Introduction

This chapter utilizes a government contractor case study to investigate how trust is constructed through internal communication. The connection between internal communication and employee engagement is also explored since the two work in tandem to create a culture rooted in trust (Cheney & Christensen, 2001), which is essential to navigating frequent organizational change. Therefore, the purpose of this chapter is to explore the interconnectedness of internal communication and employee engagement and how the two can assist in building trust between leadership and employees.

Literature Review

This chapter adopts public relations conceptualization of engagement (see Taylor & Kent, 2014), where engagement is "both an orientation that influences interactions and the approach that guides the process of interactions among groups" (Taylor & Kent, 2014, p. 384). In this way, engagement uses organizations and networks to cultivate a fully functioning society (Taylor, 2018), which helps scholars address organizational issues and situations that are often complex (Johnston & Taylor, 2018). This chapter applies this framework with a specific focus on the experiences of both leaders and employees who work for a U.S.-based government contractor.

Employee Engagement

Employee engagement is defined as the "harnessing of organization members' selves to their work roles; in engagement, people employ and express themselves physically, cognitively, and emotionally during role performances" (Kahn, 1990, p. 694). The original employee engagement model also discussed the psychological conditions that determine whether someone is willing to engage. Specifically, psychological presence is mediated by meaningfulness, safety, and availability, which leads to performance,

DOI: 10.4324/9781003195580-4

growth, and experience outcomes (Kahn, 1992). This model also includes the concept of psychological presence (Kahn, 1992).

Public relations scholars have adopted and used Kahn's (1990, 1992) original model to advance theory building by further examining the emotional, cognitive, and physical dimensions (e.g., Dhanesh, 2017; Men, 2012; Welch, 2011). Scholars in public relations have also used the first definition to extend understanding in the field. For example, Dhanesh (2017) offered a definition of engagement as the "communicative interaction" between organizations and their stakeholders (p. 926). Shen and Jiang (2019) argued that employee engagement is the process of how employees might enact their personal selves while in a working environment. Men (2012) relied on psychological presence to investigate role performances. Last, Lemon and Palenchar (2018) reconceptualized employee engagement as a mechanism for meaning making.

In addition to applying the original model and definition, public relations scholars have investigated the various antecedents that influence employee engagement such as leadership (Jiang & Luo, 2018; Jin, 2010; Men & Stacks, 2013; Meng & Berger, 2019); organizational reputation (Men, 2012); corporate social responsibility (Duthler & Dhanesh, 2018); and employee voice (Ruck et al., 2017). Most of the literature across academic disciplines examines how working conditions and available resources can create affirmative work environments, which leads to more engaged employees (Hynes, 2012). Public relations scholars are most interested in the relationship between internal communication and employee engagement.

Internal Communication

Internal communication is any exchange from those more informal like a water-cooler conversation to the more formal, top-down communication like management emails (Welch, 2011). Welch and Jackson (2007) defined internal communication as "the strategic management of interactions and relationships between stakeholders within organizations across a number of interrelated dimensions including internal line manager communication, internal team peer communication, internal project peer communication and internal corporate communication" (p. 184). This definition takes a stakeholder-centric approach, which focuses on all members within an organization. Such an approach allows internal communication to become a process shared by all employees to create meaning and cultivate organizational culture (Mazzei et al., 2012).

Organizations use a variety of channels to communicate to and with their internal audiences, including face-to-face, electronic media, social networks, and traditional printed publications (Verčič & Špoljarić, 2020). Despite the number of available internal communication channels, research has shown that face-to-face communication is still the most preferred channel by employees (e.g., Men, 2014; Mishra et al., 2014; White et al., 2010). For example, Men (2014) found that employees desire to receive information regarding decisions, changes, and policies via non-mediated channels like staff meetings or one-on-one interactions but still favored email as a mediated communication channel. Printed forms of communication like brochures, memos, and posters were not preferred by employees (2014). These preferences align with media richness theory, which suggests a continuum of communication tools with the richest mediums (e.g., face-to-face and interpersonal communication) on one end; telephone, email, and video as moderate mediums in the middle; and the least rich mediums (e.g., written statements and documents) on the other end (Daft & Lengel, 1984).

Depending on the content of the messages, employees will have different preferences for how they wish to receive the communication (Verčič & Špoljarić, 2020). To illustrate, there may be instances when face-to-face communication is not preferred since it is not always the fastest or most effective mode of communication (Mishra et al., 2014). The key to understanding preferred internal communication channels is to dedicate time and resources listening to and researching employee needs.

Several public relations scholars have examined the connection between internal communication and employee engagement to better understand how internal communication can increase employee engagement (e.g., Ewing et al., 2019; Karanges et al., 2014; Lemon, 2019; Verčič & Vokič, 2017). This research-driven connection is rooted in the fact that internal communication can serve the communication needs of employees (Welch, 2011). Specifically, if internal communication content is geared to individuals and addresses organizational issues, employees will exercise a greater willingness to engage (Walden et al., 2017). In fact, strategic internal communication can result in meaningful connections among employees in an organization and increase engagement (Karanges et al., 2015). Therefore, when leaders prompt employees to share, they are more willing to disclose feedback and opinions, which results in more employee engagement (2015). In addition to encouragement from leadership, employee sharing mechanisms like internal social media platforms create additional opportunities for employees to share feedback, which can potentially facilitate more engagement (e.g., Ewing et al., 2019; Palomares et al., 2018).

Trust

The influential role of trust has been investigated by several public relations scholars (e.g., Jiang & Luo, 2018; Meng & Berger, 2019; Yue et al., 2019). Mayer et al. (1995) initially defined trust as "the willingness of a party to be vulnerable to the actions of another party based on the expectation that the other will perform a particular action important to the trustor, irrespective of the ability to monitor or control the other party" (p. 712). Public relations scholars Hon and Grunig (1999) defined trust as "one party's level of confidence in and willingness to open oneself to the other party" (p. 2).

Ultimately, trust is the foundation of all relationships in an organization (Akiate, 2018). Trusting relationships take time to build through prior experiences and then the application of those experiences to the current situation—all of which are rooted in expectations (Tucker et al., 2012). Employees will only show their true selves at work once trust has been established since trust diminishes the fear of potential negative consequences associated with this level of vulnerability. Such levels of trust are most often established through internal communication (Lemon & Towery, 2021).

The function of internal communication helps to build and maintain trust between employees and managers (Van Dam et al., 2008). This is especially true during times of organizational change. For example, Yue et al. (2019) determined that employees mainly depend on what their managers say and do to navigate change, and if trust is present, employees will be more open to the change, which positively impacts employee engagement. However, when words and/or actions are incomplete, unfair, or unclear, trust becomes very hard to build, which impacts an organization's ability to navigate change (2019).

Research Questions

Given the connection between internal communication, employee engagement, and trust, this case study proposed two research questions. First, how do leaders of government contractors use internal communication to build trust with employees? Second, how does trust impact employee engagement for government contractor employees?

Case Description

To demonstrate the connection between internal communication and employee engagement to establish trust, this chapter utilized a case study of two government contractors located in the United States: one located in the southern U.S. and the other in the southeastern U.S. The billion-dollar sites have existed since the 1940s, which means the locations have well-established reputations in their respective cities. Both sites work on highly sensitive and top-secret work for the Department of Defense. Organizational life for government contractors is unusual in that employees experience routine changes to upper management, company values, goals, and objectives every few years, all of which require a company culture invested in employee engagement and internal communication practices to maintain trust despite the constant change.

Methodology

This study followed Yin's (2014) case study design protocol, where the goal was to attain "analytic generalization" (p. 41). Such generalizations emerge from case studies since this methodological approach allows researchers to develop a deeper understanding of the phenomenon from bounding the case based on a specific space and time (Yin, 2014). To collect data, this case study utilized a qualitative approach with management interviews and focus groups made up of non-management employees. Given the concern to protect the propriety mission of the government contractor featured in the study, no documents, such as emails or internal communication, were provided to the researcher by the organization.

Sample

The case study had 77 participants. The 7 focus groups had 56 participants with 21 participants in 3 focus groups from the southern site and 35 participants in 4 focus groups from the southeastern site. The make of focus group participants included 27 women and 29 men who varied in age, gender, positions, departments, pay type, and years with the company. The one criterion for focus group participants was that they had to be non-management employees. To capture management and internal communication staff perspectives, 21 interviews were conducted with 10 men and 11 women. Interview participants were either c-suite leaders or communication personnel with 6 participants from the southern site, 11 from the southeastern site, and 4 members of the executive leadership team. Specifically, 12 communication members, 3 site managers, 2 middle managers, and 4 executives participated in the interviews.

Data Collection

Interviews began with rapport-building and then transitioned into broad questions that asked participants to share about their professional backgrounds. From there, questions narrowed to focus more on perceptions of internal communication, employee engagement, and trust. Prompts were used to elicit more depth in participant responses. Four interviews were completed over the phone and 17 were conducted in person at the site(s). Interviews ranged from 33 to 100 minutes with the average interview length resulting in 50 minutes. A professional transcriptionist was used to transcribe the 260 pages of interview data.

The focus groups also followed a similar process that began with rapport building, which was then followed with more specific questions about internal communication, trust, and employee engagement. Prompts were also used to encourage participants to elaborate on their personal experiences. All focus groups were conducted in-person and on site, with each one lasting one hour to fit within the allotted lunch break. Food and drinks were available for each focus group. The audio recorded focus groups resulted in 144 pages of transcribed data.

Data Analysis

An inductive approach was used for data analysis across all transcripts. This approach began with open coding followed by the collapsing and adjusting of repetitive codes to develop themes that could help answer the research questions. All data analysis stages were conducted using either NVivo for Mac or Microsoft Excel.

Findings

The findings are broken into two sections based on the proposed research questions. The first section addresses how leaders use internal communication to build trust with employees. The second section covers how trust impacts employee engagement.

Using Internal Communication to Build Trust

The first research question asked how leaders of government contractors use internal communication to build trust with employees. For the participants in this study, trust is something that is earned with management over time, through more frequent, dialogic interactions. Therefore, it is not the formal, internal communication that allows management to build trust but rather more informal conversations, and both employees and management recognize the value of such communication. For example, a c-suite executive said:

> If I'm having a two-way discussion with my employees, I care about them. They know that I'm going to back them up, that I'm going to actually be their

> leader. I tell them the why and give them a big picture and create a pathway for them. That trust is gained over time. A lot of people think that due to the position they're in, that they should demand that trust. It's just not how it works.

Another manager for one of the sites said, "I think developing rapport with them, so they trust us too." The other site manager shared, "You know .... If it's informal it's better. It makes it seem like it's not an exercise." The CEO of both sites also shared, "With employees there needs to be a connection with that manager that people trust, right?" Through dialogue, trust is established, which leads to the building of connections across an organization as well as the strengthening of existing relationships.

Given the desire for more dialogic communication, one of the deterrents for building trust that management relies too heavily on is the organization's intranet. One member of the communication team said, "We rely too heavily on our intranet, and there are many employees who don't have access to the intranet. There are a lot of missives from senior management that are very dense ... most people just hit the delete button." Participants in the focus groups at both sites shared ample negative feedback regarding the intranet. One focus group participant at the southern site said, "It's hard to discern what applies to you and what's important because you see so much stuff." Another focus group participant at the other site said, "There's so much trash out there. I don't like taking the time to sort through it all."

The other deterrent that was mentioned by participants in the study is email, where too many times people rely on email instead of picking up the phone or going to someone's office to communicate a message. For example, a focus group participant in the southeast said, "Why didn't they call me? You spent two hours writing this down when you could've picked up the phone and ten minutes later, we could've solved it." Another focus group participant at the same site shared, "Instead of somebody picking up a phone and addressing an issue immediately, they feel compelled to send an email, copy their supervisor and their supervisor. Then suddenly, you have all these people helping you that you really don't need help from." A focus group participant from the southern site said, "Especially for us guys in the field. You email me, you're wasting your time .... We have craft [personnel] that don't even have accounts." Another focus group participant from the same site said, "There's a write-up that comes out on the email from our VPs. For me personally, I'm too busy to read them. I just go through there and delete them ... because it's wordy."

Part of the issue participants had with email is that such communication is rarely targeted, which means the content is not helpful for the receiver. For example, one focus group participant in the south said, "'You don't even know who I am. Why do I need to read that email? I have no interest in what you have to say. Who are you?'" Another participant shared, "I think the email, if it's directed to you, it's one thing ...When they send out a mass email, I'm like 'Oh, delete.' It can't be that important if it went to everybody, right?"

In summary, according to the participants in this study, the best internal communication to build trust included dialogic or some form of informal exchanges, whether it was in person or over the phone. Participants also suggested that the intranet and email were ineffective modes of communication since the content is not tailored to a specific audience. Therefore, such communication channels were not effective at building trust, even though they were relied upon often by management to communicate important messages.

Trust Impacts Employee Engagement

The second research question explored how the trust built with management impacts employee engagement for government contractor employees. According to the participants in this study, a direct link exists between trust and employee engagement, where a foundation of trust, rooted in dialogic exchanges, leads to more engagement from employees. For example, a focus group participant located in the southeast shared:

> I mean, everything, movement of anything, getting anything done, it is all relationship-based. There's no way without it; it's an amazing thing ...Who do you know, and do you trust them, and do they do a good job? That is actually how anything is done here.

A communication staff member for both sites explained, "We have some managers who are really good at connecting with employees, and it's just because they take the time to shake your hand and stop to talk to you." A focus group participant from the southeast said, "I think of it more of reaching out to the employees to be engaged, to make change ... one of the best supervisors I ever worked for ... He said, 'I work for you all.'" The site manager in the south said, "So, what I determined here is the folks here really want more of that personal time, so I'm probably seen out on the floor in those discussions with them a lot more."

One unique aspect of this type of communication that builds trust and employee engagement is that it needs to be genuine. A mid-level manager shared:

> I feel like people say, "Oh, we need to focus on employee engagement" but you have to care, if you're going to ask someone, you have to care what they say.

> If you want to be engaged with people, you need to care and you can tell that. I've had managers ask me, "Are you okay?" "Sure, I'm good" but then I've had managers call me while I'm not at the plant, on my cell phone, "Are you okay?" and you can just tell a difference.

Genuine communication also encourages active listening among dialogic partners. For example, one communication professional said, "Getting out and listening … I'd rather it be really hearing from employees about their perspective on how things are going, so we can react to support that." This genuine communication leads to relationship building and results in employee engagement. A communication staff member said, "You're inherently building a relationship and that direct supervisory relationship is also one of the biggest indicators of employee engagement." A c-suite executive said, "To me, that's direct employee engagement, face-to-face, hearing from employees."

In summary, this case demonstrates how the dialogic communication that is genuine and involves active listening helps build trust, which leads to employee engagement. Trust results in relationships between management and employees that ultimately encourages more engagement.

Discussion

Verčič and Špoljarić (2020) suggested that recent scholarship is limited in terms of the number of investigations into internal communication channels. Therefore, this study responds to this call by exploring government contractor employees' preferences for the types of internal communication that cultivate trust and employee engagement. The findings from this study align with Yue et al.'s (2019) work, where incomplete and unclear communication can lead to a lack of trust between management and employees, which ultimately impacts employee engagement. As demonstrated in this study, employee engagement is cultivated through dialogue and active listening, which is similar to the findings in Lemon (2019).

Contrary to Men (2014), the findings in this case study reveal that email was not necessarily an effective way to communicate major decisions as well as information regarding the organizational change. Email was discussed by participants as not being tailored to specific audiences, which impacted trust between management and employees. The richest medium of face-to-face communication was ideal. In addition, the intranet, which is considered a mid-level communication tool in terms of media richness, did not build trust nor lead to more employee engagement. This also disconfirms existing research (e.g., Ewing et al., 2019; Palomares et al., 2018), which would have assumed that since internal social media provides a feedback mechanism, employees would have seen this as an opportunity for engagement. Yet, employees in this study found the intranet to also be too impersonal.

This government contractor case study demonstrates the value of internal communication rooted in dialogue, where encouraging one-on-one communication ensures active listening, which is the best way for management to build trust. The process of building trust takes time and many frequent points of communication because one or two instances of communication are not enough to build trust among employees. However, too often, management in large organizations depends on technology to communicate, which can impact both trust and employee engagement. This dependency on technology is understandable in some ways since communicating via phone or in person to thousands of employees is not always feasible due to limited time and resources. Therefore, the goal for management is to find a way to balance email communication and intranet usage with more one-on-one communication to ensure employees feel heard and connections are built up and down the organizational hierarchy.

Suggestions for Practice

Most large organizations will face similar challenges as the government contractor featured in this case study. How do large corporations or non-profits take advantage of dialogic communication opportunities to build relationships across an organization yet ensure that all employees are adequately informed? First, as observed in this study, formal internal communication channels like intranets and email need to be tailored to specific internal audiences. Some internal audiences did not even have access to email, so how does management inform those individuals about important organizational updates or changes? In addition, the blanket email to all employees seems to be the least effective way for management to communicate. These formal communication tools are important, yet internal communication practitioners need to spend additional time creating and disseminating targeted content. This will help ensure that messages are read and not simply deleted.

Second, the internal communication strategy needs to include training for management that focuses on active listening and cultivating dialogic communication. Some of the managers who participated in this study were hired for being subject matter experts, not because they were great communicators. Therefore, the internal communication professionals need to train and equip these managers with the necessary skills to engage in dialogue that is genuine and features the active listening component to ensure their employees know they can rely on them as a resource. These exchanges should occur frequently, knowing that trust is built through informal dialogue over time, which ultimately results in employees being more willing to engage.

Learning Outcomes

1) Understand the connection between internal communication, trust, and employee engagement.
2) Gain exposure to a rarely discussed industry, the government contract sector.
3) Receive introduction to and appreciate the qualitative case study method.

Discussion Questions

1) What challenges do you think exist when pursuing face-to-face communication?
2) How has the COVID-19 pandemic changed our options for engaging in face-to-face communication?
3) Are there times when dialogic communication is not helpful or preferred? If so, describe a situation that comes to mind.

Further Readings

Ewing, M., Men, L. R., & O'Neil, J. (2019). Using social media to engage employees: Insights from internal communication managers. *International Journal of Strategic Communication, 13*(2), 110–132.

Jiang, H., & Luo, Y. (2018). Crafting employee trust: From authenticity, transparency to engagement. *Journal of Communication Management, 22*(2), 138–160. doi:10.1108/jcom-07-2016-0055

Lemon, L. L. (2019). The employee experience: How employees make meaning of employee engagement. *Journal of Public Relations Research, 31*(5–6), 176–199. doi.org/10.1080/1062726X.2019.1704288

Verčič, A. T., & Špoljarić, A. (2020). Managing internal communication: How the choice of channels affects internal communication satisfaction. *Public Relations Review, 46*, 1–7. doi.org/10.1016/j.pubrev.2020.101926

References

Akiate, Y. W. D. (2018). Employees' trust towards management and organizational Commitment after a bank's merger and acquisition: Mediated by procedural justice. *International Journal of Business & Management Science, 8*(1), 151–166.

Cheney, G., & Christensen, L.T. (2001). Organizational identity: linkages between internal and external communication. In Jablin, F., & Putnam, L. (Eds), *The new handbook of organizational communication.* Thousand Oaks, CA: Sage Publications.

Daft, R. L., & Lengel, R. H. (1984). Information richness: A new approach to managerial behavior and organizational design. *Research in Organizational Behavior, 6*, 191–233.

Dhanesh, G. S. (2017). Putting engagement in its proper place: State of the field, definition and model of engagement in public relations. *Public Relations Review, 43*, 925–933. doi.org/10.1016/j.pubrev.2017.04.001

Duthler, G., & Dhanesh, G. S. (2018). The role of corporate social responsibility (CSR) and internal CSR communication in predicting employee engagement: Perspectives from the United Arab Emirates (UAE). *Public Relations Review, 44*, 453–462.

Ewing, M., Men, L. R., & O'Neil, J. (2019). Using social media to engage employees: Insights from internal communication managers. *International Journal of Strategic Communication, 13*(2), 110–132.

Hon, L., & Grunig, J. E. (1999). *Guidelines for measuring relationships in public relations.* Institute for Public Relations. Retrieved from https://instituteforpr.org/measuring-relationships/

Hynes, G. E. (2012). Improving employees' interpersonal communication competencies: A qualitative study. *Business Communication Quarterly, 75*(4), 466–475. doi:10.1177/1080569912458965

Jiang, H., & Luo, Y. (2018). Crafting employee trust: From authenticity, transparency to engagement. *Journal of Communication Management, 22*(2),138–160. doi:10.1108/jcom-07-2016-0055

Jin, Y. (2010). Emotional leadership as a key dimension of public relations leadership: A national survey of public relations leaders. *Journal of Public Relations Research, 22*(2), 159–181. doi:10.1080/10627261003601622

Johnston, K. A., & Taylor, M. (2018). Engagement as communication: Pathways, possibilities and future directions. In A. Johnston & M. Taylor (Eds.), *The handbook of communication engagement* (1–15). Hoboken, NJ: John Wiley & Sons, Inc.

Kahn, W. A. (1990). Psychological conditions of personal engagement and disengagement at work. *Academy of Management Journal, 33*(4), 692–724. doi.org/10.2307/256287

Kahn, W. A. (1992). To be fully there: Psychological presence at work. *Human Relations, 45*(4), 321–349. doi.org/10.1177/001872679204500402

Karanges, E., Beatson, A., Johnston, K., & Lings, I. (2014). Optimizing employee engagement with internal communication: A social exchange perspective. *Journal of Business Market Management, 7*(2), 329–353.

Karanges, E., Johnston, K., Beatson, A., & Lings, I. (2015). The influence of internal communication on employee engagement: A pilot study. *Public Relations Review, 41*(1), 129–131. doi:10.1016/j.pubrev.2014.12.003

Mazzei, A., Kim, J.-N., & Dell'Oro, C. (2012). Strategic value of employee relationships and communicative actions: Overcoming corporate crisis with quality internal communication. *International Journal of Strategic Communication, 6*, 31–44.

Lemon, L. L., & Palenchar, M. J. (2018). Public relations and zones of engagement: Employees' lived experiences and the fundamental nature of employee engagement. *Public Relations Review, 44(*1), 142–155. doi.org/10.1016/j.pubrev.2018.01.002

Lemon, L. L., & Towery, N. A. (2021) The case for internal communication: An investigation into consortia forming. *Corporate Communications: An International Journal.* Early access available at doi.org/10.1108/CCIJ-07-2019-0093

Mayer, R. C., Davis, J. H., & Schoorman, D. (1995). An integrative model of organizational trust. *Academy of Management Review, 20*, 709–734. doi:10.5465/amr.1995.9508080335

Men, L. R. (2012). CEO credibility, perceived organizational reputation, and employee engagement. *Public Relations Review, 38*(1), 171–173. doi.org/10.1016/j.pubrev.2011.12.011

Men, L. R. (2014). Strategic internal communication: Transformational leadership, communication channels, and employee satisfaction. *Management Communication Quarterly, 28*(2), 264–284. doi.org/10.1177/0893318914524536

Men, L. R., & Stacks, D. W. (2013). The impact of leadership style and employee empowerment on perceived organizational reputation. *Journal of Communication Management, 17*(2), 171–192. doi:10.1108/13632541311318765

Meng, J., & Berger, B. K. (2019). The impact of organizational culture and leadership performance on PR professionals' job satisfaction: Testing the joint mediating effects of engagement and trust. *Public Relations Review, 45*, 64–75.

Mishra, K., Boynton, L., & Mishra, A. (2014). Driving employee engagement: The expanded role of internal communications. *Journal of Business Communication, 51*(2), 183–202. doi.org/10.1177/2329488414525399

Palomares, M. I., Navarro, C., & Lara, J. A. S. (2018). Determining factors of success in internal communication management in Spanish companies. *Corporate Communication: An International Journal, 23*(3), 405–422.

Ruck, K., Welch, M., & Menara, B. (2017). Employee voice: An antecedent to organizational engagement? *Public Relations Review, 43*, 904–914. doi:10.1016/j.pubrev.2017.04.008

Shen, H., & Jiang, H. (2019). Engaged at work? An employee engagement model in public relations. *Journal of Public Relations Research, 31*(1–2), 32–49. doi.org/10.1080/1062726X.2019.1585855

Taylor, M. (2018). Reconceptualizing public relations in an engaged society. In K. A. Johnston & M. Taylor (Eds.), *The handbook of communication engagement* (103–114). Hoboken, NJ: John Wiley & Sons, Inc.

Taylor, M., & Kent, M. L. (2014). Dialogic engagement: Clarifying foundational concepts. *Journal of Public Relations Research, 26*(5), 384–398. doi.org/10.1080/1062726X.2014.956106

Tucker, D. A., Yeow, P., & Viki, G. T. (2012). Communicating during organizational change using social accounts: The importance of ideological accounts. *Management Communication Quarterly, 27*(2), 184–209. doi:10.1177/0893318912469771

Van Dam, K., Oreg, S., & Schyns, B. (2008). Daily work contexts and resistance to organizational change: The role of leader-member exchange, development climate, and change process characteristics. *Applied Psychology: An International Review, 57*, 313–334. doi:10.1111/j.1464-0597.2007.00311.x

Verčič, A. T., & Špoljarić, A. (2020). Managing internal communication: How the choice of channels affects internal communication satisfaction. *Public Relations Review, 46*, 1–7. doi.org/10.1016/j.pubrev.2020.101926

Verčič, A. T., & Vokič, N. P. (2017). Engaging employees through internal communication. *Public Relations Review, 43*, 885–893.

Walden, J., Jung, E. H., & Westerman, C. Y. K. (2017). Employee communication, job engagement, and organizational commitment. *Journal of Public Relations Research, 29*(2–3), 73–89. doi.org/10.1080/1062726X.2017.1329737

Welch, M. (2011). The evolution of the employee engagement concept: Communication implications. *Corporate Communications: An International Journal, 16*(4), 328–346. doi.org/10.1108/13563281111186968

Welch, M., & Jackson, P. R. (2007). Rethinking internal communication: A stakeholder approach. *Corporate Communications, 12*, 177–198. doi:10.1108/13563280710744847

White, C., Vanc, A., & Stafford, G. (2010). Internal communication, information satisfaction, and sense of community: The effect of personal influence. *Journal of Public Relations Research, 22*(1), 65–84. doi.org/10.1080/10627260903170985

Yin, R. K. (2014). *Case study research design and methods*. Thousand Oaks, CA: Sage.

Yue, C. A., Men, L. R., & Ferguson, M. A. (2019). Bridging transformational leadership, transparent communication, and employee openness to change: The mediating role of trust. *Public Relations Review, 45*(3), 1–13.

Chapter Three

Leading Institutional Change through Digital Communication: A Case Study on the Launch of the U.S. Army Combat Fitness Test

Marc Vielledent and Chase Spears

Introduction

Change is inconvenient for organizations because it introduces uncertainty and typically creates fear (Hoffer, 1951). Regardless of the level at which change occurs, any alignment of change efforts within an organization relies on precise communication (Elving, 2005). Organizational change often results from conflict with institutional logic, that is, how broader belief systems shape behaviors. A predictable level of alignment can help leaders to identify the causes for change, understand roles and responsibilities, and execute tactics and strategies across relevant channels to support change initiatives. Predictability brings a greater assurance that public "change" events will go well, reducing the risk that, when "these events go poorly, they breed cynicism and pessimism, which can become demobilizing" (Dzur, 2019, p. 124).

In this chapter, we analyze communication related to changing the U.S. Army's physical fitness test to examine (1) how the language and actions of the change were disseminated via digital communication; (2) the initial reception from internal employees (or in this case, soldiers), and (3) how the discourse evoked various emotions from different internal groups over a five-year period. These findings reinforce previous studies and provide implications for how leaders and institutions can execute change initiatives more effectively through precise language, specific communication styles, and effective strategies.

Literature Review

The two theoretical frameworks conceptually linked to this case study examination are leadership communication and change communication. Effective change communication derives from organizational leadership (Men et al., 2018). Both the leader and the organization benefit when the environment is assessed prior to any change in communication and subsequent implementation. Communication strategies and tactics require leaders to envision the change, focus on solutions, and position themselves accordingly

DOI: 10.4324/9781003195580-5

within the team (Venus et al., 2019). This requirement is dependent upon the desired ends, potential avenues, and available means accessible for the leader to employ (Men et al., 2018). Thus, in the early stage of any effective organizational change, leadership must identify a clear and concise approach in style, language, and channel. Literature that adequately examines organizational communication within the context of organizational change is limited, leaving a gap in organizational change theory tied to leadership communication during times of change (Eisenberg et al., 1999; Frahm & Brown, 2005). Accordingly, this chapter primarily focuses on leadership communication and change communication through the digital lens.

Leaders Communicating Change

Previous research recognized the role of style, language, and channels in effective leadership communication to generate positive organizational outcomes during change (Mayfield & Mayfield, 2004; Men & Bowen, 2017; Men & Stacks, 2014). In combination with leadership behavior, leadership styles—such as transformational, visionary, ethical, and servant—have coalesced in their direct contributions to internal organizational reputation and relationships (Men & Bowen, 2017). Leaders who demonstrate a responsive communication style, classified through warm, friendly, and sensitive approaches, are perceived to be more effective communicators (Men, 2015); similarly, leaders communicating in a friendly, engaging manner are more likely to facilitate change outcomes (Solaja et al., 2016). Conversely, leaders who demonstrate an assertive communication style, classified as forceful, free, and direct, foster quality individual-organizational relationships to a lesser degree (Men & Bowen, 2017).

Individuals within the organization are more likely to respond to change in a positive way based on different types of language used by change agents (Mayfield & Mayfield, 2018). For example, direction-giving language articulates clear tasks, boundaries, role expectations, rewards, and performance feedback; whereas meaning-making language stresses reinforcement of the mission, values, and purpose. Empathetic language is classified as communication that expresses compassion, care, and encouragement to connect leaders with their followers on a more interpersonal level. This form of communication is more likely to enhance trust and commitment from stakeholders. As stakeholders perceive the potential benefits of an institutional change, they are more likely to support it (Bull & Brown, 2012).

Finally, the type and timing of strategic messages, based on context and the delivered channel, can influence audiences to generate optimal outcomes. As leaders incorporate vision into their messages, they can motivate stakeholders to participate in the change process through a mutual understanding of the current state, undesired future state, and desired future state of the organization as a whole (Men & Bowen, 2017; Men et al., 2020). Additionally, different communication channels offer leaders a decision to employ as a way to further enhance effectiveness during various stages of implementing change (Men et al., 2020). As a type of digital channel, social media represents an increasingly common way to engage stakeholders in a two-way, informal, communal manner to shape and support change efforts (Clayton, 2015). Additionally, leadership communication strategies should include aspects of authenticity, responsiveness, and transparency in their messaging to increase the likelihood of a successful change effort (Gergs & Trinczek, 2010).

The significance associated with a specific institutional change should dictate the level of leader investment. While every level within the institution relies on interaction and communication to implement change, precise leadership communication can accelerate understanding and offset barriers or resistance to change from key audiences. Thoughtful, empathetic engagement through all stages of change can further reinforce positive outcomes. During the engagement process, change agents must actively listen to their stakeholders, whether they are supporters or skeptics.

Change Communication in the Post-Digital Age

Change and developmental processes occur at various levels across an organization, to include the individual, group, organization, population, and even larger community level (Van de Ven & Poole, 1995). Communicating the purpose behind change efforts within an institution is fundamental in assuring understanding, implementation, and uniformity in behavior (Carton et al., 2014). The proliferation of digital and social technologies has provided increased opportunities for organizations and publics to build and strengthen relationships via digital communication (Men et al., 2018; Sweetser & Kelleher, 2016; Yue et al., 2020). Compared to traditional media, digital—and more specifically—social media cultivates relationships on a more interpersonal level; organizations and their representatives are more likely to cultivate meaningful relationships with stakeholders by employing personalized, interactive, conversational, open, and genuine communication (Cheng & Jiang, 2021; Tsai & Men, 2017). However, over the last few decades, communication and public relations scholars have focused on different types of relationship maintenance strategies. Yet, herein lies a gap in research based on the lack of examination in how the use of digital communication channels, particularly social media, influence the effectiveness of change communication.

During times of change, leaders should include social media analytics as part of developing an informed awareness of concerns (Men & Bowen, 2017) to better understand how the change will affect different stakeholder groups' work routine or relationships, how stakeholders may interpret change, and how to recognize stakeholder communication preferences. Given the ubiquitous nature of social media, the boundary between stakeholders and non-stakeholders for institutions and organizations has blurred, further complicating digital relationship management (Luoma-aho, 2015). Recent findings suggest there is significant potential in leveraging social media to conduct change communication. For example, an interpersonal approach provides stakeholders a chance to connect with each other while voicing their questions, concerns, and feedback about the change. While communication with direct supervisors can explain the changes in a way that is relevant to employees and easier to understand, instant feedback also reduces uncertainty and delivers a sense of control back to those affected (Allen et al., 2007). Digital channels, such as social media and online messengers, can introduce change and provide sufficient information necessary to address employees' concerns and reduce uncertainty while also representing an increasingly common way to engage employees in a two-way, informal, communal manner to shape the future, support the intended change, and offer recognition to one another (Clayton, 2015). However, digital communication often fails without socially minded leaders implementing sufficient change communication plans (Clayton, 2015). In addition to the responsive and interactive benefits digital channels provide, they offer an enhanced ability for leaders to demonstrate their expertise, guidance, and decision-making by connecting with their specific communities undergoing change (Jiang et al., 2017). Thus, organizations must be more deliberate as they prepare for situations where messages may generate unintended outcomes for the leadership, the institution, and its people.

Research Questions

This research aims to explore how organizational leadership can be more effective in change communication initiatives using digital communication. As a result, this chapter incorporates a case study and discourse analysis to examine the following research questions:

RQ1: What leadership communication styles were primarily employed during the period of change?

RQ2: What type of language and message strategies did leaders, and the institution, employ during the period of change?

RQ3: How did Army officials use social media to achieve change communication objectives?

RQ4: How did the impact and reception of the change communication differ between internal groups within the organization?

Case Summary

The U.S. Army's culture aligns many attributes, with physical fitness being preeminent among them. A common refrain around the force is "PT is the most important thing we do all day." Soldiers who do not pass the physical fitness test face negative counseling statements in writing, followed by supplemental, supervised workouts, and adverse action through "flagging"—meaning they cannot receive any awards or promotions until they rectify their score to an acceptable standard (HQDA, 2016). Fail twice in a row and individual soldiers can be processed for separation from the U.S. Army (HQDA, 2017). Even though the Army's standard physical fitness test consists of less exercise than most soldiers do on a daily basis, the career ramifications, based on how one performs on the test, make it an emotional event to the point that those being tested can feel negative physical effects from the anxiety, to include nausea, fatigue, and increased intestinal activity. This anxiety contributed to the rationale cited by U.S. Air Force officials in its changes to fitness testing in 2021, aimed at reducing the stress and stigma associated with test events (Everstine, 2019). In a similar fashion, the Space Force announced plans to do away with the annual physical fitness testing requirement in 2022, opting instead for a holistic approach to fitness for its members (Cohen, 2022). The U.S. Navy followed in November of that year, announcing that starting in 2023 it would reduce required physical fitness testing to once a year, instead of twice annually (Toropin, 2022).

The Army took a different approach to changing its physical fitness test through a design to emphasize overall physical fitness in a manner intended to reflect combat environments (Barno & Bensahel, 2018). This change in how the Army measures physical fitness required the institution to overcome resistance from those who were accustomed to, and those who excelled under the legacy Army Physical Fitness Test (APFT) regimen. Concerns among many in the force flowed beyond the Army's institutional boundaries and into the public realm, and eventually into the halls of Congress. As a result, delays in implementation led to three subsequent changes to the Army's ACFT plan.

The original APFT, introduced in 1980, was designed with feasibility and practicality in mind. All one needed to offer the test was a stopwatch, a couple of individuals to grade, and a marked two-mile running route (HQDA, 2012). On June 9, 2018, the Army formally announced the Army Combat Fitness Test (ACFT), which was said to offer a more realistic measure of capabilities required for the combat environment as compared to the three-part APFT (Kimmons, 2018). The new fitness test requires a significant amount of equipment and facilities, as the number of events doubled from three to six. Practicing many of the new events realistically requires gym use, which is sometimes prohibited for individual soldiers during official morning physical training (PT) hours at many Army installations.

The way the test was originally announced produced three primary concerns. First, the ACFT likely failed to accommodate those who have physical profiles (Kimmons, 2018). Military service is hard on the body and many soldiers develop chronic injuries along the course of their careers that interfere with their ability to take certain portions of the test (Myers, 2018). They can be exempted from portions of physical fitness testing by medical personnel with what is referred to as a temporary or permanent *profile*. When originally announced, the ACFT offered no alternative events to accommodate those who possess medically documented injuries sustained during their military service. The supporting narrative conveyed that those who could not pass the future six-part ACFT might no longer be considered fit for continued military service (Kimmons, 2018).

Second, unlike the APFT, the original AFCT did not allow for depreciating physical performance based on age (Beum, 2021). The APFT had a sliding scale for grading based on gender and age. In contrast, the ACFT, as announced in 2018, had a fixed, gender- and age-neutral scale with separate standards based on which military specialty a soldier is assigned. For example, administrative troops were assigned the lowest standard, while infantry troops were assigned the highest. Senior Army officials emphasized that the ACFT would be a harder test requiring an array of varying workouts to be successful. Finally, the original ACFT necessitated a higher level of upper body strength than the APFT, causing concerns that it may be harder for women to pass. Secretary of the Army Christine Wormuth echoed this concern at her confirmation hearing (Beynon, 2021a), and a study of the test conducted by the Rand Corporation (Hardison et al., 2022) validated her concern. These changes presented potential career impacts to tens of thousands of soldiers across the force while also eliciting the kind of emotional and public response that comes with a potential threat to continued military service.

As the change communication for this update was initiated through face-to-face touchpoints in formations from leaders to their subordinates and via digital platforms from leaders in distributed environments, collective concern and skepticism spread across the force. Much of this feedback and dialogue across the organization did not align with service officials' expectations for implementation and acceptance. As a result, service officials were forced to adapt their styles, language, and delivery methods in response to mounting criticism that culminated in a congressional order halting full implementation of the ACFT until an independent study could be conducted to determine its impact on certain institutional populations (United States House of Representatives, 2021). Conducted by Rand Corporation, this study found "the evidence base to support the ACFT is incomplete" (Hardison et al., 2022, p. vi), resulting in a fourth diagnostic version of the ACFT introduced on March 23, 2022 (Grinston & Klein, 2022).

Methodology

The purpose of this study is to explore through an interpretive approach and offer a perspective for scholars and practitioners alike. The interpretive approach is one in which researchers bridge the gap between sharing data and offering social commentary using qualitative methodologies. It is a way to work through the friction between myths and realities while acknowledging the value of sense-making (Yanow, 2011a). Thus, this chapter explores the topic through the lens of policy discourse analysis, which "focuses on the talk and action within policy: the text of policy, its meanings, and its discourses" (Gildersleeve & Hernandez, 2012, p. 6). Discourse analysis is a qualitative, interpretive approach to studying the means through which actors use words in an attempt to create new perceived realities (Gee, 2015). Merged over time with policy, cultural events, and institutional endorsement, such words, used in discourses, help to convey desired paradigms.

We identified a total of ten digital communication reflections for review (see Table 3.1.). These texts represent the major shifts in institutional narrative related to the ACFT and include communications transmitted across traditional websites, social media, a social media-enabled town hall, and e-mails to the force. They span the U.S. Army's formal announcement of the new test in 2018 through the spring of 2022. Using Gee's *Stanza Tool* and *Vocabulary Tool* (2014), this study organizes words into clusters of information by theme to aid in separating the points being communicated into three separate tiers: everyday words, words used by expert practitioners, and words used to express narrow meaning. Content analysis is conducted with multiple coders reviewing the discourse based on mutual classifications of three-tiered language. Tier 1 words are those used in ordinary conversation, such as "cat, lunch, work"; Tier 2 words are formal and more likely to be used by academics and policy experts, such as "maintain, likely, process, nation, and dominance"; Tier 3 words have narrow meanings and are most often used by experts in specific domains, such as "epistemology, rubric, lethality" (Gee, 2014).

TABLE 3.1 Discourse analyses of ACFT messages over time

Date	Topic	Language use	Messaging	Notes
July 9, 2018	Initial announcement	Tier 2	• Scientifically validated • Will change culture • Will prevent injuries • Will save money	
July 11, 2018	SMA response to concerns	Tier 2	• ACFT is realistic • May save money • Will increase readiness	Stronger language on soldiers with medical profiles
September 27, 2019	U.S. Army update	Tier 2	• Part of U.S. Natl Security	
September 27, 2019	Facebook live Q&A	Tier 2	• Is reducing injuries	Changed language about temporary medical profiles—soldiers will not be kicked out Addressed criticism of keeping the 2-mile run—contradicting a scientifically validated ACFT
June 15, 2020	SMA tweet	Tier 1 and 2	• Formally announced ACFT 2.0	Signifying a major change
June 15, 2020	U.S. Army update	Tier 1 and 2	• ACFT is evolving	Following congressional scrutiny, announced an alternate event to the leg tuck and alternative cardiovascular event for soldiers on a no-run profile
February 28, 2021	SMA tweet	Tier 1	• ACFT is fair	Counters possible impact to certain segments of population
March 22, 2021	SMA email	Tier 2	• Formally announced ACFT 3.0 • ACFT is changing culture	Signifying another major change. Signaled potential of a return to gender-based grading standards
March 22, 2021	U.S. Army update	Tier 2	• Will be data validated • Expectation to change culture	Departure from previous communication to focus on soldier feedback and performance for future versions
March 23, 2002	SMA Talks new ACFT updates	Tier 1	• Formally announced "Final ACFT version" • Should reduce injuries and improve the Army • Earlier ACFT versions not data validated • ACFT as "general" fitness test	Signified significant change, with the test returning to gender and age-based scoring Acknowledgment of concerns expressed by soldiers, now formalized in findings by the Rand Corporation Contrary themes on topics of further test evolution, the significance of changes in this fourth version, and the army having the data and equipment needed for successful implementation of the test

Note SMA refers to the Sergeant Major of the U.S. Army and is equivalent to senior leadership response.

Tier 1 = ordinary conversational; Tier 2 = formal, academic, policy speak; Tier 3 = narrow meanings used by experts in specific domains.

The justification for discourse analysis anticipates a policy's real, or anticipated, outcomes through an interpretive approach that offers space for knowledge to be subjective and reflective of the lived experience (Yanow, 2011b). This approach "focuses on the ways in which objects are constructed ... it invites us to think differently about the present by taking up a position outside our current regimes of truth" (Arribas-Ayllon & Walkerdine, 2011, p. 104). Further justification finds that discourses are a favored tool of institutions, specifically governing institutions, to foment redefinitions or change by focusing on the meanings and uses of words across time and space to create a sense of new reality (Woodside-Jiron, 2011).

Discourses are causal, bringing deliberate influence while naturally interacting and intersecting with power (Gildersleeve & Hernandez, 2012). For example, "when the discourses of policymakers are repeated over and over again, and policymakers talk about them collectively as 'the final word' or 'the most authoritative version, these texts come to be established as fact or normal when, in fact, they are simply individual texts bundled rhetorically" (Woodside-Jiron, 2011, p. 159). The Army's digital communication about the ACFT transition pointed to grand policy changes meant to shift culture and make the Army "more lethal," referring to the ability of military units to destroy the enemy (Hasson, 2019). In the context of this case study, terms such as *readiness* and *lethality* are used to convey shared values and norms that institutional members believe are essential for success and are thus repeated over time by senior military officials and added into military regulations; these terms are then adopted by the institution and accepted by policymakers and stakeholders as part of the lexicon (Woodside-Jiron, 2011).

Results and Discussion

Findings regarding leadership communication styles employed during the change (RQ1) suggest a significant presence of strong, assertive language during the early stages of the time series. It also included predictive, outcome-focused language, stating that the ACFT *will* make soldiers better at their jobs, it *will* change culture, and it *will* save money. However, this messaging contradicted data showing the Army spent at least \$63.7 million to purchase ACFT equipment, not including the cost of building and renovating facilities on military installations across the globe (Beynon, 2021b). In addition, initial language on permanent medical conditions, or profiles, was assertive and intense, with then-Sergeant Major of the Army Dan Dailey stating, "If you can't do it, then you shouldn't be a soldier," and "there is no right to wear the uniform that's guaranteed to anyone. If you're non-deployable, you're non-retainable" (Myers, 2018). By the end of the time series, as the ACFT faced congressional scrutiny, leaders became responsive and empathetic to individual soldiers and instituted new versions of the test. The subsequent version reintroduced protections for those who have approved exceptions to certain portions of physical fitness testing.

In terms of the language and message strategies (RQ2), the findings show that both the leadership and institution shifted back and forth between tier 1 and tier 2 language in attempts to engender buy-in from across the force, but ultimately demonstrating inconsistent language tone from those institutional officials across the time series. The language carried a tone of dismissiveness to concerns expressed by soldiers throughout all communication evaluated in the time sequence; however, the changes in the ACFT resulted from concerns expressed by soldiers across the force. Later ACFT communication acknowledged concerns about initial negative stakeholder perceptions and adjusted focus to (1) the ACFT evolving as the Army collects data from practice tests and (2) a heavy emphasis on the ACFT as an enabler to the institutional value of *readiness*.

Leadership communication fluctuated throughout the period of change, with several contradictory communication themes specifically related to the finality of test design, the scientific validity of the ACFT, and the testing of equipment. Examples included the theme of *cultural change* transitioning from a tone of certainty to a tone of expectation and a certainty that the ACFT *will* reduce injuries to a more hopeful tone that it *should* reduce injuries. Messaging about the test also varied in terms of its *scientifically validated* claims emphasizing that *data would inform* the final version of the test while still expecting future adjustments to this *final* test. Overall, leadership and institutional communication maintained a predominant use of technical language style up until the release of guidance that the ACFT would be informed by performance feedback. This approach resulted in a rebuke from military-focused influencers for being out of touch with the communication style desired by concerned soldiers (Barno & Bensahel, 2018; U.S. Army W.T.F! Moments, 2019). This potentially contributed to the congressional scrutiny that followed, resulting in a fourth version of the test in March of 2022, which reinstated a gender and age-based grading scale, coupled with changes to some test events and the reintroduction of alternative events that were stricken in the first version of the test.

For messages intended for all soldiers across the force, Army officials used online communication channels to communicate the introduction and implementation of the ACFT throughout the time sequence. Social media channels were used most widely (RQ3), with other online content marketed primarily across Army unit social media channels.

Digital communication via Facebook Live Q&A sessions with the Army's top senior enlisted leaders consisted of carefully scripted agendas as the strategy for steering the conversation around specific themes and talking points. Facebook's live event capability proved the main feature of social engagement strategy, in concert with threads on Twitter that carried instructional directives for soldiers to embrace the ACFT in language more commonly expected and familiar through in-person engagements between senior ranking officials and assembled units.

Finally, the impact and receptiveness of the communicated change varied significantly between internal groups (RQ4). Toward the end of the time series, communication reinforced new language stating the ACFT is fair and inclusive of all service members, which contradicted initial themes signaling potential policy changes might cause negative career repercussions to a sizeable portion of the force. In addition, those with physical profiles were initially aligned against the potential of being non-retainable, leaving thousands of soldiers who have medically validated permanent profiles to face unsettling scrutiny. Subsequent versions of the test added new alterative events to allay concerns from certain stakeholders. The version announced on March 23, 2022 (Grinston & Klein, 2022) reinstated all previously stricken alternate cardiovascular events, allowed for event exemptions based on medical profile, and replaced the leg tuck with the plank exercise, based on gender scoring data. Subsequently, a potential return to gender-specific grading scales for the ACFT marked the reversal of its initial framing as a gender-neutral test. Further, the discourses were adjusted accordingly. It is no longer branded as a test to measure combat effectiveness but now as a general fitness test. Ultimately, this communication changed the level of receptiveness from segmented publics as the result of updated data arising out of the ACFT field testing.

Implications and Future Directions

This chapter highlights several implications and contributions to both the theory and practice of public relations. First, this study reinforces previous research in leadership communication, internal public relations, and change suggesting that leaders should take caution in how and which digital channels they communicate their change message while considering the potential consequences of those messages (Ciszek & Logan, 2018; Men et al., 2020). Next, the choice of language style in leadership and change communication is likely to have a causal impact on outcomes and employee behavior. This study found that while assertive language presented a more confident approach in providing direction and dealing with difficult changes, responsive leadership communication enabled empathetic, multi-directional engagement to increase the likelihood of a sustained change within the organization.

Third, how change can be effectively communicated via digital communication is also reinforced in current literature (Venus et al., 2019), which goes into greater detail about the utility of social media specifically. In summary, aside from one-way, public-information announcements, social media enables leaders to compliment digital media and other interpersonal channels through collecting and listening outside of one-on-one and group meetings. While face-to-face, interpersonal communication remains the most effective way for military officials and members to engage, there remains a variety of options that exist across different platforms to encourage a range of publics to express their opinions, for better or worse, on specific change topics (Luoma-aho, 2015). As a result, this study highlights that consistent messaging from both leaders and organizations during times of change is more likely to elevate mutual understanding and cultivate followership while simultaneously alleviating confusion or discord within the ranks.

The fourth takeaway is that as leaders communicate change actions in a hierarchical, one-way manner via digital platforms, absent listening and data-driven support, there is a greater likelihood that stakeholders may either feel ignored within the organization or perceive flaws in changing a previously accepted institutional norm. Without empirical support, internal communication strategies that overlook multi-directional engagement during times of change risk minimizing the feedback needed from additional voices to optimize effectiveness. Finally, as previous research also highlights, organizations and leaders in the post-digital age should consider their employee's enthusiasm and meaningful purpose toward a change action (Yue, 2021), this case study further affirms the benefits digital channels provide while also examining the potential for internal discord related to change initiatives.

At the time of this writing, the future of the ACFT remains in limbo. The Army pushed ahead with making the fourth version the test of record across the force on October 1, 2022. This followed a congressionally mandated, independent review that reported findings inconsistent after nearly four years of Army messaging about the test's efficacy. As this chapter was in final edits in December, both houses of Congress passed the 2023 National Defense Authorization Act. Language in this annual appropriation require the Secretary of the Army to establish a gender-neutral physical fitness test within six months, and to brief that test to the Armed Services Committees of the House of Representatives and the Senate (United States Senate, 2022).

This case study is unique in that internal stakeholder communication forced an institution accustomed to driving policy decisions in a strong, top-down manner to adjust accordingly. Instead, open questioning and concerns from many within the force, who typically remain less apt to share their thoughts on policy changes in a public forum, drove change. Those who directed the ACFT's creation and those charged within the Army to communicate this change initiative failed to consider how assertive, nonempathetic language might be received by sub-groups within the organization on a public stage (Bernstein, 2000). The manner in which Army officials tailor communication on this change action as it continues to evolve will likely be worthy of further study. Scholars should consider exploring if an increased awareness of stakeholder perception is achieved by Army officials and how that awareness shapes the manner in which stakeholder concerns are acknowledged in future change initiatives and decision-making.

While this case study enables a specific, context-based understanding of leadership communication during change, future scholars and practitioners might use discourse analysis to further consider how organizational leaders communicate in a consistent way despite different segments, personalities, and expectations within an organization. Research questions examining other contextual, moderating roles, such as employee self-efficacy, trust, and individual vulnerabilities, could also advance theory and practice. As leaders incorporate language strategies to drive change within their organizations, how they position themselves within a traditionally hierarchical organization also raises important questions about the subsequent receptiveness, long-term satisfaction, and commitment from stakeholders. While stakeholders may remain hesitant to embrace change that directly impacts them, organizations and leaders can tailor communication to optimize response, support, and eventual long-term strategic outcomes.

Learning Outcomes

1) Understand how assertive and responsive leadership communication styles during change can influence subsequent behavior and commitment in different ways
2) Consider the power internal and external stakeholders possess in influencing organizational change via the accessibility and availability of digital communication channels
3) Understand the variance in behavior and receptiveness that change communication can have on different segmented publics

Discussion Questions

1) Where did this change-communication initially go wrong and how could Army leadership have been more effective in communicating this organizational pivot?
2) Do digital channels make change communication easier or harder in the post-digital age?
3) What leadership language style proved most effective within this case?
4) How does relationship management influence stakeholders' perception of organizational change?
5) How might leaders mitigate risk in how they communicate change to different groups within the organization?

Disclaimer: The opinions expressed in this chapter are those of the authors and do not express the official policy or position of the Department of Defense or the U.S. Government.

Further Readings

The following readings provide additional background on both this specific case as well as literature tied to leadership communication and change:

Hardison, Chaitra M., Paul W. Mayberry, Heather Krull, Claude Messan Setodji, Christina Panis, Rodger Madison, Mark Simpson, Mary Avriette, Mark E. Totten, and Jacqueline Wong. (2022). Independent Review of the Army Combat Fitness Test: Summary of Key Findings and Recommendations. Santa Monica, CA: RAND Corporation. https://www.rand.org/pubs/research_reports/RRA1825-1.html.

Brooks, I. (1996). Leadership of a cultural change process. *Leadership & Organization Development Journal, 17*(5), 31–37.

Cheng, Y. (2018). How social media is changing communication strategies: Evidence from the updated literature. *Journal of Contingencies and Crisis Management, 26*(1), 58–68.

Shirky, C. (2011). The political power of social media: Technology, the public sphere, and political change. *Foreign Affairs, 90*(1), 28–41.

References

Allen, J., Jimmieson, N. L., Bordia, P., & Irmer, B. E. (2007). Uncertainty during organizational change: Managing perceptions through communication. *Journal of Change Management, 7*(2), 187–210.

Arribas-Ayllon, M., & Walkerdine, V. (2011). Foucauldian discourse analysis. In C. Willig, & W. Stainton-Rogers (Eds.), *The Sage handbook of qualitative research in psychology* (91–108). London: Sage Publications Limited.

Barno D., & Bensahel, N. (2018, October 16). *Dumb and Dumber: The Army's New PT Test.* War on the Rocks, Retrieved from: https://warontherocks.com/2018/10/dumb-and-dumber-the-armys-new-pt-test/.

Bernstein, B. (2000). *Pedagogy symbolic control and identity: Theory, research, critique.* Bristol: Taylor & Francis.

Beum, L. (2021, May 6). *The Army Never Should Have Switched to the ACFT. Military.com.* Retrieved from: https://www.military.com/daily-news/opinions/2021/05/06/army-never-should-have-switched-acft.html.

Beynon, S. (2021a, May 13). *Army Secretary Nominee Worries the ACFT Will Push Too Many Women Out.* Military.com, Retrieved from: https://www.military.com/daily-news/2021/05/13/army-secretary-nominee-worries-acft-will-push-too-many-women-out.html.

Beynon, S. (2021b, June 2). *"Largest Purchase of Exercise Equipment Ever": How One Company Supplied Gear for the ACFT.* Military.com. Retrieved from: https://www.military.com/daily-news/2021/06/02/largest-purchase-of-exercise-equipment-ever-how-one-company-supplied-gear-acft.html.

Bull, M., & Brown, T. (2012). Change communication: The impact on satisfaction with alternative workplace strategies. *Facilities, 30*(3/4), 135–151.

Carton, A. M., Murphy, C., & Clark, J. R. (2014). A (blurry) vision of the future: How leader rhetoric about ultimate goals influences performance. *Academy of Management Journal, 57*(6), 1544–1570.

Cheng, Y., & Jiang, H. (2021). Customer–brand relationship in the era of artificial intelligence: understanding the role of chatbot marketing efforts. *Journal of Product & Brand Management.* ahead-of-print. https://doi.org/10.1108/JPBM-05-2020-2907

Ciszek, E., & Logan, N. (2018). Challenging the dialogic promise: How Ben & Jerry's support for Black Lives Matter fosters dissensus on social media. *Journal of Public Relations Research, 30*(3), 115–127.

Clayton, S. (2015, November 10). Change management meets social media. *Harvard Business Review.* Retrieved from: https://hbr.org/2015/11/change-management-meets-social-media.

Cohen, R. (2022, March 18). Here's the Space Force plan to ditch annual fitness testing. *Army Times.* Retrieved from: https://www.armytimes.com/news/your-air-force/2022/03/18/heres-the-space-forces-plan-to-ditch-annual-fitness-testing/?utm_source=facebook&utm_medium=social&utm_campaign=fb_armytimes&fbclid=IwAR1fBIiWhSbd0afscPrP2XfhrU-o9lempKTu3vX73cGUvv2Pck1dEIpCEIPg.

Dzur, A. (2019). *Democracy inside: Participatory innovation in unlikely places.* New York: Oxford University Press.

Eisenberg, N., Fabes, R. A., Shepard, S. A., Guthrie, I. K., Murphy, B. C., & Reiser, M. (1999). Parental reactions to children's negative emotions: Longitudinal relations to quality of children's social functioning. *Child Development, 70*(2), 513–534.

Elving, W. J. (2005). The role of communication in organizational change. *Corporate Communications: an International Journal, 18*(2), 176–192.

Everstine, B. W. (2019, August 5). Possible physical fitness test changes aim for holistic health. *Air Force Magazine*. Retrieved from: https://www.airforcemag.com/Possible-Physical-Fitness-Test-Changes-Aim-For-Holistic-Health/.

Frahm, J. A., & Brown, K. A. (2005, August). Building an organizational change communication theory. In *Academy of management proceedings* (Vol. 2005, No. 1, pp. C1–C6). Briarcliff Manor, NY: Academy of Management.

Gee, J. P. (2014). *How to do discourse analysis: A toolkit* (2nd ed.). London: Routledge.

Gee, J. P. (2015). Discourse, small-D, Big D. In K. Tracie, I. Cornelia, & T. Sandel (Eds.), *International encyclopedia of language and social interaction*. Hoboken: Wiley-Blackwell.

Gergs, HH, & Trinczek, R. (2010). Communication as the key factors to change management: A sociological perspective. In Holger Sievert and Daniela Bell (Eds.), *Communication and leadership in the 21st century* (141–156). Verlag Bertelsmann Stiftung, Gutersloh

Gildersleeve, R. E., & Hernandez, S. (2012). Producing (im)possible peoples: Policy discourse analysis, in-state resident tuition and undocumented students in American higher education. *International Journal of Multicultural Education, 14*(2), 1–19.

Grinston, M. A. & Klein, J. (2022, March 23). SMA talks new ACFT updates. Retrieved from: https://www.youtube.com/watch?v=pihdZskfP1Y.

Hardison, C. M., Mayberry, P. W., Krull, H., Setodji, C. M., Panis, C., Madison, R., Simpson, M., Avriette, M., Totten, M. E., & Wong, J. (2022). *Independent Review of the Army Combat Fitness Test: Summary of Key Findings and Recommendations.* Santa Monica, CA: RAND Corporation. Retrieved from https://www.rand.org/pubs/research_reports/RRA1825-1.html

Hasson, J. (2019). *Stand down: How social justice warriors are sabotaging America's military.* Washington, D.C.: Regnery.

Headquarters Department of the Army (HQDA). (2012). Field Manual 7-22: Army Physical Fitness. Retrieved from: https://armypubs.army.mil/epubs/DR_pubs/DR_a/ARN30714-FM_7-22-000-WEB-1.pdf.

Headquarters Department of the Army (HQDA). (2016). Field Manual 600-8-2: Suspensions of Favorable Personnel Actions. Retrieved from: https://armypubs.army.mil/epubs/DR_pubs/DR_a/pdf/web/ARN10794_r600_8_2_AdminFinal.pdf.

Headquarters, Department of the Army (HQDA). (2017). Field Manual 635-200: Active Duty Enlisted Administrative Separations. Retrieved from: United States. Headquarters Department of the Army. (2017). U.S. Army field manual no. 635-200: Active Duty Enlisted Administrative Separations. https://armypubs.army.mil/epubs/DR_pubs/DR_a/pdf/web/AR635-200_Web_FINAL_18JAN2017.pdf.

Hoffer, E. (1963). *The ordeal of change.* New York, NY: Harper and Brothers.

Jiang, H., Luo, Y., & Kulemeka, O. (2017). Strategic social media use in public relations: Professionals perceived social media impact, leadership behaviors, and work-life conflict. *International Journal of Strategic Communication, 11*(1), 18–41.

Kimmons, S. (2018, July 9). Army combat fitness test set to become new PT test of record in late 2020. *Army News Service*. Retrieved from https://www.army.mil/article/208189/army_combat_fitness_test_set_to_become_new_pt_test_of_record_in_late_2020.

Luoma-aho, V. (2015). Understanding stakeholder engagement: Faith-holders, hateholders & fakeholders. *RJ-IPR: Research Journal of the Institute for Public Relations, 2*(1).

Mayfield, M., & Mayfield, J. (2004). The effects of leader communication on worker innovation. *American Business Review, 22*(2), 46–51.

Mayfield, J., & Mayfield, M. (2018). *Motivating language theory: Effective leader talk in the workplace*. Palgrave MacMillan.

Men, L. R. (2015). The internal communication role of the chief executive officer: Communication channels, style, and effectiveness. *Public Relations Review, 41*(4), 461–471. https://doi.org/10.1016/j.pubrev.2015.06.021

Men, L. R., & Bowen, S. A. (2017). *Excellence in internal communication management*. New York: Business Expert Press.

Men, L. R., & Stacks, D. (2014). The effects of authentic leadership on strategic internal communication and employee-organization relationships. *Journal of Public Relations Research, 26*(4), 301–324.

Men, L. R., Tsai, W.-H. S., Chen, Z. F., & Ji, Y. G. (2018). Social presence and digital dialogic communication: Engagement lessons from top social CEOs. *Journal of Public Relations Research, 30*(3), 83–99. https://doi.org/10.1080/1062726X.2018.1498341.

Men, L. R., Yue, C. A., & Liu, Y. (2020). "Vision, passion, and care:" The impact of charismatic executive leadership communication on employee trust and support for organizational change. *Public Relations Review, 46*(3), 101927.

Myers, M. (2018, July 11). Got questions about the new PT test? The sergeant major of the Army has answers. *Army Times*. Retrieved from: https://www.armytimes.com/news/your-army/2018/07/11/got-questions-about-the-new-pt-test-the-sergeant-major-of-the-army-has-answers/.

Solaja, M. O., Idowu, E. F., & James, E. A. (2016). Exploring the relationship between leadership communication style, personality trait and organizational productivity. *Serbian Journal of Management, 11*(1), 99–117.

Sweetser, K. D., & Kelleher, T. (2016). Communicated commitment and conversational voice: Abbreviated measures of communicative strategies for maintaining organization-public relationships. *Journal of Public Relations Research, 28*, 217–231.

Toropin, K. (2022, November 15). Only one fitness test for sailors next year. *Military.com*. Retrieved from: https://www.military.com/daily-news/2022/11/15/only-one-fitness-test-sailors-next-year.html.

Tsai, W. H. S., & Men, L. R. (2017). Social CEOs: The effects of CEOs' communication styles and parasocial interaction on social networking sites. *New Media & Society, 19*(11), 1848–1867.

United States House of Representatives. (2021). William M. (Mac) Thornberry National Defense Authorization Act for Fiscal Year 2021. Washington: U.S. Government Publishing Office, Retrieved from: https://www.congress.gov/bill/116th-congress/house-bill/6395.

United States Senate. (2022). National Defense Authorization Act for Fiscal Year 2023. Washington: U.S. Government Publishing Office, Retrieved from: https://www.congress.gov/117/bills/hr7900/BILLS-117hr7900pcs.pdf.

U.S. Army W.T.F! Moments (2019, September 27). Today's U.S. Army livestream about the changes to the Army Combat Fitness Test was heavily hyped and widely watched. Facebook. https://www.facebook.com/usawtfm/posts/10158018489868606.

Van de Ven, A. H., & Poole, M. S. (1995). Explaining development and change in organizations. *Academy of Management Review, 20*(3), 510–540.

Venus, M., Stam, D., & Van Knippenberg, D. (2019). Visions of change as visions of continuity. *Academy of Management Journal, 62*(3), 667–690.

Woodside-Jiron, H. (2011). Language, power, and participation: Using critical discourse analysis to make sense of public policy. In *An introduction to critical discourse analysis in education* (2nd ed., 154–182). New York: Routledge.

Yanow, D. (2011a). Symbolic language. In *Conducting interpretive policy analysis* (42–62). Thousand Oaks, CA: Sage Publications Inc.

Yanow, D. (2011b). Underlying assumptions of an interpretive approach: The importance of local knowledge. In *Conducting interpretive policy analysis* (1–27). Thousand Oaks, CA: Sage Publications Inc. doi:10.4135/9781412983747.

Yue, A. (2021) Navigating change in the era of COVID-19: The role of top leaders' charismatic rhetoric and employees organizational identification, *Public Relations Review, 47*(5), 102–118.

Yue, C. A., Men, L. R., & Ferguson, M. A. (2020). Examining the effects of internal communication and emotional culture on employees' organizational identification. *International Journal of Business Communication.* Advance online publication. https://doi.org/10.1177/23294884.

Section II

Organizational Change

Chapter Four

Interdisciplinary Approaches in Internal Communication to Effect Successful Organizational Change: Leveraging Agile Project Management and Behavioral Neuroeconomics

Conilyn Poulsen Judge

Introduction

In early 2020, the COVID-19 pandemic forced organizations to adopt remote working practices and dramatically shift their internal communication practices (Alshaabani et al., 2021; Handscomb et al., 2021; Thaler & Sunstein, 2021). Over 500 research studies on the effects of the pandemic were published in 2020 (Verma & Gustafsson, 2020; Zhang et al., 2020), including research on the pandemic and its impact on the fields of internal communications and change management (Alshaabani et al., 2021; Fuller et al., 2020; Kim, 2018; Li et al., 2021).

Before the pandemic, organizational change has been a topic of increasing interest for practitioners and leaders for decades (Al-Haddad & Kotnour, 2015). Mastering organizational change is a critical challenge facing leaders, as the successful implementation and adoption of planned and unplanned change—such as COVID-19—has a proven impact on the organization's bottom line (Alvesson & Sveningsson, 2008). It is well-established that there is a proven cost of change failure (Burnes, 2004; By, 2005) and that strategic internal change communication is a required component of effective change management (Allen et al., 2007; Errida & Lotfi, 2021; Harkness, 2000).

As an evolving discipline, cross-disciplinary approaches to internal communication are becoming increasingly relevant (Kalla, 2005). For example, integrating individual and organizational change psychology frameworks into strategic change communications can augment supportive behavior while mitigating negative or counter-productive behavior (Li et al., 2021). Researchers suggest that further cross-disciplinary research will be valuable for change communications and internal communications (Cohen-Miller & Pate, 2019). Dianoux et al., 2019; Lemon & Macklin, 2020).

This chapter explores the interdisciplinary effect of agile project management techniques and behavioral economics strategies in promoting effective internal change

DOI: 10.4324/9781003195580-7

communication by applying a case study of a 55,000-employee Middle Eastern organization and its internal communications response to the COVID-19 pandemic.

Through this case study, the researcher explored the impact of two related fields of practice—"agile" project management and behavioral economics—to determine their effect on the success of internal change communication to drive employee behavior during the pandemic: With origins in software development, agile project management is an established model for organizations to seize opportunities and adapt to market conditions (González-Cruz et al., 2020). COVID-19 has demonstrated that organizational change requires frequent and quality internal communication (Li et al., 2021). Thus, agile is a relevant area for change communicators to explore (Handscomb et al., 2021; Malik et al., 2021). The pace of change also requires communications to be simple, fast, cost-effective, easy to mobilize, and adaptable (Li et al., 2021). Thus, behavioral economics (or "nudge") is an increasingly viable tool for change communicators (Dianoux et al., 2019; Ebert & Freibichler, 2017).

This study explored the role of internal communications in a crisis scenario and examined interdisciplinary approaches that internal communications professionals can leverage to drive behavior change. Further, the study sought to understand how agile project management principles/strategies can enable effective internal communications and drive behavior change during a crisis. Finally, the study examined how behavioral economics theories enable effective internal communications and drive behavior change.

Literature Review

Organizational Change Management

With roots in organizational development (Dievernich et al., 2016), change management is the standard business practice of supporting an organization and its people in effectively transitioning from a current state to a desired future state in response to events driven by planned or unplanned internal or external factors (Balogun & Hope Hailey, 2004; Kotter, 1996; Voehl & Harrington, 2017).

The frequency of change continues to increase in an increasingly hostile and fast-moving business environment (De Biasi, 2018; Speight, 2000), making organizational change management a necessity for success (Jayashree & Hussain, 2011). To successfully drive change, leaders must employ a systematic approach to change management that supports their unique organizational culture, structure, systems, and strategies and the situational drivers of the change (Al-Haddad & Kotnour, 2015; Dunphy & Stace, 1993).

The extant change management literature began in the 1920s, with various studies based on the change type and method (Al-Haddad & Kotnour, 2015). Continuous change is typically planned and largely dependent on senior leaders to set timetables, objectives, and procedures in advance (By, 2005). Conversely, discontinuous change usually originates with a single rapid shift in strategy, structure, or culture, may be triggered by a crisis, and requires a directive approach that often does not allow for consultation or widespread involvement (By, 2005). As discontinuous change is often unplanned, the responsibility for change must be increasingly devolved (Burnes, 2004; By, 2005; De Wit & Meyer, 2005).

Despite many cases of organizational change, research indicates that less than 30 percent of change initiatives accomplish their objectives and realize tangible benefits (Al-Haddad & Kotnour, 2015; Balogun & Hope Hailey, 2004). Change failure rates are not improving (Jacobs et al., 2013; Jansson, 2013; Michel et al., 2013; Rouse, 2011). Scholars note that organizations often rely on consultancies that offer universal change management solutions but are largely ineffectual (Jacobs et al., 2013; Ostrom, 2007; Sorge & van Witteloostuijn, 2004). Researchers have identified many reasons why change initiatives may fail, including ineffective change communication, contradictory approaches, poor planning, lack of commitment from leadership, clash of values, failure to understand the impact of change, and change fatigue/resistance (Al-Haddad & Kotnour, 2015; Burnes, 2004; Conner, 1998).

Change is the norm in today's global business environment. Across all sectors, leaders are continually under pressure to respond to a changing environment (Burnes, 2004; By, 2005). The change management discipline must continue to evolve and incorporate findings from other fields such as psychology, sociology, project management, leadership, engineering, innovation, human resources, communications, and sociology for success rates to improve (Al-Haddad & Kotnour, 2015; Voehl & Harrington, 2017).

Psychology of Change

Change occurs at the individual, team/group, and organizational levels. Individual change is a complex phenomenon involving affective, cognitive, and behavioral components (Oreg, 2006; Piderit, 2000). Change theorists rooted in psychology are either behavior-based (assuming that change is initiated based on the modification of consequences and effects) or gestalt-field-based (assuming that change is initiated by self-exploration and an acceptance of success) (Al-Haddad & Kotnour, 2015).

One of the most common reasons for the failure of organizational change is resistance by employees (Arifin, 2020; Georgalis et al., 2014; Pieterse et al., 2012). Individuals may resist change either because they fear the negative consequences of the specific change or because they are predisposed to have a negative attitude to the process of change (McCrae & Costa, 1991; Oreg, 2006). Change also causes uncertainty, making employees vulnerable and often triggering defense mechanisms (Allen et al., 2007; DiFonzo & Bordia, 2002; Yue et al., 2019.) Therefore, understanding the psychology of change is vital for change practitioners (Bouckenooghe, 2009; Lines, 2005; Singh & Gupta, 2016; van et al., 2013).

Internal Change Communications

Interest in strategic internal communication as a discipline is increasing, mainly among public relations scholars (Lee & Kim, 2021; Lee & Yue, 2020; Verčič & Vokić, 2017). Research in this growing field shows that effective internal communication is necessary to realize higher levels of performance and satisfaction (Ruck & Welch, 2012; Tourish & Hargie, 2009) and is vital during crisis scenarios (Kim, 2018; Strandberg & Vigsø, 2016).

Internal change communication is emerging as a distinctive discipline (Harkness, 2000; Luo & Jiang, 2014; Yue et al., 2019). Internal communication is crucial in driving successful organizational change, aligning content, people, and processes (Al-Haddad & Kotnour, 2015; Kitchen & Daly, 2002; van et al., 2013), and is especially critical during unplanned change (Shin et al., 2012). During the COVID-19 pandemic, the role of internal communications was vital in helping employees manage the uncertainty and anxiety that resulted from the required changes (Li et al., 2021).

Interdisciplinary Perspectives on Internal Change Communication

Internal communication is often part of corporate communication (along with public relations, media relations, marketing communications, investor relations, community relations/corporate philanthropy, government relations, and crisis management) (Argenti, 1996) or aligned with Human Resources as a driver to improve employee engagement (Mishra et al., 2014).

In a review of the current literature on internal communication, integrated, interdisciplinary approaches are increasingly common (Wakimoto, 2021) alongside domains such as business management, organizational psychology, sociology, neurology, knowledge management, innovation, and complexity theory (Al-Haddad & Kotnour, 2015; Grunewald et al., 2017; Kalla, 2005; Kim & Rhee, 2011; Lemon & Macklin, 2020; Li et al., 2021).

According to Al-Haddad and Kotnour (2015), change management has a long history of drawing from ancillary disciplines. Noted examples include Lewin's research in psychology and sociology to understand how and why people do or do not change (Lewin, 1948); Kotter's theories on management and leadership to understand how principles including planning, organizing, and directing people can help accomplish change (Kotter, 1996); and Deming's approaches to engineering management and industrial engineering to examine detailed methods of change including processes, systems, values, and skills (Deming, 1986).

Project Management: Agile and Internal Change Communications

Change management and project management typically occur in parallel, making these disciplines closely aligned (Pádár et al., 2017). Thus, trends in project management impact the field of change management (Alvesson & Sveningsson, 2008). While most researchers focus on planned or emergent change (Bamford & Forrester, 2003), change is frequently unplanned and unpredictable, making change management reactive, discontinuous, and ad hoc, mainly when triggered by a crisis (Burnes, 2004; By, 2005; De Wit & Meyer, 2005).

Established by a group of software engineers and developers in 2001, agile was developed as a more effective project management methodology in opposition to the traditional linear, "waterfall" approach used in the software industry (Cockburn & Highsmith, 2001; Serrador & Pinto, 2015). Agile's core assumption is that innovation does not proceed linearly and requires faster and lighter collaboration, continuous learning, and rapid iteration (Fowler & Highsmith, 2001; Serrador & Pinto, 2015). The "Agile Manifesto" is summarized into four values: individuals and interactions over processes and tools, working software over comprehensive documentation, customer collaboration over contract negotiation, and responding to change over following a plan (Beck et al., 2001).

Over the past two decades, "agile" has evolved and grown beyond software management to revolutionize project management and business operations (Greve et al., 2020; Morris et al., 2014). Agile practices, particularly in communications, drive psychological empowerment and result in more motivated teams (Malik et al., 2021). As a project management approach, agile projects have four times more success and one-third fewer failures than waterfall projects (Mergel et al., 2021; Serrador & Pinto, 2015).

The "modern agile movement" is now considered a critical transformational process across sectors and industries, espoused by consultancies and studied by academics

(Mergel et al., 2021) and with significant applications in internal communication (González-Cruz et al., 2020). During the COVID-19 pandemic, research findings from a joint McKinsey and Harvard University study showed that agile functions or business units responded better in customer satisfaction, employee engagement, and operational performance than non-agile counterparts (Handscomb et al., 2021).

Neuroeconomics: Behavioral Economics and Internal Change Communications

In 1946, noted change theorist Lewin proposed that previous behavior must be "discarded" before adopting new behavior (Al-Haddad & Kotnour, 2015; Burnes, 2004). However, from the 1980s, this view was criticized as impractical and unhelpful in situations that require rapid or transformational change (Burnes, 2004; By, 2005; Senior, 2002). More recently, researchers have drawn on behavioral and psychological studies to improve workers' productivity (Ebert & Freibichler, 2017).

Behavioral economics expands standard economic theory to include psychological factors in choice architecture (Dianoux et al., 2019). Rooted in neuroscience and behaviorism, "nudges" (Sunstein, 2014; Thaler & Sunstein, 2021) and "boosts'" (Grüne-Yanoff & Hertwig, 2016; Hertwig & Ryall, 2020) trigger a specific part of the brain to drive desired behavior. Nudges enable decision-making based on heuristics and automated, intuitive thinking versus systematic processing and logical thinking, which is slower (Bossaerts & Murawski, 2015; Ebert & Freibichler, 2017; Grunewald et al., 2017; Kahneman, 2011; Todorov et al., 2002). In Löfgren and Nordblom's (2020) model of decision-making, nudges can be either pure (e.g., changing default options) or preference (e.g., reminders), while boosts reduce the effort required to make a choice (Grüne-Yanoff & Hertwig, 2016; Hertwig & Ryall, 2020).

A growing interest in nudge applications by corporations stems from the fact that such tactics usually impose low or no cost, have a more significant impact than coercive tools, and can be quickly deployed (DellaVigna & Linos, 2020; Dianoux et al., 2019; Sunstein, 2014). Since 2015, nudge units have become more prevalent in the corporate world as a means of helping companies promote change and increase productivity while creating win-win outcomes for companies, employees, and customers (Gunter et al., 2019).

"Nudge Management" applies insights from behavioral science to design organizational contexts to optimize employees' fast thinking and unconscious behavior in line with the organization's objectives (Ebert & Freibichler, 2017). In contrast to many other change management approaches, the advantages of nudge management are evident: nudges are usually not very intrusive, are easily scalable, and employees are not forced to make extensive changes to their working habits (Dianoux et al., 2019; Sunstein, 2014).

In a study of HR managers, Grunewald et al. (2017) used nudge techniques (simplification and herding) to raise awareness of an incentive system and drive employee adoption. Fairness and inequality aversion are other nudge techniques used effectively to drive change with employees (Kampkötter et al., 2016; Lin et al., 2017).). During the COVID-19 pandemic, governments and companies used nudge practices, including choice architecture, social norming, and convenience/warnings to encourage behavior such as wearing masks, vaccinating, and social distancing (Thaler & Sunstein, 2021).

Further, behavioral economics research has proven to be reproducible and has a meaningful and statistically significant impact on the desired outcome (Camerer et al., 2016; DellaVigna & Linos, 2020), making it a relevant tool for internal communications and internal change communications where behavior change is desired. A meta-analysis of nudge experiments has shown that convenience-oriented nudges are more effective than intrinsic motivation interventions (Luo et al., 2021). Communicators should note that even a highly effective convenience nudge (such as automatic enrollment benefits programs) can be thwarted by impediments such as systemic barriers and unwieldy bureaucracy (sludge) and discourage employees from adopting change (Sunstein, 2021). Emerging research on nudge theory and management will lead to more personalized nudges and default rules, enabling communicators to advise leaders and more effectively drive employee behavior (Ebert & Freibichler, 2017; Thaler & Sunstein, 2021).

The study included theories developed across two interdisciplinary research streams: organizational change and internal communication. In terms of the theoretical framework, this study further expands the internal change communications research scope to include project management and behavioral economics theories.

A complex phenomenon, organizational change theories are often fragmented, cutting across disciplines including psychology, sociology, and economics, subdivided into schools of thought by discipline and representing perspectives from organizational behavior and strategic organizational change (Jacobs et al., 2013; Oreg et al., 2011; Schwarz & Huber, 2008).

Given the relatively limited depth and range of the extant literature on the cross-disciplinary study of internal change communication, the initial focus of the case study was relatively narrow to facilitate data collection and allow for generalization (Hartley, 2004; Yin, 2018).

Methodology

The researcher conducted a qualitative case study using semi-structured employee interviews, observation, and content analysis of internal sources. This case company was selected because it provided a real-life context where the phenomenon of internal change communication could be studied (Yin, 2018). Furthermore, the researcher's role as a senior advisor on change and communication at the case company made accessing people and sensitive information not in the public domain easier. It has been noted that a participant-observer within the research process can produce proper contextualization of the research phenomenon (Brereton et al., 2008; Yin, 2018); thus, observational material, in addition to interviews, forms an integral part of the data.

The primary researcher/participant-observer had a background in organizational psychology and internal communication. Before the outbreak of COVID-19, she had been retained by the case company to evaluate and establish a strategic internal communications function. As such, her perspective was informed by this position and her commitment to employing non-traditional approaches to communicate with employees during the COVID-19 pandemic.

Data collection was completed over eight weeks in the summer of 2021, consisting of content analysis of internal documents and artifacts and semi-structured virtual interviews with six participants focusing on internal change communications in response to the COVID-19 pandemic. The sample was representative of senior managers within the business continuity team. Two participants were female, while four were male. The interviews were approximately 30 minutes each, exploring participants' perspectives and experiences regarding the role of internal communication and non-traditional approaches used to engage employees during COVID-19 and their opinions about the effectiveness of these approaches and opportunities for improvement. Interviews were recorded and transcribed using Microsoft Teams.

Content analysis of internal sources included artifacts including campaign materials and recordings of six company-wide engagement sessions led by the CEO or senior leaders; over 600 pages of organizational documents, including COVID-19 task force minutes from February 2020 to June 2021; data from seven employee surveys from May 2020 to June 2021 assessing employees' feelings of safety being in the office, understanding of measures taken to increase safety, personal confidence in safety measures, and perceived feelings of safety and confidence of co-workers; Employee Engagement Survey "pulse" from December 2020; over 200 official email updates to staff issued by Group

Communications and co-developed by the COVID-19 Task Force; a dedicated intranet microsite; and an iterative strategic internal communication plan which was updated weekly during the initial stages of the pandemic and bi-weekly in subsequent stages.

All data from the interview transcripts and organizational documents were reviewed in an iterative process of identifying key concepts and themes. Analysis was informed by a deductive approach, starting with pre-determined concepts. Throughout the analysis, categories and themes were continually reviewed to ensure they reflected the data.

Case Summary

The study case is a 55,000-employee NOC (National Oil Company) based in the middle east. The 50-year-old organization comprises multiple semi-autonomous operating companies and a group headquarters. A multicultural organization, roughly half of employed personnel are local, while expatriates from over 120 regions/countries comprise the remainder. Employees are based both in office environments and on remote or even offshore production sites, commonly working alongside a large group of contracted staff employed by sub-contracted companies.

In 2016, the organization experienced a radical restructuring and leadership change. At that point, an employee engagement survey was introduced, and an internal communications practice was established. Employee engagement is improving incrementally but remains lower than established regional and industry norms. Enterprise change management is currently not an organizational practice area or discipline.

In 2021, the emergence and spread of COVID-19 disrupted the daily life of individuals and the function of most organizations, including the case company. The pandemic caused severe stress to employees and required a drastic change in behavior and management approaches as organizations needed to adjust to a rapidly shifting environment (Alshaabani et al., 2021; Thaler & Sunstein, 2021).

At the outset of the pandemic, the case company established an integrated task force led by the senior leader for health, safety, and environment (HSE) to ensure business continuity (BC) under the authority of the executive leadership team (ELT) led by the Group CEO. The BC task force included senior leaders representing medical, building services, communications, human resources, legal, safety, technology, and IT. Initially, the team met daily, eventually reducing meetings to three times a week (at the time of the document analysis and interviews.)

The corporate communications function was a key contributor to the task force as the chief marketing officer (CMO) represented internal and external communication on both the BC task force and ELT and, at times, was asked to deputize for the task force lead. Shortly after the employees of the case company were required to work remotely in March 2020, a COVID-19 Communications task force was convened to develop and execute communications plans, led by the CMO and reporting daily to the BC task force.

Case Analysis

Analysis of the qualitative comments from the participant interviews and organizational documents reflected several consistent themes regarding (1) the role of internal communication in the management of a crisis scenario, (2) the impact of agile-driven internal communications on employee adoption of unplanned change, and (3) the impact of behavioral economics-driven internal communications on employee adoption of unplanned change.

Overall, the data highlighted the critical nature of the internal communications function in developing the organization's strategic response to the pandemic and the benefits of leveraging non-traditional disciplines to support the internal communications approach. Study findings emphasized the critical benefits of agile project management and behavioral economics in supporting internal communications and contributing to positive change outcomes.

The Role of Internal Communications during COVID-19 Response

Participants shared a consistent view on the importance of internal communications during the COVID-19 response, describing it as a critically important, vital function, and integral member of the integrated project task force. Participants stated that internal communications has never been more critical to the organizations' success than during the pandemic response:

> [Internal communications] was vital to ensure engagement with all employees in the field or offices across the value chain. This would not have been done without constant communication because people need to be engaged and informed properly, especially with changing rules, regulations, testing regimes, quarantine regimes, etc.

The role of internal communications during the pandemic was to provide strategic counsel to leadership and influence decision-making to ensure the credibility and transparency of the response internally and externally. One leader, for example, stated:

> The internal comms function played a critical role throughout COVID-19 in helping the organizational leaders make the right decisions. Internal comms was often the voice of reason in the room which was important because often, a decision might have been taken without considering the negative implications on employee morale and behavior.

Findings demonstrate that internal communications during the pandemic offered a unique insight into employee sentiment and morale through ongoing sensing while ensuring rapid, consistent repetition of specific, simple messages via authoritative channels to provide definitive guidance to employees and contractors. Using a multipronged approach, the internal communications team developed and maintained various one-way and two-way channels in multiple languages to communicate updated COVID-19 messaging and reinforce desired behavior. Communication started during the initial phases of the pandemic, where staff were sent home to work remotely and continued through to subsequent stages of returning staff to offices and sites in a managed, gradual approach.

Data analysis indicates that using non-traditional disciplines to complement the development and implementation of the internal communications strategy was a critical factor in the project's success. Responding to in-house surveys, 99% of staff consistently said they had a high understanding of the organization's COVID-19 safety measures. Further, the company's bi-annual Employee Engagement Survey (conducted by an independent external provider in December 2020, ten months into the organization's response to COVID) found that 90% of staff felt the organization was responding appropriately to COVID-19, while 89% felt the company was making the right decisions at the right speed. The organization's overall engagement score improved from the previous year, primarily due to a "boost" from positive sentiment related to the COVID-19 response and increased internal communications across channels.

Agile Project Management and Internal Change Communications

Two of the participants were familiar with agile project management. The researcher explained the concepts of agile to the remainder in this context as "being continuously updated, employee-focused, owned by a cross-functional team, and using sensing to improve as compared to a more traditional, linear approach." Overall, the study found that agile was a critical success factor in developing the successful internal communications approach to the pandemic, given the rapidly changing environment.

A multi-disciplinary, multi-functional, integrated task force was established at a company level, with agreed core principles, guiding questions, and a rigorous review process to ensure responsiveness to continual change. This agile approach enabled the organization to keep up with the speed of local and global changes while enabling flows of information hierarchically, horizontally, and via inter-company networks and to allow complete, reflective learning to be turned into action very quickly. The methodology encouraged robust discussion across functions to resolve issues and strengthened the thought process to improve the end product.

For example, a robust debate was held between medical, human resources, Legal, HSE, general services, and communications to discuss the ethics of using a nudge approach to "reward" employees for being vaccinated during clinical trials. Before COVID-19, this decision would likely have been taken in isolation, without the benefit of rapid, cross-disciplinary insight to understand informed consent and the company's responsibility to support employee decision-making.

As a tenet of agile, one participant mentioned how ongoing data gathering enabled the BC team to avoid groupthink and test its assumptions regularly:

> You can easily lead yourself into believing it's all working until you get actual feedback, and the agile approach in the evolution of the communications was incredibly important. It allowed us to try things, and if they didn't work, let's go back and do something a little bit different. That mirror benefit became even more important when we were in the somewhat stable but still challenged phase – when case numbers suddenly shot up and we had to respond again quickly. Now, as we're returning to some sense of normality, that approach to try different ways of communicating the message and then adjusting has carried on.

In the case company, agile project management worked effectively in other areas during the pandemic. Participants mentioned that the information technology (IT) function leveraged agile to implement Microsoft Teams and enable remote working rapidly. IT and internal comms also used agile to develop an AI "BOT" to answer emerging employee questions around COVID-19 policy and guidelines.

In hindsight, participants noted that greater cross-representation from front-line companies and managers on the task force from the beginning would have enabled an even more agile response and improved the communications approach, especially its ability to engage contractor staff. Participants also noted the toll that agile takes on the energy of a team, mainly when working remotely, and suggested that if agile practices are to be leveraged in the long term, team members should be given guidance on how to balance this aspect.

Behavioral Economics and Internal Change Communications

The case company incorporated behavioral economics approaches to internal communications tactics. While most leaders did not fully appreciate "nudge" in the initial stages of the pandemic response, ultimately, it was seen as a key strategic response and worked alongside an authoritarian approach to ensuring compliance with policy through official reprimands for violations. One participant said, "We still have much to learn to use this thinking, but that persuasive nudge when you don't know you're being persuaded was seen as being friendly and positive."

Examples of nudges include policy change by default and restricted entry, connecting behavior to social norming, and timely reminders via SMS for tests, vaccines, and boosters. Campaigns were also developed, drawing attention to COVID-safety messaging translated into six languages, using pervasive and straightforward imagery based on color theory, strategically placed at appropriate locations, and shared via social media/WhatsApp. Participants recognized the benefits:

> The multilingual collaterals were very well constructed and proved successful in driving behavior. It wasn't about how to protect yourself. It was how to protect your family. We are your family. This is the collateral that makes people think differently that you're coming to an environment where you are protected. Using the multilanguage animation made sure everyone was grasping it, so it went through all the way, even laborers and non-English speakers. They understood the message and what was supposed to be done. I think other entities have learned from us in that regard.

Nudge was seen as particularly appropriate in this case because of the emotive nature of the choices (dealing with fear and misinformation) and the personal investment in decisions (mainly related to vaccines and the safety of family members). Participants felt that the benefits of using behavioral-science tactics were the relatively low cost and ability to implement and test outcomes quickly. While consequence management was still a part of the overall strategy, the nudge was positively oriented and helped avoid message fatigue by working on a subliminal level.

One of the participants explained:

> People fundamentally want to do the right thing; they just need to be nudged in the right direction. And that's a far more effective way to get compliance than reprimanding them for doing the wrong thing. I think it led to not only self-monitoring, but also monitoring by peers because people were quick to call each other out and say, "Hey, gentle reminder, you know you forgot to put your mask on when you left your desk." I think that it set a tone which was positive and collaborative, as opposed to reprimanding and disciplinary, which could have taken the whole tone of the company down a completely different path.

As improvements in driving behavior, participants felt that more use could have been made of incentives and recognition, using leaders as examples and inspiring behavior, and more visibly feature employee voices to demonstrate commitment.

Advancing Internal Change Communication through Additional Disciplines

The participants cited examples of other non-traditional disciplines that did or could have benefitted from internal communications to respond to COVID-19. Themes included promoting and adopting new technology, such as modeling science (traditionally used for making exploration and business decisions) to predict trends in virus spread and recovery rates according to medical/epidemiological principles and enable leaders to make interventions based on robust data. While business scenario planning played a significant role, some participants felt this approach could have been more structured and robust, especially during the early COVID-19 response.

Beyond the direct relationship with crisis communications practices, participants referenced the importance of ongoing government relations to keep abreast of changes, branding/marketing tactics, and social media to engage employees. The company also recorded documentary footage from the crisis to capture the story for the community and employees. The external perception of handling the crisis, particularly in this region, was key to influencing employees.

Participants felt that considering the psychological and emotional aspects of COVID-19 in the long term, including the stress of dealing with "long COVID," the social anxiety of returning to crowded spaces, the loss of family members, and building long-term individual resilience, would have been beneficial.

Implications for Practice

Overall, the study findings have implications and insights for large, multinational organizations to advance and enable internal change communication. As a theoretical implication, the results of this study indicate the need for internal change communication theories based on cross-disciplinary approaches that emphasize unplanned change as a catalyst. As limited theoretical attention has been paid to internal change communication and crisis scenarios in research, these findings should be added to empirical evidence. In response to calls from previous studies for deeper analysis, the findings also reflect ways for internal change communications to bridge disciplines. In other words, the role and impact of project management and psychological disciplines should be considered when a new internal change communication theory is discussed. This study further expands the scope of theoretical efforts of change and internal communications research by understanding agile and behavioral economics in unplanned internal change communications.

Learning Outcomes

1) Summarize the fundamental roles that strategic internal communications can perform during a crisis involving behavior change.
2) Demonstrate knowledge about the emerging relevance of non-traditional disciplines to advancing strategic internal change communications practice.
3) Describe how agile project management principles can augment traditional strategic internal change communications practices.
4) Describe how behavioral science "nudge" theories can support internal change communication practices.
5) Identify and analyze the application of additional disciplines to support traditional strategic internal change communications approaches.

Discussion Questions

1) Should internal communications play an active role in shaping organizational strategy and policy?
2) How has your thinking about strategic internal communication and change communication/management changed based on the case study?
3) Which discipline—agile or nudge—do you think made the biggest impact on the success of the change communications approach and why?
4) Are there ethical questions raised by aspects of the case study that should have been taken into consideration by the task force?

Further Readings

Baddeley, M. (2017). *Behavioural economics: A very short introduction (Vol. 505).* Oxford, UK: Oxford University Press.

Kahneman, D. (2011). *Thinking, fast and slow.* New York, NY: Farrar, Straus and Giroux.

Morris, L., Ma, M., & Wu, P. C. (2014). *Agile innovation: The revolutionary approach to accelerate success, inspire engagement, and ignite creativity.* New York, NY: John Wiley & Sons.

Thaler, R. H., & Sunstein, C. R. (2021). *Nudge: The final edition.* Dublin, Ireland: Allen Lane Press.

Wysocki, R. K. (2019). *Effective project management: Traditional, agile, hybrid, extreme.* New York, NY: Wiley.

References

Al-Haddad, S., & Kotnour, T. (2015). Integrating the organizational change literature: A model for successful change. *Journal of Organizational Change Management, 28*(2), 234–262.

Allen, J., Jimmieson, N. L., Bordia, P., & Irmer, B. E. (2007). Uncertainty during organizational change: Managing perceptions through communication. *Journal of Change Management, 7*(2), 187–210.

Alshaabani, A., Naz, F., Magda, R., & Rudnák, I. (2021). Impact of perceived organizational support on OCB in the time of COVID-19 pandemic in Hungary: Employee engagement and affective commitment as mediators. *Sustainability, 13*(14), 7800.

Alvesson, M., & Sveningsson, S. (2008). *Changing organizational culture: Cultural change work in progress.* Oxford, UK: Routledge.

Argenti, P. (1996). Corporate communication as a discipline. *Management Communication Quarterly, 10*, 73–97.

Arifin, K. (2020, January). Factors influencing employee attitudes toward organizational change: literature review. In *5th ASEAN Conference on Psychology, Counselling, and Humanities (ACPCH 2019)*. Gelugor: Atlantis Press (pp. 188–191).

Balogun, J., & Hope Hailey, V. (2004). *Exploring strategic change* (2nd ed). London: Prentice-Hall.

Bamford, D. R., & Forrester, P. L. (2003). Managing planned and emergent change within an operations management environment. *International Journal of Operations & Production Management, 23*(5), 546–564.

Beck, K., Beedle, M., Van Bennekum, A., Cockburn, A., Cunningham, W., Fowler, M., & Thomas, D. (2001). *Manifesto for agile software development.*

Bouckenooghe, D. (2009). Change recipients' attitudes toward change: A review study. *Vlerick Leuven Gent Working Paper Series*, 1–35.

Bossaerts, P., & Murawski, C. (2015). From behavioural economics to neuroeconomics to decision neuroscience: The ascent of biology in research on human decision making. *Current Opinion in Behavioral Sciences, 5*, 37–42.

Brereton, P., Kitchenham, B., Budgen, D., & Li, Z. (2008, June). Using a protocol template for case study planning. In *12th International Conference on Evaluation and Assessment in Software Engineering (EASE) 12* (pp. 1–8).

Burnes, B. (2004). *Managing change: A strategic approach to organisational dynamics*. Harlow: Prentice-Hall.

By, R. T. (2005). Organisational change management: A critical review. *Journal of Change Management, 5*(4), 369–380.

Camerer, C. F., Dreber, A., Forsell, E., Ho, T. H., Huber, J., ... & Wu, H. (2016). Evaluating replicability of laboratory experiments in economics. *Science, 351*(6280), 1433–1436. https://doi.org/10.1126/science.aaf0918.

Cockburn, A., & Highsmith, J. (2001). Agile software development, the people factor. *Computer, 34*(11), 131–133.

Cohen-Miller, A. S., & Pate, E. P. (2019). A model for developing interdisciplinary research theoretical frameworks. *The Qualitative Researcher, 24*(*6*), 1211–1226.

Conner, D. (1998). *Leading at the edge of chaos: How to create the nimble organization*. New York, NY: John Wiley.

De Biasi, K. (2018). *Solving the change paradox by means of trust: Leveraging the power of trust to provide continuity in times of organizational change*. New York, NY: Springer.

De Wit, B., & Meyer, R. (2005). *Strategy synthesis: Resolving strategy paradoxes to create competitive advantage* (2nd ed.). London: Thomson Learning.

DellaVigna, S., & Linos, E. (2020). *Acts to scale: Comprehensive evidence from two nudge units* (No. w27594). Cambridge, MA: National Bureau of Economic Research.

Deming, W. E. (1986). *Out of the crisis*. Cambridge, MA: MIT, Center for Advanced Engineering Study.

Dianoux, C., Heitz-Spahn, S., Siadou-Martin, B., Thevenot, G., & Yildiz, H. (2019). Nudge: A relevant communication tool adapted for agile innovation. *Journal of Innovation Economics Management, 28*(1), 7–27.

Dievernich, F. E., Tokarski, K. O., & Gong, J. (2016). *Change management and the human factor.* New York, NY: Springer International Publishers.

DiFonzo, N., & Bordia, P. (2002). Corporate rumor activity, belief and accuracy. *Public Relations Review, 28*(1), 1–19.

Dunphy, D., & Stace, D. (1993). The strategic management of corporate change. *Human Relations, 46*(8), 905–918.

Ebert, P., & Freibichler, W. (2017). Nudge management: Applying behavioural science to increase knowledge worker productivity. *Journal of Organization Design, 6*(1), 1–6.

Errida, A., & Lotfi, B. (2021). The determinants of organizational change management success: Literature review and case study. *International Journal of Engineering Business Management, 13*, 18479790211016273.

Fowler, M., & Highsmith, J. (2001). The agile manifesto. *Software Development, 9*(8), 28–35.

Fuller, R. P., Pyle, A., Riolli, L., & Mickel, A. (2020). Creating order out of chaos? Development of a measure of perceived effects of communication on the crisis organizing process. *International Journal of Business Communication.* https://doi.org/10.1177/2329488420979657.

Georgalis, J., Samaratunge, R., Kimberley, N., & Lu, Y. (2014). Change process characteristics and resistance to organisational change: The role of employee perceptions of justice. *Australian Journal of Management*, 1–25. https://doi.org/10.1177/0312896214526212.

González-Cruz, T. F., Botella-Carrubi, D., & Martínez-Fuentes, C. M. (2020). The effect of firm complexity and founding team size on agile internal communication in startups. *International Entrepreneurship and Management Journal, 16*(3), 1101–1121.

Greve, C., Ejersbo, N., Lægreid, P., & Rykkja, L. H. (2020). Unpacking Nordic administrative reforms: Agile and adaptive governments. *International Journal of Public Administration, 43*(8), 697–710.

Grunewald, M., Hammermann, A., & Placke, B. (2017). Human resource management and nudging: An experimental analysis on goal settings in German companies. *International Journal of Economics and Finance, 9*(9), 147–156.

Grüne-Yanoff, T., & Hertwig, R. (2016). Nudge versus boost: How coherent are policy and theory? *Minds and Machines, 26*(1), 149–183.

Gunter, A., Lucks, K., & Sperling-Magro, J. (2019, January 24). Lessons from the front line of corporate nudging. *McKinsey Quarterly.* https://www.mckinsey.com/business-functions/organization/our-insights/lessons-from-the-front-line-of-corporate-nudging

Harkness, J. (2000). Measuring the effectiveness of change: The role of internal communication in change management. *Journal of Change Management, 1*(1), 66–73.

Handscomb, C., Mahadevan, D., Schor, L., & Sieverer, M. (2021, June 25). An operating model for the next normal: Lessons from agile organizations in the crisis. *McKinsey Insights.* https://www.mckinsey.com/business-functions/organization/our-insights/an-operating-model-for-the-next-normal-lessons-from-agile-communications-in-the-crisis/

Hartley, J. (2004). Case study research. In C. Cassell & G. Symon (Eds.), *Essential guide to qualitative methods in organizational research* (323–333). London: Sage Publications Ltd.

Hertwig, R., & Ryall, M. D. (2020). Nudge versus boost: Agency dynamics under libertarian paternalism. *The Economic Journal, 130*(629), 1384–1415.

Jacobs, G., van Witteloostuijn, A., & Christe-Zeyse, J. (2013). A theoretical framework of organizational change. *Journal of Organizational Change Management, 26*(5), 772–792.

Jansson, N. (2013). Organizational change as practice: A critical analysis. *Journal of Organizational Change Management, 26*(6), 1003–1019.

Jayashree, P., & Hussain, S. J. (2011). Aligning change deployment: A Balanced Scorecard approach. *Measuring Business Excellence, 15*(3), 63–85.

Kahneman, D. (2011). *Thinking, fast and slow.* New York, NY: Farrar, Straus and Giroux.

Kalla, H. K. (2005). Integrated internal communications: A multi-disciplinary perspective. *Corporate Communications: An International Journal, 10*(4), 302–314.

Kampkötter, P., Mohrenweiser, J., Sliwka, D., Steffes, S., & Wolter, S. (2016, August). Measuring the use of human resources practices and employee attitudes: The linked personnel panel. In *Evidence-based HRM: A global forum for empirical scholarship.* Retrieved from https://www.econstor.eu/bitstream/10419/126534/1/843511761.pdf.

Kim, Y. (2018). Enhancing employee communication behaviors for sensemaking and sense giving in crisis situations: Strategic management approach for effective internal crisis communication. *Journal of Communication Management, 22*(4), 451–475.

Kim, J. N., & Rhee, Y. (2011). Strategic thinking about employee communication behavior (ECB) in public relations: Testing the models of megaphoning and scouting effects in Korea. *Journal of Public Relations Research, 23*(3), 243–268.

Kitchen, P. J., & Daly, F. (2002). Internal communication during change management. *Corporate Communications: An International Journal, 7*(1), 46–53.

Kotter, J. (1996). *Leading change.* Boston, MA: Harvard Business School Press.

Lee, Y., & Kim, J. (2021). Cultivating employee creativity through strategic internal communication: The role of leadership, symmetry, and feedback-seeking behaviors. *Public Relations Review, 47*(1), 101998.

Lee, Y., & Yue, C. A. (2020). Status of internal communication research in public relations: An analysis of published articles in nine scholarly journals from 1970 to 2019. *Public Relations Review, 46*(3), 101906.

Lemon, L. L., & Macklin, C. (2020). Enriching employee engagement using complexity theory. *Public Relations Inquiry.* https://doi.org/10.1177/2046147X20982524.

Lewin, K. (1948). *Resolving social conflicts, selected papers on group dynamics [1935–1946].* New York, NY: Harper.

Li, J. Y., Sun, R., Tao, W., & Lee, Y. (2021). Employee coping with organizational change in the face of a pandemic: The role of transparent internal communication. *Public Relations Review, 47*(1), 101984.

Lin, Y., Osman, M., & Ashcroft, R. (2017). Nudge: Concept, effectiveness, and ethics. *Basic and Applied Social Psychology, 39*(6), 293–306.

Lines, R. (2005). The structure and function of attitudes toward organizational change. *Human Resource Development Review, 4*(8), 8–24. https://doi.org/10.1177/1534484304273818

Löfgren, Å., & Nordblom, K. (2020). A theoretical framework of decision making explaining the mechanisms of nudging. *Journal of Economic Behavior & Organization, 174*, 1–12.

Luo, Y., & Jiang, H. (2014). Effective public relations leadership in organizational change: A study of multinationals in mainland China. *Journal of Public Relations Research, 26*(2), 134–160.

Luo, Y., Soman, D., & Zhao, J. (2021, May 27). A meta-analytic cognitive framework of nudge and sludge. https://doi.org/10.31234/osf.io/dbmu3

Malik, M., Sarwar, S., & Orr, S. (2021). Agile practices and performance: Examining the role of psychological empowerment. *International Journal of Project Management, 39*(1), 10–20.

McCrae, R. R., & Costa, P. T. (1991). The NEO personality inventory: Using the five-factor model in counseling. *Journal of Counseling & Development, 69*(4), 367–372.

Mergel, I., Ganapati, S., & Whitford, A. B. (2021). Agile: A new way of governing. *Public Administration Review, 81*(1), 161–165.

Michel, A., By, R. T., & Burnes, B. (2013). The limitations of dispositional resistance in relation to organizational change. *Management Decision, 51*(4), 761–780.

Mishra, K., Boynton, L., & Mishra, A. (2014). Driving employee engagement: The expanded role of internal communications. *International Journal of Business Communication, 51*(2), 183–202.

Morris, L., Ma, M., & Wu, P. C. (2014). *Agile innovation: The revolutionary approach to accelerate success, inspire engagement, and ignite creativity.* New York, NY: John Wiley & Sons.

Oreg, S. (2006). Personality, context, and resistance to organizational change. *European Journal of Work and Organizational Psychology, 15*(1), 73–101.

Oreg, S., Vakola, S., & Armenakis, A. (2011). Change recipients' reactions to organizational change: A 60-year review of quantitative studies. *The Journal of Applied Behavioral Science, 47*(4), 461–524.

Ostrom, E. (2007). A diagnostic approach for going beyond panaceas. *Proceedings of the National Academy of Sciences, 104*(39), 15181–15187.

Pádár, K., Pataki, B., & Sebestyén, Z. (2017). Bringing project and change management roles into sync. *Journal of Organizational Change Management, 30*(5), 797–822.

Pieterse, J. H., Caniëls, M. C. J., & Homan, T. (2012). Professional discourses and resistance to change. *Journal of Organizational Change Management, 25*(6), 798–818. https://doi.org/10.1108/09534811211280573

Piderit, S. K. (2000). Rethinking resistance and recognizing ambivalence: A multidimensional view of attitudes toward an organizational change. *Academy of Management Review, 25*(4), 783–794.

Rouse, W. B. (2011). Necessary competencies for transforming an enterprise. *Journal of Enterprise Transformation, 1*(1), 71–92.

Ruck, K., & Welch, M. (2012). Valuing internal communication; Management and employee perspectives. *Public Relations Review,* 38(2), 294–302. https://doi.org/10.1016/j.pubrev.2011.12.016.

Schwarz, G. M., & Huber, G. P. (2008). Challenging organizational change research. *British Journal of Management, 19*, S1–S6.

Senior, B. (2002). *Organisational change* (2nd ed.). London: Prentice-Hall.

Serrador, P., & Pinto, J. K. (2015). Does agile work? A quantitative analysis of agile project success. *International Journal of Project Management, 33*(5), 1040–1051.

Shin, J., Taylor, M. S., & Seo, M. G. (2012). Resources for change: The relationships of organizational inducements and psychological resilience to employees' attitudes and behaviors toward organizational change. *Academy of Management Journal, 55*(3), 727–748.

Singh, A., & Gupta, R. P. (2016). A research paper on the employees attitude towards organizational change. *Journal of Dental and Medical Sciences, 15*(2), 44–47. https://doi.org/10.9790/0853- 152124447.

Sorge, A., & Van Witteloostuijn, A. (2004). The (non)sense of organizational change: An essai about universal management hypes, sick consultancy metaphors, and healthy organization theories. *Organization Studies, 25*(7), 1205–1231.

Speight, R. (2000). Changing the way we change: Managing the soft strands of change at British Airways World Cargo. *Journal of Change Management, 1*(1), 91–99.

Strandberg, J. M., & Vigsø, O. (2016). Internal crisis communication: An employee perspective on narrative, culture, and sensemaking. *Corporate Communications: An International Journal, 21*(1), 89–102. https://doi.org/10.1108/CCIJ-11-2014-0083.

Sunstein, C. R. (2014). *Why nudge?* Cumberland, RI: Yale University Press.

Sunstein, C. R. (2021). *Sludge: What stops us from getting things done and what to do about it.* Cambridge, MA: The MIT Press.

Thaler, R. H., & Sunstein, C. R. (2021). *Nudge: The final edition.* Oxford, England: Allen Lane Press.

Todorov, A., Chaiken, S., & Henderson, M. D. (2002). The heuristic-systematic model of social information processing. *The persuasion handbook: Developments in theory and practice* (195–211).

Tourish, D., & Hargie, O. (2009). Communication and organisational success. In O. Hargie & D. Tourish (Eds.), *Auditing organizational communication* (3–37). London: Routledge.

van, D. H., Demerouti, E., & Bakker, A. (2013). How psychological resources facilitate adaptation to organizational change. *European Journal of Work and Organizational Psychology, 26*(6), 1–13.

Verčič, A. T., & Vokić, N. P. (2017). Engaging employees through internal communication. *Public Relations Review, 43*(5), 885–893.

Verma, S., & Gustafsson, A. (2020). Investigating the emerging COVID-19 research trends in the field of business and management: A bibliometric analysis approach. *Journal of Business Research, 118*, 253–261.

Voehl, F., & Harrington, H. J. (2017). *Change management: Manage the change or it will manage you* (Vol. 6). Boca Raton, FL: CRC Press.

Wakimoto, D. K. (2021). Exploring internal communication in public libraries: Challenges and opportunities for library leaders. *Library Leadership & Management, 35*(2), 1–18.

Yin, R. K. (2018). *Case study research and applications: Design and methods.* London, UK: Sage.

Yue, C. A., Men, L. R., & Ferguson, M. A. (2019). Bridging transformational leadership, transparent communication, and employee openness to change: The mediating role of trust. *Public Relations Review, 45*(3), https://doi.org/10.1016/j.pubrev.2019.04. 012.

Zhang, J., Xie, C., Wang, J., Morrison, A. M., & Coca-Stefaniak, J. A. (2020). Responding to a major global crisis: The effects of hotel safety leadership on employee safety behavior during COVID-19. *International Journal of Contemporary Hospitality Management, 32*(11), 3365–3389.

Chapter Five

Navigating Change through Chaos: A Case Study of RWJBarnabas Health's Change Communication during COVID-19

Yi Luo

Introduction

Deemed "undoubtedly one of the most complex and important endeavors in modern organizational life" (Nag et al., 2007, p. 844), organizational change occurs when an organization "changes its direction to accommodate the changing demands of internal and external customers" (Aujla & Mclarney, 2020, p. 8). Organizational change provides an opportunity for organizations to engage employees to mobilize their change-supportive attitude and behavior (Petrou et al., 2016), which accentuates the strategic role of internal communication in change management (Men et al., 2020; Schulz-Knappe et al., 2019). The current Novel Coronavirus (COVID-19) has forced significant disruptions to organizations (WHO, 2020), providing a valuable opportunity to study the impact of internal communication on change management. Specifically, this study examines how the Internal Communications team at RWJBarnabas Health (RWJBH), the most comprehensive healthcare system in New Jersey, functioned and engaged employees during this tumultuous period.

Literature Review

Organizational Change

This study focuses on the type of unplanned, sudden organizational change that occurs in response to unforeseen surprises or developments in the environment, such as the COVID-19 pandemic (Jager et al., 2021). These surprises can derail organizational members from their routine activities and overwhelm them emotionally and psychologically. To respond to unanticipated demands swiftly and effectively, organizational scholars (e.g., Bechky & Okhuysen, 2011) suggested change management focus on providing two types of vital resources: material (e.g., tools) as well as social and cognitive resources (e.g., shared expectations, peer collaboration).

DOI: 10.4324/9781003195580-8

Employee Engagement during Change

Organizational scholars (Azebedo et al., 2021; Holten et al., 2020; Ndaba & Anthony, 2015; Stigliani & Elsbach, 2018) suggested that organizations embrace employee engagement as an integral part of the change process. Employee engagement represents "a positive fulfilling, work-related state of mind that is characterized by vigor, dedication, and absorption" (Schaufeli et al., 2001, p. 74). In the context of organizational change, employee engagement refers to employee's enthusiastic emotional, psychological, and behavioral participation in the change process (Islam et al., 2021). Placing employee engagement in the context of the job demands-resource model (Schaufeli & Bakker, 2004), resources (both tangible and intangible) provided by organization can mitigate the stress from the intense physical and mental efforts associated with job demand, which in return sustain and enhance engagement (Schneider et al., 2018). Feeling valuable, worthwhile, and significant through work performance is also a major driver of employee engagement during change (Shulga, 2021).

Transparent Communication

Organizational change communication seeks to inform, involve, and encourage employees to participate in the change process (Simões & Esposito, 2014). Communication scholars have increasingly linked transparency, a vital dimension in employee communication (Jiang & Men, 2015; Men, 2014), to positive change outcomes such as openness to change (Yue et al., 2019), uncertainty reduction (Rogiest et al., 2015), and proactive coping strategies (Li et al., 2021). Transparent internal communication refers to "an organization's communication to make available all legally releasable information to employees whether positive or negative in nature—in a manner that is accurate, timely, balanced and unequivocal, for the purpose of enhancing the reasoning ability of employee, and holding organizations accountable for their actions, policies, and practices" (Men, 2014, p. 260). The concept of transparent communication involves three core components: substantial information, participation, and accountability (Rawlins, 2009).

Organizational Identity

Organizational identity defines the central, enduring, and distinctive characteristics of an organization, which answers the questions of "who we are" and "what we do" as an organization (Albert & Whetten, 1985). Grounded in organizational values as well as the mission and vision statements (Gioia et al., 2010; Sha, 2009), organizational identity provides an interpretive framework for employees to understand what their organizations stand for and in which direction they are heading (Ashforth et al., 2008). Mirroring the individual-level identity, the content of organizational identity also encompasses personal (e.g., unique attributes), relational (e.g., relationships formed with stakeholders), and social (e.g., industry membership) components (Ashforth et al., 2020). During unplanned organizational changes, a coping strategy to successfully counter the turbulent and unpredictable environmental forces lies in preserving a strong organizational identity (Piening et al., 2020; Sha, 2009). Men et al. (2020) found that top leaders' communication of vision (i.e., a manifestation of organizational identity) during change effectively fostered employees' support and cooperation. Therefore, top management and leaders can impart a sense of stability by articulating how the changes connect with the essential identities of the organization (Neill et al., 2020; Yue, 2021).

Case Summary

As the largest and most comprehensive academic healthcare system in New Jersey with over 35,000 employees, RWJBH has 14 hospitals and medical centers spanning from Northern to Southern New Jersey. The rapid surge of COVID-19 drastically transformed and upended its normal practices (Department of Health & Human Services, 2020). Hospitals were thrown into the fast-evolving vortex of inadequate capacity, supply shortage, lack of staff, the need for care redesign, financial loss, and employee burnout (Begun & Jiang, 2020). Strict hygienic rules and social distancing requirements have presented unprecedented challenges for healthcare professionals (WHO, 2020), causing significant mental, psychological, and physical stress. As a national epicenter of COVID-19, the abruptly rising pandemic cases forced RWJBH into a crisis mode almost overnight, temporarily halting its elective procedures to singularly focus all resources on providing the safest environment for patients and staff, treating COVID-19 patients and saving lives, as well as educating the community. Specifically, this case study explored the following research questions:

RQ1: What roles did Internal Communications at RWJBH play during the COVID-19 pandemic?

RQ2: How did Internal Communications at RWJBH engage employees throughout the COVID-19 pandemic?

Methodology

This study probed *how* and *what* questions about how a healthcare organization managed its internal communication programs during an ongoing global pandemic. The explorative nature of this study made a qualitative approach appropriate to examine a complex organizational reality, organizational change (Denzin & Lincoln, 2011). Particularly, this study explored the perspectives of communication leaders of RWJBH on internal communication's function and its impact on employee engagement during change. Participants of this study included the Director of Internal Communications, two Vice Presidents of the Regional Marketing Communication, and the Chief Communication Officer at RWJBH. Semi-structured interviews were used as a primary method for data collection, supplemented with interview notes and organization's literature (e.g., internal publications, email correspondence). All interviews were digitally recorded and transcribed for analysis with each interview lasting from 70 to 90 minutes. Data analysis was conducted based on Miles et al. (2020)'s three-stage data analysis, namely data reduction, data display, and conclusion drawing. Both inductive and deductive analytical approaches were adopted to allow major themes to emerge from data and identify relevant patterns based on the theoretical frameworks.

Results

Roles of Internal Communication Function

Central Information Hub

The Internal Communications team at RWJBH functioned as a central information hub during the chaotic period of COVID-19. In early January in 2020, upon sensing an imminent threat of a possible epidemic, the Internal Communications team led the efforts to build an exclusive sub-intranet housing all information related to COVID-19. To ensure consistent, timely, and accurate communication across the enterprise, all the system-wide COVID-related communication was cascaded down from the Internal Communications team at the corporate level to the local hospital leaders. Given the differences in culture, information processing, and local leaders' communication strength, each local team had the flexibility to determine how to communicate these core messages effectively. For example, some hospitals adopted townhall meetings with CEOs to interact with employees to mitigate their mounting anxieties. Given that employees trust their immediate supervisors and middle managers the most, The Internal Communications team coordinated with each local communication team to train these supervisors and middle managers to ensure that they first understood the messages and then had the skills to communicate effectively with their team members. With 14 hospitals spanning the entire region of New Jersey, it was paramount to ensure all local sites were consistently and accurately following the guidelines for patient care because deviations from the prescribed changes could potentially result in dire consequences for both patients and frontline medical staff.

Advocating and Managing Resources for Employees

Many clinical staff had to work extremely long hours and witnessed patients' rapid decline to death. To assist employees during this extraordinarily stressful period, with the help of Human Resources, the Internal Communications team quickly launched a "Connect Together" program as part of the larger Employee Assistance Program to provide social, mental, and emotional support for both employees and their families. This support program provided educational resources (e.g., virtual counseling, one-on-one coaching, webinars) on how to deal with emotional and psychological stress, peer support (e.g., support groups, group counseling), and free medical programs (e.g., telephonic coaching, text coaching, cognitive behavioral therapy, mental health counseling, etc.). Concerned about the risks that employees' children encountered during the lockdown, the organization provided employees' children with free mental health counseling and therapies. As this global pandemic created uneven risks and impact on people with different ethnicities and cultural backgrounds, RWJBH was keen to tailor its employee support programs to meet the varying expectations and social needs among employees. After recognizing that employees of color particularly were feeling isolated and disenfranchised, the Internal Communications team made employees aware of some local-based associations of black social workers and therapists who then provided niched counseling support to those employees, fostering a much-needed emotional connection to their local communities.

Sensemaker and Sensegiver

The Internal Communications team functioned as both a sensemaker and sensegiver to filter information, restore order, and provide interpretive frames for employees to alter meanings attributed to evolving situations. The team identified the following issues as the central concerns for employees during their sensemaking process: What was true? What was the scientific rationale? How did the change apply to our work? How could we ensure safe operations? To provide the most relevant information for employees, the Internal Communications team relied on two communication mechanisms to accurately interpret the complex information to easily digestible information. First, the Director of Internal Communications worked closely with the Chief Medical Officer and clinicians to process and "decipher" new information to ensure that all vital information was based on science and supported by the provider's policies. Secondly, the leaders of the Internal Communications team participated in collaborative decision makings with other essential divisions' senior leaders, which allowed the leaders of the communication team to understand and assess the impact of the COVID-related changes on each unit.

Understanding and anticipating employees' communication needs formed a foundation for the Internal Communications team to provide meanings in this chaotic change. Many part-time employees (e.g., therapists) with RWJBH also worked in other NJ hospitals with potentially different COVID-19 policies. The Director of Internal Communications engaged in active "back-door communication" with leaders of the adjoining hospitals to anticipate and understand those employees' communication needs, hence resolving their potential cognitive dissonance about why the adjustments made by RWJBH varied from other hospitals.

Empowering Other Divisions

The Internal Communications team guided employee-related communication programs across all organizational units, such as Human Resources, Business, Strategy, Finance, Quality, and others. Fast-evolving developments in COVID-19 demanded almost immediate adjustments in policies and procedures in virtually all frontline divisions (e.g., pharmacy, supply chain, urgent care, etc.). Such empowering influence from the Internal Communications team partly derived from the Director's direct access to senior management (e.g., Chief Communication Officer, Chief Medical Officer, and other SVPs, etc.). This Director was regarded as an "expert" of COVID communication by the organizational leaders. Other managers and division leaders (e.g., Supply, Operations, etc.) constantly sought guidance from the Director of Internal Communications on how to effectively communicate critical issues such as the temporary supply shortages. The empowering impact of the Internal Communications team on other divisions manifested through its expertise in communicating with employees to address their uncertainties about COVID-19 changes and in counseling division leaders to adjust policies to align with the emerging situations.

Engaging Employees during Change

Engagement through Transparent Communication

Transparent communication emerged from interviews as a critical driver for employee engagement during COVID-19. Particularly, the Internal Communications team provided substantial, truthful, and detailed information, involved employees in identifying their information needs for decision-making, and candidly sharing the organization's performances in coping with COVID. For example, to achieve transparency through disclosing substantial information, the Director of Internal Communications and her team integrated detailed facts to explain the operational impact of each relevant new development on the hospitals' operations. To provide truthful and comprehensive explanations for safety protocols, the Director guided the Chief Medical Officer on how to communicate complex medical issues in an easily digestible manner for employees to quickly absorb information and hence adjusted their work practices accordingly.

The Internal Communications team relied on various mechanisms to actively seek employees' participation in identifying their communication needs and concerns for decision-making through employee surveys, feedback from local management teams, and social media monitoring. Training and coaching were provided to middle managers on how to listen to frustrated employees and address their concerns. The Internal Communications team worked closely with each local communication team to determine the unique communication needs of employees at the local level. For example, some employees at a regional hospital voiced concerns to a division manager about the prospect of receiving a higher-grade personal protective equipments (PPEs) since they heard that the adjacent hospital staff were provided with such higher-grade PPEs. Upon receiving this feedback, the Director of Internal Communications at RWJBH immediately worked with the supply chain department to check the accurate information and dispelled the rumor.

The Internal Communications team at RWJBH communicated balanced information throughout the pandemic, which exemplified the organization's accountability, the third dimension of transparent communication. As the entire nation suffered a shortage of medical supplies during COVID-19, RWJBH communicated honestly with its employees about this challenge and the ensuing actions taken to resolve this obstacle. The highly contagious nature of COVID-19 unfortunately posed great challenges for new recruits to feel connected and assimilated with the organization. Although the Internal Communications team initiated various online and interpersonal communication programs to help new employees navigate this chaotic transitional period, some new hires still felt isolated and chose to quit. The Chief Communication Officer reflected that taking the accountability for even the negative outcome enhanced employees' commitment to the changes occurred in their jobs.

Engagement through Reinforcing Organizational Identity

The central characteristics of RWJBH are grounded in its vision to "create and sustain healthy communities together" and its mission to provide "high quality patient care, education and research to address both the clinical and social determinants of health" (RWJBH Internal Document, 2021). Particularly, high-quality patient care, safety together, and high reliability constitute the core, distinctive attributes of RWJBH's identity. Specifically, this organization's strategy to engage employees can be illustrated in three identity campaigns. First, RWJBH has launched throughout the pandemic a Heroes campaign to recognize all healthcare workers who were on the front lines and in supportive roles to care for their patients and ensure the safety of fellow employees. The campaign encouraged employees to pay tribute to colleagues on a dedicated section of the COVID-19 microsite and involved the public on social media. By recognizing employees' performance, courage, and perseverance, the organization instilled a sense of pride among its employees about their work and associated their work with the organization's defining characteristics of quality care and high reliability.

Care-Drive campaign for employees was another example of how this organization sought to engage employees through strengthening its identities. A key value in RWJBH's core identity of "Safety Together"[1] involves "You and Me Together." The Internal Communications team supported the hospital system foundation's Care-Drive campaigns (e.g., food drive, clothing drive) for employees. Employees and community partners (e.g., restaurants, nonprofits, community groups) enthusiastically donated masks, PPEs, food, clothes, and care packages to front-line employees. Feedback from employees revealed their gratitude for the supportive organization and a strong identification with the organization's identity of "You and Me Together."

The multifaceted components in RWJBH's core identity of "Safety Together"[2] enabled this organization to provide appropriate meanings attached to this identity while accommodating shifting situations in the environment. The meaning associated with an identity's consistent labels can evolve to align with the evolving expectations from the external environment (Corley & Gioia, 2004). RWJBH's "Heroes Eat Here" campaign demonstrated how this organization adapted the meanings of its "Safety Together" identity to reinforce employees' pride and bolster community relations. This campaign sought to reciprocate the generous support from local restaurants that regularly donated food to the organization's front-line employees. The broad identity component of serving the health of the communities enabled the organization to encompass the viability of the communities that it serves.

Discussion

This case underlined the strategic value of internal communication during an unplanned change triggered by an unexpected, rapidly evolving global pandemic. Effective communication programs during change can create desirable cognitive (e.g., sensemaking), affective (e.g., commitment), and behavioral (e.g., employee engagement) impacts upon employees and foster change-supportive mindset as well as behaviors. Internal Communications at RWJBH acted as a central information hub to provide consistent, accurate communication to its constituent hospitals with adjustments adapted to local needs. This case exemplified how internal communication could serve as a significant advocate for employees' well-beings, providing critical material (e.g., protective gears), cognitive (e.g., constructing meanings for change), and emotional (e.g., counseling services) support during the turbulent change period. The indispensable value of internal communication during change was also evidenced through the Internal Communications Teams' enabling role to other organizational departments based on its communication expertise in addressing changes pertaining to the pandemic. The effective engagement with employees at RWJBH during COVID-19 derived from its Internal Communications teams' transparent internal communication and various employees and community-centered campaigns aiming to reinforce the organization's core and sustaining identities.

Implications for Practice

Particularly, this study suggests the following implications for communication professionals when managing change communication. First, adopting a centralized communication system has its appeal to ensure consistency and accuracy during change in a large, geographically dispersed organization in which organizational viability relies on consistent, high-quality performance. Second, middle managers and immediate supervisors have an indispensable role to play as boundary spanners to elicit employee feedback and encourage employee participation during change. A systematic coaching program is thus desirable to guide middle managers and supervisors on how to listen to and attend to the emotional needs of employees under stress during change. Third, a focus should be placed on how to design communication programs to drive employee engagement through some core psychological factors, such as sensemaking and organizational identity, to induce employee support for change. Specifically, providing change-related senses and stressing the stability of organizational identity can elicit a strong psychological anchor, allowing employees to reconfigure meanings to interpret the unfolding change events. Such meaning alteration is conducive to mitigate employees' confusion, uncertainty, and resentment against change. Importantly, communication professionals should take advantage of the elasticity of organizational identity to incorporate revised meanings associated with the multifaceted organizational identity for employees to interpret change, thus fostering commitment and support from employees toward change. Lastly, transparent communication should be a critical component of change communication to influence employee engagement. Communication efforts need to focus on encouraging employees' active participation in identifying their concerns and information needs, involving employees in decision-making, and providing employees with truthful and substantial information about the rationales and impact of change. Such transparent communication is instrumental in mitigating stress caused by shifts in job demands and make employees feel supported through candidate feedback and coaching, which can lead to stronger dedication, higher resilience, and heightened mental efforts toward tasks (i.e., employee engagement) during change.

Learning Outcomes

1) Build awareness about the strategic role and impact of internal communication in change management.
2) Explain the important role of employees in change management.
3) Position employee engagement as a driving force for effective change management.
4) Explicate how internal communication can drive employee engagement through transparent communication and organizational identity.

Discussion Questions

1) What external circumstances have made the organizational change that occurred at RWJBH unique in comparison with other types of organizational changes?
2) How did some internal factors (e.g., organizational culture, structure, support from top management, etc.) at RWJBH affect its change communication programs?
3) How did this case study demonstrate the value of employee engagement during change?
4) How did this case study help you better understand the role of internal communication to drive employee engagement during change?

Notes

1 The six key values for "Safety Together" involves: Speak up for safety, Accurately communicate, Focus on the task, Exercise and accept a questioning attitude, Thoughtfully interact, and You and me together (RWJB Mission, Vision, and Values).

2 Safety Together is "a comprehensive process to improve our reliability, building upon past successes and using new tools and behaviors to ensure the health of our patients, workforce, and the communities we serve" (RWJB Health internal document).

Further Readings

Ernst, J., & Jensen Schleiter, A. (2021). Organizational identity struggles and reconstruction during organizational change: Narratives as symbolic, emotional and practical glue. *Organizational Studies, 42,* 891–910.

Islam, M. N., Furuoka, F., & Idris, A. (2021). Employee engagement and organizational change initiatives: Does transformational leadership, valence, and trust make a difference? *Global Business and Organizational Excellence, 40,* 50–62.

Manuti, A., & Giancaspro, M. L. (2021). The meaning of the organization or the organization of meaning? Metaphors as sensemaking tools to understand organizational change management. *Psychometrics, Methodology in Applied Psychology, 28,* 113–127.

Neill, M. S., Men, L. R., & Yue, C. A. (2020). How communication climate and organizational identification impact change. *Corporate Communications: An International Journal, 25,* 281–298.

References

Albert, S., & Whetten, D. (1985). Organizational identity. In L. L. Cummings & B. M. Staw (Eds.), *Research in organizational behavior,* Vol. 7 (pp. 263–295). Greenwich, CT: JAI Press.

Ashforth, B. E., Harrison, S. H., & Corley, K. G. (2008). Identification in organizations: An examination of four fundamental questions. *Journal of Management, 34*(3), 325–374.

Ashforth, B. E., Schinoff, B. S., & Brickson, S. L. (2020). "My company is friendly," "Mine's a rebel": Anthropomorphism and shifting organizational identity from "what" to "who." *Academy of Management Review, 45,* 29–57.

Aujla, S., & Mclarney, C. (2020). The effects of organizational change on employee commitment. *IUP Journal of Organizational Behavior, 19*(1), 7–22.

Azebedo, M. C., Schlosser, F., & McPhee, D. (2021). Building organizational innovation through HRM, employee voice and engagement. *Personnel Review, 50,* 751–769.

Bechky, B. A., & Okhuysen, A. G. (2011). Expecting the unexpected? How SWAT officers and film crews handle surprises. *Academy of Management Journal, 54,* 239–261.

Begun, J. W., & Jiang, J. (2020). Health care management during Covid-19: Insights from complexity science. Available at https://catalyst.nejm.org/doi/full/10.1056/CAT.20.0541

Corley, K. G., & Gioia, D. A. (2004). Identity ambiguity and change in the wake of a corporate spin-off. *Administrative Science Quarterly, 49*(2), 173–208.

Department of Health & Human Services. (2020). Centers for Medicare & Medicaid Services. Medicare and medicaid programs: Policy regulatory revisions in response to the Covid-19 public health emergency. https://www.govinfo.gov/content/pkg/FR-2020-04-06/pdf/2020-06990.pdf

Denzin, N. K., & Lincoln, Y. S. (2011). *The Sage handbook of qualitative research* (4th ed.). Thousand Oaks, CA: Sage.

Gioia, D. A., Price, K. N., Hamilton, A. L., & Thomas, J. B. (2010). Forging an identity: An insider-outsider study of processes involved in the formation of organizational identity. *Administrative Science Quarterly, 55*, 1–46.

Holten, A.-L., Hancock, G. R., & Bøllingtoft, A. (2020). Studying the importance of change leadership and change management in layoffs, mergers, and closures. *Management Decision, 58*, 393–409.

Islam, M. N., Furuoka, F., & Idris, A. (2021). Employee engagement and organizational change initiatives: Does transformational leadership, valence, and trust make a difference? *Global Business & Organizational Excellence, 40*, 50–62.

Jager, S. B. D., Born, M. P., Molen, H. T., & van der (2021). The relationship between organizational trust, resistance to change and adaptive and proactive employees' agility in an unplanned and planned change context. *Applied Psychology: An International Review, 25*, 1–25.

Jiang, H., & Men, R. L. (2015). Creating an engaged workforce: The impact of authentic leadership, transparent organizational communication, and work-life enrichment. *Communication Research, 44*, 225–243.

Li, J-Y., Sun, R., Tao, W., & Lee, Y. (2021). Employee coping with organizational change in the face of a pandemic: The role of transparent internal communication. *Public Relations Review, 47*(1). https://doi.org/10.1016/j.pubrev.2020.101984.

Men, L. R. (2014). Internal reputation management: The impact of authentic leadership and transparent communication. *Corporate Reputation Review, 17*(4), 254–272.

Men, R. L., Yue, C. A., & Liu, Y. (2020). "Vision, passion, and care:" The impact of charismatic executive leadership communication on employee trust and support for organizational change. *Public Relations Review, 46*(3). http://doi.org/10.1016/j.pubrev.2020.101927

Miles, B. M., Huberman, A. M., & Saldafia, J. (2020). *Qualitative data analysis: A methods sourcebook* (4th ed.). Thousand Oaks, CA: Sage.

Nag, R., Corley, K. G., & Gioia, D. A. (2007). The intersection of organizational identity, knowledge, and practice: Attempting strategic change via knowledge grating. *Academy of Management Journal, 50*, 821–847.

Ndaba, Z., & Anthony, C. (2015). The impact of employee engagement on organizational change in a telecommunications organization. In *Proceedings of the European Conference on Management, Leadership & Governance* (pp. 288–294).

Neill, M. S., Men, L. R., & Yue, C. A. (2020). How communication climate and organizational identification impact change. *Corporate Communications: An International Journal, 25*, 281–298.

Petrou, P., Demerouti, E., & Schaufeli, W. B. (2016). Crafting change: The role of employee job crafting behaviors for successful organizational change. *Journal of Management, 44*, 1766–1792.

Piening, E. P., Salge, T. O., Antons, D., & Kreiner, G. E. (2020). Standing together or falling apart? Understanding employees' responses to organizational identity threats. *Academy of Management Review, 45*, 325–351.

Rawlins, B. (2009). Give the emperor a mirror: Toward developing a stakeholder measurement of organizational transparency. *Journal of Public Relations Research, 21*(1), 71–99.

Rogiest, S., Segers, J., & van Witteloostuijn, A. (2015). Matchmaking in organizational change: Does every employee value participatory leadership? An empirical study. *Scandinavian Journal of Management, 34*(1), 1–8.

RWJBarnabas Health (2021, March 3). *Mission, Vision and Values* (Internal Document).

Schaufeli, W. B., & Bakker, A. B. (2004). Job demands, job resources and their relationship with burnout and engagement: A multi-sample study. *Journal of Organizational Behavior, 25*, 293–315.

Schaufeli, W. B., Salanova, M., González-Romá, V., & Bakker, A. B. (2001). The measurement of engagement and burnout: A two sample confirmatory factor analytic approach. *Public Relations Review, 38*(1), 128–136.

Schneider, B., Yost, A. B., Kropp, A., Kind, C., & Lam, H. (2018). Workforce engagement: What it is, what drives it, and why it matters for organizational performance. *Journal of Organizational Behavior, 39*, 462–480.

Schulz-Knappe, C., Koch, T., & Beckert, J. (2019). The importance of communicating change: Identifying predictors for support and resistance toward organizational change processes. *Corporate Communications: An International Journal, 24*, 670–685.

Sha, B.-L. (2009). Exploring the connection between organizational identity and public relations behaviors: How symmetry trumps conservation in engendering organizational identification. *Journal of Public Relations Research, 21*, 295–317.

Shulga, L. V. (2021). Change management communication: The role of meaningfulness, leadership brand authenticity, and gender. *Cornell Hospitality Quarterly, 62*, 498–515.

Simões, P. M., & Esposito, M. (2014). Improving changing management: How communication nature influences resistance to change. *Journal of Management Development, 33*, 324–341.

Stigliani, I., & Elsbach, K. D. (2018). Identity co-formation in an emerging industry: Forging organizational distinctiveness and industry coherence through sensemaking and sensegiving. *Journal of Management Studies, 55*, 1323–1355.

World Health Organization. (2020). Getting your workplace ready for COVID-19. Available at: www.WHO.int.

Yue, C. A. (2021). Navigating change in the era of COVID-19: The role of top leaders' charismatic rhetoric and employees' organizational identification. *Public Relations Review, 47*(5). http://doi.org/10.1016/j.pubrev.2021.102118.

Yue, C. A., Men, L. R., & Ferguson, M. A. (2019). Bridging transformational leadership, transparent communication, and employee openness to change: The mediating role of trust. *Public Relations Review, 45*(3). http://doi.org/10.1016/j.pubrev.2019.04.012.

Section III

Internal Issues and Crises

Chapter Six

The Myth of Emotion-Focused Employee Crisis Communication? How Information-Focused Employee Crisis Communication during COVID-19 Pandemic Job Disruption Drives Post-Pandemic Intent-to-Perform and Intent-to-Return in Hospitality Employees

Minjeong Kang

Introduction

Job disruption brought on by internal or external crises can be traumatizing to employees in that job disruption causes job security stress and uncertainties (Koul & Nayar, 2021). Situations that are mainly characterized by uncertainties, such as the COVID-19 global pandemic brought on by the novel coronavirus in 2020 and 2021, have put a lot of strains on hospitality employees (Yu et al., 2021). The hospitality industry and employees have experienced a significant job disruption brought on by the pandemic, which resulted in massive layoffs and unpaid furloughs until late 2021 (Wieczorek-Kosmala, 2021).

Organizational communication scholars (e.g., Kim, 2018) have found that employee crisis communication that is symmetrical, transparent, and empathetic can have positive post-crisis influences on employee attitudes regarding the job and the organization. When an organization undergoes a crisis, employees engage in preservation strategies to minimize any negative impacts that the crisis could personally have on them. Organizational disruption prompts the sensemaking process in employees, which provides a means to regain a sense of stability (Dougherty & Drumheller, 2006). As such, how organizations communicate with employees during a job disruption influences employees' decision to engage with their job performance and stay committed to their organization post the job disruption. This chapter explores and discusses the importance of employee-centered employee crisis communication during an organizational crisis in mitigating negative implications of crisis-induced job disruption on supportive employee attitudes, namely post-crisis trust, organizational commitment, intent-to-perform, and intent-to-return from the perspective of conservation of resources (COR) theory.

DOI: 10.4324/9781003195580-10

Theoretical Background

Many employee crisis communication studies have viewed employees as essential stakeholders in mitigating the adverse effects of the organizational crisis on external reputation and mainly have focused on utilizing internal crisis communication as mitigating tools for the negative impact of an organizational crisis (Yeoman & Bowman, 2021). Some scholars have focused on the effective use of organizational discourse (e.g., Yeoman & Bowman, 2021) or symmetrical and transparent communication (e.g., Kim, 2018) during organizational disruptions to aid employees' sensemaking. Employees engage in the sensemaking process based on their leader's discourses in communicating organizational disruptions with employees, acknowledging and providing sense-giving discourses for employees. The sensemaking theory suggests that people make retrospective sense of unexpected and disruptive events through an ongoing process of action, selection, and interpretation (Weick, 1995). For employees, sensemaking occurs to cope with ambiguity or uncertainty stemming from organizational change or crisis. Employees seek to clarify how to make sense of the situation by attending to and interpreting cues from the situation (Stieglitz et al., 2018).

COR theory can provide insights into the psychological process in which stressed employees strive to achieve such sensemaking goals (assurance and stability), motivating them to engage in resource preservation strategies (Hobfoll, 1989). Potential job loss is one of the most stressful situations in that unemployment is a major loss of resources and is related to other direct and indirect resource losses (Hobfoll et al., 2018). According to COR theory, when resource-threatening events (e.g., divorce or layoff) occur, these events tend to affect people more rapidly and strongly compared to the events of possible resource gain (e.g., marriage or promotion) because resource loss is disproportionately more saliently felt than resource gain (Hobfoll et al., 2018). Consequently, people are driven to engage in actions that could mitigate the negative consequences of resource loss, such as seeking replacement of resources (e.g., seeking another job) or investing resources for potential resource gain (e.g., signing up for a college course).

A supportive environment is vital in potential resource-loss situations and personal resources tend to emerge in a supportive environment wherein individuals are nurtured, valued, and supported via social conditions such as a supportive family and workplace (Hobfoll, 2011). During an organizational job disruption, organizations can either alleviate or exacerbate employee stress by communicating clearly with employees. Failure to alleviate employee stress during a stressful workplace situation can activate employees' self-preservation motives and self-protective behaviors. Mainly, employee-centered crisis communication addressing the emotional and the informational needs during the stressful job disruption period can appease employees' resource-conservation responses driven by resource-loss-related stress.

Job Disruption and Employees' Work Intentions as Precursors of Employee Engagement and Loyalty

As job disruption brings much stress to employees, how organizations communicate with their employees in the process of employees' sensemaking during the disruption can affect post-job employee outcomes. Work intentions emerge as employees' responses to their evaluation of the work situations to either diminish/prevent harm to their wellbeing or enhance/acquire benefits to their wellbeing (Bagozzi, 1992; Zigarmi et al., 2011). Zigarmi et al. (2009) developed a conceptual model of work intentions as outcomes of individual appraisal of their wellbeing, which employees form via cognitive and affective experiences and assessment of organizational and job characteristics. Wellbeing is one of the most important psychological resources that individuals strive to gain and maintain and it can have a profound influence on employees' cognitive and affective work experiences and the spontaneous appraisal of the work experiences, which can determine their work-related intentions such as intention to perform and intention to return (Lazarus, 1991).

While Zigarmi et al.'s (2009, 2011) models provide how organizational and work characteristics influence the formation of employees' appraisal and the subsequent intentions, the models do not address external organizational environment's impacts on employees' cognitive and affective work experiences. COR theory provides conceptual foundation explaining employees' defensive or proactive responses to external threats to prized and important resources such as the sense of wellbeing, as the theory includes both work-related and nonwork-related threats to personal resources that individual employees need to draw from to perform their work roles with passion (Hobfoll, 2011).

Intent-to-Perform

In recent years, scholars have started drawing the connection between intent-to-perform and levels of job performance as job engagement (Gollwitzer & Sheeran, 2006). Once intentions are formed, they tend to affect the likelihood for the intended behavior (performance) to occur by increasing people's investment of effort and developing various coping strategies that minimize goal and performance distractions (Baldwin & Baird,

2001; Bandura, 1986; Gollwitzer, 1999). Conceptualized by Kahn (1990) as "the simultaneous employment and expression of a person's 'preferred self' in task behaviors that promote connections to work and to others, personal presence (physical, cognitive, and emotional), and active, full role performance" (p. 700), many scholars since Kahn have defined engagement as a broad concept explaining employee job performance characterized by vigor, dedication, and absorption that employees bring in performing their job (Schaufeli & Bakker, 2004).

Kahn (1990) noted that "people employ and express or withdraw and defend their preferred selves based on their psychological experiences of self-in-role" (p. 702), which are critical influences on people's internal motivations for active full job performance. People vary their level of job performance based on the presence of three psychological conditions of meaningfulness, safety, and availability (Kahn, 1990; May et al., 2004). These conditions reflect the logic of psychological contracts in employment situations as people vary their level of job engagement according to the perceptions of benefits (meaningfulness), the safety they perceive in their workplace situations (safety), and resources individuals perceive to possess (availability) (Kahn, 1990).

Intent-to-Return

Intent-to-return refers to an employee's conscious and deliberate intention and willingness to stay with their present organization (Tett & Meyer, 1993) and is the conceptual counterpart to intent-to-leave or turnover intention (Cho et al., 2009). High employee turnover in the hospitality industry is a significant problem (Tracey & Hinkin, 2008), mainly due to overall low wages, shift schedules, and social perception of the hospitality job as an entry-level position (Dermody et al., 2004). Cho et al. (2009) found that perceived organizational support was a critical antecedent of intent-to-stay that can also decrease employee intent-to-leave among hospitality employees.

Employees' intent-to-perform and intent-to-return as precursors of job engagement and loyalty are closely linked to resources that individuals can draw up for full job performance and commitment to the organization (Zigarmi et al., 2011). Individuals need physical (e.g., strength, stamina and flexibility), cognitive (abilities to process information and think clearly), and emotional (abilities to exercise and extend affective dedication and energies) resources to have psychological availability for engagement (Kahn, 1990). More specifically, psychological availability is positively associated with resources available but negatively associated with demands from outside-work activities as the demands from nonwork aspects of lives tend to compete for limited resources (e.g., energy) from employees (May et al., 2004). As such, in a stressful work situation that signals potential and actual loss of personal resources (e.g., job or pay disruption), employees' psychological availability decreases as employees struggle to make sense of the situation and engage in resource-preservation strategies (Hobfoll, 2011). Because an organizational crisis disrupts job security and can seriously undermine employees' work intentions, it is likely to drive employees to withdraw their energy and loyalty unless the organizations provide support of resources via effective crisis communication.

Employee-Centered Crisis Communication

In organizational crisis management literature, employees often have been relegated to a functional instrument as critical mitigators of harmful effects of the crisis on organizations (Olsson, 2014). Consequently, employees as internal stakeholders who are fundamentally affected by the organizational crisis have been overlooked in crisis communication studies (Kim, 2018). While the strategic use of internal communication to shield employees from a crisis is necessary, organizations also need to communicate with employees by recognizing employees' needs for assurance and stability in a stressful workplace event (Adamu et al., 2016), not only for coping with uncertainty from the crisis in performing their job but also for making sense of the crisis in terms of personal implications.

Scholars in recent years, therefore, have begun advocating the need for employee-oriented internal communication (Ulmer, 2012), recognizing employees as agents of their situations. Employee communication during an organizational crisis hence needs to be approached as the sense-giving discourse, aiding employee's sensemaking in uncertain workplace situations (Adamu et al., 2016; Yeoman & Bowman, 2021). It is particularly important to communicate with employees from employees' perspectives by providing relevant, timely, transparent, and helpful information for employees (Olsson, 2014). However, crisis communication viewing employees as an instrument for organizational outcomes persists.

Additionally, organization studies tend to be guided by a rationality/emotionality duality in which rationality is privileged over emotions (Ashcraft, 2000; Putnam & Mumby, 1993). Dougherty and Drumheller (2006) noted that the workplace is laden with emotions. While the sensemaking process is cognitive (Fineman, 1996), emotions play a role in the outset and outcome of sensemaking in that an interruption to an organizational flow (disruption) typically brings out emotional responses to organizational members (Weick, 1995). While the sensemaking theory provides a process model of how employees make sense of organizational crises, its primary focus on cognitive-centered sensemaking provides limited insight into how organizational crises can drive employees to self-preservation from a stressful and potential resource-loss workplace situation.

According to Fiebig and Kramer (1998), unmet expectations stemming from the discrepancy between the expected and the reality can act as the catalyst for emotional experiences in the workplace. Sensemaking is not purely cognitive and emotions play a significant role in the sensemaking process (Weick, 1995), particularly when organizational flows are interrupted. Cho and Gower (2006) argued that the primacy of emotions exists during the initial stages of crisis information processing for specific crises because the publics may not evaluate crisis information based on facts or information released by organizations or the media. Similarly, Lu and Huang's (2018) dual-factor model points out that when people experience intense crisis emotions, their information processing will follow an emotion-oriented pattern.

While some crisis communication models have incorporated the influence of emotions in mostly external stakeholders' information processing, applying these models in employee communication contexts can also provide us with an understanding of how employee crisis communication may aid or hinder employees' sensemaking of the workplace crisis, which is likely to be reflected in their post-crisis work intentions. Employees play dual roles vis-à-vis the organization in that they are both its stakeholders and the organization. Employees' sensemaking during organizational crises engages them to process organizational communication as stakeholders to assess the situation critically and as the organization's members that the crisis directly disrupts and threatens their resources such as income or the sense of wellbeing. Therefore, employees experience intense stress due to heightened uncertainty and threat to resources. Employee crisis communication needs to accommodate both emotional and informational needs that employees have to make sense of the situation. Therefore, the following hypotheses are proposed:

H1: Employee crisis communication that is focused on emotion (a) and information (b) would be positively associated with intent-to-perform.

H2: Employee crisis communication that is focused on emotion (a) and information (b) would be positively associated with intent-to-return.

Case Study Analysis

Method

An online survey with full and part-time hospitality employees in North America and Europe with the panel sample from Prolific yielded 393 participants in August 2020. The survey was designed to imitate a time-lagged research design to examine the associations of employee crisis communication (information and emotion) with post-COVID employee work intentions of intent-to-perform and intent-to-stay when pre-COVID leader-member exchange (LMX) quality was controlled for. Demographic variables (gender, tenure, and position) were measured and controlled for the analysis.

Study Context

The COVID-19 pandemic had brought many aspects of life to a halt, particularly at the beginning of 2020, when the world was shocked to see the devastating tolls that the novel coronavirus took, affecting more than 500 million and killing over 6 million people worldwide as of April 24, 2022 (World Health Organization, 2022). Except for essential workers (healthcare and frontline workers), many organizations pivoted their employees to work remotely from online. On the other hand, most hospitality employees, such as food and service industry employees, were laid off or furloughed without pay due to the nature of their work that requires physical contact with customers. Further, hospitality employees tend to be transient compared to other employees in other professions, with a high rate of burnout due to high job demands and long work hours (Yu et al., 2021). Retrospectively, many employees including hospitality sector employees reported their hesitancy to return to their previous positions, as indicated in the 2021 national labor shortage as the nation prepared to come out of the pandemic slowly (Fuller & Kerr, 2022).

Data Analysis

First, exploratory factor analysis (EFA) for employee crisis communication was conducted to extract factors from 13 original crisis communication measurement items drawn from crisis communication literature. Initial EFA yielded two factors that were conceptually incongruent with low inter-item reliability. After pruning items with low-reliability coefficients, the second EFA yielded two factors that were labeled as "information-focused" (IF) and "emotion-focused" (EF) employee crisis communication (see Table 6.1 for EFA). Second, partial correlations were conducted to test the proposed hypotheses, controlling for pre-disruption (T1) LMX quality, age, gender, and tenure of the study participants' demographic characteristics (see Table 6.2).

TABLE 6.1 Exploratory factor analysis on employee crisis communication during the COVID pandemic ($N = 393$)

	Factor loading	
	1	2
Factor 1: Emotion-based crisis communication		
Individualized attention	**0.82**	0.06
Assuring	**0.88**	−0.01
Reducing uncertainty	**0.90**	−0.02
Showing empathy	**0.88**	0.03
Factor 2: Information-based crisis communication		
Correcting false information	0.02	**0.83**
Fast response	0.01	**0.78**
Timely updates	0.02	**0.84**
Total variance explained	3.04 (43.36%)	2.00 (28.62%)

Note Extraction method: Principal component analysis. Rotation method: Varimax with Kaiser normalization.

Hypothesis Test Results

H1 proposed to test if employee crisis communication would be positively associated with intent-to-perform. The test of partial correlations demonstrated that emotion-based employee crisis communication during the job disruption was not significantly associated with employees' post-disruption intent-to-perform ($r = 0.05$, $p = n.s.$) (see Table 6.2 for partial correlations result). On the contrary, information-based employee crisis communication was found to be significantly and positively correlated with employees' post-disruption intent-to-perform ($r = 0.36$, $p < 0.001$). Therefore, H1(a) was rejected, but H1(b) was supported.

TABLE 6.2 Partial correlations with descriptive statistics ($N = 393$)

	M	SD	α	T2_Cri_Emo	T2_Cri_Inf	T3_Int_Perform	T3_Int_Stay
T2_Cri_Emo	3.01	1.18	0.89	1			
T2_Cri_Inf	3.22	1.04	0.75	0.05	1		
T3_Int_Perform	4.18	.84	0.90	0.05	0.36***	1	
T3_Int_Return	75.52	28.11	N/A	0.03	0.34***	0.41***	1

Note Control Variables: Age ($M = 28.85$, $SD = 10.53$); gender (female = 63.4%); organizational tenure (mode = "2 years to less than 4 years," 24.2%); pre-COVID leader-member exchange (LMX) quality ($M = 3.44$, $SD = 0.85$).

T2_Cri_Emo = Emotion-based crisis communication during the COVID-19 pandemic; T2_Cri_Inf = Information-based crisis communication during the COVID-19 pandemic; T3_Int_Perform = Post-COVID intent to perform; T3_Int_Return = Post-COVID intent to return. *** $p < 0.001$.

H2 proposed to test if employee crisis communication that is focused on emotion (a) and information (b) would be positively associated with intent-to-return. The results of the partial correlations analysis showed that emotion-based employee crisis communication was not significantly related to employees' post-disruption intent-to-return with the organization ($r = 0.05$, $p =$ *n.s.*). On the other hand, the results showed a significant and positive association between information-based employee crisis communication and intent-to-return ($r = 0.41$, $p < 0.001$). Therefore, H2(a) was rejected, and H2(b) was supported.

Key Findings

During the early lockdown stage of the COVID-19 pandemic, many hospitality businesses were forced to shut down. Their business closure further trickled down to layoffs and unpaid furloughs of most hospitality employees. The analysis of the data from hospitality employees collected near the end of the first lockdown wave revealed the following critical insights for organizational communication with employees during this unprecedented prolonged and stressful job disruption and post-disruption employees' intent-to-perform and intent-to-return.

The results revealed the significance of IF crisis communication as the most critical component of effective employee crisis communication, which was significantly linked to intent-to-perform and intent-to return. The correlation coefficient loadings ($r = 0.36$ for intent-to-perform and $r = 0.41$ for intent-to-return) of these associations between IF crisis communication indicate a very strong association. On the other hand, EF crisis communication was insignificantly associated with employees' intent-to-perform and intent-to-return. These nonsignificant findings were inconsistent with the internal crisis communication literature, which emphasizes the importance of communicating emotional assurance to employees during an organizational crisis or change.

These findings of insignificant effects of EF employee crisis communication on intent-to-perform and intent-to-return may be partially attributed to the case study context, which brought unprecedented levels of job insecurity and uncertainty for a prolonged job disruption period. Another plausible explanation for these unexpected findings may be due to pent-up employee frustration and burnout in hospitality workers because hotels and restaurants were quick to streamline and downsize their staff to make the business operation extremely lean to survive the pandemic. Consequently, hospitality employees could have perceived their organizations' attempt at being empathetic with their communication as largely performative and empty, lacking sincere concerns for employees, which reduced their job performance intention, if they decide to return. As Fuller and Kerr (2022) noted, the trend of mass resignations of employees in the U.S. labor market is in accordance with the voluntary resignation rate for the past decade, influenced by factors such as *retirement, relocation, reconsideration, reshuffling,* and *reluctance.* Particularly noteworthy is the reconsideration factor and the reluctance factor for voluntary resignation among women and younger employees who tend to make up a large proportion of hospitality labor force by reassessing the role of work in their lives as they witnessed deaths and serious illnesses during the pandemic and struggle to care for families while holding down demanding and potentially dangerous jobs due to COVID-19 (Fuller & Kerr, 2022).

Additionally, the significant influences of IF employee crisis communication on post-disruption intent-to-perform and intent-to-return are noteworthy. These findings highlighted the crucial aspect of effective crisis communication with employees that centers around the utility of crisis communication for employees in a stressful job disruption event. This insight is consistent with the emerging notion of employee-centered crisis communication (Ulmer, 2012), which emphasizes the importance of employee crisis communication that focuses on fulfilling communication needs from the perspective of employees, rather than "feeling good" communication from the perspectives of the organization (Olsson, 2014). This study points to a possible situation that employee crisis communication that focuses on providing emotional support and assurance does not necessarily lead to supportive work intentions post crisis if emotional support is not what employees need for their stress management for their wellbeing during a job disruption. Further, this study's findings point out that employees may perceive organizations' efforts to provide concrete information regarding changes in job responsibilities, organizational responses to the crisis, and transparency in communication as genuine understanding of employee needs, while EF organizational discourses may be perceived as mainly performative and grandstanding. This insight is particularly relevant in the hospitality industry, where employees are generally more mobile than others. Many hospitality employees view their employment as temporary or financial means for other more personal goals; hence, employers' clear and timely communication might be viewed as a respectful signal of the organization's genuine understanding of employee situations and their needs for clarity in their job prospects. On a related note, the findings of this particular case study focused on hospitality employees need to be interpreted with much caution for generalizing the specific findings of the study to other industries. Rather, the findings of this case study should be accepted as a cautionary tale that reemphasizes the importance of understanding key stakeholders from the perspectives of the stakeholders and not of the organization.

Key Implications for Practice

There are several practical implications of the study. The findings suggest that an organization must anticipate and provide employees' informational needs when the organization is going through an event that disrupts regular job flow and security for employees. While employee communication that provides emotional support may seem intuitively useful to assure employees' feelings of uncertainties and anxieties during organizational turbulence, the study's findings indicate that employees might appreciate more accurate, timely, and responsive communication that provides helpful information for employees to proactively manage their stress stemming from potential resource losses. In other words, organizations must actively listen to employee concerns, anticipate employee needs brought on by organizational turbulence. Relatedly, employee communication should serve a functional utility for employees to sustain performance and retain employees, as employees are trying to make sense of the situation in terms of what the job disruption personally means for them, not only for the organization.

Additionally, the study's findings further indicate that employee-centered crisis communication that addresses employees' informational needs during a job-disruption event is essential for post-disruption job engagement and loyalty intentions. Employee job engagement requires psychological conditions of meaningfulness, safety, and availability. If meaningfulness is specific to job characteristics and safety is specific to organizational characteristics, availability condition is conducive to external factors that may prevent employees from fully engaging their mental and physical resources to job performance.

Drawing from COR theory, the findings of the current study point to the reality of stressful work situations that may trigger employees to engage in resource preservation strategies, saving energy and vigor or looking for alternative job options when the organization, seems oblivious to the struggles of employees. In order for organizations to retain and re-engage employees after a major organizational disruption, organizations need to invest and allocate resources to understand employee needs and communicate proactively to appease employee stress. The study's findings point to a very likely situation that organizations consider to be responding to employees' needs of assurance during highly uncertain organizational turbulence may in fact be quite different from what employees actually need and want in managing their stress from job uncertainties.

Learning Outcomes

1) To understand impacts of organizational disruptions on employees' sensemaking process
2) To explore types of information that employees find helpful for their sensemaking process during organizational disruptions for post-disruption job engagement and loyalty
3) To understand the critical role of employee-centered communication during organizational disruptions on post-disruption employee intents to perform and to return

Discussion Questions

1) What does it mean to be employee-centered for organizational communication?
2) What are the advantages and limitations of relying on the COR perspective in explaining employee expectations for job performance and loyalty intentions?
3) Can you think of situations when EF crisis communication can be effective for positive post-crisis employee outcomes?
4) How can or can't the findings of this case study be applied in other industries (e.g., healthcare, Information and Technologies, education, etc.)?

Further Readings

Hobfoll, S. E., Halbesleben, J., Neveu, J. P., & Westman, M. (2018). Conservation of resources in the organizational context: The reality of resources and their consequences. *Annual Review of Organizational Psychology & Organizational Behavior, 5*, 103–128.

Kahn, W. A. (1990). Psychological conditions of personal engagement and disengagement at work. *Academy of Management Journal, 33*(4), 692–724.

References

Adamu, A. A., Mohamad, B., & Rahman, N. A. A. (2016). Antecedents of internal crisis communication and its consequences on employee performance. *International Review of Management and Marketing, 6*(7), 33–41.

Ashcraft, L. K. (2000). Empowering "professional" relationships: Organizational communication meets feminist practice. *Management Communication Quarterly, 13*(3), 347–392.

Bagozzi, R. P. (1992). The self-regulation of attitudes, intentions, and behavior. *Social Psychology Quarterly, 55*(2), 178–204.

Baldwin, D. A., & Baird, J. A. (2001). Discerning intentions in dynamic human action. *Trends in Cognitive Sciences, 5*(4), 171–178.

Bandura, A. (1986). Fearful expectations and avoidant actions as coeffects of perceived self-inefficacy. *American Psychologist, 41*(12), 1389–1391.

Cho, S. H., & Gower, K. K. (2006). Framing effect on the public's response to crisis: Human interest frame and crisis type influencing responsibility and blame. *Public Relations Review, 32*(4), 420–422.

Cho, S., Johanson, M. M., & Guchait, P. (2009). Employee's intent to leave: A comparison of determinants of intent to leave versus intent to stay. *International Journal of Hospitality Management, 28*(3), 374–381.

Dermody, M. B., Young, M., & Taylor, S. L. (2004). Identifying job motivation factors of restaurant servers: Insight for the development of effective recruitment and retention strategies. *International Journal of Hospitality and Tourism Administration, 5*(3), 1–14.

Dougherty, D. S., & Drumheller, K. (2006). Sensemaking and emotions in organizations: Accounting for emotions in a rational(ized) context. *Communication Studies, 57*(2), 215–238.

Fiebig, G. V., & Kramer, M. W. (1998). A framework for the study of emotions in organizational contexts. *Management Communication Quarterly, 11*(4), 536–572.

Fineman, S. (1996). Emotion and organizing. In S. R. Clegg, C. Hardy & W. R. Nord (Eds.), *Handbook of organization studies* (289–310). London: Sage.

Fuller, J. & Kerr, W. (March 23, 2022). The Great Resignation didn't start with the pandemic. *Harvard Business Review.* Article Retrieved on June 27, 2022 from https://hbr.org/2022/03/the-great-resignation-didnt-start-with-the-pandemic

Gollwitzer, P. M. (1999). Implementation intentions: Strong effects of simple plans. *American Psychologist, 54*(7), 493.

Gollwitzer, P. M., & Sheeran, P. (2006). Implementation intentions and goal achievement: A meta-analysis of effects and processes. *Advances in Experimental Social Psychology, 38*, 69–119.

Graen, G. B., & Uhl-Bien, M. (1995). Relationship-based approach to leadership: Development of leader-member exchange (LMX) theory of leadership over 25 years: Applying a multi-level multi-domain perspective. *The Leadership Quarterly, 6*(2), 219–247.

Hobfoll, S. E. (1989). Conservation of resources: A new attempt at conceptualizing stress. *American Psychologist, 44*(3), 513–524.

Hobfoll, S. E. (2011). Conservation of resource caravans and engaged settings. *Journal of Occupational & Organizational Psychology, 84*(1), 116–122.

Hobfoll, S. E., Halbesleben, J., Neveu, J. P., & Westman, M. (2018). Conservation of resources in the organizational context: The reality of resources and their consequences. *Annual Review of Organizational Psychology & Organizational Behavior, 5*, 103–128.

Kahn, W. A. (1990). Psychological conditions of personal engagement and disengagement at work. *Academy of Management Journal, 33*(4), 692–724.

Koul, S., & Nayar, B. (2022). Combating the COVID-19 disruption: Gauging job loss grief and psychological wellbeing of hospitality employees. *Journal of Human Resources in Hospitality & Tourism, 21*(1), 82–104.

Kim, Y. (2018). Enhancing employee communication behaviors for sensemaking and sensegiving in crisis situations: Strategic management approach for effective internal crisis communication. *Journal of Communication Management, 22*(4), 451–475.

Lazarus, R. S. (1991). *Emotion and adaptation*. Oxford, UK: Oxford University Press

Lu, Y., & Huang, Y. H. C. (2018). Getting emotional: An emotion-cognition dual-factor model of crisis communication. *Public Relations Review, 44*(1), 98–107.

May, D. R., Gilson, R. L., & Harter, L. M. (2004). The psychological conditions of meaningfulness, safety and availability and the engagement of the human spirit at work. *Journal of Occupational & Organizational Psychology, 77*(1), 11–37.

Olsson, E. K. (2014). Crisis communication in public organizations: Dimensions of crisis communication revisited. *Journal of Contingencies & Crisis Management, 22*(2), 113–125.

Putnam, L. L., & Mumby, D. K. (1993). Organizations, emotion and the myth of rationality. *Emotion in Organizations, 1*, 36–57.

Schaufeli, W. B., & Bakker, A. B. (2004). Job demands, job resources, and their relationship with burnout and engagement: A multi-sample study. *Journal of Organizational Behavior: The International Journal of Industrial, Occupational and Organizational Psychology and Behavior, 25*(3), 293–315.

Stieglitz, S., Bunker, D., Mirbabaie, M., & Ehnis, C. (2018). Sensemaking in social media during extreme events. *Journal of Contingencies & Crisis Management, 26*(1), 4–15.

Tett, R. P., & Meyer, J. P. (1993). Job satisfaction, organizational commitment, turnover intention, and turnover: Path analysis based on meta-analytic findings. *Personnel Psychology, 46*(2), 342–346.

Tracey, J. B., & Hinkin, T. R. (2008). Contextual factors and cost profiles associated with employee turnover. *Cornell Hospitality Quarterly, 49*(1), 12–27.

Ulmer, R. R. (2012). Increasing the impact of thought leadership in crisis communication. *Management Communication Quarterly, 26*(4), 523–542.

Weick, K. E. (1995). *Sensemaking in organizations* (Vol. 3). Thousand Oaks, CA: Sage.

Wieczorek-Kosmala, M. (2021). COVID-19 impact on the hospitality industry: Exploratory study of financial-slack-driven risk preparedness. *International Journal of Hospitality Management, 94*(April), 1–14. https://doi.org/10.1016/j.ijhm.2020.102799

World Health Organization. (April 27, 2022). Weekly epidemiological update on COVID-19. *Emergency Situation Updates, 89*. Report Retrieved on April 27, 2022 from https://www.who.int/publications/m/item/weekly-epidemiological-update-on-covid-19—27-april-2022

Yeomans, L., & Bowman, S. (2021). Internal crisis communication and the social construction of emotion: University leaders' sense giving discourse during the COVID-19 pandemic. *Journal of Communication Management, 25*(3), 196–213.

Yu, H., Lee, L., Popa, I., & Madera, J. M. (2021). Should I leave this industry? The role of stress and negative emotions in response to an industry negative work event. *International Journal of Hospitality Management*, *94*, 102843.

Zigarmi, D., Nimon, K., Houson, D., Witt, D., & Diehl, J. (2009). Beyond engagement: Toward a framework and operational definition for employee work passion. *Human Resource Development Review*, *8*(3), 300–326.

Zigarmi, D., Nimon, K., Houson, D., Witt, D., & Diehl, J. (2011). A preliminary field test of an employee work passion model. *Human Resource Development Quarterly*, *22*(2), 195–221.

Zigarmi, D. R. E. A., & Roberts, T. P. (2012). Leader values as predictors of employee affect and work passion intentions. *Journal of Modern Economy & Management*, *1*(1), 1–28.

Appendix

Measurements

T1: Pre-COVID leader-member exchange (LMX) quality (LMX scale by Graen and Uhl-Bien (1995) (M = 3.44, SD = 0.85, α = 0.90)

- Did you usually know how satisfied your leader was with what you would do? (1 = rarely; 5 = very often)
- How well did your supervisor understand your job problems and needs? (1 = not at all; 5 = fully)
- How well did your supervisor recognize your potential? (1 = not at all; 5 = fully)
- Regardless of how much formal authority your supervisor had built into their position, what were the chances that your supervisor would use their power to help you solve problems in your work? (1 = none; 5 = very high)
- Again, regardless of the amount of formal authority your supervisor had, what were the chances that they would "bail you out" at their own expense? (1 = none; 5 = very high)
- I had enough confidence in my supervisor that I would defend and justify their decisions if they were not present to do so (1 = strongly disagree; 5 = strongly agree)
- How would you characterize your working relationship with your supervisor (prior to your job disruption)? (1 = extremely ineffective; 5 = extremely effective)

T2: Crisis communication during the COVID pandemic (developed based on review of crisis communication literature)

[During the transition period (the 1 week BEFORE and the 1 week AFTER your job was initially disrupted), think about how well your organization managed its communications about the crisis (and the job changes) at hand. Your organization's communication was … (1 = strongly disagree; 5 = strongly agree).]

T2_Cri_Emo = Emotion-based crisis communication during the COVID pandemic ($M = 3.01$, $SD = 1.18$, $\alpha = 0.89$):

- Individualized attention
- Assuring any concerns
- Reducing uncertainty
- Showing empathy

T2_Cri_Inf = Information-based crisis communication during the COVID pandemic ($M = 3.22$, $SD = 1.04$, $\alpha = 0.75$):

- Correcting false information
- Fast response
- Timely updates

T3_Int_Perform = Post-COVID intent to perform (Work Intentions_Intent-to-Perform Scale by Zigarmi & Roberts, 2012) ($M = 4.18$, $SD = 0.84$, $\alpha = 0.90$):

[If TODAY, your organization were to offer you to return to work at the same job you had before (for the same pay/compensation) … rate the following items to indicate your job performance intentions (1 = strongly disagree; 5 = strongly agree).]

- I would intend to exert the energy it would take to do my job well.
- I would intend to work efficiently to help my organization succeed.
- I would intend to achieve all my work goals.

T3_Int_Return = Post-COVID Intent to Stay (Work Intentions_Intent-to-Perform Scale by Zigarmi & Roberts, 2012) $M = 75.52$, $SD = 28.11$):

[If TODAY, your organization were to offer you to return to work at the same job you had before (for the same pay/compensation) …

- how likely would you be to choose to stay for them? (0 = extremely unlikely; 100 = extremely likely).]

Chapter Seven

To Stay Silent or Speak Up against Corporate Racial Discrimination? An Internal Public Segmentation Approach to Employee Voice and Silence Behaviors

Hyunji (Dana) Lim and Young Kim

Introduction

Racial discrimination has increasingly challenged the workplace in the United States. Big corporations, such as Amazon, Facebook, Google, and Uber, have all recently faced multiple lawsuits filed by former and current employees (Dave, 2021). According to the Pew Research Center, more than two-thirds (70%) of Americans have witnessed or experienced racial discrimination in the U.S. (Daniller, 2021). Scholars have paid attention to persistent racial discrimination in the workplace in terms of social networks, wage disparities, and hiring disadvantages (Wingfield & Chavez, 2020).

Against that backdrop, internal communication managers should consider how to communicate with their internal publics (i.e., employees), as well as assist management's decision-making processes in handling such negative trends in their organizations (Ruck et al., 2017). Employee voice behavior, as a form of upward communication, can improve management's communication of internal crises so that employees' needs and constructive ideas can be effectively communicated back to management (Kim & Lim, 2020). Nevertheless, research on employee voice and silence in internal crisis communication remains rare. Previous studies heavily centered on the lateral direction of employees' internal and external communication behaviors, but not employee voice.

Beyond that, previous studies have predominantly examined employee voice as a constructive voice behavior but failed to investigate employee silence (Morrison, 2014). Also, recent research has emphasized employee segmentation in predicting not only how employees are engaged in communication behaviors but also how internal communication managers communicate tailored crisis communication strategies (Lee, 2019). Still another line of research has indicated that enhancing employee resilience is critical for effective crisis management because resilient employees are likely to engage in proficient, proactive, and adaptive behaviors in their organizations after crises (Kim, 2020). However, there has been a lack of scholarly attention to employee segmentation considering employee resilience in voice and silence.

DOI: 10.4324/9781003195580-11

To fill those gaps, this study applies the concept of employee segmentation to the issue of racial discrimination by synthesizing employee resilience and situational perceptions to elucidate why employees do or do not speak up when they face a racial discrimination issue in the workplace. Also, internal communication managers can better understand how to effectively communicate organizational issues or crises to their employees as a means to strategically manage employee voice and silence regarding their leadership's decision-making processes.

Literature Review

Employee Voice and Silence

Employee voice, as a form of discretionary communication, means an employee's upward communication of ideas, suggestions, concerns, information about problems, or opinions about work-related issues to persons who could take appropriate action; it is intended to bring about improvement or change (Morrison, 2014). Thus, this study considers employee voice as a *constructive behavior* involving the expression of change-oriented ideas and suggestions motivated by employees' desires to improve their current situation (Ng et al., 2014).

Scholars have demonstrated that employee voice behaviors help an organization reduce errors or mistakes; increase productivity, performance, and innovation; and decrease turnover intentions (e.g., Sherf et al., 2018). In terms of the internal communication context, employee voice behaviors are considered a driver of employee engagement because organizations can benefit from employee involvement and participation by providing upward feedback (Burris et al., 2017; Ruck et al., 2017).

Therefore, employees are encouraged to engage in voice behaviors expressing ideas and concerns in their organization, but often choose not to speak up although they have useful or relevant suggestions and information about a problem (Tangirala & Ramanujam, 2008). *Employee silence* is specifically defined as an employee's intentional withholding of genuine expression about behavioral, cognitive, and/or affective assessments of organizational conditions, including potentially important work issues, to persons with the perceived authority to change the situation (Guenter et al., 2017).

Employee silence has been mainly studied as a negative factor that undermines the flow of employee feedback and suggestions on organizational weaknesses, poor managerial decisions, and the misconduct of certain organizational members (Chou & Chang, 2020). Employee silence can also have detrimental effects on organizational effectiveness related to productivity, decision making, and crisis prevention (Perlow & Williams, 2003).

Previous research has primarily explored how contextual or personal factors affect employee voice and silence (Chou & Chang, 2020). Nonetheless, researchers have recently suggested considering situational factors that could contribute to employee voice and silence by jointly interacting with other factors (Prouska & Psychogios, 2018). Employees' situational perceptions can be a critical motivator for how employees engage in active or passive communication behaviors in response to a negative issue (Lee, 2019). Moreover, employee resilience has been suggested as an important factor that induces positive outcomes—increasing work-role performance—in a post-crisis situation by helping an organization adapt quickly (Kim, 2020).

Situational Perception for Employee Voice and Silence

Perception is strong enough to influence consequent attitude and behavior (Salancik & Pfeffer, 1978). Specifically, Morrison and Milliken (2000) found that employees are less likely to interact and communicate if they perceive obstacles for speaking up (e.g., lack of upward feedback mechanisms) in their workplace. Also, perceiving a fear of retaliation was referred to as the biggest reason for employees to keep silent (Rothschild, 2008). Relatedly, scholars have indicated that employees' perceptions about an issue or crisis can influence their active communication behaviors by voluntarily seeking and disseminating valuable or organization-related information to others (Lee, 2019).

To better understand how employees engage in their communication behaviors in a crisis, Lee (2019) suggested applying the situational theory of problem solving (STOPS) as a theoretical framework. STOPS postulates situational perceptions—problem recognition, constraint recognition, and involvement recognition—as antecedents of publics' communication behaviors (Kim & Grunig, 2011). In this regard, this study uses these situational perceptions to identify different types of employees and investigate how they engage in employee voice and silence differently when encountering a racial discrimination issue.

Employee Resilience for Employee Voice and Silence

Employee resilience is defined as an employee's "capability, facilitated and supported by the organization, to utilize resources to continually adapt and flourish at work, even if/when faced with challenging circumstances" (Näswall et al., 2015, p. 1). Researchers have demonstrated that employees with high resilience are better able to respond effectively in unfamiliar or challenging situations and persevere in the face of negative issues or crises (Sutcliffe & Vogus, 2003).

Previous research has demonstrated that employee resilience plays a key role in expressing voice and stimulating individuals' proactive behaviors such as improving work methods, influencing work colleagues, or championing ideas to others (Caniëls & Baaten, 2019). Recently, Kim (2020) found that more resilient employees are likely to engage in adaptive and proactive behaviors by suggesting ideas to improve the overall effectiveness of their organizations after a crisis. Literature on silence has also shown a negative association between employee resilience and employee silence. Landau (2009) found that employees with low self-efficacy may think they are incompetent and refrain from speaking out on the organization's present predicament. Other scholars reported that employees with low self-esteem feel less deserving, capable, and outspoken, leading to employee silence (Pacheco et al., 2015).

Employee Segmentation

Research has suggested applying situational perceptions to segmented publics for effective communication about issues and crises (Grunig, 1989; Kim, 2011). The public segmentation concept has been frequently applied to identify the key publics and communicate with them more effectively in a crisis. Recently, Lee (2019) suggested employee segmentation in considering the importance of communicating with internal publics during a negative internal issue.

Management scholars have also emphasized the importance of employee segmentation because it aids in determining the efficacy of an organization's communication, leading to collaborative interaction between HR and various employee groups (Waite, 2007). Nevertheless, employee resilience has not drawn scholarly attention in employee segmentation research. Thus, this study applies the concepts of employee resilience and situational perceptions to segmentation to better understand the multifaceted motives behind employee voice and silence; we then propose more tailored communication strategies with employees for successful crisis management.

Therefore, we propose the following research questions:

RQ1: How do employee voice and silence intentions concerning racial discrimination in organizations vary by types of employees segmented in terms of their resilience and situational perceptions?

RQ2: How do employees' resilience and situational perceptions influence their voice and silence intentions concerning racial discrimination in organizations after controlling for the effects of demographic and job profile factors, such as age, gender, race, income, education, job position, and length of tenure?

Method

Case Context: Racial Discrimination in the Workplace

In July 2020, an African American manager at Facebook and two rejected job applicants filed a lawsuit against Facebook that alleged racial biases against Black employees in promotions, hiring, and recruiting (Dwoskin, 2020). In March 2021, the U.S. Equal Employment Opportunity Commission reported a systematic probe of Facebook for racial bias in hiring and promotions showing that the company's policies may be contributing to widespread discrimination (Dave, 2021). This study uses the following scenario excerpted from a published news article about the accusation of racial discrimination at Facebook:

> Today you heard that your co-workers, James and Mary, sued your company, accusing it of racial discrimination that involves treating applicants and employees unfavorably because of their race or skin color. In a complaint filed with the U.S. Equal Employment Opportunity Commission, James and Mary said that your company does not give workers who are people of color equal opportunities in their careers, and that James and Mary have long been frustrated at your company's lack of diversity. Their complaint alleged that your company violates federal and state laws by discriminating against workers and applicants who are people of color "in hiring, evaluations, promotions, and pay" and by creating a "hostile work environment."

Participants

This study conducted an online survey of 871 full-time employees working in major industries in the United States. A national survey firm, Qualtrics, recruited the participants based on the U.S. representative quotas on region and gender in May 2021. The sample was comprised of 431 women (49.5%) and 440 men (50.5%). The average age was almost 45 years old ($M = 44.99$, $SD = 15.03$). The participants had been working with the current company for an average of almost 10 years ($M = 10.49$, $SD = 9.04$). The majority ethnic group was White (82.4%, $n = 718$), followed by Black (9.6%, $n = 84$), Latino (3.8%, $n = 33$), Asian (2.6%, $n = 23$), and other races (1.5%, $n = 13$). Almost two-thirds of the participants had a bachelor's degree (32.1%, $n = 280$) or a post-graduate degree (32.6%, $n = 284$), followed by those with a two-year associate's degree or some college with no degree (24.4%, $n = 212$); nearly 10% of the participants had a high school degree or less (10.8%, $n = 95$). The participants' work tenure (total work years) for the current company ranged from less than 1 year to 50 years, with an average of around 10 years ($M = 10.48$, $SD = 9.04$). In terms of work position, less than half of the participants (43.51%, $n = 379$) worked in managerial positions (e.g., director, manager, and supervisor), while more than half (56.49%, $n = 492$) worked in non-managerial positions (e.g., specialist, associate, and technician).

Procedure

After obtaining their voluntary consent approved by the Institutional Review Board at a university in the Midwestern United States, the participants were asked to provide answers to questions about their resilience. A brief scenario describing an accusation of racial discrimination in their companies was presented to the participants to measure their situational perceptions (problem recognition, constraint recognition, and involvement recognition). Other questions asking their intentions for employee voice and silence followed. As compensation for their participation, the participants received online points for an online retailer (e.g., Amazon) equivalent to four dollars and eight cents. After conducting a pretest ($N = 100$), a main test ($N = 871$) proceeded with full-time employees working in the U.S. who did not participate in the pretest. The participants' attention was checked by a question, and none of the participants answered the question incorrectly.

Measures

This study adopted existing measurement items from previous research. All items used a 7-point Likert scale, ranging from strongly disagree (1) to strongly agree (7). Employee resilience was measured with nine items ($M = 5.89$, $SD = 0.91$, $\alpha = 0.92$) by Näswall et al. (2015). To assess situational perception, this study adopted Kim and Grunig's (2011) scales for problem recognition, constraint recognition, and involvement recognition. Each variable was measured by four items: problem recognition ($M = 5.80$, $SD = 1.16$, $\alpha = 0.81$), constraint recognition ($M = 5.26$, $SD = 1.44$, $\alpha = 0.88$), and involvement recognition ($M = 4.870$, $SD = 1.85$, $\alpha = 0.94$). To measure employee voice, considerate voice scales with eight items ($M = 5.54$, $SD = 1.42$, $\alpha = 0.94$) from Hagedoorn et al.'s (1999) modified EVLN model were adopted. Employee silence was measured with five items ($M = 3.76$, $SD = 2.02$, $\alpha = 0.96$) adopted from Tangirala and Ramanujam's (2008) scales.

Results

Segmentation

This study applied Kim's (2011) summation method to segment employees in terms of their resilience and situational perception. By taking the median point of each variable, problem recognition, constraint recognition, and involvement recognition were recoded into categorical factors of high (above median) and low (below median) and summed into a variable with two groups—active and inactive publics. Employee resilience was also categorized into two groups—high (above median) and low resilience (below median)—by taking the median point. Each dummy coded variable was summed after assigning different decimal fractions to public types (e.g., inactive: 0.10 and active: 1.00) and resilience levels (e.g., high resilience: 0.01 and low resilience: 1.02) to exclusively segment groups. As a result, almost one-third of participants were high resilient active (HRAP: 32.7%, n = 285), and nearly 16% were high resilient inactive (HRIP: 15.8%, n = 138). Less than 20% were low resilient active (LRAP: 17.0%, n = 148), while more than one-third were low resilient inactive (LRIP: 34.4%, n = 300).

Testing Research Questions

A series of one-way ANOVA were conducted to test RQ1. For employee voice, segmented employees were significantly different, $F(3, 867) = 153.32$, $p < 0.001$, $\eta^2 = 0.35$. High resilient active public (HRAP: M = 6.40, SD = 0.77) were more likely to engage in voice than other publics such as high resilient inactive (HRIP: M = 5.56, SD = 1.11), low resilient active (LRAP: M = 5.41, SD = 0.83), and low resilient inactive (LRIP: M = 4.77, SD = 1.01). Post-hoc comparison using the Tukey's HSD test revealed that each employee group was significantly different from each other ($p < 0.01$), except in a comparison between HRIP and LRAP ($p = 0.53$), for employee voice.

Regarding employee silence, segmented employees were significantly different, $F(3, 867) = 26.94$, $p < 0.001$, $\eta^2 = 0.09$. HRAP (M = 4.32, SD = 2.55) were more likely to remain silent than other publics, such as HRIP (M = 2.61, SD = 1.43), LRAP (M = 4.14, SD = 1.86), and LRIP (M = 3.57, SD = 1.42). Post-hoc comparison using the Tukey's HSD test revealed that HRAP and LRAP were not significantly different ($p = 0.79$). But HRAP and LRAP were significantly higher than HRIP and LRIP for their silence ($p < 0.05$).

This study also asked RQ2 to explore the effects of employees' resilience and situational perceptions while controlling for the effects of various control variables. To test RQ2, multiple ordinary least squares (OLS) regression analyses were conducted using

STATA 13 for employee silence and employee voice with situational perceptions (problem recognition: PR, constraint recognition: CR, and involvement recognition: IR) and factors related to demographic profile (age, gender, race, income, and education) and job profile (job position and length of tenure). The categorical factors were recoded as dichotomous variables; these factors included gender (female: 1, male: 0), race (Asian [Asian: 1, others: 0], Black [Black: 1, others: 0], Latino [Latino: 1, others: 0], and other races [other races such as Native Americans: 1, others: 0]), and job position (managerial: 1, non-managerial: 0). No regression model revealed issues with multicollinearity as no independent variable exceeded a value of 10 in the variance inflation factor (VIF) with each tolerance (*T*) value above 0.10. The independent variables in the regression models accounted for a significant portion of the variance in employee silence, $R^2 = 0.23$, $F(14, 856) = 25.17$, $p < 0.001$ and in employee voice, $R^2 = 0.46$, $F(14, 856) = 49.03$, $p < 0.001$.

The OLS regression model revealed that only PR (b = 0.16, $t = 2.50$) and IR (b = 0.32, $t = 7.23$)—not CR (b = −0.02, $t = -0.26$) and resilience (b = −0.02, $t = -0.26$)—were statistically significant for employee silence after controlling for the effects of other factors. With regard to control variables, age (b = −0.03, $t = -5.86$), gender (female) (b = −0.62, $t = -4.64$), education (b = 0.09, $t = 2.08$), Latino (b = −0.97, $t = -3.19$), and other race (b = −1.52, $t = -5.13$) appeared to be significant factors for employee silence. In the other OLS regression model, only CR (b = −0.16, $t = -3.84$) and resilience (b = 0.59, $t = 13.01$) were found to be significant factors for employee voice—not PR (b = 0.06, $t = 1.48$) and IR (b = 0.20, $t = 0.78$)—when the effects of other factors were controlled for. Among the control variables, age (b = −0.01, $t = -2.70$) was the only factor that was statistically significant for employee voice.

Discussion

The findings in this study indicated the importance of enhancing employee resilience to promote employee voice behaviors regardless of employees' activeness for a racial discrimination issue. This could be explained by employees' self-efficacy—a key component for employee resilience. Previous research has indicated that employees with high self-efficacy are likely to engage in employee voice because they are confident that their opinions are valid and would be taken seriously by management (Wang et al., 2015). Furthermore, this study showed that employees' constraint recognition (personal efficacy level) and their resilience could be the most important factors for employee voice as compared to other factors, including employees' problem and involvement recognition and factors related to their demographic and job profiles. Specifically, the finding suggests that more resilient employees with high self-efficacy and competence are likely to believe that their colleagues and supervisors will not misunderstand them when they speak up with suggestions and ideas.

Regarding employee silence intentions, this study demonstrated that more active employees (HRAP and LRAP), regardless of resilience level, are likely to remain silent about a racial discrimination issue. A possible explanation for the finding of LRAP on employee silence could be that low resilient active employees may feel self-protective motives that lead to withholding ideas and suggestions. When concerned with repercussions associated with their voice behaviors, employees are hesitant to speak up to their supervisors with their ideas and suggestions (Milliken et al., 2003). This finding was confirmed by the regression analysis that controlled for other effects. The regression analysis revealed that employees' activeness and other demographic factors (age, education, gender, and race) can be more important than their resilience in relation to employee silence. Specifically, the findings indicate that employees who (1) recognize a racial discrimination issue as important and personally connected with themselves, (2) describe themselves as Latino or other ethnic groups (e.g., Native American or Pacific Islander), and (3) are younger, female, and more highly educated are likely to choose silence on the issue.

More importantly, this study found that high resilient and active employees (HRAP) were more likely to engage in employee silence. This is plausible because employees may want to support organizations by not voicing concerns in a desire to promote good organizational citizenship (i.e., cooperative or prosocial silence) (Prouska & Psychogios, 2018). Scholars have found cooperative silence in employees who are willing to tolerate inconveniences with work; they do not complain and remain silent about issues that might disturb the functioning of the workplace (Wang et al., 2012). Also, more proactive employees choose (prosocial) silence because they want to protect the benefit of the organization based on their cooperation and altruism (Van Dyne et al., 2003).

Implications for Practice

The findings in this study have important implications for practice. First, internal communication managers can better understand how to effectively communicate organizational issues or crises to their employees as a means to encourage constructive voice regarding their leadership's strategic decision-making processes. Employees are often hesitant to engage in speaking-up communication with their supervisors because such voice behavior can be a double-edged sword. In this sense, internal communication practitioners are suggested to apply employee segmentation when collecting feedback from employees (encouraging employee voice) in an organizational crisis; they should identify potential misunderstandings and unrecognized obstacles that lead to employees' misinterpretation of internal crisis communication (Mazzei & Ravazzani, 2011).

Second, this study provides internal communication managers with a positive perspective and the need for a strategic approach to employee silence. Previous research has predominantly focused on a negative approach to employee silence, as a passive form of employee behavior, by examining risks of speaking up as an antecedent of silence to avoid detrimental organizational effectiveness (Chou & Chang, 2020). Nevertheless, findings of this study suggest that all forms of employee silence do not reflect passive and negative behaviors. Thus, this study substantiates that employee silence can become a proactive and voluntary behavior through positive motivation based on employees' situational perception and their resilience.

In this sense, internal communication managers are advised to be more conscious when communicating with employees who remain silent in a crisis. Employees could support their organization with prosocial behaviors or by deeply feeling the acceptance of organizational circumstances with the perceived constraints that they would not make a difference (Prouska & Psychogios, 2018). Hence, this study highlights the importance of internal crisis communication managers' role in the environmental scanning process to promote proactive silence and reduce negative silence by finding early signs of an issue and taking actions designed to influence the issue. Listening and environmental scanning help internal communication managers encourage employees to be more active and resilient when faced with a negative issue so that proactive silence can be promoted strategically, leading to effective internal communication. If employees perceive a crisis as a profound and long-standing issue, they are likely to choose to remain silent, because they believe that speaking up behaviors would be futile and would not result in change. At the same time, internal communication managers should consider employees' demographic factors (age, education, gender, and race) when promoting proactive silence behaviors.

Limitation and Future Research

This study has some limitations. Different forms of employee voice and employee silence (Van Dyne et al., 2003) were not included in this study. It would be interesting to examine how these different forms of employee voice and silence are influenced by employees' perceptions and resilience in future research. Relatedly, the findings in this study were limited to a racial discrimination in the workplace. Future research should investigate different issues (e.g., gender discrimination and workplace bullying) or compare other crises that could frequently occur in the workplace (Rai & Agarwal, 2019). Lastly, this study did not consider the quality of employee-organization relationships that could strongly affect publics' perceptions of crisis and employee resilience (Kim, 2020). Future research should consider pre-crisis employee relationships with their organizations and use employee segmentation to provide meaningful insights into how internal communication managers can classify employees based on their relationship status along with perceptions and resilience.

Learning Outcomes

1) Identify and analyze the importance of employees and the application of employee segmentation for effective internal crisis communication in various workplace issues.
2) Describe how employee voice and silence can be influenced by employees' situational perceptions and resilience.
3) Describe how employee silence can reflect employees' support for their organization and can be promoted by employee segmentation.

Discussion Questions

1) How would you, as an internal communication manager, communicate the issue of racial discrimination to employees?
2) How can White supervisors advocate and make space for employees of color?
3) How would you, as an employee, advocate for racial equity if you were not in a leadership position?
4) What are some examples of microaggressions related to racial discrimination in the workplace? How would you react to a microaggression if you experienced it from your co-workers and supervisors?

Further Readings

Grunig, J. E. (1989). Publics, audiences and market segments: Models of receivers of campaign messages. In C. T. Salmon (Ed.), *Information campaigns: Managing the process of social change* (197–226). Thousand Oaks, CA: Sage.

Kim, Y. (2020). Organizational resilience and employee work-role performance after a crisis situation: Exploring the effects of organizational resilience on internal crisis communication. *Journal of Public Relations Research, 32*(1–2), 47–75. https://doi.org/10.1080/1062726X.2020.1765368

Kim, Y., & Lim, H. (2020). Activating constructive employee behavioural responses in a crisis: Examining the effects of pre-crisis reputation and crisis communication strategies on employee voice behaviours. *Journal of Contingencies and Crisis Management, 28*(2), 141–157. https://doi.org/10.1111/1468-5973.12289

Lee, Y. (2019). Crisis perceptions, relationship, and communicative behaviors of employees: Internal public segmentation approach. *Public Relations Review, 45*(4), 101832. https://doi.org/10.1016/j.pubrev.2019.101832

Morrison, E. W. (2014). Employee voice and silence. *Annual Review of Organizational Psychology and Organizational Behavior, 1*, 173–197. https://doi.org/10.1146/annurev-orgpsych-031413-091328

Wingfield, A. H., & Chavez, K. (2020). Getting in, getting hired, getting sideways looks: Organizational hierarchy and perceptions of racial discrimination. *American Sociological Review, 85*(1), 31–57. https://doi.org/10.1177/0003122419894335

References

Burris, E. R., Rockmann, K. W., & Kimmos, Y. S. (2017). The value of voice to managers: Employee identification and the content of voice. *Academy of Management Journal, 60*(6), 2099–2125. https://doi.org/10.5465/amj.2014.0320

Caniëls, M. C. J., & Baaten, S. M. J. (2019). How a learning-oriented organizational climate is linked to different proactive behaviors: The role of employee resilience. *Social Indicators Research, 143*, 561–577. https://doi.org/10.1007/s11205-018-1996-y

Chou, Y. C., & Chang, T. (2020). Employee silence and silence antecedents: A theoretical classification. *International Journal of Business Communication, 57*(3), 401–426. https://doi.org/o0r.g1/107.171/2773/2932498488481471770033301

Dave, P. (2021, March 3). Exclusive: U.S. agency probes Facebook for "systemic" racial bias in hiring, promotions. *Reuters*. https://www.reuters.com/article/us-facebook-workers-exclusive/exclusive-u-s-agency-probes-facebook-for-systemic-racial-bias-in-hiring-promotions-idUSKBN2AY006

Daniller, A. (2021). *Majorities of Americans see at least some discrimination against Black, Hispanic and Asian people in the U.S.* Pew Research Center. https://www.pewresearch.org/fact-tank/2021/03/18/majorities-of-americans-see-at-least-some-discrimination-against-black-hispanic-and-asian-people-in-the-u-s/

Dwoskin, E. (2020, July 3). Complaint alleges that Facebook is biased against black workers. *The Washington Post*. https://www.washingtonpost.com/technology/2020/07/02/facebook-racial-bias-suit/

Grunig, J. E. (1989). Publics, audiences and market segments: Models of receivers of campaign messages. In C. T. Salmon (Ed.), *Information campaigns: Managing the process of social change* (197–226). Thousand Oaks, CA: Sage.

Guenter, H., Schreurs, B., van Emmerik, I., Sun, S. (2017). What does it take to break the silence in teams: Authentic leadership and/or proactive followership? *Applied Psychology: An International Review, 66*, 49–77. https://doi.org/10.1111/apps.12076

Hagedoorn, M., Yperen, N. W., Vliert, E. V., & Buunk, B. P. (1999). Employees reactions to problematic events: A circumplex structure of five categories of responses, and the role of job satisfaction. *Journal of Organizational Behavior, 20*(3), 309–321.

Kim, J.-N. (2011). Public segmentation using situational theory of problem solving: Illustrating summation method and testing segmented public profiles. *PRism, 8*(2), 1–12.

Kim, Y. (2020). Organizational resilience and employee work-role performance after a crisis situation: Exploring the effects of organizational resilience on internal crisis communication. *Journal of Public Relations Research, 32*(1–2), 47–75. https://doi.org/10.1080/1062726X.2020.1765368

Kim, J.-N., & Grunig, J. E. (2011). Problem solving and communicative action: A situational theory of problem solving. *Journal of Communication, 61*(1), 120–149. https://doi.org/10.1111/j.1460-2466.2010.01529.x

Kim, Y., & Lim, H. (2020). Activating constructive employee behavioural responses in a crisis: Examining the effects of pre-crisis reputation and crisis communication strategies on employee voice behaviours. *Journal of Contingencies and Crisis Management, 28*(2), 141–157. https://doi.org/10.1111/1468-5973.12289

Landau, J. (2009). To speak or not to speak: Predictors of voice propensity. *Journal of Organizational Culture, Communications and Conflict, 13*(1), 35–54.

Lee, Y. (2019). Crisis perceptions, relationship, and communicative behaviors of employees: Internal public segmentation approach. *Public Relations Review, 45*(4), 101832. https://doi.org/10.1016/j.pubrev.2019.101832

Mazzei, A., & Ravazzani, S. (2011). Manager-employee communication during a crisis: The missing link. *Corporate Communications: An International Journal, 16*(3), 243–254. doi:10.1108/13563281111156899

Milliken, F. J., Morrison, E. W., & Hewlin, P. F. (2003). An exploratory study of employee silence: Issues that employees don't communicate upward and why. *Journal of Management Studies, 40*(6), 1453–1476. doi:10.1111/1467-6486.00387

Morrison, E. W. (2014). Employee voice and silence. *Annual Review of Organizational Psychology and Organizational Behavior, 1*, 173–197. https://doi.org/10.1146/annurev-orgpsych-031413-091328

Morrison, E. W., & Milliken, F. J. (2000). Organizational silence: A barrier to change and development in a pluralistic world. *Academy of Management Review, 25*(4), 706–725. https://doi.org/10.5465/amr.2000.3707697

Näswall, K., Kuntz, J., & Malinen, S. (2015). Employee resilience scale (EmpRes): Measurement properties. *Resilient Organizations.* https://www.resorgs.org.nz/wp-content/uploads/2019/08/Resilient_Organisations_2015-04_Employee_Resilience_Scale.pdf

Ng, T. W., Feldman, D. C., & Butts, M. M. (2014). Psychological contract breaches and employee voice behaviour: The moderating effects of changes in social relationships. *European Journal of Work and Organizational Psychology, 23*(4), 537–553. doi:10.1080/1359432x.2013.766394

Pacheco, D. C., Moniz, A., & Caldeira, S. N. (2015). Silence in organizations and psychological safety: A literature review. *European Scientific Journal, 11*(10), 293–308.

Prouska, R., & Psychogios, A. (2018). Do not say a word! Conceptualizing employee silence in a long-term crisis context. *The International Journal of Human Resource Management, 29*(5), 885–914. https://doi.org/10.1080/09585192.2016.1212913

Perlow, L., & Williams, S. (2003). Is silence killing your company? *IEEE Engineering Management Review, 31*(4), 18–18. doi:10.1109/emr.2003.24935

Rai, A., & Agarwal, U. A. (2019). Examining the relationship between personality traits and exposure to workplace bullying. *Global Business Review, 20*(4), 1069–1087. doi:10.1177/0972150919844883

Rothschild, J. (2008). Freedom of speech denied, dignity assaulted: What the whistleblowers experience in the US. *Current Sociology, 56*(6), 884–903. https://doi.org/10.1177/0011392108095344

Ruck, K., Welch, M., & Menara, B. (2017). Employee voice: An Antecedent to organisational engagement? *Public Relations Review, 43*(5), 904–914. https://doi.org/10.1016/j.pubrev.2017.04.008

Salancik, G. R., & Pfeffer, J. (1978). A social information processing approach to job attitudes and task design. *Administrative Science Quarterly, 23*(2), 224. https://doi.org/10.2307/2392563

Sherf, E. N., Sinha, R., Tangirala, S., & Awasty, N. (2018). Centralization of member voice in teams: Its effects on expertise utilization and team performance. *Journal of Applied Psychology, 103*(8), 813–827. https://doi.org/10.1037/apl0000305

Sutcliffe, K. M., & Vogus, T. J. (2003). Organizing for resilience. In K. Cameron, J. E. Dutton, & R. E. Quinn (Eds.), *Positive organizational scholarship* (94–110). San Francisco, CA: Berrett-Koehler.

Tangirala, S., & Ramanujam, R. (2008). Employee silence on critical work issues: The cross level effects of procedural justice climate. *Personnel Psychology, 61*(1), 37–68. doi:10.1111/j.1744-6570.2008.00105.x

Van Dyne, L., Ang, S., & Botero, I. C. (2003). Conceptualizing employee silence and employee voice as multidimensional constructs. *Journal of Management Studies, 40*(6), 1359–1392. doi:10.1111/1467-6486.00384

Waite, A. (2007). HR's role in audience segmentation: How employee segmentation can help HR create tailored programs for its different employee groups. *Strategic HR Review,* 6(2), 16–19. https://doi.org/10.1108/14754390780000951

Wang, D., Gan, C., Wu, C., & Wang, D. (2015). Ethical leadership and employee voice: Employee self-efficacy and self-impact as mediators. *Psychological Reports, 116*, 751–767. https://doi.org/10.2466/01.07.PR0.116k29w9

Wang, A.-C., Hsieh, H.-H., Tsai, C.-Y., & Cheng, B.-S. (2012). Does value congruence lead to voice? Cooperative voice and cooperative silence under team and differentiated transformational leadership. *Management and Organization Review, 8*(2), 341–370. https://doi.org/10.1111/j.1740-8784.2011.00255.x

Wingfield, A. H., & Chavez, K. (2020). Getting in, getting hired, getting sideways looks: Organizational hierarchy and perceptions of racial discrimination. *American Sociological Review, 85*(1), 31–57. https://doi.org/10.1177/0003122419894335

Chapter Eight

Dealing with Employees in Crises: Examining Contingent Organization–Public Relationships (COPR) for Internal Communication

Yang Cheng, Peiyao Liu, and Callie Burnette

Introduction

Among the various definitions of crises, many focus on the inherent negative outcomes the organization must face in a crisis. In this chapter, researchers argued that a crisis could be defined as an event that "is not necessarily a bad thing. It may be a radical change for good as well as bad" (Friedman, 2002, as cited in Coombs, 2010, p. 18), such as in the case of Activision Blizzard, a company that was sued for gender discrimination and sexual misconduct in 2021. As a global entertainment holding company, Activision Blizzard is known for developing and publishing the world's top video game franchises, including World of Warcraft and Call of Duty (Matthew, 2022). However, in the lawsuit, the company and CEO Bobby Kotick were "accused of fostering a sexist culture, paying women less than men, and assigning women to lower-level jobs" (Department of Fair Employment & Housing, 2021, p. 1). Following the lawsuit's announcement, an immense amount of media coverage began, leading to even more revelations as female workers voiced their experiences with the company. Eventually, crisis responses from Activision Blizzard did not quell employee anger and led to over 2,000 employees signing a letter condemning the company's response to the allegations (Yin-Poole, 2021).

This Activision Blizzard crisis presents a valuable case to investigate the high involvement of employees, who not only called for participation in offline marches but also created a union coalition on Twitter to speak out actively. Meanwhile, the unique relationship between employees and their organizations deserves further exploration, especially within an internal crisis context. As Lee (2022) stated, more research should be conducted to understand the role of employees in relationship management. To fill the gaps, this book chapter applied the concept of contingent organization-public relationships (COPR) (cf. Cheng, 2018) to examine the dynamic internal relationship and employee engagement during Activision Blizzard's crisis. Additionally, this study also presented types of dynamic relationships between stakeholders and

DOI: 10.4324/9781003195580-12

contingency factors that influenced changes in such relationships. The following section reviewed literature on employee engagement, relationship management, and the concept of COPR.

Employee Engagement in Crises

The concept of employee engagement has attracted much attention from scholars in the past decades (e.g., Dhanesh & Picherit-Duthler, 2021; Kahn, 1990; Mazzei & Ravazzani, 2015). Kahn's (1990) study discussed the need for employee engagement and linked employee engagement to organizational effectiveness. Shuck and Wollard (2010) defined employee engagement as "an individual employee's cognitive, emotional, and behavioral state directed toward desired organizational outcomes" (p. 103). Scholars also found that employee engagement was directly linked to their work status and behavior, which could further influence the relationship management of the organization (Lee, 2022).

Employee engagement is considered a result of internal communication (Dhanesh & Picherit-Duthler, 2021; Welch, 2011). Poor internal communication leads to more crises erupting from within the organization, ultimately triggering negative employee engagement or even employee activism to seek changes on important issues (Lee, 2022). In 2021, employees at more than 50 Apple retail stores participated in a strike to protest the company's poor health measures and benefits during the pandemic (Reed, 2021). Similarly, in this case of Activision Blizzard, employees went on several walkouts to protest the company's inappropriate responses to gender discrimination and sexual harassment. Thus, both internal communication and employee engagement could significantly impact effective crisis management. Clearer and more explicit internal information exchange or communication behaviors can help employees become more actively engaged in communication behaviors when experiencing an organizational crisis (Lee, 2022). However, employees are likely to take negative actions when they believe that the organization is not fulfilling its responsibilities as it should (Coyle-Shapiro &Kessler, 2000, as cited in Lee, 2022), leading to employees acting as internal activists to pressure the organization to gain power or generate organizational change (Luo & Jiang, 2014). As internal activists with limited resources, employees often combine internal and external resources to pressure the organization, forming alliances with different individuals and organizations to achieve their requests (Luo & Jiang, 2014). In a crisis, this behavior of employees may have a further negative impact on the company's relationship management.

COPR: A Contingent Approach to Managing Relationships

Theoretical Origins of COPR

Since the 1980s, organizational-public relations (OPR) have been widely examined in empirical studies, but it still has limitations. First, most OPR research has been conducted from a public perspective rather than an organizational or co-orientation perspective (Cheng, 2018). Second, Ki and Shin's (2006) review research found that most studies analyzed the antecedents or consequences of relationships rather than the relationships themselves. In addition, OPR holds an idealized positive view of the relationship that strives for mutual benefits (Cheng, 2018). However, in reality, there is rarely two-way symmetrical communication between organizations and publics.

To fill this research gap, Cheng (2018) proposed COPR to describe a relating management process between parties. The essence of COPR is to explain a dynamic process where information is exchanged toward a common issue (Cheng, 2018). This concept also describes six modes of relationships (i.e., competing, evading, capitulating, neutral, accommodating, and cooperating ones) as events develop.

Regarding the theoretical origins, the contingency theory of accommodation (cf. Cancel et al., 1997) serves as an essential basis for COPR. Contingency theory stated that organizational stances change along a continuum, ranging from pure aggression to pure accommodation (Cancel et al., 1997). COPR followed such assumptions about dynamic stances. Furthermore, it stated that both the stances of organizations and publics should be tracked to determine the relationships (Cheng & Fisk, 2022). Meanwhile, relationship management theory provides the foundation for COPR's argument on cooperative relationships, which describes the mode where key stakeholders consider mutual benefits and accommodate each other.

In sum, to explore this dynamic relationship among the major stakeholders, Cheng (2018) suggested that it is necessary to identify the stances of each involved party first. In this chapter, studying employees' stances can help this company determine appropriate crisis responses and bring insights to enhance employee engagement as well. Thus, we posited RQ1 below.

RQ1: What were the stances of Activision Blizzard and its employees in the crisis?

Six Modes of Relationships in COPR

Based on three main types of stances, including aggression, neutrality, and accommodation, COPR has developed six relationship modes. Two main extreme modes first appeared in Figure 8.1. In the middle of these two modes are evading, capitulating, neutral, and accommodating relationships (Cheng, 2018). The competing relationship describes the status where primary stakeholders "defend their positions, defeat or reject each other's statements, omit any claims of cooperation, and focus on conflict-seeking activities" (Cheng, 2018, p. 127).

Compared to the competing relationship, the cooperating mode means both parties are willing to trust each other and actively seek solutions to issues (Cheng & Cameron, 2019). The evading relationship implies that one party wishes to avoid responses while the other party holds an aggressive stance (Cheng & Cameron, 2019). A capitulating relationship means that one side takes an aggressive stance while the other side gives up or surrenders under threats (Cheng & Cameron, 2019). The neutral relationship implies a state when both parties stop attacking each other and do not take effective actions to confront each other (Cheng & Cameron, 2019). Finally, the accommodating relationship means one party takes a neutral stance while the other takes certain steps

Six Modes of COPR	Stances of Each Party	Visual Description
Competing Relationship	Aggression vs. Aggression	
Evading relationship	Aggression vs. Neutrality	
Capitulating relationship	Aggression vs. Accommodation	
Neutral relationship	Neutrality vs. Neutrality	
Accommodating relationship	Accommodation vs. Neutrality	
Cooperating relationship	Accommodation vs. Accommodation	

FIGURE 8.1 A brief description of the six dimensions of COPR.

to achieve reconciliation. Based on the six relationship modes above, we posited RQ2 to examine the relationships between the company's management team and nonmanagerial employees in a crisis.

RQ2: What were the relationship modes between Activision Blizzard and its employees during the crisis?

Three Categories of Contingency Factors in COPR

According to Cheng and Fisk (2021, 2022), three categories of contingency factors (i.e., predisposing, situational, and proscriptive factors) could influence the relationships between organizations and their public. First, predisposing factors referred to pre-existing variables that might influence the stances of organizations or the public, which included the size and nature of organizations, organizational culture, and the power and size of the publics, etc. (Cancel et al., 1999). Second, situational factors such as the urgency of the situation, time pressure, internal threats, or potential benefits could also influence both sides' stances and strategies in crises or conflicts. Third, proscriptive factors such as moral conviction when facing the publics, legal or regulatory constraints, or other jurisdictional factors could influence choices of stances and determine types of relationships (Pang et al., 2010). Consequently, this chapter also proposed RQ3 to explore the contingency factors that might influence the changes in relationship modes.

RQ3: What were the contingency factors that influenced the state of internal relationships between Activision Blizzard and its employees during the crisis?

Method

Data Collection

We collected data across the time range of the crisis from July 20–December 31, 2021. Three channels, including LexisNexis, the Twitter platform, and Blizzard's official website, served as the sources for data collection. First, using "Activision Blizzard" as a keyword, we collected 129 news articles through LexisNexis.

Additionally, tweets were collected using the API (the Application Programming Interface). We gathered 12 companies' crisis responses from its Twitter accounts: @ActivisionBlizzard and @Blizzard Entertainment; 56 tweets from the employee affiliate account @ABetterABK; 380 tweets gathered using the hashtag #ABetterABK.

Only user-generated content was collected, excluding all retweets and quotes. Ten official statements from Blizzard's website were collected as well.

Coding Instrument

Based on the coding scheme from previous studies (e.g., Cheng, 2020; Cheng & Cameron, 2019; Cheng & Fisk, 2022), we coded and analyzed all direct and indirect statements that reflected the stances of Activision Blizzard and its employees. In each statement, the stance of both sides was defined as aggression (–1), neutrality (0), and accommodation (1). Based on the combination of these stances, we coded competing (–1, –1), evading (–1, 0), capitulating (–1, 1), neutral (0, 0), accommodating (1, 0), and cooperating relationship (1, 1).

To measure contingency factors in the crisis, we applied the coding scheme from previous literature (i.e., Cancel et al., 1999; Pang et al., 2010). Specifically, a description of the company environment (e.g., company culture, diversity) and the characteristics of the dominant coalition were coded as predisposing variables. Factors that influence the parties to solve problems during a crisis were coded as situational variables (Pang et al., 2010). In addition, factors about legal and regulatory issues are defined as proscriptive variables (Pang et al., 2010), which in this study were mainly reflected in the lawsuit filed by the State of California against Activision Blizzard.

Findings

The Activision Blizzard crisis represented an internal organizational crisis in which employees' physical and mental health were greatly threatened. For years, employees dealt with gender discrimination and sexual harassment; however, their company let these problems build up, leading to the outbreak of this scandal. Following the lawsuit from employees, media coverage also revealed the company's ongoing sexual misconduct, including the CEO's death threats toward his assistant (Fenlon, 2021). Employees also adopted Twitter to formulate their accounts that supported "A Better Activision Blizzard King (ABK)," which allowed them to freely communicate with external stakeholders on the status of the crisis (ABetterABK, 2022).

To further address RQ1 and RQ2, we made an analysis based on the main timeline of the Activision Blizzard crisis (see Figure 8.2). For each stage, we coded the stances of both sides and contingency factors that influence the stances.

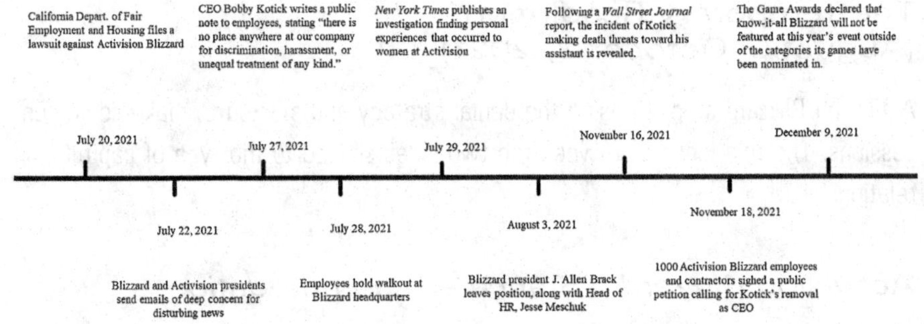
California Depart. of Fair Employment and Housing files a lawsuit against Activision Blizzard
CEO Bobby Kotick writes a public note to employees, stating "there is no place anywhere at our company for discrimination, harassment, or unequal treatment of any kind."
New York Times publishes an investigation finding personal experiences that occurred to women at Activision
Following a Wall Street Journal report, the incident of Kotick making death threats toward his assistant is revealed.
The Game Awards declared that know-it-all Blizzard will not be featured at this year's event outside of the categories its games have been nominated in.
July 20, 2021
July 27, 2021
July 29, 2021
November 16, 2021
December 9, 2021
July 22, 2021
July 28, 2021
August 3, 2021
November 18, 2021
Blizzard and Activision presidents send emails of deep concern for disturbing news
Employees hold walkout at Blizzard headquarters
Blizzard president J. Allen Brack leaves position, along with Head of HR, Jesse Meschuk
1000 Activision Blizzard employees and contractors sighed a public petition calling for Kotick's removal as CEO

FIGURE 8.2 A main timeline of the Activision Blizzard crisis.

The Outbreak of the Conflict (July 20–27, 2021)

At this stage, Activision Blizzard and its employees had aggressive stances and reacted actively to each other's statements. As a result, they had a competing relationship.

Activision Blizzard's Stance—Aggression

Activision Blizzard was accused of irresponsible behavior, threatening its operations and reputation. With news coverage and employee testimonies surfacing, the organization's operations were threatened by employee demands for a better work environment. Following its release, the organization deemed the lawsuit "inaccurate" and "distorted" (Jones & Tyrer, 2021, p. 1). In a statement released on its official website, CEO Bobby Kotick (2021) claimed, "There is no place anywhere at our company for discrimination, harassment, or unequal treatment of any kind" (p. 1). Therefore, the company was not transparent with their employees about what was happening and also denied the allegations.

Employees' Stance—Aggression

Between July 20, 2021 and July 27, 2021, a total of 18 news articles covered the event, and we saw more of the employee stances pronounced in these reports. Seventeen news reports showed the use of attack tactics by employees. For example, employees signed a statement declaring plans to protest at Activision Blizzard's headquarters on July 28, 2021, claiming that the movement was implemented because of dissatisfaction with Activision Blizzard's response to sexual harassment incidents (Robertson, 2021).

The Temporary Resolution (August 3–October 3, 2021)

Activision Blizzard stopped using the denial strategy and started to make some concessions. The relationship between the two sides shifted to the type of capitulation relationship.

Activision Blizzard's Stance—Accommodation

From August 3–October 3, 2021, Activision Blizzard released seven official statements about gender discrimination and sexual harassment cases. Six of them took the stance of accommodation, and one took an offensive stance. For instance, Activision Blizzard tweeted a statement on September 14, 2021, saying, "We announced the hiring of two senior executives who will help us build a more inclusive workplace as well as diversify and grow our revenue." Furthermore, another tweet, using an attacking tactic, claimed, "Reports incorrectly characterized the EEOC's complaint against the company as an ongoing dispute." However, it is not difficult to find that Activision Blizzard had no positive conflicts with employees, and this company took a more accommodating stance when facing its employees at this stage.

Employees' Stance—Aggression

The employees did not accept the actions taken by Activision Blizzard. ABetterABK continued to mobilize employees on Twitter to take more actions to bring more significant changes. For example, one tweet mentioned (ABetterABK, 2021), "Leadership has not yet embraced significant changes...we're hard at work building a movement that will continue to take action until the real, tangible change is enacted."

The Re-Escalation of the Conflict (November 16–19, 2021)

On November 16, 2021, Activision Blizzard (2021) again issued a rebuttal to a report from Wall Street Journal, which led to another employee protest on November 18, 2021. The relationships between these two parties once again returned to a competing one.

Activision Blizzard's Stance—Aggression

On November 16, 2021, Activision Blizzard (2021) issued another statement declaring that "the Wall Street Journal's report about the company is untrue … the company has the most inclusive workplace underway." The statement argued that the *Wall Street Journal*'s views on Activision Blizzard and the CEO were misleading.

Employees' Stance—Aggression

The crisis came to a head on November 18, 2021, when employees launched a protest calling for firing of Activision Blizzard CEO Bobby Kotick. For instance, ABetterABK adopted a strategy of attack by responding to all three tweets posted on November 16, 2021. The employee organization declared that if the CEO is not replaced, they will not keep silent and they will continue to strike (Pal, 2021).

Activision Blizzard's Compromise (November 21–December 9, 2021)

This crisis finally turned for the better on November 21 when Activision Blizzard began to take practical action to express its corporate stance. Employees began to stop attacking the company. The relationship between the two sides turned into an accommodating relationship.

Activision Blizzard's Stance—Accommodation

Activision Blizzard (2021) announced "the creation of a Workplace Responsibility Committee to oversee the company's success in improving workplace culture and eliminating all forms of harassment and discrimination at the company." At the same time, Activision Blizzard acknowledged that the company remained flawed on the issue of sexual harassment and gender discrimination. The official website stated, "While the company, with the board's support, has been making important progress in improving workplace culture, it is clear that current circumstances demand increased board engagement."

Employees' Stance—Neutrality

After continued actions such as demonstrations and strikes employees' demands were successfully met. The employees' union also shifted its attention more to the issues within the game industry and the Blizzard contract workers, forming a neutral stance. An accommodating relationship emerged.

In summary, we found that the company and its employees' relationships were dynamic and complex during the crisis. In the first stage, the relationship between the company and the employee was a competing one. However, after provoking a strong reaction from the employee, the relationship was quickly transformed into a capitulating relationship. In the second phase, Activision Blizzard adopted an accommodation stance. Although not completely gaining the employees' understanding, it still significantly eased the relationship. In the third phase, Activision Blizzard again took an aggressive stance, provoking a revolt from its employees. It was not until the final complete back down that the relationship was eased.

To answer RQ3, we analyzed three major categories of factors and their impacts on stances and relationships.

Predispositions

First, we identified two predisposing factors: the cultural environment and the characteristics of the dominant coalition. As many employees stated, "Blizzard needs to eliminate the toxic and predatory workplace culture," and "they [Activision executives] treat the culture of fear as fun." Employees drastically impacted the company's culture, processes, leadership, and policies, and they made it clear in the lawsuit that the workplace environment was unsuitable, which had formulated an irresponsible image of the company (Department of Fair Employment & Housing, 2021).

The characteristics of the dominant coalition also had a significant impact on the relationships. After initially denying claims, the management team passively supported the employees' efforts, notably the CEO Bobby Kotick, who directly stated that this company does not have any discrimination, harassment, or unequal treatment (Allen, 2022). While employees felt the CEO was heavily responsible for allowing the unsafe work environment to persist (Allen, 2022), Activision Blizzard had continued to highlight game releases and updates to protect its business continuity throughout the crisis. The organization tried to maintain the operations fully during the crisis, focusing their messaging on normal business operations rather than the handling and effects of the crisis within their organization.

Situational Variables

Internal threats served as the most threatening situational factor when corporate corruption and negligence of employee opinions ultimately led to the crisis. Employees' revelations on media platforms further worsened the company's reputation. As a creator of many popular video games, Activision Blizzard faced extreme backlash from the gaming community, damaging its reputation.

Proscriptive Variables

Legal or regulatory restraints influenced the stance and relationship between the two parties. Employees chose to sue Activision Blizzard when they realized that internal communication was no longer effective. Only through a lawsuit were they able to resolve the issue, and the company's poor internal responses led employees to choose an aggressive stance. The California government's lawsuit led Activision Blizzard to take an accommodative stance to resolve the issue.

As the crisis continues, Activision Blizzard has taken steps to repair its relationship with its employees. On March 29, 2022, Activision Blizzard agreed to "enhancing policies, practices, and training to prevent harassment and discrimination in the workplace … and hire a neutral, third-party equal employment opportunity consultant to be approved by the EEOC" (Press Release, 2022, p. 1). The following month, Activision Blizzard appointed a new Chief Diversity, Equity, and Inclusion Officer (Press release, 2022, p. 1). These developments were appraised by the employees' "ABetterABK" account, indicating an improved relationship.

Discussion and Conclusion

As internal communication is the driver of employee engagement (Welch, 2011), this chapter suggested that organizations should adopt more active internal communication to effectively manage internal activism and prevent further activism from causing more serious corporate crises. For example, Activision Blizzard may not have thought in advance that ignoring employee inputs would lead to lawsuits and internal activism, ultimately leading to damages to its reputation. Employers thus should engage in appropriate internal communication to understand the needs of their employees and the potential impact of their behavior.

Additionally, this study enriched the discussion of COPR by analyzing and emphasizing the impact of employees, who were identified as the most affected group of internal stakeholders. These employees expected fair and equal treatment in their working environment, no matter gender, race, or sexuality. Serving as influential social media users, they also took certain information forms to relay their experiences and stories with the company. However, the organization was not meeting these expectations, becoming one of the driving forces that inspired the crisis. This study supported past studies, which have shown that the external publics trusted employees as sources of crisis information, which could shape an organization's online reputation (Helm, 2011).

Learning Outcomes

1) Understand stances and the six modes of relationship between organizations and their employees in crises.
2) Analyze what impact employee engagement had on the company's relationship management.
3) Identify contingency factors that influenced the internal communication on Activision Blizzard's relationships with its employees.

Discussion Questions

1) What strategies that Activision Blizzard and its employees have employed in the crisis?
2) If you were the CEO of Activision Blizzard, how do you plan to manage this crisis?
3) As a global entertainment company, what are your suggestions for the relationship management of Activision Blizzard?

Further Readings

Cheng, Y. (2020). Contingent organization-public relationship (COPR) matters: Reconciling the contingency theory of accommodation into the relationship management paradigm. *Journal of Public Relations Research, 32*(3–4), 140–154. https://doi.org/10.1080/1062726X.2020.1830405

Cheng, Y., & Cameron, G. T. (2019). Examining six modes of relationships in a social-mediated crisis in China: An exploratory study of contingent organization–public relationships (COPR). *Journal of Applied Communication Research, 47*(6), 689–705. https://doi-org.prox.lib.ncsu.edu/10.1080/00909882.2019.1695874

References

ABetterABK [@ ABetterABK]. (2021, August 11). It's been two weeks since our walkout, and leadership has yet to embrace significant change. With thousands of ABK employees on our side, we're hard at work building a movement that will continue to take action until real, tangible change is enacted [Tweet]. Twitter. https://twitter.com/ABetterABK/status/1425483151237783552

ABetterABK. (@ABetterABK) (2022). Tweets (Twitter Profile). Twitter. Retrieved April 23, 2022. https://twitter.com/ABetterABK?ref_src=twsrc%5Egoogle%7Ctwcamp%5Eserp%7Ctwgr%5Eauthor

Activision Blizzard (2021, November 16). Activision Blizzard issues statement regarding recent Article. Investor.activision.com. https://investor.activision.com/news-releases/news-release-details/activision-blizzard-issues-statement-regarding-recent-article

Allen, V. E. (2022). Activision Blizzard: A brief timeline of everything, from the lawsuit to now. Destructoid. https://www.destructoid.com/activision-blizzard-lawsuit-timeline-industry-ceo-bobby-kotick-report/

Cancel, A., Cameron, G., Sallot, L., & Mitrook, M (1997). It depends: A contingency theory of accommodation in public relations. *Journal of Public Relations Research, 9*(1), 31–63. https://doi.org/10.1207/s1532754xjprr0901_02

Cancel, A. E., Mitrook, M. A., & Cameron, G. T. (1999). Testing the contingency theory of accommodation in public relations. *Public Relations Review, 25*(2), 171–197.

Cheng, Y. (2018). Looking back, moving forward: A review and reflection of the organization-public relationship (OPR) research. *Public Relations Review, 44*(1), 120–130. https://doi.org/10.1016/j.pubrev.2017.10.003

Cheng, Y. (2020). Contingent organization-public relationship (COPR) matters: Reconciling the contingency theory of accommodation into the relationship management paradigm. *Journal of Public Relations Research, 32*(3–4), 140–154. https://doi.org/10.1080/1062726X.2020.1830405

Cheng, Y., & Cameron, G. T. (2019). Examining six modes of relationships in a social-mediated crisis in China: An exploratory study of contingent organization–public relationships (COPR). *Journal of Applied Communication Research, 47*(6), 689–705. https://doi-org.prox.lib.ncsu.edu/10.1080/00909882.2019.1695874

Cheng, Y. & Fisk, A. (2021). Toward a contingency theory of relating management: Exploring organization-public relationships (OPRs) in conflicts. *Negotiation and Conflict Management Research, 15*(1), 32–51. https://doi.org/10.34891/20210921-523

Cheng, Y., & Fisk, A. (2022). Contingency theory informs relationship management: Exploring the contingent organization-public relationships (COPR) in a crisis of Mainland China. *Public Relations Review, 48*(2), 102178. https://doi.org/10.1016/j.pubrev.2022.102178

Coombs, W. T. (2010). Crisis communication and its allied fields. In W. T. Coombs & S. J. Holladay (Eds.), *Handbook of crisis communication* (54–64). New York: Wiley-Blackwell.

Coyle-Shapiro, J., & Kessler, I. (2000). Consequences of the psychological contract for the employment relationship: A large scale survey. *Journal of Management Studies, 37*(7), 903–930. https://doi.org/10.1111/1467-6486.00210

Department of Fair Employment & Housing. (2021, July 21). DFEH sues California gaming companies for equal pay violations, sex discrimination, and sexual harassment. (Press Release). https://www.dfeh.ca.gov/wp-content/uploads/sites/32/2021/07/BlizzardPR.7.21.21.pdf

Dhanesh, G. S., & Picherit-Duthler, G. (2021). Remote internal crisis communication (RICC)—role of internal communication in predicting employee engagement during remote work in a crisis. *Journal of Public Relations Research*, 1–22. https://doi.org/10.1080/1062726x.2021.2011286

Fenlon, W. (2021). Everything that's happened since the Activision Blizzard lawsuit went public. PC Gamer. https://www.pcgamer.com/activision-blizzard-lawsuit-controversy-timeline-explained/#section-everything-so-far

Friedman, M. (2002). *Everyday crisis management: How to think like an emergency physician.* Naperville, IL: First Decision Press.

Helm, S. (2011). Employees awareness of their impact on corporate reputation. *Journal of Business Research, 64*(7), 657–663. https://doi.org/10.1016/j.jbusres.2010.09.001

Jones, A. & Tyrer, B. (2021). Activision Blizzard lawsuit and investigations explained Gamesradar. https://www.gamesradar.com/the-activision-blizzard-lawsuit-explained/

Kahn, W. A. (1990). Psychological conditions of personal engagement and disengagement at work. *Academy of Management Journal, 33*(4), 692–724. https://doi.org/10.2307/256287

Ki, E. J., & Shin, J. H. (2006). Status of organization–public relationship research from an analysis of published articles, 1985–2004. *Public Relations Review, 32*(2), 194–195. https://doi.org/10.1016/j.pubrev.2006.02.019

Kotick, B. (2021, July 27). Activision Blizzard | A Letter From CEO Bobby Kotick to All Employees. Investor.activision.com. https://investor.activision.com/news-releases/news-release-details/letter-ceo-bobby-kotick-all-employees

Lee, Y. (2022). The rise of internal activism: Motivations of employee's responses to organizational crisis. *Journal of Public Relations Research, 33*(5), 387–406. https://doi.org/10.1080/1062726X.2022.2034630

Luo, Y., & Jiang, H. (2014). Empowerment and internal activism during organizational change: A relocation story in China. *International Journal of Strategic Communication, 8*(1), 1–28. https://doi.org/10.1080/1553118x.2013.810628

Matthew, J. (2022). How Activision Blizzard makes money. *Investopedia.* https://www.investopedia.com/how-activision-blizzard-makes-money-4799286

Mazzei, A., & Ravazzani, S. (2015). Internal crisis communication strategies to protect trust relationships: A study of Italian companies. *International Journal of Business Communication, 52*(3), 319–337. https://doi.org/10.1177/2329488414525447

Pal, R. (2021, November 17). 150 Activision Blizzard employees are planning a walkout from the organization and here's why. https://www.sportskeeda.com/esports/150-activision-blizzard-employees-planning-walkout-organization

Pang, A., Jin, Y., & Cameron, G. T. (2010). Contingency theory of strategic conflict management: Directions for the practice of crisis communication from a decade of theory development, discovery and dialogue. In W. T. Coombs, & S. J. Holladay (Eds.), *The handbook of crisis communication* (pp. 425–448). Hoboken, NJ: Wiley-Blackwell.

Press Release (2022). Court to approve activation agreement with EEOC. https://www.sec.gov/Archives/edgar/data/718877/000110465922040197/tm2210789d1_ex99-1.htm

Reed, K. (2021, December 29). Apple employees mount one-day strike on Christmas Eve to demand COVID-19 protections and better working conditions. World Socialist Web Site. https://www.wsws.org/en/articles/2021/12/29/appl-d29.html

Robertson, S. (2021, July 27). Report: Activision Blizzard employees to strike on July 28 outside Blizzard HQ in response to handling of sexual harassment lawsuit. Dot Esports. https://dotesports.com/business/news/report-activision-blizzard-employees-strike-july-28

Shuck, B., & Wollard, K. (2010). Employee engagement and HRD: A seminal review of the foundations. *Human Resource Development Review, 9*(1), 89–110. https://doi.org/10.1177/1534484309353560

Welch, M. (2011). The evolution of the employee engagement concept: Communication implications. *Corporate Communications: An International Journal, 16*(4), 328–346. https://doi.org/10.1108/13563281111186968

Yin-Poole, W (2021, July 27). Over 2000 current and former Activision Blizzard employees sign petition calling company response to discrimination lawsuit "abhorrent and insulting." *Eurogamer.* Retrieved from https://www.eurogamer.net/over-2000-current-and-former-activision-blizzard-employees-sign-petition-calling-company-response-to-discrimination-lawsuit-abhorrent-and-insulting

Section IV

Employee Activism

Chapter Nine

Internal Communication and Employee Activism: Netflix's Dave Chappelle Woes and Perspectives from the Field

Arunima Krishna, Raymond L. Kotcher, and Donald K. Wright

Introduction

On October 20, 2021, Netflix employees staged a walkout from the company's headquarters in Los Gatos, CA, to protest comedian Dave Chappelle's recent Netflix special and the company's handling of complaints against it (Paul, 2021). Chappelle's special, which included jokes about transgender people and a reference to himself as "Team TERF," or trans-exclusionary radical feminists, which refers to people who argue that people's biological sex at birth, especially women, cannot be changed, had been criticized by many, including GLAAD (Koblin, 2021) and Netflix's own employees. Despite mounting internal criticism, Netflix executives continued to defend Chappelle and their decision to air the special, even suspending trans employees who had publicly criticized the special, culminating in employee walkouts and protests outside the company headquarters. Coordinated by the company's trans employee resources group (ERG), these walkouts and protests were attributed to poor listening communication by Netflix leaders, with co-CEO Ted Sarandos admitting that he "screwed up ... internal communication" (Jones, 2021, para 14).

Netflix's employee walkout is one in a series of instances of employee activism that corporate America has witnessed in the last decade. From Hootsuite (Moreno, 2020) and Wayfair (Hames, 2019) employees' swift and vocal opposition to their respective companies' dealings with the controversial federal agency ICE, Google employees' protests against their handling of sexual harassment cases (Wakabayashi et al., 2018) to Walmart (Gurchiek, 2019) and Amazon (Wingard, 2020), examples of employee activism are plentiful. Indeed, a 2019 Weber Shandwick study found that nearly 4 in 10 employees say they have "spoken up to support or criticize their employers' actions over a controversial issue that affects society" (Gaines Ross, 2019), emphasizing the importance of transparent and clear internal communication when addressing employee activism, and of being mindful of issues on employees' minds, i.e., listening.

DOI: 10.4324/9781003195580-14

As the corporate world grapples with how to navigate this new wave of employee activism, public relations and communication scholarship has sought to provide theoretically grounded explorations of employee activism. Although still relatively in its infancy, public relations scholarship has examined employee advocacy and activism, especially in the form of case studies. For example, Curtin (2016) explored employee activists' discourses to pressure their employers to act responsibly. Similarly, Luo and Jiang (2014) sought to understand the empowerment strategies used by employee activists to urge their employer to reverse an unpopular policy. Most recently, Krishna (2021) offered a conceptually and practically sound definition of employee activism, defining it as "goal-oriented efforts organized and negotiated by individual and/or groups of employees to internally and/or externally advocate for or against organizational policy and/or decision making to generate social change" (p. 119). The present study adopts this definition of employee activism.

Given the increasing importance of employee activism in business in general and the practice of public relations in particular, a key question facing business and communication professionals is how best to address employee activism. Although traditional management and public relations scholarship tended to view activists as opposition (Dozier & Lauzen, 2000), more recent advances in both practice and scholarship have provided a more nuanced perspective of how organizations should view activism, particularly internal activism. As Reitz and Higgins (2022) noted, "We are entering an age of employee activism that may well upend our assumptions about power within organizations" (p. 1). Thus, for internal communicators to be able to best address and embrace employee activism, it is important to understand the best practices that public relations and communications professionals have adopted in understanding and engaging with employee activists, as well as the tensions they face in their work as the bridge between employee activists and organizational leadership. The following research questions, thus, guide this study:

RQ1: What are some best practices related to employee activism reported by public relations/communications professionals?

RQ2: What are some tensions experienced by public relations/communication professionals related to employee activism?

Method

The data reported in this study are part of a larger annual research project that aims to assess the state of the public relations field. The annual Bellwether Survey is a collaboration between Boston University's College of Communication and *PRWeek*, an international public relations trade publication. Subscribers of *PRWeek* were invited to respond to a 10–15 minute-long survey which included several open-ended and close-ended questions. The survey was also distributed among members of the Public Relations Society of America and contacts of the BU research team (i.e., the authors of this chapter), yielding a total of 689 completed responses from public relations and communication practitioners. The survey was fielded between April and June 2022.

In order to answer the research questions, the survey included an open-ended question, which read, "A recent study discussed employee activism as employees' efforts to advocate for or against organizational policy to generate social change. In what ways has your organization/clients experienced such employee activism? In what ways has the PR/Comms function been involved in helping address employee activism?" A total of 333 participants responded to this question, and thus were included in the final sample. Of these, 101 participants reported being from agencies or consulting firms, 85 were corporate employees, 53 worked for nonprofits, and 41 worked for governmental organizations. Seventeen participants were with educational institutions and 36 responded with "other." The sample consisted of 205 women and 123 men, with the remaining five participants choosing not to respond. More than two-thirds of the participants described themselves as senior managers or executives ($n = 224$), 84 were mid-career professionals, and 23 were early-career public relations professionals. The sample was distributed across generations, as 99 participants (30%) identified themselves as being Boomers, 137 (41.52%) were Gen-X, 77 (23.33%) were Millennials, and 9 participants were Gen-Z.

Data Analyses

To understand public relations practitioners' experiences related to employee activism in their organizations, their qualitative responses to the question noted in the previous section were analyzed. A total of 333 responses were analyzed to understand and identify internal communication and engagement best practices and tensions experienced by the participants related to employee activism. Data analyses involved a thematic analysis (Braun & Clarke, 2006) of all responses to identify themes related to the research question. The first author read and re-read all the data, putting together initial codes and patterns. These initial codes were then consolidated and synthesized into potential themes. The voices of the participants were prioritized throughout the analyses, and the constant comparative method (Charmaz, 2006) was used to review and refine themes. The authors then re-read the data to ensure that all relevant ideas were captured and reported, and alternative interpretations were considered and discussed to achieve consensus on the findings.

Findings

RQ1: What Are Some Best Practices Related to Employee Activism Reported by Public relations/ communications Professionals?

Our research question necessitated the identification of themes related to public relations practitioners' reported best practices related to employee activism in their workplaces. Three broad themes were identified and are reported in the sections that follow along with exemplar quotes from the participants.

Importance of Listening

One of the most prominent themes discussed by the participants when it comes to employee activism was the importance of listening to employees and their perspectives. Several participants discussed how crucial listening had been to their and their clients' internal communication strategy and to address employee activism. For example, an agency professional noted the following:

> An advocacy-focused client hired my agency for internal communications support. Within the organization, a group of employees felt unheard and had begun implementing advocacy tactics like sign-on letters. This caused a [rift] with client leadership. My agency conducted listening sessions with client leadership and the employees to diagnose the issues and suggest internal communications tactics to build trust.

Even respondents whose organizations did not experience a lot of employee activism and pushback about social issues emphasized the importance of listening to employees and being mindful of their feedback. An in-house practitioner noted the importance of actively and purposefully listening to employees as a way of issues management, stating, "We have had limited activism. However, it tends to arise in direct response to official comms announcements internally and on social media platforms. Comms/PR are very attuned to this and engage in social listening to help ID issues quickly as they arise and clarify any positions quickly with employees."

Other respondents similarly reported engaging in active listening to employees as a form of internal communication to proactively manage issues and employee activism, noting, "We haven't experienced employee activism though we do have a monthly open dialogue on critical topics where employees are encouraged share their thoughts, experiences and point of views on issues that are important to them. We all learn by listening." This focus on active listening as part of internal communication was echoed by another participant, who discussed how employee activism and feedback was embedded in the executive leadership's strategy. This respondent said:

> We have an open line of communication with all of our employees and our executive leadership team. Our ELT takes time to answer questions from employees. We also have quarterly eNPS surveys, and we take action on the feedback we receive, and try to implement/change policies/procedures as needed based on employee feedback.

Several participants alluded to the aftermath of George Floyd's murder in May 2020 as being an inflexion point in how their organizations handled employee activism, attributing this inflexion to listening. One participant articulated how their organization revised and adjusted their policies on taking a stand on social issues:

> In 2020, we heard from employees across the country about their dismay we hadn't taken a stand advocating diversity; typically we avoid weighing into cultural waters. However, their feedback was helpful, and we ultimately created a diversity council, chaired by our CEO, with representatives from each of our employee resource groups. Our LGBTQ+ ERG also has worked with HR to ensure our benefits cover domestic partners, that people can identify as LGBTQ+ if they choose (as they can identify race, for instance) and that they have choices beyond male and female when self-identifying. We also had employee protests and some resignations when we required vaccination or reasonable accommodation.

An agency professional wrote about how ignoring employee activism and the lack of a listening framework resulted in a social media crisis and complete overhaul of the leadership and culture:

> Following the George Floyd murder, one company's employee base asked the leadership of that organization to take a stand that "Black Lives Matter." The leadership did nothing. Six months later, they had a social media crisis as frontline employees took their frustration to the court of public opinion. As such that organization's board hired my agency to address the crisis, and the focus 100% shifted to external and internal communications and leadership. As such the company leadership team has changed, the board leadership has changed, and internal processes now exist to thoughtfully consider employee feedback and customer engagement.

An agency professional related the story of how employee activism and listening forced leadership to apologize for their actions, stating, "A certain client, led by a Covid-denying Trump supporter, had such pushback from his harmful and hurtful comments in all-hands meetings that he had to apologize." In these ways and more, participants emphasized the role of listening in internal communication, especially related to employee activism.

Listening Mechanisms

In addition to articulating the importance of listening as a crucial aspect of internal communication best practices related to employee activism, participants also enumerated mechanisms through which they conducted listening. One of the most important listening mechanisms discussed by participants was employee (or enterprise) resource groups (ERGs henceforth). One in-house professional noted, "We have channeled and supported activism through the formation of ERGs (Enterprise resource groups) and incorporated their input into national training activities (e.g., implicit bias training) and even national marketing promotions." Another public relations practitioner discussed how ERGs in their organization were a result of employees' requests rather than a top down decision. They said:

> We have established several Employee Resource Groups as part of our diversity, equity and inclusion activities. These have all been employee led – the ask was bottom up. Employees are invited to contribute stories to internal newsletters and share their experience in anonymous surveys every two weeks which are review by management and acted upon.

This bottom-up movement toward ERGs was echoed by another public relations professional, who said, "Supporting employee resource groups through our diversity, equity and inclusion program. Many of the events and groups have been formed from a bottom up perspective." Similarly, another participant discussed the role of ERGs in informing corporate policy, stating, "We work to take into account feedback from colleagues and employee resource groups to inform internal and external positions and such." Another participant noted, "We have an active set of employee resource groups which have been revamped over the past two years to not just be a gathering place for employees but to be ways in which employees engage with the larger community, assist in recruiting, etc."

The second listening mechanism identified in participants' responses was formal listening opportunities offered by the management or public relations teams. For example, one participant stated, "We send annual engagement and quarterly pulse surveys and use that feedback to evaluate sentiment and make necessary program changes (or identify new opportunities)" in addition to learning from ERGs and diversity, equity, and inclusion (DEI) groups. Another participant mentioned conducting "quarterly eNPS surveys" among employees. Similarly, an agency professional noted that "My agency has created affinity groups, done surveys and created employee working groups to ensure we are keeping up with employee needs." Another respondent stated:

> Being a smaller organization, and having had a diverse makeup of employees for years I don't think we've encountered what other organizations have. We do employee engagement surveys (via a third party) and analyze demographics to spot gaps in employee morale and makeup annually. This has helped us stop issues from getting too big before solutions are introduced.

Manifestations of Employee Activism

In response to the survey question, participants also discussed a variety of ways in which employee activism had manifested in their respective organizations. Three broad categories of employee activism manifesting in the organization emerged. First, as indicated by prior findings is organizational movement on DEI initiatives and the establishment of ERGs. For example, a participant stated:

> Our PR/Comms function has been leading a diversity and inclusion initiative in our organization since the George Floyd event. We have about 1/3 of the company involved in initiating change both within the company and in the community. We are working to bring more people of color into the advertising industry and our organization.

Another participant discussed how employee activism had led to the formation of ERGs, noting, "The creation and strengthening of three internal BRGs related to LGBTQ+ community, Women in the Workplace, and BIPOC community as well as a commitment to discussing diversity issues." A similar sentiment was echoed by another participant, who said, "Supporting employee resource groups through our diversity, equity and inclusion program. Many of the events and groups have been formed from a bottom up perspective." A participant discussed how employees self-organized into a task force and how it shaped internal and external communication, writing, "We had a group of employees organize into a DEI task force to advocate for the creation of an explicitly anti-racist organization. PR/Comms has been involved in shaping and drafting messages for external stakeholders that reflect new state of the organization."

A participant explained the communication team's role in navigating employees' expectations related to activism versus the corporate strategy and how the former helped shape internal and external communication, stating, "We have experienced an increase in employees' expecting the company in North America to make public statements about societal issues, even if those issues are not related directly to our business. George Floyd. Juneteenth. War. Natural Disasters. Hate crimes." Another participant discussed how employees' activism had shaped internal communication and policy related to DEI, stating:

> My agency's been consistently open to employees [advocating] on behalf of social justice causes - we're a social justice focused agency, after all. Employees have made recommendations (which have been considered + accepted) on language used to refer to specific identity groups (Latinx v Latino, etc.), how we communicate internally (for instance, avoiding gifs that unintentionally stereotype Black/BIPOC people), etc.

Similarly, a participant discussed the activism of employee-led groups in helping generate social change, saying:

> Our company's enterprise is to generate social change, so generally we are already having open discussion about the causes of the day. We have some employee-created and -led groups focused on those causes, and our strategic comms team serves either as advisor to or has staff that are involved in. However, all branded external and mass-internal communications get reviewed, edited, and approved by our team.

Another participant noted, "Following the murder of George Floyd and the global social protests that arose in response, our employees successfully drove development of a formal corporate program to address diversity and expand opportunities for previously under-represented groups in our industry. PR/Comms informs the company and promotes the program externally."

A second manifestation of employee activism noted by participants was in the form of corporate purpose and giving. One participant described employee activism as paid volunteering time, saying, "Our agency supports activism. We have paid time off for volunteering, company match for donations and internal groups to support DEI, etc."

Another participant had a similar thought regarding employee activism, noting that "We are allowed to offer pro-bono time on the clock, as long as we keep track of the hours (up to 15–20% of our day)." An agency employee further underscored their employers supporting pro-bono work as an employee activism manifestation, stating, "Every agency, including my own, either has or should take on a pro Bono client in a relevant space. We make time to allow the teams to pursue the causes they have the ability to influence."

One participant connected employee activism to corporate purpose and corporate responsibility, stating that:

> We have a purpose team that meets to discuss CSR projects, VTO, and purpose driven measures within the company and in our community. Employees are able to advocate for the pro bono clients we take on, and go after the VTO opportunities we wish to pursue. We give 8 hours each calendar year to VTO as cross-functional teams that go into the community to serve. PR has helped communicate these opportunities, spearhead some of the initiatives and outreach, and build cohesion.

Another participant discussed how the changing demographics of the workforce are forcing organization-wide changes to corporate responsibility. This participant stated that:

> As a nonprofit, employee activism and advocacy is part of the culture. One big shift we have seen since Black Lives Matter protests in 2020 is that client CSR programs and more employee-driven and focused on women and BIPOC. Client employees tend to be Millennials and Gen Z so clients use CSR for employee retention and recruitment.

Finally, a few participants reported focus on and investment in ESG as a result of employee activism, at least in part. A participant stated, "We are seeing employee activism in both DI&E issues and also with ESG. Our comms function has helped to create our positioning on both these issues, including the creation of our annual corporate citizenship review." Another participant discussed the changes their clients had made related to a number of including social and environmental sustainability. They said.

> My agency is focused on telling our clients' stories and communicating their efforts related to social justice, equality and environmental sustainability. Some of my clients have a long-term focus on these issues, while others have

> been inspired to take significant action more recently, at the behest of their employees, customers and other stakeholders. For example, addressing racial justice in the wake of the murder of George Floyd, or by bringing much needed healthcare resources to underserved communities in the wake of COVID-19, or by addressing the significant and growing threat of climate change by reducing their carbon footprints.

Similarly, another participant noted:

> As a global social justice funder, our employee activism is very strong on concerns on two fronts. First, how we manage our investment portfolio concerning climate change and criminal justice reform to advocate that the organization divests from fossil fuels and private prisons which we have done. Second, internal debates on issues like our position about not defunding the police, Middle East relations, vaccine inequity, etc.

RQ2: What Are Some Tensions Experienced by Public Relations/Communication Professionals Related to Employee Activism?

Although the themes discussed as part of the previous research question seem to indicate employee activism having a socially progressive effect on internal communication and policies, some participants did not share such enthusiasm. Several participants discussed the tensions that rose within their organizations in the wake of employee activism, either due to generational differences between management and workforce, as well as ideological differences between them. One participant discussed the ideological disconnect between the workforce and executive leadership as follows:

> BLM movement opened executive management's eyes. They didn't realize the newer members of the workforce cared about those things and wanted their employer to have values. Forced some hard discussions for them to admit it was important - especially for a more conservative company/leadership team. Next up was climate change and a Net Zero commitment. There was TREMENDOUS resistance to "far-left propaganda" and "consultants creating new industries." We ended making a commitment and it actually drove our entire evolving ESG strategy once they realized it was a competitive advantage and our customers cared.

Some participants even lamented the lack of empowerment felt by the public relations teams to do anything or effect any change due to the internal culture. As one participant stated:

> Communications is deeply involved in, if not driving these decisions in our company. Key for us is authenticity. Are we actually in a position to "do something" or do we feel like we should say something because other companies are? We stop ourselves from saying words that are not backed with action. Sometimes, it can be hard to get our employees on board with this strategy, but we strive to be consistent in our approach so that when we do speak out, our employees, customers and community can trust that we are genuine.

The position of public relations within the organizational structure also created some tension regarding addressing employee activism, as one participant noted:

> Food insecurity has some focus for our company; but often defaults to tactical execution instead of a well-thought out 360 strategic activation. This holds true for animal welfare issues. Both are due to Marketing owning and funding PR and having a rather antiquated, non-inclusive approach to PR. Climate change is another area and we are working on sorting through the science to activation.

Similarly, a participant reported experiencing tension due to internal communication being under human resources rather than public relations, stating:

> HR (where internal communications traditionally lives in my organization) has started to lean heavily on PR/Comms to draft internal announcements and reactions to breaking news situations. Employees expect to be addressed after breaking news and HR does not feel equipped to speak about sensitive news issues.

Discussion

The present study sought to explore the best practices and tensions experienced by public relations and communication professionals when addressing, handling, and managing employee activism. A qualitative thematic analysis of public relations practitioners' open-ended responses uncovered four broad themes, three related to best practices and one related to tensions. In particular, participants highlighted generational differences between leadership and employee base and the attendant differences in expectations of corporations about speaking up about social issues as a key tension. Additionally, participants noted internal cultures and the position of the public relations function within the corporate structure as a key barrier to being able to effectively address employee activism. However, participants discussed several best practices that they had experienced as part of their work at the intersection of internal communication and employee activism, which are discussed next.

Theoretical Implications

Two key points of learning emerge from these analyses. First, this study served to underscore the importance of organizational listening as a key component of internal communication, especially when addressing employee activism. Failure to listen and understand employee concerns and sentiment may lead to the escalation of employee activism from internal to external, as was seen in the case of Hootsuite, Wayfair, Amazon, and numerous others. Although organizational listening has been theorized and discussed in management (e.g., Cooper & Husband, 1993) and public relations and communication literature (e.g., Macnamara, 2016), only recently has organizational listening been discussed as a key component of excellent internal communication (Neill & Bowen, 2021; Qin & Men, 2021). The findings of this present study situate listening as a central practice not just for effective internal communication and the facilitation of two-way, mutually beneficial relationships (Macnamara, 2016) but also as a means of thoughtfully and carefully navigating employee activism. Several participants articulated how important listening has been to their practice, especially in their handling of employee activism, and outlined several mechanisms of active internal listening as part of best practices related to internal communication and employee activism. Future scholarship may serve to further articulate how internal listening can be improved and how internal communicators may best leverage listening into their practice.

Second, the present study emphasized the crucial role played by employee resource groups (ERGs) in internal communication and employee activism. Several participants highlighted not only ERGs' role in active internal listening but also how ERGs helped shape policy and acted as consultants to top leaders. Failure to recognize the voices and mobilization potential that ERGs hold may result in disruptions to the organization's functioning, as Netflix's executive leadership found out to their detriment. Furthermore, participants also discussed the establishment of new ERGs as one of the manifestations of employee activism, representing employees' mobilization and organizing efforts to advocate for change within their organizations. Interestingly, although few public relations studies explore or address ERGs, the role of employee groups as agents of mobilization and employee activism has long been studied in management literature. Reitz and Higgins (2022) noted that "employee resource groups can also help steer leaders" toward decision making that helps generate social change. Indeed, employee groups have a long history of organizing and mobilizing around issues of diversity and social identity to help affect internal change (Friedman, 1996). More recently, Maks-Solomon & Drewry (2021) investigated the role of internal activism from employee groups in promoting companies' pro-LGBT activism and found that companies with LGBT ERGs with highly educated workforces to predict pro-LGBT corporate activism, a point of learning for Netflix. The results of the present study point to the importance of studying ERGs from a communication lens, and call for scholars to undertake research that helps provide theoretically grounded insights into ERGs, how they mobilize and organize, and the impact they may have on organizational decision-making.

Implications for Netflix

The findings discussed in this study not only provide points of learning for organizations trying to address employee activism and outrage, like Netflix, but also help us better understand why and how employee activism was necessary in the first place. Some of the tensions discussed by the participants related to ideological differences, for instance, may provide insight into Netflix's decision to defend Dave Chappelle despite employee criticism. Indeed, some participants pointed to differences between conservative leaders' assumptions and ideologies clashing with their more liberal workforces who expect them to take a stand on social issues, and resorting using extreme descriptors and labels to delegitimize criticism. Such strategies adopted by some leaders echoes Dave Chappelle's use of the phrase "Team TERF" to delegitimize criticisms of his own anti-trans rhetoric, which eventually resulted in employee walkouts at Netflix, the platform upon which his special was broadcast.

The findings also help contextualize and explain the mobilization power demonstrated by Netflix's trans ERG in organizing the employee walkouts. ERGs, when incorporated into the organization's employee listening strategy, can be crucial in helping management understand employee sentiment and making decisions accordingly. As active vocal groups within the organization, ERGs can exert influence on internal culture and wield control that can bring organizational functioning to a halt, as Netflix found out to its detriment. The findings from this study point to a need for Netflix management to undertake relational rebuilding and healing with its workforce, and sincere engagement with the ERG may be an important first step, given the key role the ERG played in mobilizing employee activism. Netflix would also be served well to establish robust internal listening mechanisms in order to avoid being caught off guard by their employees' ire, as seemed to be the case with the Dave Chappelle controversy.

Learning Outcomes

1) Understand the role of listening as a key internal communication tool in addressing employee activism
2) Understand how ERGs are influential in employee activism for mobilization and internal listening
3) Identify different manifestations of employee activism
4) Unpack how generational differences between organizational leaders and a Gen-Z and Millennial-dominated workforce may result in tensions and differences in corporate expectations

Discussion Questions

1) How can public relations practitioners effectively navigate the tensions related to generational differences when addressing employee activism?
2) Is employee activism inherently good or bad? What are some considerations organizations should keep in mind when addressing employee activism?
3) This chapter identified internal listening as a crucial element of internal communication in understanding employee activism. What are some listening mechanisms communicators may utilize for effective listening?
4) What are some key considerations to keep in mind when working with ERGs, especially marginalized communities' employee groups?

Further Readings

"Employees Rising: Seizing the Opportunity in Employee Activism." (n.d). *Weber Shandwick*. Retrieved from https://www.webershandwick.com/uploads/news/files/employees-rising-seizing-the-opportunity-in-employee-activism.pdf

Anderson, D. S. (1992). Identifying and responding to activist publics: A case study. *Journal of Public Relations Research*, *4*, 151–165, https://doi.org/10.1207/s1532754xjprr0403_02

Austin, L., Overton, H., McKeever, B. W., & Bortree, D. (2020). Examining the rage donation trend: Applying the anger activism model to explore communication and donation behaviors. *Public Relations Review, 46*(5), 1–8. https://doi.org/10.1016/j.pubrev.2020.101981

Badigannavar, V., & Kelly, J. (2005). Why are some union organizing campaigns more successful than others? *British Journal of Industrial Relations, 43*(3), 515–535 https://doi.org/10.1111/j.1467-8543.2005.00367.x

Berger, B. K. (2005). Power over, power with, and power to relations: Critical reflections on public relations, the dominant coalition, and activism. *Journal of Public Relations Research, 17*(1), 5–28. https://doi.org/10.1207/s1532754xjprr1701_3

Briscoe, F., & Gupta, A. (2016). Social activism in and around organizations. *The Academy of Management Annals, 10*(1), 671–727. https://doi.org/10.1080/19416520.2016.1153261

Bryan, J. (2019, July 3). Corporate advocacy of social issues can drive employee engagement. Smarter with Gartner. Retrieved from https://www.gartner.com/smarterwithgartner/corporate-advocacy-of-social-issues-can-drive-employee-engagement/

Chen, Y. R. R., Hung-Baesecke, C. J. F., & Kim, J. N. (2017). Identifying active hot-issue communicators and subgroup identifiers: Examining the situational theory of problem solving. *Journalism & Mass Communication Quarterly, 94*(1), 124–147. https://doi.org/10.1177/1077699016629371

Gautam, N., & Carberry, E. (2020). Understanding Employee Activism in the High-Tech Sector: A Comparative Case Analysis. In *Academy of Management Proceedings* (Vol. 2020, No. 1, p. 20523). Briarcliff Manor, NY 10510: Academy of Management.

Kim, J. N., & Rhee, Y. (2011). Strategic thinking about employee communication behavior (ECB) in public relations: Testing the models of megaphoning and scouting effects in Korea. *Journal of Public Relations Research, 23*(3), 243–268. https://doi.org/10.1080/1062726X.2011.582204

Krishna, A. (2022). Employee-Organization Identity Fusion: Connecting Leadership and Symmetrical Internal Communication to Identity-and Engagement-Related Outcomes. *International Journal of Business Communication.* https://doi.org/10.1177/23294884221130744

Krishna, A., & Kim, S. (2015). Confessions of an angry employee: The dark side of de-identified "confessions" on Facebook. *Public Relations Review, 41*(3), 404–410.

Lee, Y. (2020). A Situational Perspective on Employee Communicative Behaviors in A Crisis: The Role of Relationship and Symmetrical Communication. *International Journal of Strategic Communication, 14*(2), 89–104. https://doi.org/10.1080/1553118X.2020.1720691

Luo, Y., & Jiang, H. (2014). Empowerment and internal activism during organizational change: a relocation story in China. *International Journal of Strategic Communication, 8*(1), 1–28. https://doi.org/10.1080/1553118X.2013.810628

Maiorescu, R. D. (2017). Using online platforms to engage employees in unionism. The case of IBM. *Public Relations Review, 43*(5), 963–968. https://doi.org/10.1016/j.pubrev.2017.07.002

Mazzei, A., Kim, J. N., Togna, G., Lee, Y., & Lovari, A. (2019). Employees as advocates or adversaries during a corporate crisis. The role of perceived authenticity and employee empowerment. *Sinergie Italian Journal of Management, 37*(2), 195–212. https://doi.org/10.7433/s109.2019.10

McCown, N. (2007). The role of public relations with internal activists. *Journal of Public Relations Research, 19*(1), 47–68.

Skoglund, A., & Böhm, S. (2020). Prefigurative partaking: Employees' environmental activism in an energy utility. *Organization Studies, 41*(9), 1257–1283. https://doi.org/10.1177/0170840619847716

Thelen, P. D. (2020). Internal communicators' understanding of the definition and importance of employee advocacy. *Public Relations Review, 46*(4), 1–11. https://doi.org/10.1016/j.pubrev.2020.101946

References

Braun, V., & Clarke, V. (2006). Using thematic analysis in psychology. *Qualitative Research in Psychology, 3*(2), 77–101.

Charmaz, K. (2006). *Constructing grounded theory: A practical guide through qualitative analysis.* London: Sage.

Cooper, L. O., & Husband, R. L. (1993). Developing a model of organizational listening competency. *International Listening Association Journal, 7*(1), 6–34. https://doi.org/10.1080/10904018.1993.10499112

Curtin, P. A. (2016). Exploring articulation in internal activism and public relations theory: A case study. *Journal of Public Relations Research, 28*(1), 19–34. https://doi.org/10.1080/1062726X.2015.1131696

Dozier, D. M., & Lauzen, M. M. (2000). Liberating the intellectual domain from the practice: Public relations, activism, and the role of the scholar. *Journal of Public Relations Research, 12*(1), 3–22. https://doi.org/10.1207/S1532754XJPRR1201_2

Friedman, R. A. (1996). Defining the scope and logic of minority and female network groups: Can separation enhance integration? *Research in Personnel and Human Resources Management, 14*, 307–349.

Gaines Ross, L. (2019, September 20). 4 in 10 American workers consider themselves social activists. *Quartz at Work*. Retrieved from https://qz.com/work/1712492/how-employee-activists-are-changing-the-workplace

Gurchiek, K. (2019, September). Employee activism is on the rise. *SHRM*. Retrieved from https://www.shrm.org/hr-today/news/hr-news/pages/employee-activism-on-the-rise.aspx

Hames, A. (2019, July 2). The rise of employee activism: Lessons from the Wayfair walkout. *Employee Benefit News*. Retrieved from https://www.benefitnews.com/opinion/wayfair-walkout-exemplifies-importance-of-company-culture

Jones, Z. C. (2021, October 25). Netflix employees stage walkout over Dave Chappelle special. CBS News. Retrieved from https://www.cbsnews.com/news/dave-chappelle-netflix-employees-walkout/

Koblin, J. (2021, October 14). Netflix loses its flow as critics target Chappelle special. *The New York Times.* Retrieved from: https://www.nytimes.com/2021/10/14/business/media/dave-chappelle-closer-netflix.html

Krishna, A. (2021). Employee activism and internal communication. In Men, L. R. and Verčič, A. T. (Eds.), *Current trends and issues in internal communication: Theory and practice.* Cham, Switzerland: Springer Nature.

Luo, Y., & Jiang, H. (2014). Empowerment and internal activism during organizational change: A relocation story in China. *International Journal of Strategic Communication, 8*(1), 1–28. https://doi.org/10.1080/1553118X.2013.810628

Macnamara, J. (2016). Organizational listening: Addressing a major gap in public relations theory and practice. *Journal of Public Relations Research, 28*(34), 146–169. https://doi.org/10.1080/1062726X.2016.1228064

Maks-Solomon, C., & Drewry, J. M. (2021). Why do corporations engage in LGBT rights activism? LGBT employee groups as internal pressure groups. *Business and Politics, 23*(1), 124–152. https://doi.org/10.1017/bap.2020.5

Moreno, J. E. (2020, September 24). Hootsuite reverses after criticism of contract with ICE. *The Hill.* Retrieved from https://thehill.com/policy/technology/518091-hootsuite-reverses-after-criticism-of-contract-with-ice

Neill, M. S., & Bowen, S. A. (2021). Employee perceptions of ethical listening in US organizations. *Public Relations Review, 47*(5), 1–8. https://doi.org/10.1016/j.pubrev.2021.102123

Paul, K. (2021, October 20). Netflix employees join wave of tech activism with walkout over Chappelle controversy. *The Guardian.* Retrieved from https://www.theguardian.com/media/2021/oct/20/netflix-employees-activism-walkout-dave-chappelle-controversy

Qin, Y. S., & Men, L. R. (2021). Why does listening matter inside the organization? The impact of internal listening on employee-organization relationships. *Journal of Public Relations Research, 33*, 365–386. https://doi.org/10.1080/1062726X.2022.2034631

Reitz, M., & Higgins, J. (2022). Leading in an age of employee activism. *MIT Sloan Management Review, 63*(2), 1–7.

Wakabayashi, D., Griffith, E., Tsang, A., & Conger, K. (2018, November 1). Google walkout: Employees stage protest over handling of sexual harassment. *The New York Times.* Retrieved from https://www.nytimes.com/2018/11/01/technology/google-walkout-sexual-harassment.html

Wingard, J. (2020, January 10). Employee activism is the new normal. So why is Amazon leadership freaking out? *Forbes.* Retrieved from https://www.forbes.com/sites/jasonwingard/2020/01/10/employee-activism-is-the-new-normal-so-why-is-amazon-leadership-freaking-out/#3110658827f1

Chapter Ten

What Makes Employees Become Activists? Investigating Employee Activism in the AI Community

Jie Jin and Leping You

Introduction

The advent of artificial intelligence (AI) technology has raised extensive ethical concerns. In addressing such concerns, employees of technology companies are essential actors, as they are more integral members of the AI community than the business owners (Belfield, 2020). Over time, employees have become activists in the AI community, promoting positive social impacts and ethics in AI research and development, in response to concerns about the risks AI poses to human security, as well as the risks of societal inequality and discrimination (Belfield, 2020). Two critical examples of employee activism in this field are the suspension of Project Maven and employee mobilization against the departure of Timnit Gebru.

In late 2017, Google began working with the U.S. Department of Defense on Project Maven, which integrates AI into battlefield technology by using "machine-learning to automatically label images, buildings, and other objects captured by cameras on drones, helping Air Force analysts identify unique targets" (Fang, 2019, para. 6). But the project's potentially lethal outcomes were seen as violating a core Google value–*Don't Be Evil*—as well as the ethics and safety principles of AI research and development (Fang, 2019; Shane & Wakabayashi, 2018). Employees at Google drafted and signed a letter of petition, urging Google to suspend the project. In June 2018, Google announced it would not renew its Project Maven contract with the military (Fang, 2019; Shane & Wakabayashi, 2018).

The ouster of Timnit Gebru, who was a co-leader of the Ethical AI research team at Google, also ignited a collective movement among Google employees. The departure of Timnit Gebru was due to a research paper she co-authored, advocating for ethical AI research and application. Specifically, she argued for the ethical application of deep-learning systems in the natural language processing field, which could mitigate harm to marginalized populations, though "most language technology is built to serve the needs of those who already have the most privilege in society" (Bender et al., 2021,

DOI: 10.4324/9781003195580-15

p. 613). However, Google terminated the leaders of the Ethical AI research team, suggesting to some that the tech giant only cared about AI research that aligned with their business interests (GoogleWalkout, 2020). Google employees were furious that Google censored AI research in this way, and that it downplayed the Diversity, Equity, and Inclusion principles of AI development (GoogleWalkout, 2020). As a result, employees created the *#MakeAIEthical* campaign, calling for the AI community to stand in solidarity with the Ethical AI team by declining cooperative, collaborative, and funding opportunities from Google (Vincent, 2021). The backlash to Project Maven and to censorship of AI research at Google showed that employees could be a driving force in ethical AI research. In that sense, employees become internal activists at the organization, regulating its performance to ensure its business practices are ethically and socially responsible. Although many studies have examined how activist groups regulate organizational governance, little research has explored employee activism through the lens of internal communication. This chapter aims to explore the factors that make employees into activists demanding the organization to behave responsibly. More specifically, we began by defining employee activism in the context of internal communication, followed by exploring the factors that motivate employees to engage in collective actions.

Literature Review

Defining Employee Activism

Until recently, collective action was rare among high-tech workers because they were well paid and satisfied with their working conditions (Nedzhvetskaya & Tan, 2019). Evidence suggests that tech employees are most likely to engage in collective action inside the organization when their high-tech identities are no longer sustained and supported by the organizational image (Milton, 2003). Employees holding high-tech identities are concerned about technology-related issues. For example, when a tech company makes unethical decisions regarding the development and deployment of AI, its employees may find an inconsistency between their individual moral identity and their perception of the organization's image (Alahmad & Robert, 2020).

Activism is one major way the public puts pressure on an organization to change its policies and practices (Kalodimos & Leavitt, 2020), to share power and address their collective concerns (Berger, 2005; McCown, 2007). While activists do not always bring sweeping changes to organizations, they have facilitated the empowerment of female employees in the workplace (Almeleh et al., 1993) and the adoption of LGBTQ-inclusive policies (Raeburn, 2004), and improved corporate environmental performance (Yang et al., 2018). Employees, like their external counterparts, become internal activists when engaging in actions and organizing as groups to press demands on an organization (McCown, 2007).

However, it is important to notice that the bargaining power of activists can vary, depending on the costs to the organization if it fails to address activists' concerns and demands (Belfield, 2020). Shareholders usually take the ownership position and thus have a louder voice at the company's decision-making table (Sjöström, 2008). Tech employees today are often compensated by their organizations in the form of stock grants (Conger, 2018), so these equity-holding employees become active shareholders, submitting shareholder proposals that publicly urge companies to take action on issues like climate change, workplace equality, immigration policy, ethical use of AI, human rights violations, etc. (Miles et al., 2021). Moreover, the AI talent market is still in short supply and demand is likely to stay high in the future, ensuring high-tech talent can have a say at the bargaining table (Belfield, 2020). Furthermore, as compared to outsider activists, tech employees who are insider activists can use their internal knowledge of organizations to persuade companies and leaders to embrace the causes they support (Briscoe & Gupta, 2016).

This study defines employee activism as employees who lack institutional channels to top management decision-making engaging in collective action to gain influence inside the organization (King & Soule, 2007; Milton, 2003). Even though tech employees have the power to force change at tech giants, existing research gives scant attention to the potential for employee activism, let alone that of highly skilled tech workers (Briscoe & Gupta, 2016). In light of tech activism's rise, the current study proposed a set of research questions that examined the factors that turn tech employees into internal activists.

Drivers of Employee Activism

Transparent Communication

Transparent internal communication has been identified as a critical driver of quality employee-organization relationships (Men & Jiang, 2016), corporate reputation (Men, 2014), and employee engagement (Chanana, 2020). Scholars have equated transparency with accountability, accessibility, openness, and credibility (Rawlins, 2008; Tapscott & Ticoll, 2003). The purpose of transparent communication is not limited to increasing the flow of information but also enhancing mutual understanding (Men, 2014). For organizational communication to be transparent, organizations must make information relevant to employees available and accountable, whether it is about organizations' actions, decisions, or policies (Rawlins, 2008; Taiminen et al., 2015). Transparency makes sense only if organizations pay attention to employees' concerns and enable employees' "active participation in acquiring, distributing, and creating knowledge" (Cotterrell, 1999, p. 419). Transparency is one ethical concern facing tech companies' AI practices. Such companies do not always behave accountably or provide enough information regarding their privacy policies for AI-enabled products, their AI-related management decisions, or the procedures and processes of the AI research and projects they fund (Du & Xie, 2021; R. Metz, 2021). As AI-powered systems are increasingly applied to decision-making processes in social-organizational settings, the underlying logic of reasoning and justification for AI systems to act and think should be explainable and accountable to users (Ehsan et al., 2021). All this gives rise to our study's first research question:

> **RQ1:** In face of unethical development and deployment of AI, how do Google employees perceive and interpret the impact of the organization's transparent communication efforts on their intention to engage in the #MakeAIEthical campaign?

Moral Obligation

Moral obligation is concerned with the extent to which someone feels motivated by their moral principles (rather than their personal interests) to *do the right thing* (Vilas & Sabucedo, 2012). Moral obligation may be involved in employees' intention to engage in activist actions in morally relevant situations (Gorsuch & Ortberg, 1983), which are characterized by having significant consequences if moral rules are not followed or respected (Hart et al., 2012). This is certainly the case with activism by tech employees, who have recognized that a wide range of AI-related ethical challenges needs to be addressed by tech companies, or the AI community more broadly (Conger, 2021). Of all the risks that AI products may pose, tech workers are most concerned about how AI may endanger human security and social justice (Du & Xie, 2021). Now, the perception of unethical AI practices within the organization is likely to arouse a moral obligation for Google employees to participate in collective action aimed at mitigating the harm caused by unethical AI use (Najibi, 2020). Indeed, it is Google employees' moral convictions that help them interpret their reality and then justify their participation in collective action (Vilas & Sabucedo, 2012). For instance, Google's famous former motto *Don't be evil* has also been used by Google employees to interpret and legitimize their activist actions against unethical AI decisions within the organization (Barbaschow, 2021). This leads to our second research question:

> **RQ2:** In the face of Google's unethical development and deployment of AI, how do Google employees perceive and interpret the relationship between employees' moral obligation to promote ethical AI practices and employees' intention to engage in #MakeAIEthical Campaign?

Method

We used the case study method to answer the research questions of the study. By definition, a case study "consists of a detailed investigation, often with empirical material collected over a period of time from a well-defined case to provide an analysis of the context and processes involved in the phenomenon" (Rashid et al., 2019, p. 5). Case study is appropriate for this study because it allows us to aggregate in-depth qualitative data from multiple sources about the examined real-life phenomenon (e.g., the #MakeAIEthical campaign) (Yin, 1994). With the versatile materials, case study also allows us to identify essential factors, patterns, and processes to interpret research questions contextualized in the #MakeAIEthical campaign (Rashid et al., 2019).

We gathered secondary qualitative data from a variety of sources to investigate the #MakeAIEthical campaign. These sources include news coverages of the campaign from the credible news agencies, including *The New York Times*, *Reuters*, *Business Insider*, *Bloomberg*, etc. We also analyzed Google employees' voices that appeared on the website of *Google Walkout For Real Change*, which documented materials related to the #MakeAIEthical campaign such as the communications among Google employees, the open letters written to Google employees and AI community, and public announcements. Our analysis focuses on identifying salient themes and patterns associated with why the campaign was catalyzed and developed over time and how the employees reacted to it.

Results

In the following section, we introduce the case of #MakeAIEthical campaign. Following the case overview, two relevant research questions are addressed individually to increase our understanding of this emerging phenomenon.

Overview of the Case: #MakeAIEthical Campaign

#MakeAIEthical is a movement in response to the firing of Timnit Gebru and Margaret Mitchell, both were core AI researchers in Google's Ethical AI team. Gebru, a prominent black woman in AI ethics research, was abruptly fired in December 2020 after sending an internal email expressing dissatisfaction with the internal censorship of not-yet-public research papers and the diversity crisis within the workplace. Nonetheless, more details of Gebru's exit point to the culmination of disagreement and conflict between ethics researchers like Gebru and Google over AI-relevant research. Specifically, Gebru's study highlights the potential risks of large language models, which are crucial to Google's bottom line. The four main risks of developing and sustaining large-scale AI models include environmental and financial costs, the growing problem of systemic discrimination, manipulation of human behavior, and misguided research efforts that may not be conducive to understanding (Hao, 2020). Following Gebru's departure, Mitchell, another fierce critic of Google's internal censorship, was fired in February 2021 for her public defense of Gebru (C. Metz, 2021).

Google's treatment of Gebru and Mitchell is seen as the company's retaliation toward employees' efforts to stop the company from building an unethical and harmful AI system. With more than 1,500 Google employees signing a petition to CEO Sundar Pichai, a few engineers' resignations, and the #MakeAIEthical campaign, Google's employees took collective action to pressure the company to make a real change (Lytvynenko, 2022). Specifically, they asked members of the AI community to adopt the following: (a) academic conferences should not accept research papers from business institutions such as Google that have corporate lawyers edit papers examining the potential harms of AI technology, (b) organizations such as Google should be more transparent about their research and publication approval process, (c) launched the #RecruitMeNot campaign to call on students and researchers to decline recruitments and offers from Google recruiters, (d) academic institutions and other research organizations should refuse to accept grants from Google until it meets basic standards of research integrity, and (e) state and national legislatures should provide more comprehensive and robust whistleblower protections that allow employees to disclose the development and use of harmful technologies by private entities (The future must be ethical: #MakeAIEthical, 2021).

Analysis of the Case

We analyzed this case to understand how former and current Google employees perceive and interpret employee engagement in the #MakeAIEthical Campaign, and how

Google's AI-related communication practices facilitate the formation of employee activist groups inside Google and the AI community.

Findings for RQ1. In the case of #MakeAIEthical Campaign, Timnit Gebru, the former co-leader of Google's Ethical AI team, was fired after asking Google for more accountability and transparency around research and publication processes affiliated with Google (Grant, 2021). Gebru's departure, together with Google's subsequent dismissal of another ethical AI expert, Margaret Mitchell, stimulated Google's existing internal activists to unionize, and one of their calls is for more transparency in all aspects of work (Dean, 2021). After the abrupt firing of Gebru, more than 2,600 out of Google's 13,500 employees signed petition demanding Google to explain why it rejected a research paper Gebru coauthored that looked at the potential ethical risks of language models (Langley, 2020; Paul, 2021).

Unlike Microsoft and Facebook, which give somewhat independence and publicity to their research centers, Google's research center is under strict scrutiny (R. Metz, 2021). To prevent researchers from publishing papers that negatively impact Google's AI technology, Google has introduced a filter system to oversee the research about sensitive topics and its publication process (Dastin & Dave, 2021; GoogleWalkout, 2020). Google's internal emails also revealed that it had asked its lawyers to extensively revise their AI research papers to make them sound more neutral and nicer in tone (Dastin & Dave, 2021). In some cases, Google's lawyers had even asked their researchers to remove references to Google technology and other negative findings of AI technology (Dastin & Dave, 2021). As a matter of fact, nearly 2,700 Google employees and more than 4,000 supporters within the academy and industry signed a petition demanding more transparency about Google's research, projects, and employment (GoogleWalkout, 2020). In their petition, they demanded Google make its decision-making process more public, as well as provide clearer guidelines on how AI-related research should be reviewed within the organization (GoogleWalkout, 2020).

Findings to RQ2. #MakeAIEthical Campaign is a result of accumulated dissatisfaction with unethical development and deployment of AI technology at Google. Gebru, the former leader of Google's ethical AI team, said now was not the right time to sell facial recognition technology to police departments because it could exacerbate racial and gender discrimination (Ovide, 2020). Gebru pointed out that people with darker skin are more vulnerable to facial-recognition systems as they use historical data reflecting societal inequalities to make decisions and projections (Keith, 2021).

More broadly, the rise of AI may increase employment polarization, diminish individuals' self-worth, erode public trust, and create feelings of isolation and disconnection (Du & Xie, 2021; Wright & Schultz, 2018). As Gebru pointed out, to build larger and more powerful language models, tech companies like Google seldom think about how to avoid bringing bias and inequalities from human society into the AI systems (Perrigo, 2022). However, after internally voicing her views on the ethical risks associated with large AI models and trying to get Google to explain the process used to review her research, Gebru was abruptly fired (Wong, 2020). While researchers like Gebru and Mitchell had been working to demonstrate that the design and use of current AI technologies may exacerbate social problems, Google has not actively addressed these researchers' concerns; instead, Google chose to fire these researchers, both Gebru and Mitchell in 2020 and Zoubin Ghahramani, a former vice president at Google Research in 2022 (Wakabayash & Metz, 2022). As doubts about the technology are likely to be silenced at Google, the tension between Google and its AI researchers will persist and fuel bottom-up resistance (O'Gorman, 2021). For instance, Googlers rallied on Twitter and used the hashtag #MakeAIEthical to express their support for Gerbu and pressured Google to make real change. Two engineers quit because of Google's mistreatment toward Gebru and other underrepresented employees (Paul, 2021).

Discussion

While organizations with excellent internal public relations practices encourage open internal communication and share decision making with their employees (McCown, 2007), some organizations neither listen to employees' voices nor respond to their concerns, causing employees to become active public or internal activists (Reitz et al., 2021; Reyes, 2021). There are potential downsides to employee activism, which may distract employees from being engaged in work tasks and harm work productivity; it may also alienate employees who disagree with the employee activists on some issues and increase polarization in the workplace (Miles et al., 2021). However, organizations taking actions to restrict employee activism can lower employee morale and motivation, thus impairing employee engagement and increasing the resignation rate (Reitz et al., 2021; Zafft, 2021). In the face of employee activism, mishandling communication with employees can damage the organization's reputation and functioning (Briscoe & Gupta, 2016).

Before answering the question of how organizations should respond to employee activism, the current study argues that we should first understand what makes tech employees internal activists. A closer examination of the #MakeAIEthical Campaign reveals that lack of transparent communication and moral obligation are the most salient drivers for tech employees at Google to become internal activists. Google employees tend to lose trust in the organization where transparent internal communication regarding AI development is missing. Also, Google's unethical AI practices violate their employees' belief in moral business conduct, thus leading employees to become activists. In other words, dissatisfaction with Google's moral performance drives tech employees to agitate for organizational changes to address ethical issues they are concerned about and to sustain their valued moral identities (Milton, 2003; Smith & Ferguson, 2001).

Practically, this study helps highlight that Google cannot simply view employee activism as contradictory to organizational goals. In essence, employee activism in the tech industry reflects how tech employees balance their relationship with the organization to address power issues (Berger, 2005; McCown, 2007). There is no one-size-fits-all approach that can discourage employee activism or employees' determination to rally against companies (MacLellan, 2020; Reitz et al., 2021). To address employee activists' concerns, it is crucial to understand what factors make employees internal activists, especially considering that high-tech employees hold highly moral identities as well as considerable bargaining power (Belfield, 2020; Milton, 2003). Future studies could go further by exploring the role of public relations in responding to employee activism. For instance, before employees turn into activists, leading to business disruption, organizations might use issue management, crisis communication, and risk communication to counter the impact of employee activism at different stages (Aronczyk, 2018; Reyes, 2021).

Learning Outcomes

1) Describe and demonstrate four major ethical concerns surrounding Google's development and use of AI technology.
2) Identity and analyze the role of organizational communication in influencing tech employees' intention to engage in activism actions.
3) Justify how personal attributes such as moral obligation drive tech employees to challenge their organization's unethical AI practices.

Discussion Questions

1) Search for an employee activism case that happened after 2021 and discuss what factors as explored in this chapter can be used to explain the case you found.
2) What new factors that were not identified in the chapter do you think can be applied to the case you found?
3) Why is it important for organizations to address employees' concerns and needs timely and responsively? Can you think of a reason as to why employees' requests might not matter?
4) What advantages do public relations professionals have in balancing the interests of the organization and their employees?

Further Readings

Belfield, H. (2020, February). Activism by the AI community: Analysing recent achievements and future prospects. In *Proceedings of the AAAI/ACM Conference on AI, Ethics, and Society* (pp. 15–21). https://doi.org/10.1145/3375627.3375814

Campbell, A. H. (2018, October 18). *How tech employees are pushing Silicon Valley to put ethics before profit.* Vox. https://www.vox.com/technology/2018/10/18/17989482/google-amazon-employee-ethics-contracts

Conger, K. (2021, January 4). Hundreds of Google employees unionize, culminating years of activism. *The New York Times.* https://www.nytimes.com/2021/01/04/technology/google-employees-union.html

Du, S., & Xie, C. (2021). Paradoxes of artificial intelligence in consumer markets: Ethical challenges and opportunities. *Journal of Business Research, 129,* 961–974.

Harwell, D., & Tiku, N. (2020, December 3). Google's star AI ethics researcher, one of a few Black women in the field, says she was fired for a critical email. *The Washington Post.* https://www.washingtonpost.com/technology/2020/12/03/timnit-gebru-google-fired/

Kim, J. N., & Grunig, J. E. (2011). Problem solving and communicative action: A situational theory of problem solving. *Journal of Communication, 61*(1), 120–149.

McCown, N. (2007). The role of public relations with internal activists. *Journal of Public Relations Research, 19*(1), 47–68.

Tomašev, N., Cornebise, J., Hutter, F., Mohamed, S., Picciariello, A., Connelly, B., … Clopath, C. (2020). AI for social good: Unlocking the opportunity for positive impact. *Nature Communications, 11*(1), 1–6.

Wright, S. A., & Schultz, A. E. (2018). The rising tide of artificial intelligence and business automation: Developing an ethical framework. *Business Horizons, 61*(6), 823–832.

References

Alahmad, R., & Robert, L. (2020). Artificial intelligence (AI) and IT identity: Antecedents identifying with AI applications. *AMCIS 2020 Proceedings.* (pp. 1–10). In the *Americas Conference on Information Systems.* https://doi.org/10.48550/arXiv.2005.12196.

Almeleh, N., Soifer, S., Gottlieb, N., & Gutierrez, L. (1993). Women's achievement of empowerment through activism in the workplace. *Affilia, 8*(1), 26–39.

Aronczyk, M. (2018). Public relations, issue management, and the transformation of American environmentalism, 1948–1992. *Enterprise & Society, 19*(4), 836–863. https://doi.org/10.1017/eso.2017.69

Barbaschow, A. (2021). *Google employees form Alphabet Workers Union to bring back the "Don't be evil" motto.* ZDNet. https://www.zdnet.com/article/google-employees-form-alphabet-workers-union-to-bring-back-the-dont-be-evil-motto/

Belfield, H. (2020, February). Activism by the AI community: Analysing recent achievements and future prospects. In *Proceedings of the AAAI/ACM Conference on AI, Ethics, and Society* (pp. 15–21).

Bender, E. M., Gebru, T., McMillan-Major, A., & Shmitchell, S. (2021, March). On the dangers of stochastic parrots: Can language models be too big? In *Proceedings of the 2021 ACM Conference on Fairness, Accountability, and Transparency* (pp. 610–623). https://doi.org/10.1145/3442188.3445922

Berger, B. K. (2005). Power over, power with, and power to relations: Critical reflections on public relations, the dominant coalition, and activism. *Journal of Public Relations Research, 17*(1), 5–28. https://doi.org/10.1207/s1532754xjprr1701_3

Briscoe, F., & Gupta, A. (2016). Social activism in and around organizations. *Academy of Management Annals, 10*(1), 671–727. https://doi.org/10.5465/19416520.2016.1153261

Chanana, N. (2020). Employee engagement practices during COVID-19 lockdown. *Journal of Public Affairs, 21*(4), e2508.

Conger, K. (2021). Hundreds of Google employees unionize, culminating years of activism. *The New York Times.* https://www.nytimes.com/2021/01/04/technology/google-employees-union.html

Conger, K. (2018). Tech workers got paid in company stock. They used it to agitate for change. *The New York Times.* https://www.nytimes.com/2018/12/16/technology/tech-workers-company-stock-shareholder-activism.html

Cotterrell, R. (1999). Transparency, mass media, ideology and community. *Journal for Cultural Research, 3*(4), 414–426.

Dastin, J., & Dave, P. (2021, February 25). Exclusive: Google pledges changes to research oversight after internal revolt. *Reuters.* https://www.reuters.com/article/us-alphabet-google-research-exclusive/exclusive-google-pledges-changes-to-research-oversight-after-internal-revolt-idUSKBN2AP1AC

Dean, G. (2021, January 4). Google workers in the US and Canada have formed a union after years of clashes between staff and execs. *Business Insider.* https://www.businessinsider.com/google-alphabet-workers-form-union-us-canada-contractors-2021-1

Ehsan, U., Liao, Q. V., Muller, M., Riedl, M. O., & Weisz, J. D. (2021, May). Expanding explainability: Towards social transparency in ai systems. In *Proceedings of the 2021 CHI Conference on Human Factors in Computing Systems* (pp. 1–19). http://dx.doi.org/10.1145/3411764.3445188.

Fang, L. (2019, March 1). Google hedges on promise to end controversial involvement in military drone contract. *The Intercept.* https://theintercept.com/2019/03/01/google-project-maven-contract/

GoogleWalkout. (2020, December 3). *Standing with Dr. Timnit Gebru—#ISupportTimnit #BelieveBlackWomen. Google Walkout For Real Change.* https://googlewalkout.medium.com/standing-with-dr-timnit-gebru-isupporttimnit-believeblackwomen-6dadc300d382

Google Walkout For Real Change. (2021, March 8). The future must be ethical: #MakeAIEthical. *Medium.* https://googlewalkout.medium.com/the-future-must-be-ethical-makeaiethical-9eb3edd7cf3c

Gorsuch, R. L., & Ortberg, J. (1983). Moral obligation and attitudes: Their relation to behavioral intentions. *Journal of Personality and Social Psychology, 44*(5), 1025–1028.

Grant, N. (2021, January 28). Google CEO says internal rancor over AI due to transparency. *Bloomberg.* https://www.bloomberg.com/news/articles/2021-01-28/google-ceo-says-internal-rancor-over-ai-due-to-transparency

Hao, K. (2020, December 4). We read the paper that forced Timnit Gebru out of Google. Here's what it says. *MIT Technology Review.* https://www.technologyreview.com/2020/12/04/1013294/google-ai-ethics-research-paper-forced-out-timnit-gebru/

Hart, H. L. A. *The concept of law* (3rd ed.). Oxford: Oxford University Press.

Kalodimos, J., & Leavitt, K. (2020). Experimental shareholder activism: A novel approach for studying top management decision making and employee career issues. *Journal of Vocational Behavior, 120*, 103429. https://doi.org/10.1016/j.jvb.2020.103429

Keith, P. (2021). Why Timnit Gebru isn't waiting for big tech to fix AI's problems. *Time.* https://time.com/6132399/timnit-gebru-ai-google/

King, B. G., & Soule, S. A. (2007). Social movements as extra-institutional entrepreneurs: The effect of protests on stock price returns. *Administrative Science Quarterly, 52*(3), 413–442.

Langley, H. (2020, December 4). More than 1,000 Google employees have signed a letter demanding answers from leadership after a top AI researcher was suddenly fired. *Business Insider.* https://www.businessinsider.com/more-than-1000-google-employees-signed-petition-over-researcher-firing-2020-12

Lytvynenko, J. (2022, February 7). Why the balance of power in tech is shifting toward workers. *MIT Technology Review.* https://www.technologyreview.com/2022/02/07/1044760/tech-workers-unionizing-power/

MacLellan, L. (2020). Can Coinbase ward off employee activism with its new hardline policy? *Quartz.* https://qz.com/work/1910563/coinbase-is-taking-a-hard-line-on-employee-activism/

McCown, N. (2007). The role of public relations with internal activists. *Journal of Public Relations Research, 19*(1), 47–68. https://doi.org/10.1080/10627260709336595

Men, L. R. (2014). Internal reputation management: The impact of authentic leadership and transparent communication. *Corporate Reputation Review, 17*(4), 254–272. https://doi.org/10.1057/crr.2014.14

Men, L. R., & Jiang, H. (2016). Cultivating quality employee-organization relationships: The interplay among organizational leadership, culture, and communication. *International Journal of Strategic Communication, 10*(5), 462–479. https://doi.org/10.1080/1553118X.2016.1226172

Metz, C. (2021, February 19). A second Google A.I. researcher says the company fired her. *The New York Times.* https://www.nytimes.com/2021/02/19/technology/google-ethical-artificial-intelligence-team.html

Metz, R. (2021, March 11). How one employee's exit shook Google and the AI industry. *CNN.* https://www.cnn.com/2021/03/11/tech/google-ai-ethics-future/index.html

Miles, S. A., Larcker, D. F., & Tayan, B. (2021). Protests from within: Engaging with employee activists. *Stanford Closer Look Series.* https://www.gsb.stanford.edu/facultyresearch/publications/protests-within-engaging-employee-activists

Milton, L. P. (2003). An identity perspective on the propensity of high-tech talent to unionize. *Journal of Labor Research, 24*(1), 31–53.

Najibi, A. (2020). Racial discrimination in face recognition technology. *SITN.* https://sitn.hms.harvard.edu/what-is-sitn/

Nedzhvetskaya, N., & Tan, J.S. (2019). What we learned from over a decade of tech activism. *The Guardian.* https://www.theguardian.com/commentisfree/2019/dec/22/techworker-activism-2019-what-we-learned

O'Gorman, M. (2021, April 1). Google's union of activists highlights the need for ethical engineering. *The Conversation.* https://theconversation.com/googles-union-of-activistshighlights-the-need-for-ethical-engineering-155850

Ovide, S. (2020, June 9). A case for banning facial recognition. *The New York Times.* https://www.nytimes.com/2020/06/09/technology/facial-recognition-software.html

Paul, K. (2021). Two Google engineers quit over company's treatment of AI researcher. *The Guardian.* https://www.theguardian.com/technology/2021/feb/04/googletimnit-gebru-ai-engineers-quit

Perrigo, B. (2022, January 18). Why Timnit Gebru isn't waiting for big tech to fix AI's problems. *Time.* https://time.com/6132399/timnit-gebru-ai-google/

Rashid, Y., Rashid, A., Warraich, M. A., Sabir, S. S., & Waseem, A. (2019). Case study method: A step-by-step guide for business researchers. *International Journal of Qualitative Methods, 18,* 1–13. https://doi.org/10.1177/1609406919862424

Rawlins, B. (2008). Give The emperor a mirror: Toward developing a stakeholder measurement of organizational transparency. *Journal of Public Relations Research, 21*(1), 71–99.

Raeburn, N. C. (2004). *Changing corporate America from inside out: Lesbian and gay workplace rights (Vol. 20).* Minneapolis, MN: University of Minnesota Press.

Reitz, M., Higgins, J., & Day-Duro, E. (2021). The wrong way to respond to employee activism. *Harvard Business Review.* https://hbr.org/2021/02/the-wrong-way-to-respond-toemployee-activism

Reyes, C. (2021). Spinning at the border: Employee activism in "Big PR." *Media and Communication, 9*(3), 133–143. http://doi.org/10.17645/mac.v9i3.4118

Shane, S., & Wakabayashi, D. (2018, April 4). "The business of war": Google employees protest work for the Pentagon. *The New York Times.* https://www.nytimes.com/2018/04/04/technology/google-letter-ceo-pentagon-project.html

Sjöström, E. (2008). Shareholder activism for corporate social responsibility: What do we know? *Sustainable Development, 16*(3), 141–154. https://doi.org/10.1002/sd.361

Smith, M. F., & Ferguson, D. P. (2001). Activism. In R. L. Heath (Ed.), *Handbook of public relations* (291–300). Thousand Oaks, CA: Sage.

Taiminen, K., Luoma-aho, V., & Tolvanen, K. (2015). The transparent communicative organization and new hybrid forms of content. *Public Relations Review, 41*(5), 734–743. https://doi.org/10.1016/j.pubrev.2015.06.016

Tapscott, D., & Ticoll, D. (2003). *The naked corporation: How the age of transparency will revolutionize business.* New York: Free Press.

Vilas, X., & Sabucedo, J.-M. (2012). Moral obligation: A forgotten dimension in the analysis of collective action. *Revista de Psicología Social, 27*(3), 369–375.

Vincent, J. (2021, April 13). *Google is poisoning its reputation with AI researchers: The firing of top Google AI ethics researchers has created a significant backlash.* The Verge. https://www.theverge.com/2021/4/13/22370158/google-ai-ethics-timnit-gebru-margaretmitchell-firing-reputation

Wakabayashi, D., & Metz, C. (2022, May 2). Another firing among Google's A.I. brain trust, and more discord. *The New York Times.* https://www.nytimes.com/2022/05/02/technology/googlefires-ai-researchers.html

Wong, J. C. (2020). More than 1,200 Google workers condemn firing of AI scientist Timnit Gebru. *The Guardian.* https://www.theguardian.com/technology/2020/dec/04/timnit-gebru-google-ai-fired-diversity-ethics

Wright, S. A., & Schultz, A. E. (2018). The rising tide of artificial intelligence and business automation: Developing an ethical framework. *Business Horizons, 61*(6), 823–832. https://doi.org/10.1016/j.bushor.2018.07.001

Yang, A., Uysal, N., & Taylor, M. (2018). Unleashing the power of networks: Shareholder activism, sustainable development and corporate environmental policy. *Business Strategy and the Environment, 27*(6), 712–727. https://doi.org/10.1002/bse.2026

Yin, R. K. (1994). Discovering the future of the case study. Method in evaluation research. *Evaluation Practice, 15*(3), 283–290. https://doi.org/10.1177/109821409401500309

Zafft, R. (2021, April 28). Wokeness at work: Is the pendulum swinging back? Coinbase, Basecamp & Google. *Forbes.* https://www.forbes.com/sites/robertzafft/2021/04/28/35-yearslater-coinbase-and-basecamp-catch-up-with-my-grandma--will-othersfollow/?sh=1e5b7b36269e

Section V

Internal Communication and Emerging Technologies

Chapter Eleven

Internal Social Media and Employee Engagement in a Danish Bank

Vibeke Thøis Madsen

Introduction

Internal social media (ISM) facilitates communication between organizational members across hierarchies, departments, and geographical distances. It can be an integrated part of the intranet, a separate social software such as Microsoft Teams, Yammer, or Slack or a closed group on LinkedIn, Facebook, or Twitter (Leonardi et al., 2013). Regardless of the setup, everyone in the organization can contribute, and the communication is visible to all organizational members (Treem & Leonardi, 2012). As a result, communication on ISM has been linked to participatory and transparent internal communication (Madsen, 2022) that can engage employees (Ewing et al., 2019; Men et al., 2020). However, far from all organizations unleash the potential of ISM (Madsen, 2017; Ruck, 2015; Sievert & Scholz, 2017; Werling, 2020) and, based on a case study in a Danish bank, this chapter explores how participatory communication on ISM can develop and why it might lead to employee engagement. Before the case study is presented, a brief literature review connects literature on internal communication and ISM with a Communication Constitutes Organizations (CCO) perspective on engagement to create a theoretical understanding of how engagement might emerge from employee communication on ISM.

Literature Review

Internal communication plays a vital role in organizations (Dahlman & Heide, 2020; Men & Bowen, 2017; Ruck, 2015). It coordinates activities, informs about the strategic direction of the organization, helps employees make sense of their work and the organization, and builds relationships between employees. Internal communication thus helps employees become part of and identify with the organization, and has thus been found to be key to employee engagement (Men et al., 2020; Ruck, 2015), especially if employees experience organizational practices of internal communication as acceptable and appropriate (Welch, 2012) and can voice their opinion, are listened to and have a say in organizational decisions (Ruck et al., 2017). In other words, symmetrical communication based on trust, credibility, openness, and reciprocity can improve the relationship between employees and their organizations and thus

DOI: 10.4324/9781003195580-17

enhance employee engagement (Kang & Sung, 2017; Taylor & Kent, 2014). The organizational context is therefore of great importance, not just by providing appropriate human resource management, having a transparent and authentic management style, and involving internal communication, but also by trusting, empowering, and listening to employees (Gode et al., 2019; Mazzei, 2018). ISM provides an informal vertical and horizontal communication arena where mutual conversations can take place. Using ISM for internal communication has been linked to employee engagement (Gode et al., 2019; Madsen, 2020; Men et al., 2020). However, the introduction of ISM does not in itself lead to participatory communication and employee engagement. In a study of eleven organizations, Madsen (2018) found that three different types of communication arenas can develop when ISM is introduced: *A quiet or empty communication arena*, *a knowledge-sharing communication arena*, and *a participatory communication arena*. An assumption could be that the quiet arenas that are often found in organizations (Madsen, 2017; Sievert & Scholz, 2017) do not create employee engagement, while the participatory and to some extent the knowledge-sharing communication arena has the potential to do so.

The question is how communication on ISM can lead to employee engagement. Heide and Simonsson (2018) identified two different and contrasting perspectives on employee engagement: a managerial perspective and an alternative, employee-centered perspective, which is grounded in a CCO understanding. According to the managerial perspective, engagement is a psychological state that grows out of employees experiencing meaningfulness, safety, and availability (Kahn, 1990; Welch, 2011) after listening to inspiring talks of CEOs and managers. However, from the CCO perspective, engagement is constructed within social, interactive sensemaking processes (Weick, 1995). Engagement thus "emanates from "within," from being an active partner in an interactive sensemaking process characterized by trust, mutual commitment, and shared creation of meaning" (Heide & Simonsson, 2018, p. 210).

The CCO perspective on engagement emerges from an understanding of employees as active communicators and co-constructors of organizational communication rather than as passive receivers of internal communication. Therefore, it could be argued that employees are also co-constructors of engagement (cf. Heide & Simonsson, 2011). According to Taylor and Kent (2014), real dialogue only takes place if the participants are engaged (p. 390). Employees only point out improvements, innovations, and learn from mistakes and discuss on ISM with other employees or managers when they care about their organization (Madsen, 2016), and when they experience that they can influence processes and decision-making (Ewing et al., 2019). Furthermore, the CCO perspective embraces the idea that organizations are built bottom-up and that they are multivocal and polyphonic (Heide & Simonsson, 2018). Contradictions, tensions, and paradoxes are therefore an inherent part of organizational communication, and it could be argued that engagement grows out of the interaction of different viewpoints. If all organizational members agree on the direction of the organization, there is not much to discuss, but if they have to argue for and defend their viewpoints, they become more aware of the situation of the organization and how they perceive the organization. In other words, the polyphonic or multivocal organization is a source for engaging conversations about the identity of an organization (Kopaneva & Sias, 2015).

After their presentation of the two perspectives on engagement, Heide and Simonsson (2018) advocated for more research into how dialogue, critical voice, and peer communication relate to engagement. Communication on ISM is visible to all organizational members, and thus is a good arena for studying interactions between organizational members. The aim of this chapter is, therefore, to answer the following research question: *How and why does ISM increase employee engagement?*

Methodology

An explorative single case study (Yin, 2014) was conducted to explore the relationship between communication on ISM and employee engagement. Jyske Bank, the third biggest bank in Denmark, with 3,300 employees and 98 locations in 2021, was selected as a critical case (Flyvbjerg, 2006). The bank is known for its open communication climate, supportive CEO, and for trying to be a bank that is different from other banks (Madsen, 2016). A discussion forum was introduced on the intranet in 2004, and in 2014 it was placed on the front page of a new social intranet called *JB United* to signal the importance of listening to employees. Here, employees could not only comment on but also like posts from other employees, and when they did so, their pictures, names, job position, and location appeared next to their comment or like. In this respect, the communication made *people*, *communication* and *interactions* visible to all organizational members (Treem et al., 2020). The case study consisted of screenshots of three months of discussions on ISM in 2013 and three months in 2018, as well as semi-structured interviews with 24 employees conducted in 2014 and 2015. The employees selected for the interviews were identified after studying the communication on ISM as they represented different job positions, locations, and types of communication behavior, and were furthermore inspired by Brandtzaeg and Heims' (2011) typology of five different social networking sites users, namely debaters, actives, socializers, lurkers, and sporadics. The interviewees included both men and women, young and old employees. The interviews were conducted face-to-face, and they lasted, on average, one hour.

Analyzing the Empirical Material

A netnographic study (Kozinets, 2015) was conducted to make sense of the communication on ISM. First, all the screenshots showing communication on ISM were read to get an idea of the content and themes discussed, the number of employees commenting and liking, the number of interactions on ISM, and who communicated with whom. Second, posts that developed into discussions were analyzed more in-depth to study the dynamics of communication on ISM. Third, a thematic analysis (King, 2012) of the transcripts of the interviews was carried out to explore the employees' perspectives on communication on ISM. The codes were clustered into four overall themes: visibility of communication on ISM, perceived internal communication, perceived communication on ISM, and perceived value of communication on ISM.

Findings

Employee Voice and Ventriloquism

Analysis of the screenshots revealed that many employees posted, commented, and liked content on ISM. Some employees were more active than others, while others would only appear from time to time, only like content, or not be visible at all.

The four topics that could develop into longer discussions were:

1) *Customers and products*: Sharing knowledge, generating ideas, finding solutions to challenges, and other task-related communication.
2) *Working conditions*: Discussing IT systems, work routines, and employee benefits.
3) *Organizational issues*: Discussing organizational issues and organizational identity.
4) *ISM-specific issues*: Metacommunication about how to communicate on ISM.

The distinction between the different topics was not clear-cut. A discussion might both be about an IT-system and a meta-discussion about how to communicate on ISM;

alternatively, it might start as a discussion about a product and end as a discussion about organizational identity. The presentation of the four topics thus indicates what topics the employees cared about and were willing to invest their time and energy in discussing. The topics about customers and products were closely related to their daily tasks, as were discussions about IT-systems and work routines. In that respect, they were engaged in discussing job-related issues, and it seemed to be linked to a desire to act as a professional bank adviser and offer customers relevant and competitive products. For example, a discussion about a product for young people being out of date and not able to match the product of competitors led to the following comments:

> "… I just have to say that Jyske Bank is REALLY way behind on the concept for young people. We have nothing to offer that is not matched by other banks …" … "If the concept is not improved, we will lose customers in the long run."
>
> *From an initial post by a bank adviser*

> "It is not only the 18:27 concept that has to be looked at. 12:17 ought to be looked at as well, if we are to maintain good experiences and preserve the customer relationship."
>
> *From a comment by another bank adviser*

The employees clearly criticize the products and perhaps even the bank for not paying attention to the market and customers' needs. It is unclear whether this is just employees wishing to complain or dedicated and engaged employees wishing to improve the organization. They risk a lot by engaging in the ISM communication arena that is visible to all organizational members: they risk their job and their reputation in the organization (Madsen & Verhoeven, 2016). In other words, they have a lot at stake, and still choose to raise their voice. The open communication climate in the bank therefore seems to invite the employees to raise their concerns on ISM, and these employees took up the invitation. Furthermore, when one employee raises an issue, others feel inclined to develop and add their perspectives to the discussion. And when they try to challenge or make sense of organizational decisions, they talk as members of the organization. The bank advisers in the previously mentioned examples use the collective "we," which is addressee-inclusive (De Cillia et al., 1999). It signals that they feel they belong to the organization. Furthermore, in discussions on ISM, the employees use slogans and phrases used by management such as "the customer relationship" to argue their case. This could be perceived as an act of ventriloquism (Cooren, 2012) where "things are made to speak and act through what we say or do" (p. 5). Ventriloquism is especially present in conversations that develop into discussions about organizational identity. Here, employees consciously use slogans and phrases from the bank to build their arguments (Madsen & Johansen, 2019). For example, an employee from one of the branches shares an experience with a customer who compares the bank to one of the bank's competitors due to the malfunctioning telephone system. This prompts the following comment from a bank adviser: "That is a nasty comparison. Something has to be done about it. It should not sound like that in *Denmark's most customer-oriented bank*" (my emphasis). Thus, the managerial discourse used to construct the identity of the organization speaks through the employees when they negotiate and reconstruct organizational identity (Madsen, 2016).

Ambient Awareness and Empowerment

The interviews with the 24 employees provided insights into their perception of communication on ISM—both the employees who contributed to the discussions and the employees who followed the discussions. The initiator of the first post about the product for young people had the following reflection about creating posts:

> "I just hope that those who develop the products will make it better. And in this way, you know that it has been said. It gives you some sort of satisfaction. If things are not said, you can just sit there and be frustrated."
>
> *Interview 12*

In other words, if opinions are not expressed, this can lead to disengagement. Communication on ISM was thus found to contribute to a healthy communication climate.

> "It is like a listening tube in the organization. I see it as a valve where everyone can bring something to the table. Positive and negative criticism. If you have something you want to get out in the open, this is a targeted way of doing it."
>
> *Interview 3*

ISM was not only about letting off steam. It also provided a way of influencing and changing decisions.

> "You actually force the responsible person to respond, since now everyone has seen that this might be an option."
>
> *Interview 6*

Due to the visibility of ISM, employees perceived that they were listened to and their voice had an impact. At the same time, visibility made it possible for all organizational members to follow the discussions on ISM which created "ambient awareness" (Leonardi & Neeley, 2017):

> "I use it to keep up with what is going on in the organization. Which direction are we heading? Are there things we need to react to? It indicates how the organization is doing. How does the workplace function?
>
> *Interview 23*

At the same time, communication on ISM gave insights into the polyphonic nature of the organization:

> "I think it is very interesting to hear people's opinions. Someone might like it. Someone has input pointing in another direction, seeing things from a different perspective. It can help open your eyes because you might have a one-sided way of seeing things."
>
> *Interview 1*

The discussions of the different viewpoints continued across the desks, at lunch, and at the coffee machine, helping the employees make sense of their work and the organization. Even employees who said they did not follow the different threads on ISM were aware of the issues being discussed. ISM provided an opportunity to voice an opinion; it created awareness of the organization and made the employees feel valued:

> "Now I can compare with the bank where I was employed previously, where I felt like a rather ordinary employee number and a piece in a chess game. This is not how I think it is in Jyske Bank. Here, I believe that people are interested in knowing what we ordinary soldiers think - and I appreciate that."
>
> *Interview 21*

> "You are welcome to voice your opinion. Your opinion is valued. Everyone is part of the community. It creates cohesion."
>
> *Interview 9*

As the quotations from the interviews illustrate, the employees stated that communication on ISM created cohesion and awareness of the plurality of voices in the organization. They felt empowered and that they mattered as individual employees.

Discussion and Conclusion

The chapter set out to explore how and why ISM might create employee engagement. The case study in Jyske Bank indicates that there is a link and why this is the case. ISM provided a communication arena where employees felt invited to voice their opinion, and they found that managers had to respond due to the visibility of the communication. ISM therefore provided a communication arena where they could point out shortcomings, make suggestions and get the attention of top managers instead of feeling frustrated, and this made them feel empowered and able to influence decisions in the organization. Empowerment has among other things been linked to engagement (Mazzei, 2018), and based on the interviews with the 24 employees, one could argue that the employees experienced meaningfulness, safety, and availability (Kahn, 1990). Furthermore, employees participating in discussions on ISM were prepared to risk their reputation for the sake of the organization, and when they did so, they spoke as a member of the organization using the inclusive "we" and ventriloquizing managerial discourses. In this respect, the employees were engaged dialogue partners (Taylor & Kent, 2014).

From a CCO perspective, engagement developed in at least two ways. First, employees became engaged when they interacted with other employees or managers on ISM. They could start a discussion, make a comment, or like content, and these discussions often departed from contradictions, tensions, and paradoxes, such as how they could be a customer-oriented bank if they did not pick up the phone? Regardless of whether they made a comment or liked content, they had to decide about their perspective on the issue discussed. Thus, it can be argued that employees became engaged when they interacted with communication on ISM, in the same way as employees become engaged when they contribute to innovation (Gode et al., 2019). Second, employees who followed the discussions on ISM became engaged when they tried to make sense of the interactions on ISM in discussions with colleagues over lunch. In both cases, employee engagement emerged out of or happened in social, interactive sensemaking processes (Weick, 1995) with participatory communication on ISM.

According to the interviewees, it was not only communication on ISM that made employees satisfied with their job. It was just as much organizational culture, style of management, colleagues, and working conditions. So, it could be argued that participatory communication on ISM (Madsen, 2018) is only likely to develop if the organization has a culture or style of management that not only supports employee voice on ISM but also responds to and actively uses input from the employees. The question is then what it takes to make employees feel inclined to criticize organizational practices and products, or challenge the identity of the organization as they seem to do in Jyske Bank. An argument could be that they should identify with the organization and really care about their organization. In other words, they need to be engaged. An open communication climate sets the stage for engagement, and employees become engaged when they interact with each other and try to challenge or make sense of organizational decisions either on ISM or over lunch.

Implications for Practice

Communication on ISM has the potential to engage employees if they perceive that their voice on ISM is welcome and they can influence organizational decisions. It requires courage from the organization to let go of control, and managers should be prepared to receive criticism and respond in a constructive manner that encourages critical voices in the future (Madsen & Johansen, 2019).

Organizations should not fear employees adding negative comments as their self-censorship will make them communicate in a constructive manner, and other employees will comment if someone steps out of line (Madsen & Verhoeven, 2016). Actually, communicative rules and moderating might be counterproductive and prevent employees from communicating on ISM.

Introducing ISM sends a signal to the employees that the organization and managers are interested in listening to the employees, so just having the media is a promise of transparency and participation, and if the organization is not ready to fulfill this promise, it might be better not to introduce ISM.

Employees prefer in-person internal communication to other internal communication channels (Ruck, 2015), and even if ISM offers transparent organizational communication, it cannot replace in-person communication that is better suited to mutual dialogue (Taylor & Kent, 2014). However, especially in organizations that are scattered across different locations or perhaps even countries, ISM offers fast and interactive communication that is more symmetrical and informal than other types of written internal communication. The pictures of the employee and the opportunity to comment and like posts bring aspects from oral conversations into writing.

Learning Outcomes

1) Describe how management should phrase the introduction of ISM to the employees, when it is implemented.
2) Describe a list of initiatives a communication department can do to start conversations on ISM and how they can ensure that comments are answered from relevant employees or managers.
3) Reflect on the possible benefits from not interfering in negative discussions and what it could do to the organization if the communication department removed or deleted some comments.

Discussion Questions

1) What will happen if an organization introduces ISM without allowing criticism and debate?
2) What can an organization gain from openly discussing organizational challenges?
3) What can organizations do to encourage employees to openly voice their opinion on ISM?
4) What can an organization do to prepare managers to tackle communication on ISM?

Further Readings

Heide, M., & Simonsson, C. (2018). Coworkership and engaged communicators: A critical reflection on employee engagement. In *The handbook of communication engagement*. Hoboken, NJ: John Wiley and sons, (205–220).

Madsen, V. T. (2020). Communicative leadership on internal social media: A way to employee engagement? In A. T. Verčič, R. Tench, & S. Einwiller (Eds.), *Joy (advances in public relations and communication management)* (93–114). Bingley: Emerald Publishing Limited. https://doi.org/10.1108/S2398-391420200000005008.

References

Brandtzaeg, P. B., & Heim, J. (2011). A typology of social networking sites users. *International Journal of Web Based Communities*, *7*(1), 28–51.

Cooren, F. (2012). Communication theory at the center: Ventriloquism and the communicative constitution of reality. *Journal of Communication*, 62, 1–20.

Dahlman, S., & Heide, M. (2020). *Strategic internal communication: A practitioner's guide to implementing cutting-edge methods for improved workplace culture*. London: Routledge.

De Cillia, R., Reisigl, M., & Wodak, R. (1999). The discursive construction of national identities. *Discourse & Society, 10*, 149–173.

Ewing, M., Men, L. R., & O'Neil, J. (2019). Using social media to engage employees: Insights from internal communication managers. *International Journal of Strategic Communication, 13*(2), 110–132.

Flyvbjerg, B. (2006). Five misunderstandings about case-study research. *Qualitative Inquiry, 12*, 219–245.

Gode, H. E., Johansen, W., & Thomsen, C. (2019). Employee engagement in generating ideas on internal social media: A matter of meaningfulness, safety and availability. *Corporate Communications: An International Journal, 25*(2), 263–280.

Heide, M., & Simonsson, C. (2011). Putting coworkers in the limelight: New challenges for communication professionals. *International Journal of Strategic Communication, 5*(4), 201–220.

Kang, M., & Sung, M. (2017). How symmetrical employee communication leads to employee engagement and positive employee communication behaviors: The mediation of employee-organization relationships. *Journal of Communication Management, 12*(1), 82–102.

Kahn, W. A. (1990). Psychological conditions of personal engagement and disengagement at work. *The Academy of Management Journal, 12*(1), 692–724. https://doi.org/10.2307/256287

King, N. (2012). Doing template analysis. In G. Symon & C. Cassell (Eds.), *Qualitative organizational research: core methods and current challenges* (426–450). London: Sage.

Kopaneva, I., & Sias, P. M. (2015). Lost in translation: Employee and organizational constructions of mission and vision. *Management Communication Quarterly, 29*(3), 358–384.

Kozinets, R. V. (2015). *Netnography: Redefined*. London: Sage.

Leonardi, P., & Neeley, T. (2017). What managers need to know about social tools. *Harvard Business Review, 95*(6), 118–126.

Leonardi, P. M., Huysman, M., & Steinfield, C. (2013). Enterprise Social media: Definition, history, and prospects for the study of social technologies in organizations. *Journal of Computer-Mediated Communication, 19*, 1–19. https://doi.org/10.1111/jcc4.12029.

Madsen, V. T. (2016). Constructing organizational identity on internal social media: A case study of coworker communication in Jyske bank. *International Journal of Business Communication, 53*(2), 200–223. https://doi.org/10.1177/2329488415627272.

Madsen, V. T. (2017). The challenges of introducing internal social media—the coordinators' roles and perceptions. *Journal of Communication Management, 21*(1), 2–16. https://doi.org/10.1108/JCOM-04-2016-0027.

Madsen, V.T. (2018). Participatory communication on internal social media—a dream or reality? Findings from two exploratory studies of coworkers as communicators. *Corporate Communications: An International Journal, 23*(4), 614–628. https://doi.org/10.1108/CCIJ-04-2018-0039

Madsen, V. T. (2020). Communicative leadership on internal social media: A way to employee engagement? In A. T. Verčič, R. Tench, & S. Einwiller (Eds.), *Joy (advances in public relations and communication management)* (93–114). Bingley: Emerald Publishing Limited. https://doi.org/10.1108/S2398-391420200000005008.

Madsen, V. T. (2022). Internal social media: A promise of participatory communication and organizational transparency. In J. Falkheimer & M. Heide (Eds.), *Research handbook in strategic communication*. Cheltenham: Edward Elgar Publishing, 431–444.

Madsen, V. T., & Johansen, W. (2019). A spiral of voice? When employees speak up on internal social media. *Journal of Communication Management, 23*(4), 331–347. https://doi.org/10.1108/JCOM-03-2019-0050

Madsen, V.T., & Verhoeven, J.W. (2016). Self-censorship on internal social media: A case study of coworker communication behavior in a Danish bank. *International Journal of Strategic Communication, 10*(5), 387–409. https://doi.org/10.1080/1553118X.2016.1220010

Mazzei, A. (2018). Employee engagement. In R. Heath & W. Johansen (Eds), *The international encyclopedia of strategic communication*. John Wiley & Sons. https://onlinelibrary.wiley.com/doi/10.1002/9781119010722.iesc0068

Men, R. L., & Bowen, S. A. (2017). *Excellence in internal communication management*. New York, NY: Business Expert Press.

Men, L. R., O'Neil, J., & Ewing, M. (2020). Examining the effects of internal social media usage on employee engagement. *Public Relations Review, 46*(2). https://doi.org/10.1016/j.pubrev.2020.101880

Ruck, K., Welch, M., & Menara, B. (2017). Employee voice: An antecedent to organisational engagement? *Public Relations Review, 43*(5), 904–914.

Ruck, M. K. (Ed.). (2015). *Exploring internal communication: Towards informed employee voice*. Farnham: Gower Publishing, Ltd.

Sievert, H., & Scholz, C. (2017). Engaging employees in (at least partly) disengaged companies. Results of an interview survey within about 500 German corporations on the growing importance of digital engagement via internal social media. *Public Relations Review, 43*(5), 894–903. https://doi.org/10.1016/j.pubrev.2017.06.001.

Taylor, M., & Kent, M. L. (2014). Dialogic engagement: Clarifying foundational concepts. *Journal of Public Relations Research, 26*(5), 384–398.

Treem, J. W., & Leonardi, P.M. (2012). Social media use in organizations: Exploring the affordances of visibility, editability, persistence, and association. In *Communication yearbook*, Vol *36* (143–189). New York, NY: Routledge.

Treem, J. W., Leonardi, P. M., & van den Hooff, B. (2020). Computer-mediated communication in the age of communication visibility. *Journal of Computer-Mediated Communication, 25*(1), 44–59. https://doi.org/10.1093/jcmc/zmz024

Weick, K. E. (1995). *Sensemaking in organizations*. Thousand Oaks, CA: Sage.

Welch, M. (2011). The evolution of the employee engagement concept: Communication implications. *Corporate Communications: An International Journal, 16*(4), 328–346.

Welch, M. (2012). Appropriateness and acceptability: Employee perspectives of internal communication. *Public Relations Review, 38*(2), 246–254.

Werling, K. N. (2020). Influencing factors for employees' usage intention of internal social media communication technologies. *European Journal of Business and Management Research, 5*(2), 1–8.

Yin, R. K. (2014). *Case study research: Design and methods* (5th ed.). Thousand Oaks, CA: Sage.

Chapter Twelve

Nice-to-Know: Role Expectations on Enterprise Social Media in the Aviation Industry

Joost Verhoeven and Ward van Zoonen

Introduction

Enterprise social media (hereafter ESM) refer to "web-based platforms that allow workers to (I) communicate messages with specific coworkers or broadcast messages to everyone in the organization; (II) explicitly or implicitly reveal particular coworkers as communication partners (III), post, edit, sort text and files linked to themselves or others; and (IV) view the messages, connections, text, and files communicated, posted, edited, and sorted by anyone else in the organization at any time of their choosing" (Leonardi et al., 2013, p. 2).

As such, ESM provide unique opportunities for organizational communication that were hard, or impossible to achieve before these technologies entered the workplace (Treem & Leonardi, 2013). Despite some apparent benefits to ESM use, their adoption and use in organizations is sometimes plagued by diverging expectation about how and why ESM should be used possibly leading to underutilization (Rode, 2016). At the root of this problem is the often voluntary and noncommittal nature of ESM use. Many ESM platforms are introduced as technologies that *could* (rather than should) be used, while its content is frequently classified as "nice to know" rather than "need to know." As a direct result of the noncommittal, nonessential classification of communication, employees can construct diverse communicative role perceptions and expectations (Pekkala, 2020). Consequentially, users may approach these platforms with a wide variety of expectations about their and others' roles.

In this chapter we present an analysis of ESM use in a large European aviation company. We will draw on role theory and social media literature to develop the conceptual boundaries of our case study. Subsequently, we discuss the use and role expectations of various user groups in this case: (I) the cabin crew, (II) platform moderators, (III) experts (office employees), and (IV) managers. In any community, users come together and establish an understanding of the roles that each person should play. These roles consist of behavioral expectations. In the context of this case, these expectations concern how different user groups ought to use ESM.

DOI: 10.4324/9781003195580-18

We will use role theory as a lens to interrogate how users define their and others' roles within an online community. There is a rich history of studying social roles and behaviors in social communities (Mead, 1934) and, more recently, online communities (Holtzblatt et al., 2013). Work in this area has studied and conceptualized various types of users inter alia "active contributors," "moderate contributors," and "readers" (Holtzblatt et al., 2013). However, when considering ESM, the organizational context and roles individuals play and bring to the platform should be considered too. As such, literature on role theory and organizational behavior helps to delineate the scope of the analysis and bring the discussion into focus.

Specifically, in this chapter, we will describe the context-specific roles that employees in this aviation company play on ESM. And shed light on how the role expectations shape the experiences of users on this ESM platform. In doing so, we seek to answer three interrelated questions: (I) Which roles do users on ESM play? (II) What do users expect of each other in these roles on ESM? And (III) How do the role expectations of users shape their own experiences of ESM use?

Role Theory

Human behavior is strongly guided by socially designed roles. Role theory is concerned with the ways in which (social) expectations define various roles within broader social contexts and how these expectations and roles shape subsequent behaviors (e.g., Katz & Kahn, 1978). In recent years, role-based understandings of organizational life have been criticized for not being flexible enough, failing to provide an authentic account of human agency and creativity as individuals navigate their social contexts. Especially in the context of ESM a more dynamic perspective on user roles might be fruitful. For instance, ESM have been construed as technologies that transcend formal hierarchies and roles in organizations, create more egalitarian communication structures, and knit together the enterprise in ways that were previously impossible (Meske et al., 2020). Indeed, ESM hold various benefits for knowledge sharing (van Zoonen & Sivunen, 2020), organizational learning (Leonardi, 2014), and task performance (Chen et al., 2019). Coupled with the notion that ESM platforms in organizations are often expected to be adopted by employees but not required to be adopted (Rode, 2016) a more granular understanding of employees' roles—i.e., beyond in-role versus extra-role role dichotomies—is needed (Borman & Motowidlo, 1997).

Roles have been conceptualized in different ways ranging from relatively fixed notions of roles as inherently related to specific positions in an organization, as a functionalist perspective would assume, to roles as symbolic meanings enacted by social actors, as an interactionist perspective would assume (Järventie-Thesleff & Tienari, 2016). Regardless, roles are important as they help establish (a temporary) sense of coherence and provide a framework for understanding how meaning is constructed in relational interactions. Hence, understanding the relational interactions within online communities requires an understanding of the different roles that users play in these communities (Akar et al., 2019).

The interaction between people is typically enabled and constrained by the social structure within which these interactions take place. Social roles provide a framework of meaning that defines social structure and articulates the expectations and conditions for communication (Gleave et al., 2009). Conversely, Laitinen and Sivunen (2020) suggested that employees construct their role on ESM by considering their personal privacy boundaries, the responsibilities attached to their professional roles, and the uncertainties surrounding the exact nature of their online audience. On ESM professional role expectations are important in defining what is accepted and what is expected from other users and their communication. Hence, role expectations may enable and constrain the information that is shared on ESM.

Role theory was initially developed to explain the predictability of human behavior in relation to particular scripts and parts individuals played. In other words, a role makes the behavior of the role occupant predictable. A role is constituted by a set of behavioral expectations. However, roles are also constructed through interactions, and different perspectives on the same roles may co-exist. That makes it important to study the (different) roles and expectations that may shape ESM use and user experiences.

In the context of role-related boundaries, individuals are found to expressly share their role preferences and confront those who violate expectations (Walden, 2019). Expectancy denotes an enduring pattern of anticipated (communication) behavior (Burgoon, 1993). Building on Expectancy Violation Theory (Burgoon & Jones, 1976), communication expectancies are based on several factors, such as the salient features of the communicator (e.g., communication style), the relationship between communicators (e.g., status) and the context of communication (e.g., privacy, formality). Together these factors dictate the expectancies one can have of a given encounter. These expectancies in turn serve as framing devices in interpersonal interactions people use to plan and adapt their communication and anticipate the communication of other actors. Violations of expectations represent a positively or negatively valanced deviation from expected behavior (Burgoon & Walther, 1990), which may impact interaction patterns and outcomes. This may affect communication efficiency and lead to arousal and distractions among users (Piercy & Underhill, 2021).

In the present case study, we review the communicative role expectations of different user groups and focus on the ways in which these role expectations affect user experience.

Methods

Study Design

Semi-structured interviews were carried out with 23 employees of a large European airline company about their use and experiences with ESM. Both authors conducted the interviews, either face to face at the crew center or at one of the office buildings, or through video conferencing. All interviews were carried out between May and October 2019 and were recorded and transcribed. The participants received no compensation for their participation. Participants were asked about the role they played at work, the frequency with which they used Yammer, the role they played on Yammer, and their experiences on the ESM platform. We engaged in purposive sampling to select participants in different roles. Of the participants, 11 worked as Cabin Crew (4 flight attendants, 4 pursers, and 3 senior pursers), 7 were part of the management, 1 worked for the labor union, 2 participants worked as staff trainers, 2 were community managers, and 1 participant worked in HR. Please note that this does not add up to the total of 23 because the airline company works with ancillary positions that combine a cabin crew role with some support role (e.g., community manager or trainer).

Case Summary

The study was carried out in the Inflight division. The Inflight division is responsible for all inflight services, which includes the staffing of flights, as well as the logistics that are necessary for flights, ranging from inflight hardware (e.g., tableware, comfort items and trolleys), catering, groceries, and beverages, and for hotel accommodation for crew, duty travelers and stranded passengers. The Inflight division faces many communication challenges, ranging from keeping cabin crew informed about the latest changes to the safety and service procedures, to bridging the socio-spatial boundaries between cabin crew and the support staff "under the wings." Often, the workforce is globally dispersed, and cabin crew spends very little time at the airline's home base. Their access to the Internet is often unreliable or unavailable (e.g., during the flights), hindering synchronous communication.

The case company implemented Yammer (a large Microsoft-based ESM platform), to support the inflight crew and bridge the gap between the personnel "under the wings" and those "flying." All employees of the Inflight division have access to an Inflight Yammer group, where they can post messages and respond to threats. This includes cabin crew (i.e., flight attendants, pursers and senior pursers), as well as line managers and community managers. All the cabin crew members are equipped with tablets that they are expected to bring at all times, during the flights. Cabin crew is expected to use Yammer while off work. Support staff "under the wings," such as logistic managers, catering managers, and schedulers, attain access to the Yammer group when they are tagged by moderators. A team of community managers moderates the Yammer community. They are available daily from 8 a.m. to 10 p.m. Community managers usually hold ancillary positions, combining their work as cabin crew with community management.

Findings

On the basis of qualitative data, we will report (1) which roles employees play on Yammer, (2) which expectations users hold of each other, and (3) how users experience the enactment of these roles and violations of role expectations.

We will first outline the generic behavioral expectations that users hold of each other and expectations of the platform itself. Then, we will elaborate on more specific expectations that employees hold of the moderator role, the expert role, and the managerial role on Yammer.

Generic Behavioral Expectations

Employees Are Expected to Be Up-to-Date

The aviation industry is a very dynamic one where work procedures are standardized to a large extent, but procedures are also constantly updated. Therefore, to deliver a consistently high level of service it is vital that employees, particularly cabin crew, make sure to "have all the right information" (Participant 4, moderator). Remaining up-to-date can be challenging, considering the amount of information that is available in the organization, the complexity of the service, and the low frequency with which some employees fly. When employees face conflicting information, they have a need for some authority that can settle the conflict. In such cases, they may turn to Yammer and either post a new question or use the search-functionality to check whether somebody else posted that question before. Since some users consider Yammer an "official" corporate channel, they treat the answers given by moderators and experts as the "correct" information, that can overrule information from other channels.

> On Facebook, you can ask a colleague a question and then .... You ask one question and receive six different answers. Which is the right answer? Ask it on Yammer, and you know which answer [company name] finds the correct answer. That is the power of Yammer.
>
> *Participant 4*

However, not all users share this expectation, because the use of Yammer is generally considered voluntary and nonessential for your performance, as participant 17 explained: "For us, Yammer is 'nice-to-know.' So what you read or post there is not required information. You don't have to treat it as the truth" (Participant 17, cabin crew).

Direct Communication

Secondly, participants expect ESM to enhance their social connectivity within the organization, because it enables them to quickly form associations with people in the organization that would be hard to establish otherwise (Treem & Leonardi, 2013).

> The principle of Yammer is to establish direct lines between [name organization] and the concerning departments that are supposed to do something about it. Let's imagine that there is a shortage of sugar sachets on board. Well, you post that on Yammer: There are not enough sugar sachets. Ok, we will go straight to catering services: There are too few sugar sachets. Then, that will be solved quickly.
>
> *Participant 22, cabin crew*

These direct associations on ESM are expected and appreciated, not because they improve the social lubricant in the organization, but because they support collaborative problem solving with little effort (Li et al., 2020).

In addition, through short lines of contact on Yammer, some more senior employees expect decision-making in the organization to become more democratic. These users aim to exercise power by establishing strategic relations, by engaging in direct open dialogues with management, and by mobilizing others to exert pressure on decision-makers.

This does not only concern policymaking but also advances regular business processes. For instance, because of a malfunctioning chair in business class, a senior purser tried to arrange a refund for a traveler. After this traveler notified the purser that no refund had been received yet, he decided to post it on Yammer.

> So, you can also use it [Yammer] to speed up processes within the company or put pressure on it. That works really nicely, I think .... So, you get a larger basis for addressing things. At the same time, it is not one-way communication anymore. You receive feedback, you get a response from unexpected directions that can be very useful for you.
>
> *Participant 1, cabin crew*

However, even when users in such instances receive online support for their cause, this often does not result in the desired change. While ESM are often praised for their ability to disrupt organizations and stimulate change (Archer-Brown & Kietzmann, 2018), participants were usually disappointed with the results of their change efforts and, when asked, could hardly mention examples of changes that were initiated on Yammer. Participant 1 explained that, when trying to push for change, "you hope to influence processes, and, in practice, you get disappointed" (Participant 1).

Communication Style and Respect

Yammer is understood as an "official" corporate channel, which means that users expect other users to treat each other respectfully and refrain from using emotional language: "This is a professional forum where we help each other by posing questions. ... leave out the emotions!" (Participant 21, cabin crew). Users expect each other to "take out the emotion and describe the message in a factual way" (Participant 2, cabin crew). Even though self-censorship is to some extent the norm on Yammer, senior staff generally feel less restrained in their communication, as participant one explains: "Ever since I am senior purser, which is the highest rank on board, I feel less restrained to react. I can imagine that you won't post everything, when you have one or two stripes (red: on you uniform)."

Specific Role Expectations

Besides the above-mentioned more generic role expectations, three more specific roles emerged on the platform: that of the moderator, manager, and expert. For these groups, participants held more specific behavioral expectations.

Moderator Role

In general, participants were very satisfied with the role that moderators play on Yammer: "I think they do that very well" (Participant 15, cabin crew). Some users even form positive parasocial relations with the moderator. Participant 18 (cabin crew) developed "a bit of a soft spot for these two [moderators]."

Moderators are first supposed to serve a liaison role: they are expected to send questions directly to the concerning departments" (Participant 22). In addition, moderators are expected to "keep an eye on the platform" (Participant 4), to monitor the compliance to written and unwritten rules. In particular, when users express rude language, engage in personal attacks, or when conversations get heated up, moderators are expected to terminate conversations, remove messages, and confront users. By doing so, they ascertain that the online space remains a safe, pleasant place to express oneself. When moderators are perceived to violate this expectation, users feel unsafe and may decide to leave the platform.

> I placed a critical remark and then I was treated ridiculously, and in a personal way, totally unprofessional. Then, I would have expected the moderator to say: hey, listen, what you say to [Name], that is not the point. I cannot even recall, but it was very unpleasant, I thought "Hey guys, forget it!"
>
> *Participant 22*

In addition, moderators are expected to track the progress of the query and make sure that experts follow up on their responsibilities. When talking about the moderator role, one flight attendant mentioned: "What I find important, is that when something is posted, that it also comes back to somebody. That there is feedback" (Participant 11, cabin crew).

While moderators are certainly perceived to serve this role, some participants have expressed concerns. In particular, some participants think that moderators "... are not impartial. That is understandable, to some extent, because they are in a [company name] position. So, they will allow some speakers more freedom than others. That can be frustrating" (Participant 1).

Managerial Role

There are diverging expectations and perceptions of the managerial role of Yammer. First of all, some managers consider Yammer a place "for the crew amongst themselves" (Participant 6, manager), where managers are not expected to play an active role at all.

Rather, this manager played a passive role to "see what is going on, to see what the themes are, to taste the atmosphere, and to check whether there are things that I can or should address" (Respondent 6).

However, more senior employees expected management to be available, open, and transparent on ESM and invite others to the democratic process. Some participants got disappointed with managers' involvement on Yammer, when they believe that the management "uses it [Yammer] to influence our group, but when you actually ask for answers, they don't respond … It reflects an improper use of Yammer" (Participant 1). Some cabin crew members got discouraged from posting their constructive feedback, because they perceived the management as very strategic in the topics that they chose to address and ignore on Yammer.

Expert Role

Experts are generally expected to provide quick, complete, and unambiguous information that answers questions and solves problems. Experts on the other hand feel pressured because users (and sometimes moderators) hold unrealistically high expectations of them. These elevated expectations make it "awful to answer something on there [Yammer], because it was never good enough, never fast enough" (Participant 5, expert loyalty program). Experts find responding to questions challenging because "it always involves something that people are unhappy about" (Participant 13, HR expert).

Many experts are uncomfortable or even anxious to be active on Yammer, because "there is a lot of negativity; when there are policies or political issues, they play the man, not the ball. That bothered me in the beginning and kept me up at night" (Participant 5). Furthermore, they experience it as an unsafe social environment, in which "you have to be careful what you write, because when you use one wrong way, it goes like Bam, Bam, Bam!" (Participant 13).

Discussion

First, the data support the notion that role expectations help users collaborate and solve problems efficiently. Behavioral expectations form a script that disciplines users, prescribing how, in this case, cabin crew, moderators, experts, and managers are expected to contribute to collaborative problem-solving (Li et al., 2020). In particular, the platform enables cabin crew to connect with experts and managers directly and quickly, who, in turn, are expected to provide clarity and practical solutions.

Moderators facilitate this process by serving a liaison and policing role. As such, ESM helps employees to collaboratively solve everyday problems in complex and dispersed organizational contexts.

However, this study also reveals that providing employees with a digital platform by no means implies that they will share similar expectations regarding its use and the roles of other users. Clearly, rather than passively complying with existing scripts for ESM use, users continuously construct and calibrate scripts through improvisation and negotiation. Role-crafting is an ongoing process. Even though all users acknowledged that Yammer is first and foremost a platform for internal servicing, expectations diverged with respect to the role managers should play, or the speed with which experts should provide answers. These diverging expectations cause friction, which can lead to frustration, conflicts, and ultimately disengagement.

Finally, like many other organizations, this aviation company cultivated the notion that information on ESM is "*nice to know*" rather than "*need to know.*" Because of the non-essential nature of the platform, users may be more likely to allocate their resources (i.e., time and energy) to other communication channels and tasks that are considered more formal parts of their occupational roles and ignore socially constructed expectations related to ESM use. Since employees are free to decide whether they use the platform, users also presume more liberty to use, or not use, at their discretion, avoiding normative role expectations.

Implications for Practice

The case study presented here provides multiple concrete implications for practitioners and organizations using ESM to facilitate communication and collaboration between members. ESM can be powerful tools for internal organizational communication, but the value of these platforms depends on the extent to which and the ways in which members participate (Rode, 2016). Hence, a tenacious organizational challenge is to grow and maintain use, but more often, enthusiasm about ESM use swiftly drops soon after these platforms are implemented (Veeravalli & Vijayalakshmi, 2019). The findings provide further insight into the roles that several groups are expected to play on ESM. Diverging role expectations and usage patterns may generate frictions and frustrations that can lead employees to abandon the platform. The voluntary nature of ESM use as platforms that offer "nice-to-know" information rather than "need-to-know" information is oil to the fire, providing users even more leeway in defining their own user roles. We argue that it would behoove organizations and practitioners to pay attention to the mutual expectations that different user groups on ESM have. This starts with clearly articulating a value proposition for an ESM platform. Why is the ESM implemented? What needs does it address? How should different users contribute? How does the ESM relate or complement existing information and communication technologies? Once these questions are adequately answered, organizations and their members can articulate the different roles users play, within this shared framework. The findings illustrate how ESM behaviors are shaped by behavioral norms and expectations (cf. Barker, 1993). As different users hold divergent beliefs about these norms, and these norms may evolve over time because of positive and negative experiences, ongoing meta-communication (Madsen, 2017) is needed to align usage norms and prevent friction. Platform moderators can play a pivotal role in this discourse because they oversee ESM dialogues and often have some authority in the community. In case of friction, they can inventory users' beliefs about behavioral norms, and they can lay out some basic rules of engagement. For instance, if ESM are used as employee service channels, what service level agreements apply to different user groups such as managers and experts? If the platform serves multiple purposes (e.g., social engagement and employee service channel), are there designated channels or groups?

Hence, for organizations and practitioners to develop a thorough implementation strategy that covers why a platform is needed, by whom it should be used, in what specific ways. Our findings suggest that considering the complete digital work environment and employees (communicative) role expectation is crucial to the successful implementation of ESM.

Learning Outcomes

1) Describe users' expectations of an ESM platform in a large aviation company.
2) Describe users' mutual expectations regarding online behaviors in an ESM platform in a large aviation company.
3) Identify and analyze the frictions that emerge when users hold diverting expectations on ESM.

Discussion Questions

1) Can an ESM platform enhance engagement without enticing people to use the platform in the first place by facilitating everyday problem solving?

2) How can moderators manage communication on ESM in an objective and neutral way?
3) Does the nonessential status of ESM hamper the professionalization of communication on ESM?

Further Reading

Hacker, J. V., Bodendorf, F., & Lorenz, P. (2017). A framework to identify knowledge actor roles in enterprise social networks. *Journal of Knowledge Management, 21*(4), 817–838. https://doi.org/10.1108/JKM-10-2016-0443

References

Akar, E., Mardikyan, S., & Dalgic, T. (2019). User roles in online communities and their moderating effect on online community usage intention: An integrated approach. *International Journal of Human–Computer Interaction, 35*(6), 495–509. https://doi.org/10.1080/10447318.2018.1465325

Archer-Brown, C., & Kietzmann, J. (2018). Strategic knowledge management and enterprise social media. *Journal of Knowledge Management, 22*(6), 1288–1309. https://doi.org/10.1108/JKM-08-2017-0359

Barker, J. R. (1993). Tightening the iron cage: Concertive control in self-managing teams. *Administrative Science Quarterly, 38*(3) 408–437. https://doi.org/10.2307/2393374

Borman, W. C., & Motowidlo, S. J. (1997). Task performance and contextual performance: The meaning for personnel selection research. *Human Performance, 10*(2), 99–109. https://doi.org/10.1207/s15327043hup1002_3

Burgoon, J. K. (1993). Interpersonal expectations, expectancy violations, and emotional communication. *Journal of Language and Social Psychology, 12*(1–2), 30–48. https://doi.org/10.1177/0261927X93121003

Burgoon, J. K., & Jones, S. B. (1976). Toward a theory of personal space expectations and their violations. *Human Communication Research, 2*(2), 131–146. https://doi.org/10.1111/j.1468-2958.1976.tb00706.x

Burgoon, J. K., & Walther, J. B. (1990). Nonverbal expectancies and the evaluative consequences of violations. *Human Communication Research, 17*(2), 232–265. https://doi.org/10.1111/j.1468-2958.1990.tb00232.x

Chen, X., Wei, S., Davison, R. M., & Rice, R. E. (2019). How do enterprise social media affordances affect social network ties and job performance?. *Information Technology & People, 33*(1), 361–388. https://doi.org/10.1108/ITP-11-2017-0408

Gleave, E., Welser, H. T., Lento, T. M., & Smith, M. A. (2009, January). A conceptual and operational definition of "social role" in online community. In *2009 42nd Hawaii International Conference on System Sciences* (1–11). IEEE. https://doi.org/10.1109/HICSS.2009.6

Holtzblatt, L., Drury, J. L., Weiss, D., Damianos, L. E., & Cuomo, D. (2013). Evaluating the uses and benefits of an enterprise social media platform. *Journal of Social Media for Organizations, 1*(1), 1–21. http://www2.mitre.org/public/jsmo/pdfs/01-01-evaluating-uses.pdf

Järventie-Thesleff, R., & Tienari, J. (2016). Roles as mediators in identity work. *Organization Studies, 37*(2), 237–265. https://doi.org/10.1177/0170840615604500

Katz, D., & Kahn, R. L. (1978). *The social psychology of organizations* (Vol. 2, 528). New York: Wiley.

Laitinen, K., & Sivunen, A. (2020). Enablers of and constraints on employees' information sharing on enterprise social media. *Information Technology & People, 32*(2), 642–665. https://doi.org/10.1108/ITP-04-2019-0186

Leonardi, P. M. (2014). Social media, knowledge sharing, and innovation: Toward a theory of communication visibility. *Information Systems Research, 25*(4), 796–816. https://doi.org/10.1287/isre.2014.0536

Leonardi, P. M., Huysman, M., & Steinfield, C. (2013). Enterprise social media: Definition, history, and prospects for the study of social technologies in organizations. *Journal of Computer-Mediated Communication, 19*(1), 1–19. https://doi.org/10.1111/jcc4.12029

Li, K., Huang, L., & Song, Z. (2020). Understanding the emergence of collaborative problem-solving practices in enterprise social media: The roles of social factors. *IEEE Access, 8*, 210066–210080. https://doi.org/10.1109/ACCESS.2020.3039239

Madsen, V. T. (2017). The challenges of introducing internal social media—the coordinators' roles and perceptions. *Journal of Communication Management, 21*(1), 2–16. https://doi.org/10.1108/JCOM-04-2016-0027

Mead, G. H. (1934). *Mind, self and society* (Vol. 111). Chicago: University of Chicago Press.

Meske, C., Kissmer, T., & Stieglitz, S. (2020). Bridging formal barriers in digital work environments—investigating technology-enabled interactions across organizational hierarchies. *Telematics and Informatics, 48*, Article 101342. https://doi.org/10.1016/j.tele.2020.101342

Pekkala, K. (2020). Managing the communicative organization: A qualitative analysis of knowledge-intensive companies. *Corporate Communications: An International Journal, 25*(3), 551–571. https://doi.org/10.1108/CCIJ-02-2020-0040

Piercy, C. W., & Underhill, G. R. (2021). Expectations of technology use during meetings: An experimental test of manager policy, device use, and task-acknowledgment. *Mobile Media & Communication, 9*(1), 78–102. https://doi.org/10.1177/2050157920927049

Rode, H. (2016). To share or not to share: The effects of extrinsic and intrinsic motivations on knowledge-sharing in enterprise social media platforms. *Journal of Information Technology, 31*(2), 152–165. https://doi.org/10.1057/jit.2016.8

Treem, J. W., & Leonardi, P. M. (2013). Social media use in organizations: Exploring the affordances of visibility, editability, persistence, and association. *Annals of the International Communication Association, 36*(1), 143–189. https://doi.org/10.1080/23808985.2013.11679130

van Zoonen, W., & Sivunen, A. (2020). Knowledge brokering in an era of communication visibility. *International Journal of Business Communication, 60*(1), 313–330. https://doi.org/10.1177/2329488420937348

Veeravalli, S. & Vijayalakshmi, V. (2019). A morphological review of enterprise social media literature. *Journal of Organizational Computing and Electronic Commerce, 29*(2), 139–162. https://doi.org/10.1080/10919392.2019.1583456

Walden, J. (2019). Communicating role expectations in a coworking office. *Journal of Communication Management, 23*(4), 316–330. https://doi.org/10.1108/JCOM-09-2018-0097

Chapter Thirteen

Management of Cybersecurity through Internal Communication

Solyee Kim and Jeonghyun Janice Lee

Introduction

In the age of digital communication, organizations have experienced growing threats to cybersecurity, such as data theft, manipulation, and fraud. With the COVID-19 pandemic, organizations expect to face more challenges related to cybersecurity due to more transitions to working from home (Parker et al., 2020). For instance, working from home poses various threats due to unsecured home networks, different technologies, personal devices, unauthorized access, and irresponsible behaviors (Ramadan et al., 2021). To preserve confidentiality, integrity, and availability of organizations' information systems, employees' information security awareness is as important as technological countermeasures against cyberattacks (Khando et al., 2021). However, research (Callanan et al., 2016; Khando et al., 2021) indicates that many employees are not aware of the Personal Data Protection laws including EU's General Data Protection Regulation (GDPR), Fair Information Practices (FIPs), and Personal Data Protection Act (PDPA), which protects various stakeholders' data privacy and rights.

Despite the growing importance of employees' policy awareness and compliance regarding cybersecurity, the topic needs more attention in the field of communication literature. Internal communication plays a pivotal role in driving employee engagement with organizational initiatives (Mishra et al., 2014). To better understand perceptions on cybersecurity among communications professionals, this chapter provides findings from a survey conducted among 1,046 communication professionals in the United States and Canada, as part of the Plank Center's North American Communications Monitor (NACM) 2020–2021. Moreover, the chapter shares various insights applicable for organizations' internal communication to better manage emerging threats to cybersecurity through employee engagement.

Internal communication presents a number of opportunities to prevent and mitigate crises related to cyberattacks and data thefts. In this chapter, we provide definitions and fundamental understandings of cybersecurity, cyberattacks, and cybersecurity management in the context of communication. First, we define cybersecurity as a set of

DOI: 10.4324/9781003195580-19

guidelines, technologies, and training that provide protection of an organization's data and of its computer and digital communication infrastructure (Schatz et al., 2017). Based on this definition, we provide experiences and perceptions of cybersecurity among communication professionals in North America. Next, we provide more understandings of cyberattacks, which are defined as deliberate attempts by unauthorized entities to access systems of Information and Communication Technology (Fisher, 2016), and their impacts on communication management. We also discuss communication professionals' experiences and perceptions around such cyberattacks. Lastly, we apply three phases of crisis management (Coombs & Holladay, 2010) to identify challenges and opportunities related to cybersecurity management and communications.

Literature Review

Whereas internal communications can effectively engage employees in fostering cybersecurity culture (Baskin, 2019), there is a growing need for more research on cybersecurity and cyberattacks in the communication field (DiStaso, 2018). Because cybersecurity and cyberattacks are concerns beyond IT or legal departments affecting the entire organization (DiStaso, 2018), identifying and addressing communication challenges and opportunities are critical.

Role of Internal Communication in Cybersecurity Management

Cybersecurity has grown rapidly, both as an industry and as an organizational function, because cyberattacks, data theft, manipulation, and fraud have become a large driver of organizational and corporate risk (Tatar et al., 2021). This makes cybersecurity a highly relevant issue in all fields, including communications.

Defined as a set of guidelines, technologies, and training that provide protection of an organization's data and of its computer and digital communication infrastructure (Schatz et al., 2017), cybersecurity is increasingly considered as a critical part of organizational culture (Stackpole, 2022). Research indicates that building cybersecurity culture is fundamental to raise awareness and change attitudes and behaviors among employees (Alshaikh, 2020). Highlighting the role of internal communication, Da Veiga and colleagues (2020) define cybersecurity culture as:

> contextualized to the behavior of humans in an organizational context to protect information processed by the organization through compliance with the

> information security policy and an understanding of how to implement requirements in a cautious and attentive manner as embedded through regular communication, awareness, training and education initiatives.
>
> *(p. 19)*

However, because attitudinal and behavioral changes take time, management should understand employees' knowledge, assumptions, values, and beliefs regarding the organization's information assets and communicate and direct cybersecurity policies and practices with a clear vision. As employees' cybersecurity behaviors can negatively or positively impact trust of other stakeholders as well, organizations need proactive employee engagement in cybersecurity issues.

Cyberattacks on Communication Department or Agency

Although cyberattacks are not new, prevalence and sophistication of cyberattacks make every organization at risk (DiStaso, 2018). Cyberattacks refer to deliberate attempts by unauthorized entities to access systems of Information and Communication Technology, including theft, disruption, and damage (Fisher, 2016). Experts (DiStaso, 2018; Fisher, 2016; Weldon, 2016) warned that the frequency and severity of cyberattacks will increase.

Fisher (2016) identified four different impacts of cyberattacks that have high significance for communication management. First, cybertheft can exfiltrate critical organizational and personal data including information pertinent to finance and proprietary rights. Second, denial-of-service can cause delays or block legitimate stakeholders from using the system. Third, botnet malware can activate a system to attack other systems. Fourth, attacks on industrial systems can seriously destroy or disrupt the supply system of an organization. Given that communication departments and agencies heavily rely on digital data and infrastructure in many ways, assessing perceptions of likelihood of various cyberattack incidents is critical.

Cybersecurity Management and Communications

In recent years, cybersecurity has become one of the primary concerns for businesses and organizations. With growing interest in cybersecurity, the media has given increased attention to cybersecurity. Consequently, the media has influenced and reflected the public's interest in the phenomenon as well (DiStaso, 2018).

For successful cybersecurity management, effective communication is paramount (Wang & Park, 2017). During three phases of pre-crisis, crisis response, and post-crisis (Coombs & Holladay, 2010), cybersecurity management requires cyber crisis communication strategies and tactics. For instance, in the pre-crisis phase, communication professionals are responsible to prepare and prevent cyber crises in multiple ways including developing communication plans and internal guidelines and providing education and training on cybersecurity. Responding to cyber crisis incidents, communication professionals are required to orchestrate internal and external stakeholder communication in a timely manner. In the post-crisis phase, communication professionals extend their crisis response strategies and enhance organizational learning (Coombs & Holladay, 2010). Considering various responsibilities throughout different phases, understanding the level of communication professionals' engagement with varying crisis communication activities for their department/agency and organization/client offers a meaningful assessment of the role of communication in cybersecurity management.

Communication professionals actively engage in protecting their organizations by handling problems as well as changing structure when crises such as cyberattacks or data theft occur. Primarily, there are five strategies which they can prepare for fighting cyber criminality (Schatz et al., 2017): (1) managing crisis communication (internal/external) in case of cyberattacks, (2) addressing cybersecurity in internal communications, (3) educating employees in cybersecurity, (4) developing cybersecurity guidelines, and (5) implementing cybersecurity technologies.

Given the increasing needs to better understand cybersecurity issues in workplaces and the role of communication professionals in cybersecurity management, the research questions are as follows:

RQ1: What is the role of internal communication in cybersecurity management?

RQ2: What are the strategies that the communication professionals use in response to cyberattacks?

Methods

To answer the research questions, we examined the responses from the Plank Center's North American Communication Monitor 2020–2021 survey among 1,046 communication professionals. The Plank Center for Leadership in Public Relations conducts biannual surveys to provide contemporary understandings of communication management practice in North America. In its 2020–2021 project, communication professionals reported their personal and organizational experiences related to cyberattacks or data threat; internal information management to enhance cyber security; and perceptions of likelihood of attacks from cybercriminals. The survey includes complete responses from 1,046 communication professionals practicing in varying areas of communications in the United States and Canada.

Participants

In the survey, 778 communication professionals in the United States and 268 in Canada provided their responses. The average age of the professionals was 41.2 years ($SD = 11.3$). Of the participants, 545 identified as women (52.1%) and 499 as men (47.7%). In terms of racial and ethnic identities, nearly three in four ($n = 753$, 72.0%) identify as White/Caucasians, 9.1% Black/African Americans ($n = 95$), 8.9% Asian/Asian Americans ($n = 94$), 5.4% Hispanics ($n = 57$), and 4.6% other racial and ethnic minorities ($n = 47$).

A vast majority of the survey participants worked as in-house communication professionals in communication departments in different types of organizations: private companies ($n = 427$, 40.8%); public organizations ($n = 234$, 22.4%); governmental organizations ($n = 136$, 13.0%); and nonprofit organizations ($n = 83$, 7.9%) whereas 15.9% worked at agencies or as independent consultants ($n = 166$). The sample ($n = 447$) includes 42.7% with more than 10 years of professional experience in communication management and public relations, followed by 32.5% ($n = 340$) with 6–10 years of experience.

As for positions, 30.9% ($n = 323$) held leadership positions such as head of communication or CEO of an agency and 47.2% ($n = 494$) were unit or team leaders in an agency or an organization. These demographic and professional backgrounds indicate that the responses were largely based on experienced communication professionals.

Results

Overall, the survey indicated that cyberattacks or incidents of data theft are common among organizations; more than half of the respondents (50.9%, $n = 531$) had experienced cyberattacks or incidents of data theft in their organization. Specifically, the data showed that 18.5% of respondents ($n = 193$) experienced cyberattacks multiple times. Furthermore, the survey revealed that communication professionals in the United States and Canada were aware of the relevance of cybersecurity issues to their daily work in communications. Of the respondents, 62.3% (n = 651) said cybersecurity was relevant for the daily work of their communication department. The communication professionals' perception of relevance of cybersecurity to their daily work was higher in the following types of organizations: 67.1% of communication professionals in public companies (n = 701), 63.8% of those who work in consultancies and agencies (n = 665), and 62.3% of those in private companies (n = 651).

However, some discrepancies were found in terms of perceptions of the relevance of cybersecurity to their work depending on positions. Heads of communication/CEOs (n= 323, 30.9%) were more likely to perceive cybersecurity more relevant to their daily work compared to unit or team leaders (n = 494, 47.2%), and team members (n = 229, 21.9%) in an agency or an organization. On the 5-point Likert scale (1 = *not at all*; 5 = *to a great extent*), the heads of communication/CEOs rated 3.92 (SD = 1.06) on average whereas the mean of team leaders' rating was 3.65 (SD=1.13) and team members' rating was 3.58 (SD=1.16), respectively. However, there was no statistically significant difference between team leader and member groups (Figure 13.1).

When it comes to giving attention to the debate about cybersecurity (Figure 13.1), the average score of all responses was 3.53 (SD = 1.16), which is slightly lower than the relevance score (M=3.72, SD=1.12). While overall average score revealed that all respondents had given some attention to the cyber security discourse, respondents' rates varied

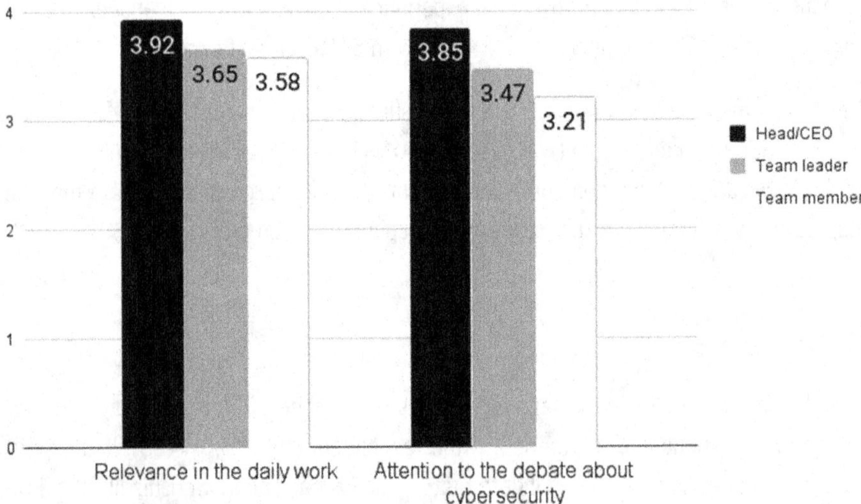

FIGURE 13.1 Perceived relevance of cybersecurity by positions: Head/CEO, Team leaders, and Team members. *Source*: NACM Report 2020–2021.

depending on their positions. Heads of communication/CEOs showed the highest level of attention ($M = 3.85$, $SD = 1.13$), followed by team leaders ($M = 3.47$, $SD = 1.12$) and team members ($M = 3.21$, $SD = 1.16$). This result indicated that respondents in higher positions showed more attention to cybersecurity issues.

Moreover, based on Fisher's four impacts, communication professionals were asked how likely they were to experience the cybercrimes such as stealing data about their stakeholders, closing down the digital infrastructure, hacking their website or social media accounts, and leaking sensitive information, such as communication strategies, budgets, and evaluations. Of the four different types of cybercrimes, communication professionals were more likely to identify hacking websites and/or social media accounts and leaking sensitive information of their organization as greater threats.

The communication professionals responded that their organization's website or social media accounts were more likely to be a target of cybercriminals ($n = 395$, 39.0%). Also, their organizations' sensitive information (e.g., communication strategies, budgets, evaluations, etc.) was often targeted by cybercriminals ($n = 378$, 37.5%).

When looking into responses by organization types (Figure 13.2), public companies appeared more concerned with criminal attacks on their sensitive information and digital infrastructure. Respondents from public companies indicated that cybercriminals tried to leak their sensitive information, which was only shared internally or in their department ($n = 111$, 49.8%) or to close down digital infrastructure, such as employees'

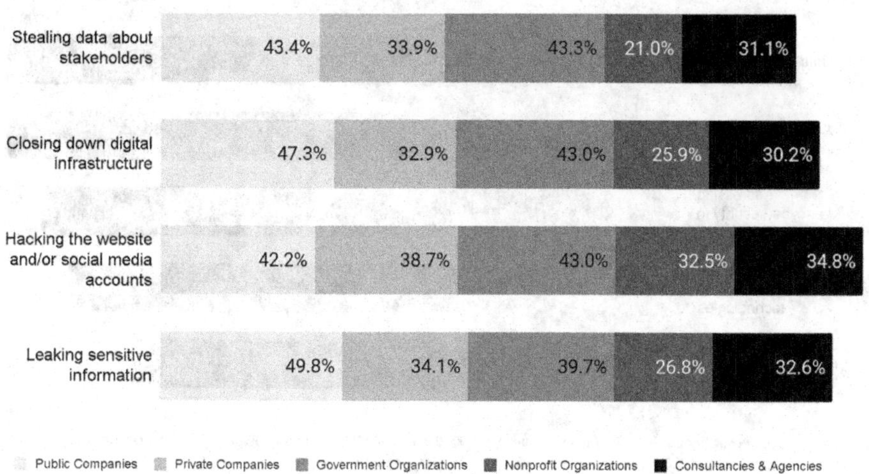

FIGURE 13.2 Percentage of cybercrime cases by organization types. *Source*: NACM Report 2020–2021.

computers and content management systems ($n=105$, 47.3%). Similarly, private companies revealed that they had previously experienced incidents of sensitive information leak ($n=140$, 34.1%). However, they were more likely to be attacked by crimes related to their organization's websites and/or social media accounts ($n=160$. 38.7%). On the other hand, government organizations were more concerned about data associated with their internal stakeholders ($n=58$, 43.4%).

In sum, communication professionals experienced various types of cybercrimes including data leaks and thefts although organizations were differently focusing on each incident. In general, respondents expressed their concerns about hacking incidents of their communication channels, including official websites and/or social media accounts. Since those platforms are at the forefront of their organization, it is plausible that those are more likely to be victims of cybercriminals. This indicates that cybersecurity management has become a highly relevant topic in employee engagement and organizational communication.

Communication professionals in the United States and Canada were also asked what strategies they were using to do cybersecurity communication management. Overall, organizations not only focused on handling problems by actively communicating internally and externally but also strove to prepare for cyberattacks. The result indicated that managing communication in case of cyberattacks and educating employees in cybersecurity are some of the primary strategies that communication professionals use (Figure 13.3).

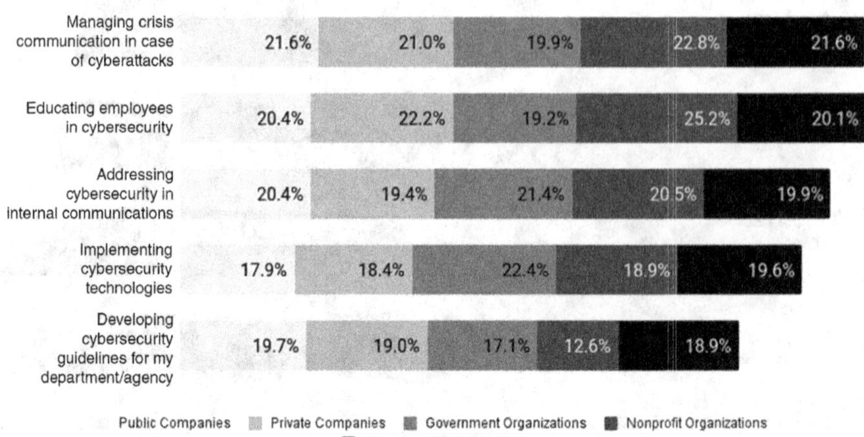

FIGURE 13.3 Percentage of cybersecurity management strategies for employee engagement implemented in organizations. *Source*: NACM Report 2020–2021.

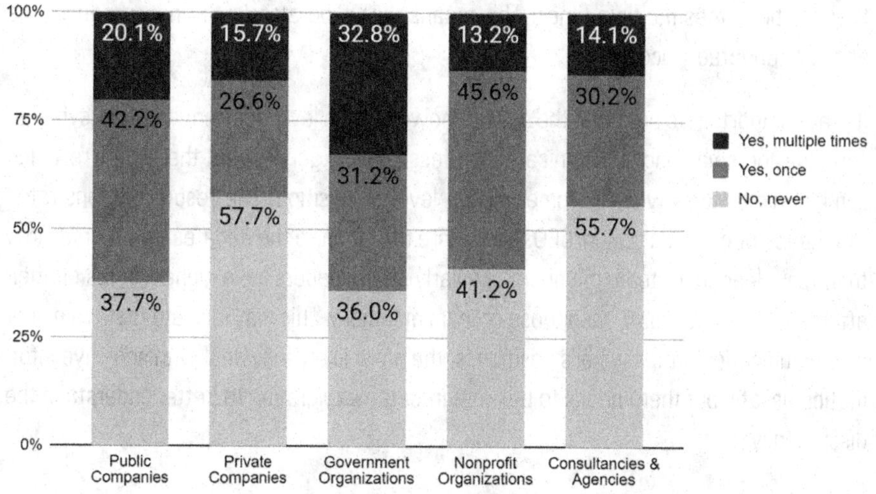

FIGURE 13.4 Percentage of experienced cyberattacks or incidents of data thefts by organization types. *Source*: NACM Report 2020–2021.

The result indicated that organizations used varying strategies to different extent depending on organization types (Figure 13.4). Whereas nonprofit organizations are more likely to focus on managing crisis communication and educating employees in cybersecurity, governmental organizations put their efforts on internal communication pertaining to cybersecurity and implementing cybersecurity technologies. This corresponds to the result of cybercrime attacking governmental organizations more frequently. More governmental organizations ($n = 41$, 32.8%) reported that they experienced cybercrimes multiple times, which is higher than other organizations (i.e., public companies ($n = 40$), 20.1%; private companies ($n = 63$), 15.7%, consultancies and agencies, 14.1% ($n = 21$), and nonprofit organizations ($n = 9$), 13.2%). Governmental organizations may consider that it is more important to be ready for protecting an organization's resources including data. This indicates that different types of organizations have varying experiences and strategies of cybersecurity management.

Discussion

Communication professionals in North America were aware of the urgency of cyberattacks and their relevance to their daily work. The 2020–2021 NACM revealed that more than half of them had experienced cyberattacks or data thefts. For example, 32.8% of the respondents working at government organizations reported that they had been a victim of cybercrimes multiple times. This means that cyberattacks are not rare incidents and can repeatedly occur.

It is also important to note that the survey showed a high level of attention to the cybersecurity discourse among communication professionals in general, but the results revealed some discrepancies when it comes to the level of position. The results demonstrated that heads of communication/CEOs paid more attention to the debates on cybersecurity than team leaders or team members. Similarly, team leaders gave higher scores on their attention to cybersecurity than those of team members. This may indicate that the higher a communication professional's position is, the more likely they deal with sensitive information assets, but there needs to be more in-depth exploration to better understand the discrepancy.

When it comes to specific incidents of cybercrimes, communication professionals indicated that some of the most commonly experienced incidents were hacking into their websites or social media accounts and data stealing. Because official websites and social media accounts of the organizations are often easily accessible to publics including organizations' stakeholders, the websites and social media accounts can be perceived to be more vulnerable to cyberattacks. Given the roles and responsibilities communication professionals have in an organization, it makes sense that the respondents shared that communication channels that they manage are vulnerable to cybersecurity incidents. However, it is important to note that those cybersecurity risks pose threats to all employees. Therefore, communication professionals should identify communication challenges and opportunities for enhanced cybersecurity management as well as crisis prevention and response.

With growing urgency and importance of cybersecurity, communication professionals have significant roles in protecting organizations' data, sensitive information, and resources using various strategies of cybersecurity management and internal communication. The survey revealed that internal communication plays a critical role in managing cybersecurity crises. Governmental organizations put substantial efforts to address the issue internally and implement cybersecurity technologies. Other types of organizations also use internal communication to educate employees in cyber security. Often, cybersecurity issues in communication focus on external communication, but the findings of the survey suggest the importance of internal communication and employee engagement on cybersecurity issues. The case summary in the following illustrates how an employee's mistake can lead to a serious data breach incident.

Case Summary

In July 2022, it was reported that the international hotel chain Marriott was hit by data breach, which resulted in 20GB of stolen data including customer payment information and confidential business documents (Faife, 2022; Page, 2022). This 20GB data breach occurred due to a mistake of an employee in Maryland who was tricked by hackers (Page, 2022).

Since 2014, the hotel chain had a number of data breach cases (Faife, 2022; Page, 2022). Various sources reported that Marriott's data breach incidents have resulted in various costly lawsuits including one of the largest class-action lawsuits (Garfinkle, 2022; Schaffer, 2022). This case demonstrates the importance of employees' day-to-day engagement in cybersecurity and organizations' long-term commitment to cybersecurity management.

Implications for Practice

The fast-paced advancement in technology and communication calls for a strong need to provide timely, updated, and engaging workshops and training to employees on cybersecurity. In this environment, employees' awareness and knowledge of cybersecurity are highly valued and the educators can help meet these organizational demands through incorporating data protection and privacy education into the curriculum. Through a secondary data analysis, we addressed highlights of the survey that can provide effective tools and examples communication educators and professionals can use to advance cybersecurity management through communication.

Scholars have discussed that employee relations and employee monitoring are some of the most important factors that influence employees' information security behavior (Yaokumah et al., 2019). Organizations have put increasing efforts to enhance employees' awareness and knowledge to mitigate cybersecurity threats including cyberattacks (Yaokumah et al., 2019). However, programs related to security education, training, and awareness have not turned out to be as successful as organizations hoped and human vulnerability has been deemed one of the primary factors of cyber vulnerabilities (Sharma & Bashir, 2020). Furthermore, some studies have also indicated that employees feel bored and experience cybersecurity fatigue (Reeves et al., 2021a; Reeves et al., 2021b).

To combat such aversion or wariness toward organizational cybersecurity efforts, Reeves and colleagues (2021b) identified four strategies to enhance employee engagement in cybersecurity programs. First, customization of content, style (e.g., humorous, dramatic), and delivery (e.g., in-person, online, hybrid) of the cybersecurity education, training, and awareness programs depending on employees' demographics can increase employee engagement. Second, it is critical to highlight cybersecurity as a part of management and organizational culture. Because employees' attitudes and behaviors are influenced by their colleagues and management, cultivating the perception of cybersecurity as a cultural norm can help drive employee engagement. Third, organizations should regularly evaluate their organization's structure, systems, and industry trends related to cybersecurity. Because of the fast-paced advancement of technology, organizations' cybersecurity systems should stay up to date, so they are not lagging behind. Finally, organizations should be aware of preconceptions, experiences, and understandings of the cyber threats shared among employees. Because of personal convenience and habits, employees' behaviors and decision-making can deviate from organizations' policies and best practice recommendations. In implementing these strategies to enhance employees' engagement, communication can collaborate with human resources and information and technology departments in providing cyber education and cybersecurity plans (DiStaso, 2018).

As digital communication has become prevalent in communication practice, communication professionals use a great deal of user information gathered on the Internet and social media platforms (Meng et al., 2022; White & Boatwright, 2020). In communications education, cybersecurity, including data and privacy issues, has been scantly discussed despite its growing importance and prevalence in communications industries and professions. Given that cybersecurity issues not only pose critical ethics questions for communication professionals (Meng et al., 2022; Ward et al., 2020) but also can be applied to crisis and risk communication and management (DiStaso, 2018), educators can introduce and present cybersecurity cases in varying communication topics.

Learning Outcomes

1) To capture contemporary perceptions of communication professionals in the United States and Canada on cybersecurity and cyberattacks in relevance to the field of communication.
2) To understand the role of employee engagement in organizational cybersecurity management.
3) To raise awareness of various trainings and certificate programs on cybersecurity:
   a) **General Data Protection Regulation** (GDPR; https://gdpr.eu/): GDPR is a set of rules from the European Union (EU) to put more control over customers'

information by harmonizing data privacy laws across Europe. Although this is created by the EU, it affects organizations not only located within the EU but also outside of the region if they monitor the behavior of EU data subjects. Therefore, it applies to all companies processing and holding the personal data regardless of the company's location. It directly affects any communication professionals who deal with data. Under GDPR, There will be limits on the amount of data because an organization can only gather necessary data for the purpose. The purpose and the use of customer's data should be stated clearly in a consent form before data gathering. Since information providers (i.e., customers) have a right to be forgotten, they can withdraw the use of personal data at any time. Also, organizations should prepare a data protection plan for customers. If those are violated, penalties could lead to fines as high as $24.6 million or 4% of global annual revenue, whichever is larger.

b) **International Association of Privacy Professionals** (IAPP; https://iapp.org/): IAPP, a nonprofit organization, provides various resources for privacy management. The resources include best practices, training, and latest trends in privacy management. IAPP offers three certification programs: (1) Certified Information Privacy Professional (CIPP), (2) Certified Information Privacy Manager (CIPM), and (3) Certified Information Privacy Technologist (CIPT).

Discussion Questions

1) Studies suggest that employees' demographics such as age, working industry, and education level, have substantial effects on the awareness and compliance of information security policies. Based on this understanding, please choose an organization and discuss what are some of the considerations for the organization to make to customize training programs on cybersecurity.
2) Due to the COVID-19 pandemic, there is a growing number of employees working from home. What do you think makes it challenging to engage remote employees in cybersecurity? What role does internal communication play to manage the challenges?
3) What are the specific activities communication professionals can prepare for cybersecurity in each stage of crisis or risk communications: pre-crisis, during crisis, and post-crisis?
4) Given the case of the frequent data breach at the hotel chain Marriott as discussed in the case summary, what are some of the ways to increase employee engagement in cybersecurity management?

Further Readings

Coombs, W. T. (2007). Protecting organization reputations during a crisis: The development and application of situational crisis communication theory. *Corporate Reputation Review, 10*(3), 163–176. https://doi.org/10.1057/palgrave.crr.1550049.

Meng, J., Reber, B. H., Berger, B. K., Gower, K. K., & Zerfass, A. (2021). *North American Communication Monitor 2020–2021. The impact of COVID-19 pandemic, ethical challenges, gender issues, cybersecurity, and competence gaps in strategic communication.* Tuscaloosa, AL: The Plank Center for Leadership in Public Relations. ISBN (electronic): 978-0-578-90837-3.

Wolford, B. (n.d.) What is GDPR, the EU's new data protection law? GDPR.EU. Retrieved from: https://gdpr.eu/what-is-gdpr/#:~:text=The%20General%20Data%20Protection%20Regulation,to%20people%20in%20the%20EU.

References

Alshaikh, M. (2020). Developing cybersecurity culture to influence employer behavior: A practice perspective. *Computers & Security, 98.* https://doi.org/10.1016/j.cose.2020.102003.

Baskin, E. (October 9, 2019). Using internal communications to engage employees in cybersecurity, *Forbes*, Retrieved from https://www.forbes.com/sites/forbesagencycouncil/2019/10/09/using-internal-communications-to-engage-employees-in-cybersecurity/?sh=2a69581454f4

Callanan, C., Jerman-Blažič, B., & Blažič, A. J. (2016). User awareness and tolerance of privacy abuse on mobile internet: An exploratory study. *Telematics and Informatics, 33*, 109–128, http://dx.doi.org/10/1016/j.tele.2015.04.009.

Coombs, T., & Holladay, S. J. (2010). Parameters of crisis management. In T. Coombs & S. J. Holladay (Eds.), *The handbook of crisis communication* (pp. 17–53). Hoboken, NJ: Wiley-Blackwell.

Da Veiga, A., Astakhova, L. V., Botha, A., & Herselman, M. (2020). Defining organizational information security culture—Perspectives from academia and industry. *Computer & Security, 92*, Article 101713, https://doi.org/10.1016/j.cose.2020.101713

DiStaso, M. (2018). Communication challenges in cybersecurity. *Journal of Communication Technology, 1*(1), 43–60. https://joctec.org/articles/1-1/114.pdf.

Faife, C. (July 6, 2022). The Marriott hotel has been hit by another data breach. *The Verge.* Retrieved from: https://www.theverge.com/2022/7/6/23196805/marriott-hotels-maryland-data-breach-credit-cards.

Fisher, E. A. (2016). *Cybersecurity issues and challenges: In brief.* Washington D.C.: Library of Congress. Congressional Research Service. https://sgp.fas.org/crs/misc/R43831.pdf.

Garfinkle, M. (July 7, 2022). Marriott just got hit by another data breach—for at least the 7th time since 2010. *Entrepreneur.* Retrieved from: https://www.entrepreneur.com/article/430988.

Khando, K., Gao, S., Islam, S. M., & Salman, A. (2021). Enhancing employee's information security awareness in private and public organizations: A systematic literature review. *Computer & Security, 106*, 1–22. https://doi.org/10.1016/j.cose.2021.102267.

Meng, J., Kim, S., & Reber, B. (2022). Ethical challenges in an evolving digital communication era: coping resources and ethics trainings in corporate communications. *Corporate Communications: An International Journal*, ahead-of-print. https://doi.org/10.1108/CCIJ-11-2021-0128.

Mishra, K., Boynton, L., & Mishra, A. (2014). Driving employee engagement: The expanded role of internal communications, *International Journal of Business Communication, 51*(2), 183–202. https://doi.org/10.1177/2329488414525399.

Page, C. (July 6, 2022). Hotel giant Marriott confirms yet another data breach. *TechCrunch*. Retrieved from: https://techcrunch.com/2022/07/06/marriott-breach-again/.

Parker, K., Horowitz, J. M., & Minkin, R. (2020). How the coronavirus outbreak has—and hasn't—changed the way Americans work. *Pew Research Center*. Retrieved from: https://www.pewresearch.org/social-trends/2020/12/09/how-the-coronavirus-outbreak-has-and-hasnt-changed-the-way-americans-work/.

Ramadan, R. A., Aboshosha, B. W., Alshudukhi, J. S., Alzahrani, A. J., El-Sayed, A., Dessouky, M. M. (2021). Cybersecurity and countermeasures at the time of pandemic. *Journal of Advanced Transportation, 2021*, 1–19. https://doi.org/10.1155/2021/6627264.

Reeves, A., Delfabbro, P., & Calic, D. (2021a). Encouraging employee engagement with cybersecurity: How to tackle cyber fatigue. *SAGE Open, January-March*, 1–18. https://doi.org/10.1177/21582440211000049.

Reeves, A., Calic, D., Delfabbro, P. (2021b). "Get a red-hot poker and open up my eyes, it's so boring": Employee perceptions of cybersecurity training. *Computers & Security, 106*, 1–13. https://doi.org/10.1016/j.cose.2021.102281

Schaffer, A. (May 27, 2022). The Marriott lawsuit explores the conundrum of how to value stolen data. *The Washington Post*. Retrieved from: https://www.washingtonpost.com/politics/2022/05/27/marriott-lawsuit-explores-conundrum-how-value-stolen-data/

Schatz, D., Bashroush, R., & Wall, J. (2017). Towards a more representative definition of cyber security. *Journal of Digital Forensics, Security and Law, 12*(2), 53–74. https://doi.org/10.15394/jdfsl.2017.1476

Sharma, T. & Bashir, M. (2020). An analysis of phishing emails and how the human vulnerabilities are exploited. I. Corradini, E. Nardelli, T. Ahram (Eds), *Advances in Human Factors in Cybersecurity: AHFE 2020 Virtual Conference on Human Factors in Cybersecurity*, July 16–20, 2020, USA (pp. 49–55). Cham, Switzerland: Springer. https://doi.org/10.1007/978-3-030-52581-1_7

Stackpole, B. (2022). How to build a culture of cybersecurity. *MIT Management*. Retrieved from: https://mitsloan.mit.edu/ideas-made-to-matter/how-to-build-a-culture-cybersecurity.

Tatar, U., Nussbaum, B., Gokce, Y., & Keskin, O. F. (2021). Digital force majeure: The Mondelez case, insurance, and the (un) certainty of attribution in cyberattacks. *Business Horizons, 64*(6), 775–785.

Wang, P. & Park, S.-A. (2017). Communication in cybersecurity: A public communication model for business data breach incident handling. *Issues in Information Systems, 18*(2), 136–147. https://doi.org/10.48009/2_iis_2017_136-147.

Ward, J., Luttrell, R., & Wallace, A. (2020). PR ethics literacy: Identifying moral and ethical values through purposeful ethical education. *Journal of Public Relations, 6*(3), 66–80. https://aejmc.us/jpre/wp-content/uploads/sites/25/2020/12/WARD-ET-AL-PR-ethics-literacy-Identifying-moral-and-ethical-values-through-purposeful-ethical-education-from-JPRE-6.3.pdf.

Weldon, D. (2016, August 24). A deeper look at business impact of a cyberattack. *CIO.* Retrieved from: https://www.cio.com/article/3112617/data-breach/a-deeper-look-atbusiness-impact-of-a-cyberattack.html.

White, C. L., & Boatwright, B. (2020). Social media ethics in the data economy: Issues of social responsibility for using Facebook for public relations. *Public Relations Review, 46*(5), 101980, https://doi.org/10.1016/j.pubrev.2020.101980.

Yaokumah, W., Walker, D. O., & Kumah, P. (2019). SETA and security behavior: Mediating role of employee relations, monitoring, and accountability. *Journal of Global Information Management, 27*(2), 102–121. https://doi.org/10.4018/JGIM.2019040106.

Section VI

Internal CSR/CSA

Chapter Fourteen

The Roles of Internal Communication in Driving Corporate Volunteering among Chinese Employees: An Integrated Approach of Social Influence and Volunteering Motivations

Yi-Ru Regina Chen, Minqin Ma, and Chun-Ju Flora Hung-Baesecke

Introduction

Corporate volunteering (CV) has been found to generate significant benefits to the charity/NGO, the corporation, and the employee (Caligiuri et al., 2013). In the United States, 90% of corporations have initiated a CV program (Cook & Geldenhuys, 2018). However, only about 50% of their counterparts in mainland China (hereinafter China) have done so (Hu et al., 2016). Additionally, employee volunteer recruitment and retention seem to be a challenge in China. More importantly, the literature has suggested that Chinese employees, especially the younger generation, have distinct social and cultural characteristics, and they are taking a more leading role in planning their firms' CV activities than before (HCVCChina, 2019). This book chapter explicates the role of internal communication in driving employees' CV participation in China by first proposing a framework that integrates social influence theory, motivation-based theory of volunteerism, and internal communication matrix. It then conducts a case study on Tencent (a 2020 Fortune 200 Chinese corporation), using mixed methods of interviewing and content analysis, to validate the framework. Implications of the findings are also proposed for academics and managers who seek to understand or implement CV in China.

Literature Review

Internal CV Communication: Definition and Levels

Internal communication is understood as the structured, strategic communication of an organization to advance its missions and goals by managing interactions and relationships at all levels of the organization (Malouf et al., 2016; Verčič et al., 2012; Welch & Jackson, 2007). As taking part in volunteering is an individual employee's decision, moving beyond business and job responsibilities, internal communication related to CV (i.e., internal CV communication) is often conducted formally and informally. Internal CV communication is defined, in this chapter, as all forms of communication about CV

DOI: 10.4324/9781003195580-21

conducted at all levels of an organization. Guided by Welch and Jackson's (2007) internal communication matrix, this chapter analyzes an organization's internal CV communication on three levels: (1) management-employee CV communication, (2) supervisor-subordinate CV communication, and (3) peer-peer CV communication.

Management-Employee CV Communication

Adapted from Welch and Jackson's (2007) matrix, management-employee CV communication refers to the CV communication between an organization's top management (e.g., Chief Executive Officers (CEO) or the Chief Communication Officers) and its entire body of employees (as a stakeholder). Top management engages in CV communication with employees to deliver transparent and clear information about the organization's CV goals and policies to employees, to give employees a voice in decision-making, to foster awareness and favorable attributions toward CV activities, and to engage employees in CV (Chen & Hung-Baesecke, 2014; Du et al., 2010; Duthler & Dhanesh, 2018). Management-employee CV communication is *often* one-way, top-down communication from the centralized source (e.g., the top management) to the employees via the organization's own channels (e.g., internal social media platforms, intranet, emails, newsletters, and public speeches) (Potoski & Callery, 2018).

Existing literature has suggested that to motivate employees' CV participation effectively, management-employee CV communication should not only contain sufficient information about the CV activity (Malouf et al., 2016) but also signify how the activity aligns with the organization's purpose, values, CSR strategy, core know-hows and competitive advantages (Aguilera et al., 2007; D'Amato et al., 2010; Malouf et al., 2016; Opoku-Dakwa et al., 2018). Furthermore, top leaders' advocacy and recognition (e.g., giving awards or compliments to employee volunteers in official events) are critical for employees to sustain their CV participation and to maintain a positive self-concept and self-assessment (Grant, 2012; Hu et al., 2016; Wang et al., 2017).

The CV literature shows that 62 percent of the programs are employee-led (Malouf et al., 2016; Wainwright, 2005). Management-employee CV communication, therefore, could be bottom-up when the top management empowers the employee in planning and decision-making about CV programs or CV policies (Gammons, 2018; Malouf et al., 2016).

Supervisor-Subordinate CV Communication

Supervisor-subordinate CV communication refers to supervisors' CV-related information behaviors (i.e., information sharing, seeking, and exchanges) with subordinates collectively (as an entire group) or individually (one-to-one) (Welch & Jackson, 2007; Yammarino & Dubinsky, 1992). This CV communication occurs between a department/unit responsible for CV and (whole or individual) employees or between a mid- or low-level line manager and his or her immediate subordinates. Guided by Welch and Jackson (2007), the content of supervisor-subordinate CV communication includes: assigning employee roles (e.g., a CV program leader), setting program targets, assigning work for effective and successful CV implementation (Potoski & Callery, 2018), and clarifying organizational policies about CV (e.g., performance expectations, official responsibilities, and benefits; Nifadkar et al., 2019). In Wang et al.'s (2017) study, employees in China reported their line managers' incompetence in implementing CV on-site as a critical obstacle to their CV participation. Hence, supervisor-subordinate CV communication should also consider how supervisors' support is provided and seek feedback from the employee volunteers to optimize future CV programs.

Peer-Peer CV Communication

Combining Welch and Jackson's (2007) internal team peer communication and internal project peer communication categories, peer-peer CV communication refers to CV-related communication among employees (within a unit or across units). Employees may talk about CV programs with a colleague with whom they interact for work assignments as a conversation topic or with whom they collaborate in a CV program as a task-related topic. Compared to the previous two levels of internal CV communication, peer-peer communication is more effective in driving employees' participation in the programs (Miller & Fyke, 2020; Potoski & Callery, 2018) for two reasons. Firstly, Wang et al. (2017) found that Chinese employees are eager to exchange their CV experience, stories, and intrinsic rewards (e.g., happiness and peace of mind) with colleagues through the organization's internal and public social media platforms or in face-to-face communication. Consequently, more than 42 percent of Chinese employees obtain CV-related information from their colleagues (Wang et al., 2017). Secondly, value-based and emotional information sharing about CV by coworkers is seen as more credible than the traditional hierarchical communication from the top management or supervisors whose motivations might be questionable (Potoski & Callery, 2018). Indeed, Cao et al. (2021) found that an employee's sharing of stories about CV experiences is essential to drive CV participation among other employees.

Social Influence Theory

Social influence theory posits how behavioral changes occur through social influence (Kelman, 1958)—the influence from the real or implied presence of significant others

(Hogg & Vaughan, 2011, p. 236). In the CV context, the top management and coworkers are two sources of social influence in motivating the employee's CV participation (e.g., Chen & Hung-Baesecke, 2014; Hu et al., 2016) because of their respective power over the employee.

The social power approach posits that people who possess power (e.g., valued resources) can influence others toward behavioral change (Fiske & Berdahl, 2007). In this vein, Kelman (1958) proposed three types of social power (i.e., means-control, attractiveness, and credibility) an agent possesses to make others change their behavior through the mechanisms of compliance, identification, and internalization, respectively. According to Kelman (1958), the *compliance* mechanism occurs when the influencer uses his/her control of specific resources (e.g., rewards or punishments) to gain the target's acceptance by threatening to withdraw the resources if the target fails to comply. The *identification* mechanism takes place when the influencer gains acceptance by his/her attractiveness and the representativeness of his/her group. To be attractive, one must construct "a positive identity as virtuous and held in high regard" (Maclean et al., 2015, p. 1627). Furthermore, being liked, respected, and affiliated are the keys to exercising the identification route of social influence (Cialdini & Goldstein, 2004). The target, in this context, complies with maintaining a relationship with the influencer or the influencer's group (Kelman, 1958). By sharing their CV experiences and enthusiasm with their peers, employee volunteers may build a positive identity to attract their peer colleagues to participate in CV activities or be a part of the CV teams (Cialdini & Goldstein, 2004; Hu et al., 2016). The *internalization* mechanism happens when the influencer's recommendation, driven by his/her credibility or expertise, is consistent with the target's value system toward the issue. Scholars further reorganized Kelman's influence mechanisms as normative social influence versus informational social influence (Burnkrant & Cousineau, 1975; Lord et al., 2001). The former (including compliance and identification) refers to behavioral change implemented to fit the expectation of other individuals or groups, while the latter (internalization) refers to the credible information and value agreement that underpins the behavioral change.

The top management controls organizational and social resources desired by employees and the leaders in an organization often possess some level of credibility and charisma through authority and strong delivery (Gardner, 2003). As a result, the more resources a leader can award an employee and the more credible and charismatic the leader is, the more powerful he or she can be in shaping employees' CV behaviors through compliance, identification, and internalization. Indeed, by providing recognition, presenting awards, making positive assessments, and giving promotional opportunities to employee volunteers, leaders can exert a compliance route of social influence on employees' CV participation (Kelman, 1958). Furthermore, leaders' modeling behavior of CV participation not only enhances the awareness of CV among the employees (D'Amato et al., 2010) but also signifies the organization's expectation for employees to participate in CV (Peloza & Hassay, 2006). Therefore, top managers can perform CV with advocacy to drive employees' CV participation through the mechanisms of identification and internalization (Chen & Hung-Baesecke, 2014; Hu et al., 2016; Peloza & Hassay, 2006). However, it is crucial to align leaders' CV behavior with CV advocacy for the leaders to exert the above-mentioned influences (Chen & Hung-Baesecke, 2014; D'Amato et al., 2010).

Theoretically, supervisors (mid- or low-level managers) play a similar role to that played by leaders but are less powerful in driving employee CV participation. It is because compared to leaders, they control fewer resources and usually have less authority or charisma; thereby, they are less likely to be effective role models in CV to employees. Practically, supervisors mobilize their subordinates' CV engagement when their top managers prioritize CV as a strategic goal or when they have a personal value in CV (Vlachos et al., 2014). The extant CSR/CV literature thus neglects the role of middle managers in CSR strategy and communication (Vlachos et al., 2014). Furthermore, a corporation's CV is often overseen by a supporting department (e.g., public relations, public affairs, community outreach, or human resources; Wang et al., 2017) and thus, mid- or low-level line managers are seldom involved in CV management. Regarding the head of the supporting department, he or she has little social influence on individual employees other than his or her subordinates in the department unless the head is in the corporation's dominant coalition.

Coworkers do not obtain resources from fellow employees, but they frequently interact with them at work and in their lives and thus they significantly affect the employee's emotions and experiences (Cialdini & Goldstein, 2004). This frequent interaction generates a high demand for acceptance and fits within the workgroup. As a result, coworkers aggregately exercise normative influence on a fellow employee's behavior, including his/her CV participation through identification and internalization (Cao et al., 2021; Cialdini & Goldstein, 2004; Hu et al., 2016).

Volunteering Motivations of Employees

The existing literature has frequently suggested that employee volunteerism could have mixed motives—altruistic (the desire to help and to do good deeds) and egoistic (employees looking to progress their careers) (Burns et al., 2006). Peloza and Hassay (2006), and Peloza et al. (2009) contended that the third motive, the desire to be a good corporate citizen, should be part of the motives contributing to a more effective corporate volunteer program. An analysis by Peloza et al. (2009) revealed that egoistic and organizational citizenship motives were the most important drivers for employees participating in volunteering programs.

More detailed categorizations of volunteering motivations can be found in Clary et al.'s (1998) research. Using a functional approach, six motivations have been identified when discussing employee volunteering. These motivations include values (altruistic and humanitarian concerns about others), understanding (acquisition of knowledge, skills, and competences), enhancement (personal growth/self-esteem and psychological development), social (strengthening relationships with others), protective (minimizing the guilt of feeling more fortunate than others or solving problems), and career (career benefits resulting from participating in volunteering activities). Houle et al. (2005) found that employees take part in different volunteering tasks based on their own motives, and the benefits coming from the tasks.

Inspired by Clary et al.'s (1998) work, Pajo and Lee (2011) further identified the following motives: altruism (a desire to help, to give back, to assist those who are less fortunate), meaningfulness (a desire driven by the meaningfulness, impact, worth or significance of the volunteer activity), organizational citizenship (a desire to reciprocate positive treatment from the employer, to support the company or to present a favorable image of the enterprise), role variety (driven by the opportunity to do something different from "normal" work), relational and social task characteristics (driven by positive affective judgment about the activity and the relational and/or social aspects of the tasks), networking (driven by the opportunity to get to know others in the organization and/or build their own profile), and personal (driven by individual and personalized reasons for volunteering). The research also reported that to have a satisfying employee volunteering experience, it is critical to enhance perceptions of task significance and meaningfulness and to incorporate relational elements into the volunteer programs. In terms of the motives relative to age differences, Briggs et al. (2010) found that young adults are more likely to be motivated by personal factors (e.g., peer pressure, concerns about self-image, and the need for personal development), while older adults are more likely to be motivated by other reasons and values (sense of responsibility toward the community and the motivation to contribute to the well-being of others).

The Integrative Framework

Based on the literature review, we proposed a theoretical framework (Table 14.1) that integrates the motivation-based theory of volunteerism with social influence theory (Cialdini & Goldstein, 2004; Kelman, 1958) and internal communication dimensions (Welch & Jackson, 2007) to examine the roles of internal communication in driving CV behaviors.

TABLE 14.1 The integrative framework for internal communication roles in driving corporate volunteering motivations.

	Leader (e.g., CEO) communication	**Supervisor communication**	**Coworker communication**
Communication source	Leaders	Mid- or low-level line managers or the manager responsible for the corporation's CV function	Employees (who are usually volunteers)
Means of influence	• Advocacy (one-to-many communication) • Compensations and other tangible supports • Actual volunteering: sending a strong value/mission signal	• Advocacy (one-on-one or one-to-many communication) • Limited tangible and intangible supports • Actual volunteering: sending a strong value/mission and expectation signal	• Advocacy (one-on-one or group communication) • Actual volunteering: sending a strong expectation signal
Sources of influence	• Having great influence attempts and impacts on employees	• Having a wide range of influence attempts and impacts on subordinates (depending on the supervisor's valuation of CV)	• Facing the same situation (e.g., CV)—competition or comparison • Daily close interaction—social acceptance
Form of influence	• As a single source of influence	• As a single source of influence	• In an aggregate form of influence
Communication usage	• Advocacy • Public recognition • Value co-creation • Decision-making	• Advocacy • Public recognition • Experience sharing • Project planning and execution	• Advocacy • Experience sharing • Project planning and execution
Motivations triggered	• Value • Reward (recognition/awards and positive assessments) • Career (promotions)	• Value • Reward (recognition and positive assessments) • Career (promotions) • Socializing (relationship cultivation)	• Value • Understanding (knowledge, skills) • Enhancement (self-growth, self-esteem) • Socializing • Reward (reputation) • Protective (escaping from negative feelings about work)

The literature has suggested that leaders (e.g., CEO of an organization) and coworkers can motivate employees' participation in CV through communicating with the employees. However, their communication has different effects on driving employee motivations. The framework explicates the two communication mechanisms, respectively. As the organization's top decision-maker, the CEO sets its vision and leads it to perform. Employees are highly aware of the CEO's words and actions and thus, they affect them. For example, the CEO can initiate and implement organizational policies (e.g., paid leaves for CV or CV as a performance criterion) to encourage CV participation. Thus, the CEO is a single powerful source of influence on employees' CV behavior (Cialdini & Goldstein, 2004). As the top authority figure who controls the organization's resources at large, the CEO's plea for CV participation may elicit employee compliance to gain rewards, such as recognition, awards, positive assessments, or career advancement (Cialdini & Goldstein, 2004). When the CEO is a charismatic figure or especially liked by employees, the employee may comply with the CEO's plea for CV participation to mimic the CEO or to build a relationship with him/her. When the CEO advocates CV by linking it to the organization's values and/or his/her actual volunteering, the employee may imitate the CEO's CV behavior by treating the CEO as a role model. In summary, the CEO's communication to the employees (in a type of one-to-many) can be used for the purposes of advocacy CV, recognizing employees' CV behaviors, co-creating meaning and value of CV with employees, and engaging employees with decision-making about CV practice. Such communication can trigger the prosocial value motivation, reward motivation, and career motivation of the employees' CV participation.

As non-authority figures who usually control little or no resources over others in the organization, coworkers influence the employees' CV participation through identification and internalization. An employee's feelings and experiences at work are directly impacted by the employee's relationship with his/her coworkers. Thus, an employee is likely to perform CV to be socially accepted, especially when many of his/her coworkers are doing so (i.e., identification). Coworkers often share their experiences in CV activities with one another, including what they witnessed about the problem/people they serve, and how they feel after volunteering, on their networks, and thereby drive their colleagues' CV participation via value congruence (i.e., internalization). In addition to advocacy and experience sharing, coworker communication (peer-peer communication) about CV often occurs in order to plan and execute CV programs. As a result, coworker communication can trigger the employees' CV motivations of prosocial value, understanding (knowledge, skills, and leadership), enhancement (self-growth and self-esteem), socializing, reward (reputation), and protection.

As previously discussed, supervisors in general exert weaker social influences on employees in their CV participation. Supervisors have a similar role as top managers in inducing employee CV participation because they are low-level leaders. Like their coworkers, employees have the desire to be socially accepted by supervisors because they directly work with and are evaluated by their supervisors. As a result, the framework suggests that supervisors can utilize a combination of influence means and communication tactics that are exclusive to leaders and coworkers to enhance a wide range of motivations of employees for CV.

Case Study: Tencent

Tencent Volunteer Association

Founded in 1998 and listed on the Hong Kong Stock Exchange in 2004, Tencent Holdings (hereinafter Tencent) is one of China's technology conglomerates providing Internet services to individuals and companies. Tencent Foundation and Tencent Volunteer Association (TVA) were set up in 2007 to oversee the company's volunteering practice. Following the company's newly issued vision and mission—*Value for Users, Tech for Good*—the company merged Tencent Foundation with Tencent charity and CSR practices to form a new division, titled Tencent Sustainable Social Value Organization (SSVO), in April 2021. SSVO is responsible for producing the company's shared value projects that aim to leverage the company's core technologies and business capabilities to innovatively conduct charitable activities (Tencent, 2021). TVA is now the sole unit that oversees Tencent's CV function.

TVA is a virtual unit under the Department of Tencent Culture. It has only one staff member (with a title of association chair) responsible for the company's internal and external volunteering programs and activities. For example, when SSVO needs employee volunteers to support its events, TVA will recruit volunteers and (co-)manage their volunteering assignments for SSVO. According to the TVA Chair, TVA currently has more than 7,000 volunteers in 28 branches. It has appointed 200 Tencent employee volunteers (hereinafter Tencent volunteers) in various departments of the company as CV directors, who lead in organizing CV programs (Interpersonal Communication, July 3, 2021).

Methodology

This case study used mixed methods of interviewing and content analysis to examine the internal CV communication at Tencent and the effects of that communication on the employees' CV participation. Eight telephone interviews were conducted in July 2021 with the TVA Chair and seven active Tencent volunteers. The content for analysis included the top management's two letters to employees and media reports about Tencent's volunteering activities on the company's website, as well as the 19 CV postings on the TVA WeChat account (i.e., TVA's official communication platform) issued after the new corporate vision and mission were announced. The two letters were sent to the employees on the date of SSVO's launch and Tencent's 99 Giving Day Campaign, respectively, and were identified by the interviewees as being very important communication pieces about CV. Three of the WeChat postings were about the top management's speeches at Tencent's annual Volunteer Conference, a significant event for the Tencent volunteers.

Results

Tencent's Management-Employee CV Communication

This level of internal CV communication at Tencent takes a top-down approach: communication is initiated by its 18-member Executive Committee (e.g., the CEO Pony Ma and the Executive Director and President Martin Lau) to the employees via emails and speeches given at the company's mega events (i.e., Tencent's launch of the SSVO, annual Volunteer Conference, and annual 99 Giving Day Campaign). Management-employee CV communication not only draws much attention from the employees but also makes them understand how CV links to the company's corporate culture and values. For example, the interviewees associated integrity (a value of Tencent) and "Tech for Good" (Tencent's mission) with the company's general CV direction: CV through technologies. Six Tencent volunteer interviewees recognized the launch of SSVO as signaling the determination of Tencent to upgrade its charity efforts, including CV. As the programmer interviewee put it, "[Hearing about the news of the establishment of SSVO] deeply touched me because it meant that the company wishes to be more professional in CV execution, or to push [its CV function] to a higher level." And the TVA Chair further explained:

> This action [establishing SSVO] signifies the company's increasing investment in philanthropy and social responsibility to the public. As for CV, although it is not a KPI of the company, we will make greater investments in this area, which is indicated by our organizational restructure.

Compliance-Directed Social Influence of the Top Management

To encourage CV behaviors via rewards (i.e., resource control), Tencent's top management publicly recognizes devoted Tencent volunteers by paying them compliments and bestowing awards at the company's annual Volunteer Conference. The awards include Excellent Volunteers, Outstanding Director of Volunteer Branch, Excellent Volunteer Team, and Tencent Light Innovation Challenge Winners. The social influence is effective for compliance when the targets believe their activities are noticed and recognized by others (Burnkrant & Cousineau, 1975). Tencent employees at large view the Volunteer Conference as a high-profile company event. As the TVA Chair put it, "[the Conference] is akin to a festival to the Tencent volunteers who are excited to attend it." Indeed, the interviewee in customer service mentioned: "Our Volunteer Conference is specially designed for all employee volunteers to receive extensive publicity, encouragement, and recognition in the company to motivate more employees to participate in CV activities." A product-manager interviewee further claimed that many employee volunteers attend the Conference to shine among other employees by actively sharing their volunteering experiences in front of the Conference participants, including the top management.

Identification-Directed Social Influence of the Top Management

To exercise identification influence, the top management communicated with the employees via the two letters to remind them of the ways Tencent builds a positive identity through its CV efforts. The contents of the letters focused on three attributes of Tencent—leadership, meaningfulness, and advocacy. The letters argued that Tencent, as an industry leader in China and worldwide, should commit to charity (i.e., being "the first charity organization of the Internet industry") to generate meaningful, positive impacts. For instance, the letters addressed Tencent's 99 Giving Day Campaign as a "one of a kind" charity initiative for businesses and organizations in China to make a positive impact by helping re-distribute resources and wealth among people in society through CV behaviors and donations.

Internalization-Directed Social Influence of the Top Management

The top management's letters to employees and speeches at the Volunteer Conference aim to deliver an internalization route of social influence, which supplies credible information to indicate the congruence between the company's behavior and its value system, thereby advocating for the employees' behavior to achieve a value congruence with the company (Fiske & Berdahl, 2007; Kelman, 1958). The speeches and letters illustrated how Tencent establishes its value of "Tech for Good" through commitment, strategic thinking, persistence, and outcomes with facts and statistics, so as to encourage internalization in its employees. For example, Tencent's 99 Giving Day Campaign attracted 48 million donors. Tencent also set up a Chinese Renminbi 1.5 billion (approximately 0.235 million U.S. dollars) anti-pandemic fund and mobilized 12,000 Tencent volunteers to fight against COVID-19 as well as developing 14 businesses to deliver its "Tech for Good" value to consumers. The speeches and letters also repeated the terms "digitalized public welfare," "technological public welfare," and "Tech for Good" throughout the content.

Tencent's Supervisor-Subordinate CV Communication

The interview data suggested that this level of CV communication only occurs between the TVA Chair and the employees (volunteers and non-volunteers), the TVA Chair and the CV directors, and the CV directors and Tencent volunteers. Line managers did not engage in CV communication with their subordinates. CV Communication content included promoting CV programs, assigning CV roles, providing CV support, planning and managing CV activities, and seeking feedback on CV activities. Communication for CV promotion mainly took a top-down approach, while communication for CV execution took a dialogic approach. For example, the product manager interviewee reported that the TVA Chair issues all calls for Tencent's CV participants. Additionally, the TVA Chair received feedback on Tencent volunteers' CV participation experiences through their informal chats. For instance, the programmer interviewee mentioned his dialogue with the TVA Chair, where he suggested how to better execute a CV program after participating in a CV activity by saying that "[the TVA Chair] usually accepted my suggestions for actions when implementing the follow-up CV activities."

In addition, the TVA Chair strategically utilized various communication platforms to promote CV programs to the employees at large, including the official TVA WeChat account, company email systems, Tencent KM (the company's intranet), and new staff orientation. The interviewees indicated emails as their most preferred communication channel with the TVA. Each of the 28 branches and existing CV programs had formed a group chat on WeChat. Communication between the TVA Chair and the directors and the directors and Tencent volunteers was predominantly through the group chats on WeChat because of convenience and promptness.

Compliance-Directed Social Influence of the TVA

As a virtual unit with one full-time staff member, the TVA aimed to drive CV participation by publicly *recognizing* the contribution of Tencent volunteers to society and the company via frequently expressing the company's gratitude to them and sharing their CV stories with others on its official WeChat account to boost their positive image and reputation. However, it should be noted that none of the six volunteer interviewees indicated that their CV participation is fostered by this means. An exemplar of the TVA WeChat post reads:

> On June 1, the International Children's Day this year, Tencent employee volunteers delivered gifts to the long-term child patients at the Shenzhen City Children's Hospital and the children in Daliangshan [*an impoverished mountainous area in Sichuan Province*]. It is the best Children's Day gift and the nicest surprise for them. Thanks to all our loving Tencent volunteers who participated in this June 1 Children's Day activity.

Identification-Directed Social Influence of the CV Directors

Tencent volunteers admired their CV directors for their excellent CV organization competence and citizenship. As the interviewees pointed out, the directors are not only capable but also highly committed to conducting CV activities that deliver good experiences to Tencent volunteers. The directors use their communication and behaviors to convey their passion and enthusiasm for CV activities. As a result, the directors drive the CV participation of Tencent volunteers (e.g., to continue their CV participation or to take the role in organizing a CV program) by means of the volunteers' desire to cultivate their relationship with them. As the interviewee in online gaming design described a CV director with whom he worked:

> I like the director very much because I think he/she is very kind, and secondly, he/she has been doing CV for so many years on a regular basis. Whenever there is a problem, he/she will go the extra mile to solve it. Although we never have any interactions at work, I think this person must have good communication skills. And I think I would like to become a good friend with him/her.

Tencent's Peer-Peer CV Communication

The interview data revealed that the Tencent volunteers are extremely self-driven in launching and organizing the CV programs. For instance, the interviewee from the Corporate Culture Department mentioned:

> We have many CV programs initiated and developed by Tencent volunteers from a small idea into a large-scale program project utilizing their organizational and leadership skills. Some good examples are the Planting in Tenggeli Program and Starry Color Autistic Children Care Program.

The interview data also showed that coworkers have a stronger impact on driving employee CV participation at Tencent than the top management do. Tencent volunteers generated identification and internalization influence on their peers' CV participation by sharing their CV stories on their personal WeChat moment (equivalent to Facebook wall) and the TVA WeChat account and through face-to-face communication. For instance, the interviewee from the Corporate Culture Department claimed that his coworkers' CV stories shared at the Volunteer Conference emotionally motivate him to sustain his CV participation.

Identification-Directed and Internalization-Directed Social Influence of Peers

The interview data revealed identification-directed and internalization-directed social influence of Tencent volunteers on their fellow employees through perceived positive identity toward the Tencent volunteers and the value congruence between the Tencent volunteers and their coworkers, respectively. When explaining the identification-directed social influence through peer-peer CV communication, the interviewees suggested that Tencent volunteers' communication about their CV experience on WeChat and in-person motivates not only the employees to participate in CV programs but also the volunteers to sustain their CV participation by delivering a positive identity and showing attractiveness to their peers. For instance, all the interviewees reported that as Tencent volunteers, they often share their CV experiences and thoughts with people in their networks on WeChat moment. The sharing usually gained positive responses from their coworkers, such as praise and the creation of positive images as "virtuous and excellent people with good time management skills," as suggested by the senior manager interviewee. Furthermore, the TVA WeChat account also published Tencent volunteers' stories and experiences, which further built the volunteers' fame and reputation among their coworkers. The product manager interviewee claimed that she was praised by her coworkers when they found out she was a member of the TVA and her coworkers further asked her how to join the TVA to practice CV.

Tencent volunteers' sharing of their CV stories or beliefs also drives other employees' CV participation when the stories and beliefs align with the value system of the other employees (i.e., internalization-directed social influence). For example, three interviewees reported that they become active Tencent volunteers because of another Tencent volunteer who is dedicated to CV and devotes his time to CV participation on a regular basis. The interviewees agreed with the value of CV devotion, thereby modeling the behavior of the Tencent volunteer.

Conclusion and Discussion

CV has become an increasingly important aspect of CSR because of its positive impact on the organization, the employee, the collaborating NGOs, and society. This chapter advances the body of knowledge of CSR and internal communication by using a case study to validate the proposed integrative framework that explicates what and how the motives of employees toward CV are driven by leaders and coworkers, respectively, through their communication within an organization to increase/sustain CV.

Theoretical Contributions

The case study demonstrates the applicability of the proposed framework to analyze how internal CV communication can foster employee CV participation through the mechanisms suggested by social influence theory. It is also evident that internal CV communication by leaders and coworkers functions differently in enhancing the motivations to induce employees' CV participation, while the direct impacts of CV communication by supervisors on CV participation are limited. Therefore, future research should move from treating internal CV communication as a whole to communication-level analysis when examining its function(s) in driving employee CV participation. To refine the proposed framework, researchers should further examine how CV communication by mid- or low-level supervisors who are active in CV affect employee CV participation in their corporations. In addition, future research should examine how to use internal CV communication to drive other outcomes for employees, such as employee engagement, well-being, and productivity. For example, it is worth examining if involving employees to co-create the values and purposes of an organization, using leader-employee communication in a dialogic mode, enhances the level of affective and behavioral engagement of the employee volunteers in the CV activities derived from these co-created values and purposes. This inquiry is especially relevant to Chinese organizations with large numbers of Generation Z employees, who seek opportunities that offer intrinsic meaning (Kelly, 2021).

Practical Implications

Drawing on the findings of the case study, several implications are presented below for both academics and managers concerning CV in China. First, since the COVID-19 outbreak in 2019, there have been increasing expectations of purpose-led businesses from various stakeholders, including employees (Palsule & Chavez, 2020). Corporate leaders in China have communicated internally about CV using a more strategic communication approach than before, by linking CV with the firm's values and mission. However, the leaders' internal communication still centers on CV advocacy and promotion of the firm's CV success through publicizing the activities of the employees at large, with little or no sharing of their own CV experiences. This might explain why only 8% of Tencent's employees have participated in CV, as reported by the TVA chair. Leaders' actual CV behavior plays a pivotal role in sustaining employees' CV participation.

Second, CSR/CV managers (mid-level supervisors) should organize an internal communication structure that optimizes the integration of communication efforts by leaders and coworkers to employees via their end-to-end volunteering journey. For example, a crowdsourcing platform that allows leaders and employee volunteers to share with others the knowledge and skills necessary for improving the performance of CV activities could be part of the structure. Such a platform could not only increase volunteer satisfaction by means of pre-volunteering self-training and post-volunteering sharing but also motivate CV participation through the manifested benefits of self-enhancement and social interaction with leaders and coworkers. The organization of such a structure, also driven by technologies, should be explored in detail in future studies. Last but not least, the internal CV communication, initiated by the supervisor, who is the head of the supporting department or unit that oversees the corporation's CV function, must be more strategically planned than leader communication or coworker communication to achieve its objective. It is because the supervisor as the source of communication has weaker social influence than the leader or the coworker does in general.

Learning Outcomes

1) Identify how internal communication at different levels in a corporation engages in CV communication and its effects on CV participation.
2) Describe how social influence theory can inform internal CV communication practices.
3) Understand why and how top managers and coworkers are social agents within a corporation who can significantly influence the employees' CV participation by considering employee CV motivations.

Discussion Questions

1) What are the similarities and differences between internal CV communication in China and the United States?
2) How can CSR/CV managers apply the integrative framework to develop the internal CV communication strategy for their organization?
3) What is an effective means for CSR/CV managers to persuade the top management to participate in CV activities?
4) What are the data necessary for organizing an organization's internal communication structure in order to optimize the integration of communication efforts by leaders and coworkers to employees via their end-to-end volunteering journey?

Further Readings

Miller, K. (2012). *Organizational communication: Approaches and processes.* 6th Edition. Boston, MA: Wadsworth Cengage Learning.

Rodell, J. B., Breitsohl, H., Schröder, M., & Keating, D. J. (2016). Employee volunteering: A review and framework for future research. *Journal of Management, 42*(1), 55–84. http://doi.org/10.1177/0149206315614374

Ryan, R., & Deci, E. (2000). Self-determination theory and the facilitation of intrinsic motivation, social development, and well-being. *American Psychologist, 55*(1), 68–78. http://doi.org/10.1037/0003-066X.55.1.68

Spears, R. (2021). Social influence and group identity. *Annual Review of Psychology, 72*(1), 367–390. https://doi.org/10.1146/annurev-psych-070620-111818

References

Aguilera, R. V., Rupp, D. E., Williams, C. A., & Ganapathi, J. (2007). Putting the S back in corporate social responsibility: A multilevel theory of social change in organizations. *Academy of Management Review, 32*(3), 836–863. https://doi.org/10.5465/amr.2007.25275678

Briggs, E., Peterson, M., & Gregory, G. (2010). Toward a better understanding of volunteering for nonprofit organizations: Explaining volunteers' pro-social attitudes. *Journal of Macromarketing, 30*(1), 61–76. https://doi.org/10.1177/0276146709352220

Burnkrant, R. E., & Cousineau, A. (1975). Informational and normative social influence in buyer behavior. *Journal of Consumer Research, 2*(3), 206–215. https://doi.org/10.1086/208633

Burns, D. J., Reid, J. S., Toncar, M., Fawcett, J., & Anderson, C. (2006). Motivations to volunteer: The role of altruism. *International Review on Public and Nonprofit Marketing, 3*, 79–91. https://doi.org/10.1007/BF02893621

Caligiuri, P., Mencin, A., & Jiang, K. (2013). Win-win-win: The influence of company-sponsored volunteerism programs on employees, NGOs, and business units. *Personnel Psychology, 66*(4), 825–860. https://doi.org/10.1111/peps.12019

Cao, Y., Pil, F. K., & Lawson, B. (2021). Signaling and social influence: The impact of corporate volunteer programs. *Journal of Managerial Psychology, 36*(2), 183–196. https://doi.org/10.1108/JMP-06-2020-0332

Chen, Y. R. R., & Hung-Baesecke, C. J. F. (2014). Examining the internal aspect of corporate social responsibility (CSR): Leader behavior and employee CSR participation. *Communication Research Reports, 31*(2), 210–220. https://doi.org/10.1080/08824096.2014.907148

Cialdini, R. B., & Goldstein, N. J. (2004). Social influence: Compliance and conformity. *Annual Review of Psychology, 55*, 591–622. https://doi.org/10.1146/annurev.psych.55.090902.142015

Clary, E. G., Ridge, R., Stukas, A., Snyder, M., Copeland, J., Haugen, J., & Miene, P. (1998). Understanding and assessing the motivations of volunteers: A functional approach. *Journal of Personality and Social Psychology, 74*, 1516–1530. https://doi.org/10.1037/0022-3514.74.6.1516

Cook, G., & Geldenhuys, D. J. (2018). The experiences of employees participating in organisational corporate social responsibility initiatives. *SA Journal of Industrial Psychology, 44*, 10 pages. https://doi.org/10.4102/sajip.v44i0.1481

D'Amato, A., Eckert, R., Ireland, J., Quinn, L., & Van Velsor, E. (2010). Leadership practices for corporate global responsibility. *Journal of Global Responsibility, 1*(2), 225–249. https://doi.org/10.1108/20412561011079371

Du, S., Bhattacharya, C. B., & Sen, S. (2010). Maximizing business returns to corporate social responsibility (CSR): The role of CSR communication. *International Journal of Management Reviews: IJMR, 12*(1), 8–19. https://doi.org/10.1111/j.1468-2370.2009.00276.x

Duthler, G., & Dhanesh, G. S. (2018). The role of corporate social responsibility (CSR) and internal CSR communication in predicting employee engagement: Perspectives from the United Arab Emirates (UAE). *Public Relations Review, 44*(4), 453–462. https://doi.org/10.1016/j.pubrev.2018.04.001

Fiske, S. T., & Berdahl, J. L. (2007). Social power. In A. Kruglanski & T. Higgins (Eds.), *Social psychology handbook of basic principles* (678–692). 2nd Edition. The Guilford Press.

Gammons, S. (2018). *Can participants of an employee volunteering programme be catalysts for change when they return to their organisation?* Roffey Park Institute. https://documents.pub/document/can-participants-of-an-employee-participants-of-an-employee-volunteering-programme.html

Grant, A. M. (2012). Giving time, time after time: Work design and sustained employee participation in corporate volunteering. *The Academy of Management Review, 37*(4), 589–615. https://doi.org/10.5465/amr.2010.0280

Gardner, W. L. (2003). Perceptions of leader charisma, effectiveness, and integrity: Effects of exemplification, delivery, and ethical reputation. *Management Communication Quarterly, 16*(4), 502–527. https://doi.org/10.1177/0893318903251324

HCVCChina. (2019). *The development report on Chinese corporate volunteering in 2019*. Horizon Corporate Volunteer Consultancy. http://www.hcvcchina.com/h-nd-632.html

Hogg, M. A., & Vaughan, G. M. (2011). *Social psychology*. 6th Edition. Pearson Education Limited.

Houle, B. J., Sagarin, B. J., & Kaplan, M. F. (2005). A functional approach to volunteerism: Do volunteer motives predict task preference? *Basic and Applied Social Psychology, 27*(4), 337–344. http://doi.org/10.1207/s15324834basp2704_6

Hu, J., Jiang, K., Mo, S., Chen, H., & Shi, J. (2016). The motivational antecedents and performance consequences of corporate volunteering: When do employees volunteer and when does volunteering help versus harm work performance? *Organizational Behavior and Human Decision Processes, 137*, 99–111. https://doi.org/10.1016/j.obhdp.2016.08.005

Kelly, J. (2021, January 4). China's Gen-Zers are slacking off, refusing to work overtime and playing on their phones in protest of long hours and low pay. *Forbes*. https://www.forbes.com/sites/jackkelly/2021/01/04/chinas-gen-zers-are-slacking-off-refusing-to-work-overtime-and-playing-on-their-phones-in-protest-of-long-hours-and-low-pay/?sh=7f812e6f1fdb

Kelman, H. C. (1958). Compliance, identification, and internalization: Three processes of attitude change. *Journal of Conflict Resolution, 2*(1), 51–60. http://doi.org/10.1177/002200275800200106

Lord, K. R., Lee, M.-S., & Choong, P. (2001). Differences in normative and informational social influence. *Advances in Consumer Research, 28*(1), 280–285.

Maclean, M., Harvey, C., Gordon, J., & Shaw, E. (2015). Identity, storytelling and the philanthropic journey. *Human Relations, 68*(10), 1623–1652. https://doi.org/10.1177/0018726714564199

Malouf, A., Selakovic, M., & Ljepava, N. (2016). Exploring the relationship between corporate volunteering and internal communications in multinational organizations. *Communication Management Review, 1*(2), 6–22. https://doi.org/10.22522/cmr20160208

Miller, K. E., & Fyke, J. P. (2020). Communication professionals' sensemaking of CSR: A case study of a financial services firm. *Business and Professional Communication Quarterly, 83*(2), 184–203. https://doi.org/10.1177/2329490620903737

Nifadkar, S. S., Wu, W., & Gu, Q. (2019). Supervisors' work-related and nonwork information sharing: Integrating research on information sharing, information seeking, and trust using self-disclosure theory. *Personnel Psychology, 72*(2), 241–269. https://doi.org/10.1111/peps.12305

Opoku-Dakwa, A., Chen, C. C., & Rupp, D. E. (2018). CSR initiative characteristics and employee engagement: An impact-based perspective. *Journal of Organizational Behavior, 39*(5), 580–593. https://doi.org/10.1002/job.2281

Pajo, K., & Lee, L. (2011). Corporate-sponsored volunteering: A work design perspective. *Journal of Business Ethics, 99*(3), 467–482. https://doi.org/10.1007/s10551-010-0665-0

Palsule, S., & Chavez, M. (2020). *Rehumanizing leadership: Putting purpose back into business.* Duke Corporate Education.

Peloza, J., & Hassay, D. N. (2006). Intra-organizational volunteerism: Good soldiers, good deeds and good politics. *Journal of Business Ethics, 64*(4), 357–379. https://doi.org/10.1007/s10551-005-5496-z

Peloza, J., Hudson, S., & Hassay, D. (2009). The marketing of employee volunteerism. *Journal of Business Ethics, 85*(2), 371–386. http://doi.org/10.1007/s10551-008-9734-z

Potoski, M., & Callery, P. J. (2018). Peer communication improves environmental employee engagement programs: Evidence from a quasi-experimental field study. *Journal of Cleaner Production, 172*, 1486–1500. https://doi.org/10.1016/J.JCLEPRO.2017.10.252

Tencent. (2021, April 19). *Tencent unveils blueprint of sustainable innovations for social value as core development strategy: Initial investment of RMB 50 billion for the new initiative.* Tencent. https://static.www.tencent.com/uploads/2021/05/27/c947815a6b7558d6843b24741ffac5e9.pdf

Verčič, A. T., Verčič, D., & Sriramesh, K. (2012). Internal communication: Definition, parameters, and the future. *Public Relations Review, 38*(2), 223–230. https://doi.org/10.1016/j.pubrev.2011.12.019

Vlachos, P. A., Panagopoulos, N. G., & Rapp, A. A. (2014). Employee judgments of and behaviors toward corporate social responsibility: A multi-study investigation of direct, cascading, and moderating effects. *Journal of Organizational Behavior, 35*(7), 990–1017. https://doi.org/10.1002/job.1946

Wainwright, C. (2005, July). Building the case for corporate volunteering. *Business Community Intelligence*, 40–42. https://www.ourcommunity.com.au/files/bci_firstedition.pdf

Wang, Z., Chen, H., Zhang, Y., & Li, Y. (2017). 中国企业志愿服务报告 [A report on volunteering in China]. In China Volunteer Service Federation (Ed.), *Blue book of voluntary service: Annual report on development of voluntary service in China* (144–197). Social Sciences Academic Press.

Welch, M., & Jackson, P. R. (2007). Rethinking internal communication: A stakeholder approach. *Corporate Communications, 12*(2), 177–198. https://doi.org/10.1108/13563280710744847

Yammarino, F. J., & Dubinsky, A. J. (1992). Superior-subordinate relationships: A multiple levels of analysis approach. *Human Relations, 45*(6), 575–600. https://doi.org/10.1177/001872679204500603

Chapter Fifteen

Engaged Employees through Internal CSR Communication: A Case Study of Home Depot

Chuqing Dong and Baobao Song

Introduction

Home Depot, a famous home improvement supplies retailer, was founded by Bernie Marcus and Arthur Blank in 1978. Today, the hardware giant has over 2,200 stores across North America (The Home Depot, 2021a). Deeply rooted in its prosocial corporate values, Home Depot dedicates itself to doing the right thing for its employees, the environment, and the community. The company has three flagship corporate social responsibility (CSR) programs, including improving the lives of U.S. veterans, training tradespeople to fill the labor gap, and supporting communities impacted by natural disasters.

Team Depot, Home Depot's official employee volunteer force, is one of the most important driving forces to fulfill these long-term strategic goals. In 1993, the company marshaled its employee volunteers and founded Team Depot. Within two years, Team Depot received the President's Service Award from President Clinton, the highest honor given to volunteers by the President to date (The Home Depot, 2018). Home Depot's active internal CSR communication is led by more than 2,200 community captain leaders, spanning across all levels of employees (The Home Depot, 2021b).

Based on Home Depot's successful CSR activities, this chapter provides a case study of the internal CSR communication at Home Depot. The chapter begins with an overview of academic research on internal CSR, explaining the concept of employee CSR engagement and classic CSR communication strategies. Next, by examining company's annual CSR reports and conducting interviews with Home Depot Foundation managers, this study reveals Home Depot's communication efforts that facilitate employees' CSR engagement. Internal CSR communication implications are highlighted afterward.

Literature Review

Employee CSR Engagement

CSR describes a wide range of discretionary business practices that aim to meet stakeholder expectations of organizations' economic, legal, ethical, and philanthropic

DOI: 10.4324/9781003195580-22

responsibilities (Lee & Carroll, 2011). Based on stakeholder theory, organizations are under pressure from both external stakeholders, such as consumers, and internal stakeholders, such as employees, to engage in socially responsible behaviors. Employees are increasingly recognized as integral stakeholders for their roles as organizational ambassadors (Edinger-Schons et al., 2019), internal customers (Bhattacharya et al., 2007), and important enablers of their organizations' socially responsible actions (Rupp et al., 2006).

Employee engagement is a multifaceted construct that encompasses individuals' cognitive, emotional, and physical expression of themselves when performing an organizational role (Duthler & Dhanesh, 2018; Jiang & Shen, 2020). In this study, employee engagement in CSR refers to the extent to which employees are cognitively focused on, emotionally linked to, and physically devoted to the CSR activities organized by their employer. Cognitively engaged employees demonstrate their attention and dedication (Rothbard, 2001) by being mentally available to process CSR information and engage in CSR activities. Emotionally engaged employees experience positive affection and empowerment when they are part of an organization's CSR initiative (Kang et al., 2010). Physically engaged employees participate in actions to support the employer's CSR activities, such as donations and volunteer programs in which employees invest their time or skills to achieve CSR goals (Chen & Hung-Baesecke, 2014; Im et al., 2016). Employees can also participate in CSR by offering suggestions on CSR policy or engaging in an organization's CSR decision-making (Kim et al., 2010).

It is important to examine employee CSR engagement for several reasons. First, employee engagement in CSR facilitates the effective delivery of CSR activities because employees are the "primary enactors" in CSR activities (Bhattacharya et al., 2007, p. 23). Chen and Hung-Baesecke (2014) suggested that CSR represents a "dynamic internal process relying on employee involvement in its development and implementations" (p. 210). In addition, employee engagement in CSR activities reflects an organization's culture and values, separate from the organization's external prosocial behaviors aimed at image building. Third, employee CSR engagement leads to numerous positive individual and organizational outcomes, including employee satisfaction and commitment (Barakat et al., 2016), employer-employee relationship quality (Chen et al., 2019), employee identification (Brammer et al., 2015), and organizational citizenship and employee advocacy behaviors (Du et al., 2010; Newman et al., 2015).

Companies, however, face several challenges as they attempt to promote employee CSR engagement. Even if employees have a positive attitude toward CSR, many psychological and environmental factors may still prevent them from engaging in organizational CSR activities (Bekmeier-Feuerhahn et al., 2017). For example, inflexible giving programs, unclear information about the cause, pressure from employers and colleagues, and employees' limited ability to donate or volunteer can push employees away from participating in CSR. Other studies have found that limited knowledge about CSR and lack of time are important barriers preventing employees from participating in CSR activities (Bekmeier-Feuerhahn et al., 2017; Young et al., 2010). Communication also plays a critical role in informing and engaging stakeholders. Given that employees are the most vital internal stakeholders, CSR scholars have searched for effective communication strategies to improve internal CSR engagement (Bekmeier-Feuerhahn et al., 2017; Jiang & Luo, 2020; Lim & Greenwood, 2017). The following section presents the theoretical framework of CSR communication.

Internal CSR Communication

Internal communication is a fast-growing area of research and practice specialization in public relations that has generated interdisciplinary interests from fields like organizational communication, management, organizational psychology, and corporate communication (Lee & Yue, 2020; Verčič et al., 2012). Serving both managerial and communication functions, internal communication can be defined as purposeful, organization-planned efforts fostering the interactions and relationships between stakeholders at all levels in an organization (Lee & Yue, 2020). Public relations scholars have suggested that although both internal and external communication can be integrated, internal communication emphasizes social responsibility and contributes to organizational effectiveness in unique ways. Based on the excellence theory of public relations, strategic internal communication emphasizes two-way, symmetrical communication, and engagement when cultivating relationships with employees (Men, 2014; Men & Bowen, 2017). However, practitioners and leaders in the field tend to agree that it is concerning when one-way information dissemination is a predominant component of internal communication, and there is a gap between practice and theory (Verčič et al., 2012).

In the context of CSR, previous research has drawn on both instrumental and constitutive approaches to conceptualizing CSR communication. From an instrumental perspective, CSR communication is defined as "communication that is designed and distributed by the company itself about its CSR efforts" (Morsing 2006, p. 171; also cited in Kim, 2019). This approach emphasizes the managerial function of CSR communication by identifying strategies that can effectively deliver CSR messages to target stakeholders and accomplish organizational goals. From a constitutive perspective, CSR communication is a participatory process involving the co-creation of the meaning of CSR through dialogue, negotiation, and symbolic interaction (Golob et al., 2013). However, internal CSR communication is still relatively underdeveloped compared to external CSR communication. The paucity of studies on internal communication, in general, and internal CSR communication, in particular, is a scholarly call that needs to be addressed in public relations research (Duthler & Dhanesh, 2018).

Drawing on both internal communication and CSR communication literature, we define internal CSR communication broadly as any communication designed and distributed by an employer to its employees about its CSR endeavors. Grounded in stakeholder theory and Grunig and Hunt's (1984) models of public relations, Morsing and Schultz (2006) proposed a typology that incorporates both instrumental and constitutive approaches, which can serve as a robust theoretical framework to understand internal CSR communication.

According to Morsing and Schultz (2006), companies can strategically engage with stakeholders using three key CSR communication strategies: *information, response, and involvement*. The information strategy is aligned with the public information model, in which one-way communication occurs from an organization to its employees. This type of communication is the organization's monologue to disseminate information simply. The goal of communication is to raise awareness about the company's CSR activities. The company assumes that employees will make sense of the CSR activities based on the available information.

In contrast, the response strategy follows a two-way asymmetrical model of public relations, in which messages flow between an organization and its employees. Companies may research employees' expectations and collect feedback on CSR to influence their attitudes and behaviors and encourage them to be more engaged. Companies can modify and improve their CSR programs using this strategy. However, since this type of communication is still sender-oriented, employees may passively respond to corporate actions.

The final type of communication is the involvement strategy, which represents a two-way, dialogical approach. It is the most advanced and ethical model of public relations. Using this strategy, an organization takes a balanced position in the relationships with its employees, values the relationships, and ensures that employees' voices are heard and incorporated into CSR decision-making and implementation. Open, ongoing dialogues are encouraged as the company listens to employees' different and even contentious opinions. The company also facilitates negotiations and accepts the potential risks and changes as a result of dialogic communication.

Compared to external CSR communication, internal CSR communication has been relatively less studied (Duthler & Dhanesh, 2018). This study aims to make connections between theory and practice by asking the following research questions about a nationwide corporation known for employee engagement in CSR–Home Depot:

RQ1: How do Home Depot's employees engage in its CSR activities?

RQ2: What strategies does Home Depot employ to communicate CSR to employees?

RQ3: What factors enable internal CSR communication with Home Depot employees?

Method

This study adopted a qualitative case study approach, which allowed the researchers to build and examine theories based on comprehensive and in-depth data collection from two primary sources, including in-depth interviews with two managers of Home Depot Foundation and a careful examination of seven corporate responsibility reports from 2015 to 2021. Home Depot's recent annual Corporate Responsibility and Sustainability Reports (2015 to 2020) are essential data sources disclosing the company's employee-related CSR activities. To analyze the CSR reports, the authors read the full reports line by line to understand the entire data set. Texts describing employee-related CSR activities (e.g., Team Depot) were identified, followed by a textual analysis of CSR communication strategies and employee engagement. To code CSR communication strategies, we adopted a deductive approach using Morsing and Schultz's (2006) typology, paying particular attention to the words and phrases used to describe the company's internal CSR communication efforts and strategies. To code employee engagement with CSR activities, we used descriptive coding to identify the different ways, forms, and types of employee engagement with CSR reported by the company. In both phases of coding, the authors met regularly to engage in intensive discussion about the coding process, resolve coding discrepancies, and review the data for consistency.

Two semi-structured, in-depth telephone interviews were conducted. The interviews lasted 48 and 61 minutes, respectively. The interviewees were two Home Depot Foundation managers whose job responsibilities included CSR partnership management, finance, and community grants administration for the Home Depot Foundation. The two managers had 5 and 12 years of work experience with Home Depot. The interviews were de-identified and transcribed for data analysis. The semi-structured interview protocol asked the participants about (1) their job, (2) overall work experience, (3) the companies' CSR activities and internal communication, and (4) their engagement with the company's CSR activities. Two researchers coded the transcripts together. Taking the same deductive approach as the one used to analyze the annual reports, the researchers identified codes reflecting Morsing and Schultz's (2006) CSR communication strategies. In addition, the researchers inductively coded and conceptualized additional themes that reflected other relevant theoretical constructs and drew patterns among the themes under the guidance of the research questions. During this process, we approached introspection through the techniques of reflexive thematic analysis recommended by Byrne (Braun & Clarke, 2013).

Findings

Employee Engagement in CSR Activities

The process, forms, and scope of employee CSR engagement were thoroughly reported in the annual reports in three formats: CEO letters, employee anecdotal stories, and statistical summaries. Our findings revealed that employees mainly engaged in Home Depot's three flagship CSR programs: improving the lives of U.S. veterans, training tradespeople to fill the labor gap, and supporting communities impacted by natural disasters (The Home Depot, 2021a). The reports revealed a growing pattern of employees' time commitment to CSR engagement, increasing from 150,480 hours in FY2016 to 315,000 in FY2019. The annual CSR reports included associates' personal stories to describe their engagement with CSR. For example, a CEO letter stated, "... our associates have impacted more than 22,000 veterans; housing units over the past three years by generously giving their time and hard work through our Team Depot projects" (2015 Sustainability Report, p. 5). Detailed anecdotal and statistical evidence was also frequently presented to demonstrate Home Depot's commitment to and accountability for employee CSR engagement. For example, "54,000 associates volunteered for Team Depot projects in 2019" (2020 Responsibility Report, p. 120); and in combating COVID, "more than 95% of our stores have donated essential Covid-19 supplies locally" (2020 Responsibility Report, p. 21).

The scope of employee CSR engagement covers all associate levels across the company and has expanded to other countries (e.g., Mexico) in recent years. Notably, employees took the initiative to lead CSR activities locally, showing a bottom-up approach to CSR engagement. For example, by fixing a veteran's home to be move-in ready, employees were able to give back to the communities where they live and work. More than 2,000 associates at all levels of the company led Team Depor activities in 2020. Nonprofit partners are an important venue for employee CSR engagement. Home Depot has collaborated with thousands of nonprofit organizations (e.g., All Hands and Hearts, the American Red Cross, Convoy of Hope, Team Rubicon), through which employees can engage in volunteer work and matching donations.

The Application of Information, Response, and Involvement Strategies

The interviews with the two CSR managers of the Home Depot Foundation revealed that its internal CSR communication includes information, response, and involvement strategies, but there was substantial variation in the specific tactics for each communication strategy. The information communication strategy has been used consistently and frequently through weekly email newsletters to inform store associates about Home Depot Foundation's CSR programs and decisions. The response strategy was used less frequently and was applied as reactive communication to employees' reports to the organization. Home Depot used three tactics to implement the response strategy. First, at the end of each CSR project, a team of independent store associates, the store manager, or the Team Depot Captain would send a report to the Home Depot Foundation. In response, the corporation would broadcast the outcomes and value of the reported project to the entire organization. However, reporting of the projects is not mandatory for employee participants unless the Foundation financially funds the activities. It is worth noting that the Home Depot Foundation financially funds only about 30% of the employees' field activities. Each year, Home Depot also hosts an annual survey and training event for all Home Depot Captains called "the voice of the associates" to hear from and give feedback to the store associates. The survey serves as a corporate listening channel, and the training sessions educate Team Depot Captains and ensure that Captains understand the company's scale of CSR efforts, progress, and long-term plans. Team Depot Captains are the liaisons between the company and the employees under the response communication strategy. The regional vice presidents of Home Depot also do store walks to hear from the store associates and address their concerns directly.

The third strategy, the involvement strategy, is utilized most frequently at the store level. Team Depot Captains, the self-elected leaders of CSR activities at each Home Depot store, are the primary practitioners of the involvement strategy. This strategy is also enabled by the high level of autonomy Home Depot gives its employees who want to engage in CSR efforts. At the local level, average Team Depot members have the autonomy to propose and drive a CSR project that matches their passions and interests. The Team Depot Captains and members collectively negotiate and make decisions on the actual community projects. Team Depot Captains serve as the central communication hubs within their own team using the involvement communication strategy. This strategy allows internal CSR communication to grow naturally and organically for each associate volunteer team.

Factors Influencing Internal CSR Communication and Employee Engagement

Home Depot Foundation managers discussed prosocial values, servant leadership, and decentralized communication infrastructure as three key enablers of internal CSR communication. The values of "giving back" and "doing the right thing" were common themes in the interviews with the managers. They reported that Home Depot employees "live and believe" these corporate values in every aspect of the business operation. The company's long-term commitment to these prosocial corporate values has not only propelled the company to thoroughly embrace all levels of CSR communication strategies but also encouraged employees' extra-role helping behaviors, manifested by the broad mobilization of employee volunteerism. Home Depot's prosocial corporate culture cultivates an environment where both managers and employees hold strong beliefs in the value of CSR, actively communicate CSR through diverse channels, and voluntarily engage in CSR activities.

The second enabler is servant leadership, which is characterized by follower orientation, service to subordinates, and moral elevation (Sendjaya et al., 2008). In particular, servant leaders encourage employees to learn and grow by offering them autonomy in the workplace (Bass, 2000). At Home Depot, servant leadership is thoroughly implemented from the top to mid-level management. In addition to "pushing the idea of giving back … and doing what's right in the communities," the leaders listen to employees' needs and concerns, provide ample support for employees' creativity and innovation, and trust employees "to get things done," according to one of the Home Depot Foundation managers. The servant leadership style of the managers encourages Home Depot employees to engage in CSR activities.

Lastly, Home Depot has a decentralized communication infrastructure, which enables the CSR involvement in communication strategy at the bottom level of the company.

Instead of implementing a hierarchical structure, the company's internal CSR activities are decentralized. Since the company operates in all U.S. states as well as in other countries (e.g., Mexico and Canada), the corporation only functions as a "support center." Team Depot Captains in individual stores negotiate and organize employees' routine engagement in CSR programs. This decentralized structure and small-scale Team Depot teams successfully empower a CSR involvement communication strategy, which is often the most difficult strategy to implement, especially in large corporations.

Implications for Practice

Based on Home Depot's CSR and internal communication literature, interviews with the managers, and an analysis of the CSR reports, we provide four suggestions for internal CSR strategy development. First, companies should consider using a combination of information, response, and involvement strategies. Each strategy has its benefits and weaknesses. For example, weekly newsletters are a convenient way to disseminate CSR information to less engaged employees. However, the effects of generating awareness and engagement are not guaranteed by the information strategy alone. Blending the different communication strategies could achieve optimum communication effects.

Second, corporate values that are deeply rooted in managers' and employees' desires are the most fundamental drivers of effective internal CSR communication and employee CSR engagement. Managers could strengthen employees' beliefs in the value of CSR and motivate them to participate by fostering a prosocial corporate culture. Adopting the servant leadership style could also effectively facilitate employee engagement by empowering employees to exercise autonomy in CSR.

Third, instead of adopting a hierarchical communication structure, decentralized CSR communication could effectively boost employee engagement, especially in large corporations. A "transversal" communication infrastructure could effectively complement the involvement strategy. Instead of having only one department in charge of CSR communication, a designated CSR leader in every department at all levels would improve the embeddedness of CSR into the corporate fabric and propel the implementation of the involvement strategy (Beckman et al., 2009). Managers could also segment workers into small groups depending on their interest in a social cause to create CSR activities and track the success of CSR involvement in a decentralized manner.

Finally, collaboration with nonprofit organizations that specialize in certain CSR areas (e.g., disaster response) can provide professional training and support so that employees can engage in targeted CSR, and thus increase the social impact of their CSR participation. The localization of CSR can also help employees conveniently engage in CSR because of the proximity to the neighborhood needs.

Learning Outcomes

1) Comprehend the theoretical foundations of internal CSR communication and employee CSR engagement.
2) Analyze the case of Home Depot and understand how the information, response, and involvement CSR communication strategies are implemented using different communication tactics.
3) Assess strengths and weaknesses of different internal CSR communication strategies in practice.

Discussion Questions

1) To what extent do you think Home Depot's success in internal CSR communication can be replicated in other companies in the retail industry? Are there any differences for companies in other industries? Why or why not?
2) What expectations do younger employees have for their employers' CSR efforts? How would their expectations help shape our understanding of internal CSR and CSR communication?
3) How can the internal communication strategies discussed in this chapter be applied to address employees' emerging CSR expectations? What additional tactics or strategies can be developed besides or based on these strategies?

Further Readings

Deloitte. (2020). *The Deloitte Global Millennial Survey 2020*. Retrieved from: https://www2.deloitte.com/global/en/pages/about-deloitte/articles/millennialsurvey.html.

Donia, M. (2020, January 29). *Employees want genuine corporate social responsibility, not greenwashing.* Retrieved from: https://theconversation.com/employees-want-genuine-corporate-social-responsibility-not-greenwashing-130435.

Rodell, J. B., Breitsohl, H., Schröder, M., & Keating, D. J. (2016). Employee volunteering: A review and framework for future research. *Journal of Management, 42*(1), 55–84.

References

2015 Sustainability Report. (2015). https://corporate.homedepot.com/sites/default/files/THD_0039_2015_Sustainability_Report_Online_Nov_10.pdf

2020 Responsibility Report. (2020). Retrieved from https://ir.homedepot.com/~/media/Files/H/HomeDepot-IR/documents/ESG%20Page/2020_Responsibility%20Report_FINAL.pdf

Bass, B. M. (2000). The future of leadership in learning organizations. *Journal of Leadership Studies*, *7*(3), 18–40.

Barakat, S. R., Isabella, G., Boaventura, J. M. G., & Mazzon, J. A. (2016). The influence of corporate social responsibility on employee satisfaction. *Management Decision*, *54*(9), 2325–2339.

Beckman, T., Colwell, A., & Cunningham, P. H. (2009). The emergence of corporate social responsibility in Chile: The importance of authenticity and social networks. *Journal of Business Ethics*, *86*(2), 191–206.

Bekmeier-Feuerhahn, S., Bögel, P. M., & Koch, C. (2017). Investigating internal CSR communication: Building a theoretical framework. In *Handbook of integrated CSR communication* (89–107). Cham: Springer.

Bhattacharya, C. B., Sen, S., & Korschun, D. (2007). Corporate social responsibility as an internal marketing strategy. *Sloan Management Review*, *49*(1), 1–29.

Brammer, S., He, H., & Mellahi, K. (2015). Corporate social responsibility, employee organizational identification, and creative effort: The moderating impact of corporate ability. *Group & Organization Management*, *40*(3), 323–352.

Braun, V., & Clarke, V. (2013). *Successful qualitative research: A practical guide for beginners*. London: Sage.

Chen, Y. R. R., & Hung-Baesecke, C. J. F. (2014). Examining the internal aspect of corporate social responsibility (CSR): Leader behavior and employee CSR participation. *Communication Research Reports*, *31*(2), 210–220.

Chen, Z. F., Hong, C., & Occa, A. (2019). How different CSR dimensions impact organization-employee relationships: The moderating role of CSR-culture fit. *Corporate Communications: An International Journal*, *21*(1), 63–78.

Du, S., Bhattacharya, C. B., & Sen, S. (2010). Maximizing business returns to corporate social responsibility (CSR): The role of CSR communication. *International Journal of Management Reviews*, *12*(1), 8–19.

Duthler, G., & Dhanesh, G. S. (2018). The role of corporate social responsibility (CSR) and internal CSR communication in predicting employee engagement: Perspectives from the United Arab Emirates (UAE). *Public Relations Review*, *44*(4), 453–462.

Edinger-Schons, L. M., Lengler-Graiff, L., Scheidler, S., & Wieseke, J. (2019). Frontline employees as corporate social responsibility (CSR) ambassadors: A quasi-field experiment. *Journal of Business Ethics*, *157*(2), 359–373.

Golob, U., Podnar, K., Elving, W. J., Nielsen, A. E., Thomsen, C., & Schultz, F. (2013). CSR communication: Quo vadis? *Corporate Communications: An International Journal*, *18*(2), 176–192.

Grunig, J. E., & Hunt, T. (1984). *Managing public relations*. Fort Worth, TX: Harcourt Brace Jovanovich College Publishers.

Im, S., Chung, Y., & Yang, J. (2016). Employees' participation in corporate social responsibility and organizational outcomes: The moderating role of person–CSR fit. *Sustainability, 9*(1), 28. https://doi.org/10.3390/su9010028

Jiang, H., & Luo, Y. (2020). Driving employee engagement through CSR communication and employee perceived motives: The role of CSR-related social media engagement and job engagement. *International Journal of Business Communication*. https://doi.org/10.1177/2329488420960528

Jiang, H., & Shen, H. (2020). Toward a relational theory of employee engagement: Understanding authenticity, transparency, and employee behaviors. *International Journal of Business Communication*. https://doi.org/10.1177/2329488420954236.

Kang, K. H., Lee, S., & Huh, C. (2010). Impacts of positive and negative corporate social responsibility activities on company performance in the hospitality industry. *International Journal of Hospitality Management, 29*(1), 72–82.

Kim, S. (2019). The process model of corporate social responsibility (CSR) communication: CSR communication and its relationship with consumers' CSR knowledge, trust, and corporate reputation perception. *Journal of Business Ethics, 154*(4), 1143–1159.

Kim, H. R., Lee, M., Lee, H. T., & Kim, N. M. (2010). Corporate social responsibility and employee–company identification. *Journal of Business Ethics, 95*(4), 557–569.

Lee, S. Y., & Carroll, C. E. (2011). The emergence, variation, and evolution of corporate social responsibility in the public sphere, 1980–2004: The exposure of firms to public debate. *Journal of Business Ethics, 104*(1), 115–131.

Lee, Y., & Yue, C. A. (2020). Status of internal communication research in public relations: An analysis of published articles in nine scholarly journals from 1970 to 2019. *Public Relations Review, 46*(3), 101906.

Lim, J. S., & Greenwood, C. A. (2017). Communicating corporate social responsibility (CSR): Stakeholder responsiveness and engagement strategy to achieve CSR goals. *Public Relations Review, 43*(4), 768–776.

Men, L. R. (2014). Strategic internal communication: Transformational leadership, communication channels, and employee satisfaction. *Management Communication Quarterly, 28*(2), 264–284.

Men, L. R., & Bowen, S. A. (2017). *Excellence in internal communication management*. New York, NY: Business Expert Press.

Morsing, M. (2006). Corporate social responsibility as strategic autocommunication: On the role of external stakeholders for member identification. *Business Ethics: A European Review, 15*(2), 171–182.

Morsing, M., & Schultz, M. (2006). Corporate social responsibility communication: Stakeholder information, response and involvement strategies. *Business Ethics: A European Review, 15*(4), 323–338.

Newman, A., Nielsen, I., & Miao, Q. (2015). The impact of employee perceptions of organizational corporate social responsibility practices on job performance and organizational citizenship behavior: Evidence from the Chinese private sector. *The International Journal of Human Resource Management, 26*(9), 1226–1242.

Rothbard, N. P. (2001). Enriching or depleting? The dynamics of engagement in work and family roles. *Administrative Science Quarterly, 46*(4), 655–684.

Rupp, D. E., Ganapathi, J., Aguilera, R. V., & Williams, C. A. (2006). Employee reactions to corporate social responsibility: An organizational justice framework. *Journal of Organizational Behavior, 27*(4), 537–543.

Sendjaya, S., Sarros, J. C., & Santora, J. C. (2008). Defining and measuring servant leadership behaviour in organizations. *Journal of Management Studies, 45*(2), 402–424. https://doi.org/10.1111/j.1467-6486.2007.00761.x

The Home Depot. (2018, January 25). *From the archives: Team Depot celebrates 25 years of giving back.* Retrieved from: https://corporate.homedepot.com/newsroom/team-depot-celebrates-25-years-giving-back

The Home Depot. (2021a, August, 10). *About us.* Retrieved from https://corporate.homedepot.com/about

The Home Depot. (2021b). *2021 ESG report.* Retrieved from: https://corporate.homedepot.com/sites/default/files/THD_2021ESGReport_singlepages_2_0.pdf

Verčič, A. T., Verčič, D., & Sriramesh, K. (2012). Internal communication: Definition, parameters, and the future. *Public Relations Review, 38*(2), 223–230.

Young, W., Hwang, K., McDonald, S., & Oates, C. J. (2010). Sustainable consumption: Green consumer behaviour when purchasing products. *Sustainable Development, 18*(1), 20–31.

Chapter Sixteen

The Impact of Corporate Social Advocacy: A Case Study on Building Employee-Company Relationships through Corporate Engagement in the Fight against Asian Hate

Keonyoung Park

Introduction

On March 16, 2021, six Asian women were killed by a lone shooter at several spas in the Atlanta, Georgia area (Liu, 2022). It was an extreme example of the increased anti-Asian sentiment in the U.S. since the COVID-19 pandemic. In response to an increasing number of reports of Asian hate crimes, some organizations such as Nike, Clinique, and HBO have voiced their public support for the #StopAsianHate movement (General, 2021). However, other organizations have remained silent. Corporate social advocacy (CSA) refers to the various ways in which a corporation shows support for controversial socio-political movements (Dodd & Supa, 2014). This chapter presents a recent case of CSA in the U.S. as these corporations raised their voices to support #StopAsianHate.

The present study sheds light on how organizations' engagement in #StopAsianHate influenced their employees' engagement in the workplace. Since Asians make up only about 7% of the U.S. overall population (Pew Research Center, 2021), engaging in #StopAsianHate might not promote broad support from the general public. In addition, most people have low involvement in Asian-related issues or they may prioritize these issues less. People have also taken different positions on the #StopAsianHate movement. However, CSA can signal an organization's sincere commitment to an issue and society (e.g., Park, 2021), because organizations take a risk of negative responses from groups of people who oppose the stance (Baur & Wettstein, 2016). This study expects that organizations' engagement in #StopAsianHate will promote a positive organizational identity that is admired by the public including employees.

There have been academic attempts and social discourse exploring the #StopAsianHate movement since the COVID-19 pandemic surged (He et al., 2021). Although previous studies have provided meaningful insights into understanding the influence of #StopAsianHate, the research outcomes have tended to suggest broad implications in general (e.g., Gover et al., 2020; Tessler et al., 2020). Based on internal communication

DOI: 10.4324/9781003195580-23

perspectives, this study focuses on employee-employer relationships when organizations take a stance and make their voices heard on current social issues. Successful internal communication creates workplace relationships with shared values (Karanges et al., 2015) and sense of community (Shen & Jiang, 2021). Building on the insights from social identity theory (Tajfel & Turner, 1986), the results have meaningful implications for organizations and public relations practitioners regarding how to manage controversial social issues to effectively communicate with employees and maintain a mutually beneficial relationship.

Literature Review

Role of Organizations' Social Engagement in Employee-Employer Relationships

Organizations have often engaged in social issues to contribute to a better society. Even if their corporate social responsibility (CSR) activities are not directly connected to organizational profits, organizations expect relational benefits in terms of social investment, such as positive attitudes, trust, loyalty, and mutual commitment from the public (Du et al., 2010). The benefits of CSR have also been extended to employee-employer relationships. How organizations communicate about their CSR activities can impact employee engagement. For example, when organizations provide interactive and stakeholder-engaged CSR communication, employees are more likely to perceive that the organization and its CSR activities are authentic and, in turn, engage in supportive activities (Jiang & Luo, 2020). Duthler and Dhanesh (2018) provided empirical evidence that organizations' CSR activities in social and sustainable dimensions encourage employees to be more socially and affectively engaged.

Employee-Company Identification (ECI)

CSA is when a corporation takes a stance on a controversial socio-political issue (Dodd & Supa, 2014). As a progressive form of CSR, this study posits that CSA may have a stronger effect on employee engagement than traditional CSR initiatives that do not let an organization's voice be heard. Since CSA is when an organization definitively discloses their stance on controversial social issues (Dodd & Supa, 2014), the public may need to determine what the organization's issue stance is and if the organization has a sincere social commitment (Park & Jiang, 2020). When organizations take a stand, employees can recognize their employer's social identity compared to their own identity.

Social identity theory explains how individuals define themselves based on their social group's identity. People form their self-identity based on their group membership(s), which cultivates a sense of belonging (Tajfel & Turner, 1986). In addition, when people recognize a positive characteristic of their organization, they attempt to identify themselves with the organization so they can benefit as a member (Ashforth & Mael, 1989).

Employee communication scholars have adopted the social identity approach to understanding the relationships between employers and employees (Scott, 2007). A corporation may motivate its employees to perceive organizational characteristics more positively. As a result, employees accept the organization's identity to represent their self-image, referred to as ECI. Kim et al. (2010) showed that when employees perceive more external prestige based on their organizations' characteristics, the employees may have a higher level of ECI. Previous research has also suggested that ECI enhances employees' subjective well-being (Yang, 2014) and organizational commitment (Kim et al., 2010; Turker, 2009) and decreases turnover intentions (Haque et al., 2019).

Organization-Based Self-Esteem (OBSE)

The groups to which a person belongs are significant sources of self-esteem (Tajfel & Turner, 1986). When an organization's CSA engagement Organization-Based Self-Esteem influences employees' identity, organization-based self-esteem (OBSE) may mediate the connection. OBSE refers to the self-perception of employees' competence and self-worth in relation to other organizational members (Pierce et al., 1989). Unlike general self-esteem, self-evaluations are taken into account in OBSE specifically in a workplace context. Pierce et al. (1989) claimed that employees with a high level of OBSE tend to regard themselves as "important, meaningful, effectual, and worthwhile within their employing organization" (p. 625).

Organizations' social engagement has been shown to be a crucial factor in employees' OBSE. Employees' OBSE is likely to rise when they have organizational pride and a positive self-image that is fostered by organizational membership (Dutton et al., 2010). For example, Hur et al. (2022) suggested that an organization's social reputation based on its CSR activities during the COVID-19 crisis may have fostered frontline workers' self-image and OBSE in addition to identification with the organization.

Previous research has also shown that employees' OBSE can enhance employee relationships and organizational outcomes. For example, Hui and Lee (2000) showed that employees were less receptive to a sense of organizational uncertainty (i.e., job insecurity and anticipation of organizational changes) when they had high levels of OBSE. Moreover, employees' intrinsic motivation, organizational commitment, and absenteeism were affected differently by the moderating effects of OBSE.

Employee Engagement

This study places employee engagement as the final outcome variable that is influenced by CSA. In terms of work roles in an organization, employees are expected to engage in "occasional innovative and cooperative behavior" (p. 388) that goes beyond their required work roles (Katz & Kahn, 1966). Employee engagement has also been discussed with a focus on employees' attitudes (e.g., vigorous, devoted, and immersed in the workplace environment) with a pleasant, rewarding, and work-related mindset (Schaufeli & Bakker, 2004). Based on this view, engagement from an organizational perspective can be defined as an individual's experiences that are psychologically inspired over time through interactions with an organization that is distinguished by emotional commitment, positive affectivity, and empowerment, leading to motivated behavioral results (Kang, 2014).

Both OBSE and ECI are considered antecedents of employee engagement (Wollard & Shuck, 2011). Because a positive self-concept based on organizational membership can bring relational rewards, employees may become motivated to be more involved as a result of the rewards (Saks, 2006). Therefore, building on the literature review, this study suggests the following hypotheses and theoretical model in the context of CSA related to the #StopAsianHate movement (see Figure 16.1):

H1: An employer's CSA is positively related to employees' OBSE.

H2: An employer's CSA is positively related to ECI.

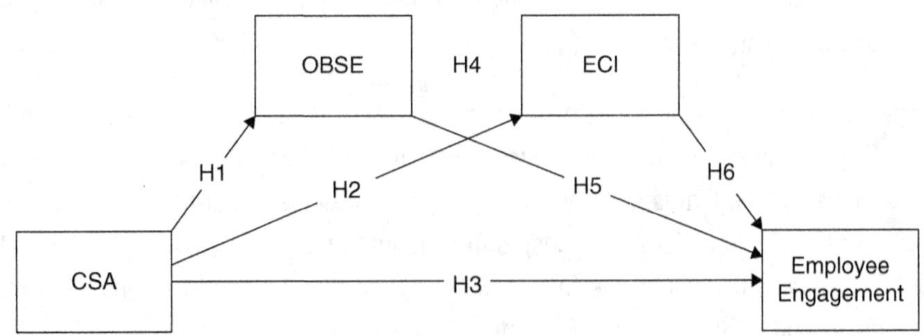

FIGURE 16.1 Theoretical model and hypotheses of this study.

Note: CSA: corporate social advocacy, OBSE: organization-based self-esteem, ECI: employee-company identification, Hypothesized indirect effects (H7: CSA → OBSE → Employee Engagement, H8: CSA engagement → ECI → Employee Engagement, H9: CSA → OBSE → ECI→ Employee Engagement).

H3: An employer's CSA is positively related to employee engagement.

H4: Employees' OBSE is positively related to ECI.

H5: OBSE is positively related to employee engagement.

H6: ECI is positively related to employee engagement.

H7: OBSE mediates the relationship between an employer's CSA and employee engagement.

H8: ECI mediates the relationship between an employer's CSA and employee engagement.

H9: OBSE and ECI mediate the relationship between an employer's CSA and employee engagement.

Method

This study collected data from an online survey ($n = 798$) via Qualtrics, an online survey platform. Survey participants were recruited through Daynata. Only full-time employees working in the U.S. were invited to participate in the survey. Prior to completing the main questionnaire, survey participants read a brief introduction about CSA and Asian hate crimes in the U.S. The participants were asked to answer the survey questions thinking about their own organizations and social engagement related to the issue of stopping Asian hate.

Sample Profile

Of the 798 survey participants, 56.5% were males and 43.2% were females. The distribution of age is as follows: 8.5% participants were 18 to 24 years old, 11.2% were 25 to 29, 18.2% were 30 to 34, 21.3% were 35 to 39, 14.3% were 40 to 44, 9.5% were 45 to 49, 4.1% were 50 to 54, 5.6% were 55 to 59, 3.4% were 60 to 64, 7.2% were 65 to 69, 2.5% were 70 to 74, and 0.3% were 75 or above ($SD = 11.65$). In terms of race, most participants (72.3%) were Caucasian, followed by African (9.5%), Latino or Hispanic (7.8%), East Asian (3.1%), South Asian (2.6%), mixed (2%), other races (1.6%), Middle Eastern (0.5%), and Caribbean (0.5%). In total, 74.5% of the participants had an annual income of $30,000 to $149,999. As for the highest level of education, 87.4% of the participants had college experience. In terms of the organizational size, 72.9% had between 250 and 50,000 employees.

Measures: Main Variables

Employer's CSA engagement was measured by asking participants' perceived strength of organizations' issue identification. Four measurement items were borrowed from previous research (Park & Jiang, 2020) and modified for the context of #StopAsianHate. Sample questions are, "*Regarding the issue of #StopAsianHate,* my company defines itself as a supporter of the issue" and "my company is confident that the political/social option it has chosen is the best" ($M = 5.77$, $SD = 1.04$). We measured **OBSE** with ten items from Pierce et al.'s (1989) study. Sample statements are, "I count around here," "I am taken seriously around here," and "I am important around here" ($M = 5.86$, $SD = 0.93$). **Employee-Company Identification (ECI)** was adopted to measure an employee's perceived quality of the relationship with his/her employer. To measure the concept, we took six items from Ali et al.'s (2020) study. Items include, "When someone criticizes my company, it feels like a personal insult," "I am very interested in what others think about my company," and "When I talk about this company, I usually say 'we' rather than 'they'" ($M = 5.60$, $SD = 1.08$).

Lastly, we measured **employee engagement** with five emotional engagement items. Previous research has suggested that employee job engagement includes physical, emotional, and cognitive engagement. Considering that emotional engagement motivates both physical and cognitive engagement, we adopted emotional engagement to test the effect of CSA. Example items are, "When *my company participates in a corporate social advocacy (CSA),* I feel energetic at the job assigned to me," and "I am interested in the job assigned to me" ($M = 5.78$, $SD = 1.01$). All items were measured on a 7-point Likert scale.

Data Analysis

The reliability of all the main variables was examined before testing the hypotheses. All the variables revealed statistically satisfactory reliability (*Cronbach's* $\boldsymbol{\alpha}_{\text{employer's CSA engagement}} = 0.89$, $\boldsymbol{\alpha}_{\text{OBSE}} = 0.94$, $\boldsymbol{\alpha}_{\text{ECI}} = 0.91$, $\boldsymbol{\alpha}_{\text{employee engagement}} = 0.86$).

Using Hayes' (2013) PROCESS Model 8 as a guide, this study conducted a conditional process model test to examine both the direct and indirect influences depicted in Figure 16.1. The PROCESS model was used to assess the two mediator-related hypotheses of the study. The PROCESS model provides effect sizes and bootstrap confidence intervals (CIs) for both direct and indirect channels, as well as estimates for indirect effects that are mediated by the two factors (Hayes, 2013).

Results

Testing Hypotheses

The results of the PROCESS model analysis revealed statistically significant correlations among the four important variables: perceived CSA engagement strength, OBSE, ECI, and employee emotional engagement. To remove unexpected effects, the PROCESS model added control variables, including participants' demographic information (i.e., age, gender, ethnicity, income, and education), employment history (i.e., number of employees in the organization, work period, position), and perceived involvement in the #StopAsianHate issue.

The findings indicated that employees' perceived that the strength of CSA engagement of their organization on the issue of #StopAsianHates was directly connected to employees OBSE (H1 supported, Coeff. = 0.18, $t = 5.42$, $p = 0.00$), ECI (H2 supported, Coeff. = 0.57, $t = 22.97$, $p = 0.00$), and employees' emotional engagement in their workplace (H3 supported, Coeff. = 0.21, $t = 7.55$, $p = 0.00$). Employee's OBSE was also positively associated with employees' ECI (H4 supported, Coeff. = 0.67, $t = 17.49$, $p = 0.00$) and emotional engagement (H5 supported; Coeff. = 0.31, $t = 10.97$, $p = 0.00$). Lastly, there was a positive relationship between ECI and emotional engagement (H6 supported; Coeff. = 0.43, $t = 12.16$, $p = 0.00$).

This study confirmed the indirect effects of the main antecedent (i.e., perceived strength of CSA) on the final outcome variable (i.e., employee's emotional engagement), estimating bootstrapping CIs with 5,000 times the samplings. Employees' perceived strength of CSA on the issue of #StopAsianHate was statistically significantly positive for employees' emotional engagement in their workplace when the relationship was mediated by either OBSE (H7 supported; Coeff. = 0.06, BootSE = 0.01, $p < 0.01$) or ECI (H8 supported; Coeff. = 0.25, BootSE = 0.04, $p = 0.00$). Both mediators together (OBSE as the first mediator and ECI as the second mediator) also indicated a relationship between the strength of CSA and emotional engagement (H9 supported; Coeff. = 0.12, BootSE = 0.02, $p = 0.00$) (see Figure 16.2).

Discussion/Application

This case study explored how CSA generates employee engagement in the context of the #StopAsianHate movement. Building on social identity theory, the current study proposed a theoretical model and tested it empirically using an online survey. According

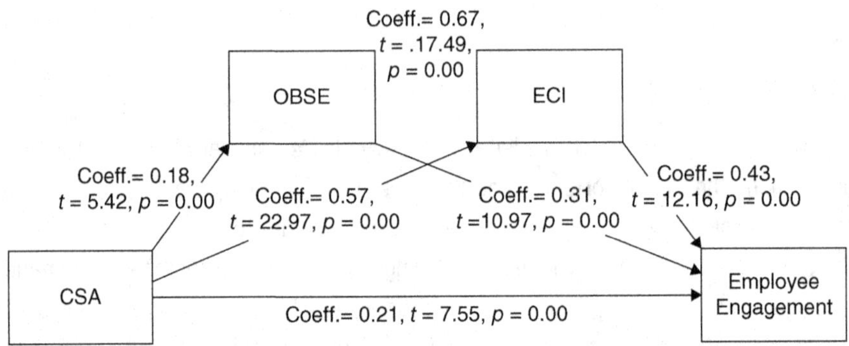

FIGURE 16.2 Results of hypothesis testing.

Notes: CSA: corporate social advocacy, OBSE: organization-based self-esteem, ECI: employee-company identification, Hypothesized indirect effects, Indirect effects (H7: CSA → OBSE → Employee Engagement (Coeff. = .06, BootSE = .01, p = .00), H8: CSA engagement → ECI → Employee Engagement (Coeff. = .25, BootSE = .04, p = .00), H9: CSA → OBSE → ECI → Employee Engagement (Coeff. = .12, BootSE = .02, p = .00).

to social identity theory, people tend to perceive that their self-concept reflects their relevant group's characteristics (Tajfel & Turner, 1986). Public relations researchers have suggested that organizations may develop employee relations and enhance their emotional satisfaction by cultivating an organizational identity (Kim et al., 2010; Turker, 2009; Yang, 2014). In this line of research, the present study showed that organizations' active engagement in social issues (i.e., CSA) can be an attractive identity that motivates employees to engage in the workplace. Our survey results also showed that the stronger employees perceived their organizations' CSA, the higher they perceived OBSE, ECI, and engagement in the workplace. Specifically, employee engagement based on their perception of CSA was mediated by OBSE and ECI. Thus, this case study extends the application of social identity theory to the CSA literature.

This study also provides insights into the impact of CSA in the context of employee communication. Given that previous academic and corporate interest in CSA has tended to focus on the influence of CSA on external stakeholders or on business return, this case study is a bridge between the CSA and employee relations literature. The findings of this study suggest lessons on effective internal communication based on the co-value creation process and identity sharing. As Shen and Jiang (2021) claimed, internal public relations can be more sustainable when approached with a community-building perspective where both organizations and employees are full members with a strong sense of belonging. In this line, this study provides an example of the community-building process between an organization and employees, which starts from CSA and connects to employees' OBSE and ECI.

Moreover, considering that the result showed the connection between CSA, OBSE, ECI, and employee engagement, this study may add an implication to employee engagement literature. Scholars expect internal communication to develop workplace relationships with significance and value that can be represented to employee engagement (Karanges et al., 2015). The finding of this study suggests the way CSA enhances strong relationships between organizations and employees that connect to employee engagement.

This case study contributes to employee communication literature by providing practical guidelines on how corporations should manage controversial socio-political issues, especially when not all employees are deeply involved in the issues. Although corporations have diverse internal stakeholders from various social backgrounds, they are not immune to social pressure. Although this study provides empirical evidence on the impact of companies that spoke out against Asian hate crimes, the expected outcome of this study is that it provides a compelling example of how corporations can strengthen relationships with their employees by supporting social issues, even if they are controversial. Recent research has shown that quality relationships between employees and their organizations enhance employees' work-related outcomes, leading to not only increased employee engagement but also a decrease in job burnout, and intention to quit (Ali et al., 2020).

The findings of this study may also have broad implications for corporations hoping to remain neutral in the face of an increasingly polarized world. For example, considering the diversity of employee backgrounds in global corporations, a corporation's definitive stance on a controversial issue may be perceived as favoring one group over another. However, by remaining silent, a corporation could be construed as having abandoned a group. Thus, practitioners and scholars should discuss the optimal level of CSA to enhance employee relationships and employee engagement for everyone.

Learning Outcomes

1) Understand that corporations can develop employee-employer relationships by actively engaging in social issues.
2) Explain how CSA has an impact on employee engagement in the workplace.
3) Recognize that CSA engagement with a controversial social issue, such as #StopAsianHate, can be a positive corporate characteristic to encourage employees to have OBSE and identify themselves with their organization.

Discussion Questions

1) Explain the underlying process of the relationship between employees' perceptions of CSA and their emotional engagement in the workplace.
2) What are the similarities and differences between traditional CSR activities and CSA? Of the two types of corporate social engagement, which one could more effectively motivate employees to become engaged in their job? Why?
3) When taking a supportive position on the #StopAsianHate issue, how should corporations communicate with employees who do not support the movement?
4) Can the findings of this study be applied broadly to other CSA contexts around diverse social issues?

Further Readings

Baur, D., & Wettstein, F. (2016). CSR's new challenge: Corporate political advocacy. In M. C., Coutinho de Arruda, B. Rok (Eds.), *Understanding ethics and responsibilities in a globalizing world* (171–187). Cham, Switzerland: Springer.

Dodd, M. D., Supa, D. W. (2014). Conceptualizing and measuring corporate social advocacy communication: Examining the impact on corporate financial performance. *Public Relations Journal, 8*(3), 2–23.

He, L. S., Zhou, W., He, M., Nie, X. H., & He, J. (2021). Openness and COVID-19 induced xenophobia: The roles of trade and migration in sustainable development. *PLoS One, 16*(4), e0249579.

References

Ashforth, B. E., & Mael, F. (1989). Social identity theory and the organization. *Academy of Management Review, 14*(1), 20–39.

Ali, I., Ali, M., Grigore, G., Molesworth, M., & Jin, Z. (2020). The moderating role of corporate reputation and employee-company identification on the work-related outcomes of job insecurity resulting from workforce localization policies. *Journal of Business Research, 117*, 825–838.

Dodd, M. D., & Supa, D. W. (2014). Conceptualizing and measuring corporate social advocacy communication: Examining the impact on corporate financial performance. *Public Relations Journal, 8*(3), 2–23.

Du, S., Bhattacharya, C. B., & Sen, S. (2010). Maximizing business returns to corporate social responsibility (CSR): The role of CSR communication. *International Journal of Management Reviews, 12*(1), 8–19.

Duthler, G., & Dhanesh, G. S. (2018). The role of corporate social responsibility (CSR) and internal CSR communication in predicting employee engagement: Perspectives from the United Arab Emirates (UAE). *Public Relations Review, 44*(4), 453–462.

Dutton, J. E., Roberts, L. M., & Bednar, J. (2010). Pathways for positive identity construction at work: Four types of positive identity and the building of social resources. *Academy of Management Review, 35*(2), 265–293.

General, R. (2021, February 23) *Major Brands Around the World Share #StopAsianHate in Solidarity.* Yahoo News. https://news.yahoo.com/major-brands-around-world-share-211203162.html

Gover, A. R., Harper, S. B., & Langton, L. (2020). Anti-Asian hate crime during the COVID-19 pandemic: Exploring the reproduction of inequality. *American Journal of Criminal Justice, 45*(4), 647–667.

Haque, A., Fernando, M., & Caputi, P. (2019). The relationship between responsible leadership and organisational commitment and the mediating effect of employee turnover intentions: An empirical study with Australian employees. *Journal of Business Ethics, 156*(3), 759–774.

Hayes, A. F. (2013). *Introduction of mediation, moderation, and conditional process analysis: A regression-based approach.* New York, NY: The Guilford Press.

He, L. S., Zhou, W., He, M., Nie, X. H., & He, J. (2021). Openness and COVID-19 induced xenophobia: The roles of trade and migration in sustainable development. *PLoS One, 16*(4), e0249579.

Hui, C., & Lee, C. (2000). Moderating effects of organization-based self-esteem on organizational uncertainty: Employee response relationships. *Journal of Management, 26*(2), 215–232.

Hur, W. M., Rhee, S. Y., Lee, E. J., & Park, H. (2022). Corporate social responsibility perceptions and sustainable safety behaviors among frontline employees: The mediating roles of organization-based self-esteem and work engagement. *Corporate Social Responsibility and Environmental Management, 29*(1), 60–70.

Jiang, H., & Luo, Y. (2020). Driving employee engagement through CSR communication and employee perceived motives: The role of CSR-related social media engagement and job engagement. *International Journal of Business Communication*, Online First, https://doi.org/10.1177/2329488420960528

Kang, M. (2014). Understanding public engagement: Conceptualizing and measuring its influence on supportive behavioral intentions. *Journal of Public Relations Research, 26*(5), 399–416.

Karanges, E., Johnston, K., Beatson, A., & Lings, I. (2015). The influence of internal communication on employee engagement: A pilot study. *Public Relations Review, 41*(1), 129–131.

Katz, D., & Kahn, R. L. (1966). *The social psychology of organizations.* New York, NY: Wiley

Kim, H. R., Lee, M., Lee, H. T., & Kim, N. M. (2010). Corporate social responsibility and employee–company identification. *Journal of Business Ethics, 95*(4), 557–569.

Liu, M. C-M. (2022, March 16). *A year after the Atlanta shootings, Asian women live in fear: 'How are we all going to stay safe?'* Washington Post. https://www.washingtonpost.com/lifestyle/2022/03/16/anti-asian-attacks-nyc-atlanta/

Park, K. (2021). The mediating role of skepticism: How corporate social advocacy builds quality relationships with publics. *Journal of Marketing Communications*, 1–19. https://doi.org/10.1080/13527266.2021.1964580

Park, K., & Jiang, H. (2020). Signaling, verification, and identification: The way corporate social advocacy generates brand loyalty on social media. *International Journal of Business Communication*, Online First. https://doi.org/10.1177/2329488420907121

Pew Research Center. (2021, April 29). *Key facts about Asian Americans, a diverse and growing population.* https://www.pewresearch.org/fact-tank/2021/04/29/key-facts-about-asian-americans/

Pierce, J. L., Gardner, D. G., Cummings, L. L., & Dunham, R. B. (1989). Organization-based self-esteem: Construct definition, measurement, and validation. *Academy of Management Journal, 32*(3), 622–648.

Saks, A. M. (2006). Antecedents and consequences of employee engagement. *Journal of Managerial Psychology, 21*(7), 600–619.

Schaufeli, W. B., & Bakker, A. B. (2004). Job demands, job resources, and their relationship with burnout and engagement: A multi-sample study. *Journal of Organizational Behavior: The International Journal of Industrial, Occupational and Organizational Psychology and Behavior, 25*(3), 293–315.

Scott, C. R. (2007). Communication and social identity theory: Existing and potential connections in organizational identification research. *Communication Studies, 58*(2), 123–138.

Shen, H., & Jiang, H. (2021). Rethinking internal public relations: Organizations and publics as community members. *Journal of Public Relations Research, 33*(6), 415–428.

Tajfel, H., & Turner, J. C. (1986). The social identity theory of intergroup behaviour. In S. Worchel & W. G. Austin (Eds.), *Psychology of intergroup relations* (7–24). New York, NY: Nelson-Hall.

Tessler, H., Choi, M., & Kao, G. (2020). The anxiety of being Asian American: Hate crimes and negative biases during the COVID-19 pandemic. *American Journal of Criminal Justice, 45*(4), 636–646.

Turker, D. (2009). How corporate social responsibility influences organizational commitment. *Journal of Business Ethics, 89*(2), 189–204.

Wollard, K. K., & Shuck, B. (2011). Antecedents to employee engagement: A structured review of the literature. *Advances in Developing Human Resources, 13*(4), 429–446.

Yang, C. N. (2014). Does ethical leadership lead to happy workers? A study on the impact of ethical leadership, subjective well-being, and life happiness in the Chinese culture. *Journal of Business Ethics, 123*(3), 513–525.

Section VII

Diversity, Equity, and Inclusion

Chapter Seventeen

How Higher Education Engages Employees into DE&I: A Thematic Analysis of Strategic Plans and Chief Diversity Officer Job Duties of the California State University System

Cheng Hong

Introduction

Today's workplace has become more than ever diverse with an increasing number of women, minorities, foreign-born individuals, people with disabilities, and people from other under-represented groups working in the public and private sectors. In response, diversity, equity, and inclusion (hereafter referred to as DE&I) issues have drawn attention among various types of organizations across the United States. In higher education, many universities and colleges have created and appointed Chief Diversity Officers (CDOs), who serve as an institution's highest-ranking diversity administrators and report to the president and/or provost, to achieve an inclusive and equitable community that values diversity and fosters mutual respect and understanding (Williams & Wade-Golden, 2013). Some people regard the appointment of CDOs as symbolic, while others consider it as an intentional action toward transformational change at the institutions (Parker III, 2020). At the same time, DE&I issues have been written into higher education institutions' strategic plans, aiming to create a cohesive and supportive infrastructure for students, faculty, and staff from diverse backgrounds. University strategic plans usually act as a blueprint for improvements desired by one higher education institution and target at increasing enrollment and diversity across the campus (Gardner, 2021).

This chapter sets out to analyze and discuss DE&I issues in higher education from the perspectives of internal communication and employee engagement. Specifically, the author focuses on how university strategic plans address DE&I issues to engage employees (i.e., faculty and staff) into the building of a diverse, inclusive, and equitable community. Additionally, this chapter explores the roles of CDOs in internal communication about DE&I strategies and initiatives. A thematic analysis of strategic plans and job descriptions of CDOs across 23 campuses of California State University system was conducted.

DOI: 10.4324/9781003195580-25

Literature Review and Relevant Theories

Recent years have witnessed the increasing need to align diversity goals with institutional missions in higher education, which gave rise to the job positions of CDOs and the incorporation of DE&I initiatives into university strategic plans (Nixon, 2013). As an executive-level role, CDOs are expected to provide strategic guidelines for diversity planning and implementation at higher education institutions and exert significant impact on diversity hiring and promotion, admission criteria, curriculum, and so on. The National Association of Diversity Officers in Higher Education (NADOHE) has published standards of professional practice for CDOs, including employment training and removing the structural barriers to the access and success of students, faculty, and staff who belong to marginalized and oppressed groups (NADOHE, 2020; Worthington et al., 2020). Higher education literature has also addressed the critical role of university strategic plans in providing a forum for campus-wide conversations about important decisions, including DE&I issues (Hinton, 2012). Meanwhile, scanning of internal environment is deemed as essential when making strategic plans; in other words, a strategic plan should reflect the internal view of an institution in setting its approach and priorities (Hinton, 2012).

Previous investigation of CDOs and university strategic plans has rarely drawn on perspectives of strategic internal communication and employee engagement. To fill in the research gap, this chapter aims to adopt the theoretical lens of stakeholder theory (ST) and employee engagement (Saks, 2006; Taylor & Kent, 2014). ST posits that organizations need to build relationships and create values for all stakeholders who are interdependent on each other (Freeman & Dmytriyev, 2017) and that organizations should be managed in the interest of all their constituents (Laplume et al., 2008). This theory concerns knowing how to engage stakeholders to create useful solutions to problems the organization faces (Freeman et al., 2020). To do so, organizations need to segment stakeholders, understand their interests, and predict their behaviors (Laplume et al., 2008). Employer organizations should be long-term oriented and consciously build trust and foster agility among their stakeholders (Freeman et al., 2020). Prior research has adopted ST to empirically examine corporations' strategies to achieve stakeholder support, manage reputation, increase organizational identity; and workplace diversity has been identified as one significant facet of stakeholder management (Laplume et al., 2008). Furthermore, value creation ST, as one strand of ST, argues that the distinctive elements of ST include individual stakeholders' interactions in value creation within an organization (Freeman et al., 2020).

Employee engagement has been defined in multiple ways. For example, Schaufeli et al. (2002) posited that employee engagement is a "positive, work-related state of mind that is characterized by vigor, dedication and absorption" (p. 74). Saks (2006) conceptualized employee engagement as cognitive, emotional, and behavioral components associated with individual role performance, and thus operationalized engagement with a slightly different approach, including two dimensions of job engagement (i.e., about performing the specific task role) and organizational engagement (i.e., about performing the role as a member of the organization). Saks' (2006) conceptualization highlights the influence of individual employees on the employer organization, which is relevant to this current study context where university employees are motivated to engage into the practice of diversity, equity, and inclusion initiatives to exert impact on organizational culture as members of their employer institution. In addition, employee engagement has also been understood from an organization's perspective (Jeung, 2011). To be specific, empirical evidence has shown that positive organizational behaviors/factors such as organizational support (e.g., Saks, 2006) and congruence between individual and organizational values (e.g., Rich et al., 2010) can motivate employees to engage at the workplace as a member of their employer organization. From this perspective, this chapter seeks to discuss what efforts the CSU campuses have made to engage their employees in the DE&I initiatives.

Case Summary

This case study mainly investigated the DE&I strategies and narratives of the California State University (Cal State or CSU). CSU is a public university system in California with 23 campuses and seven off-campus centers across the state of California. As the largest four-year public university system in the United States, CSU educates approximately 477,000 students who are ethnically, economically, and academically diverse, and hires nearly 56,000 faculty and staff who also come from diverse backgrounds (CSU Fact Book, 2022). One value the whole CSU system holds is diversity and inclusion, aiming to seek out a diversity of ideas, disciplines, and backgrounds. The 23 CSU campuses, though varying by their location, setting, and size, all embrace and practice the value of diversity and inclusion in their own way, connecting the university with the greater community. To be specific, the 23 campuses are CSU Bakersfield, CSU Channel Islands, Chico State, CSU Dominguez Hills, Cal State East Bay, Fresno State, Cal State Fullerton, Cal Poly Humboldt, Cal State Long Beach, Cal State Los Angeles, Cal Maritime, CSU Monterey Bay, CSUN,

Cal Poly Pomona, Sacramento State, Cal State San Bernardino, San Diego State, San Francisco State, San José State, Cal Poly San Luis Obispo, CSU San Marcos, Sonoma State, and Stanislaus State. Each campus has established its own office of diversity, appointed (or in the process of searching for) a CDO, and created a strategic plan that contains DE&I-related initiatives and statements. To engage employees into DE&I issues, CDOs oversee communicating such initiatives and narratives to university faculty and staff. They are also expected to face and handle a diversity of voices among internal stakeholders. Thus, this case study explores the following research questions:

RQ1: What roles do CDOs play in communicating DE&I issues internally among university employees (i.e., faculty and staff) at 23 campuses of CSU system?

RQ2: How do university strategic plans address DE&I issues internally to engage CSU employees into the building of a diverse, equitable, and inclusive campus community?

Methodology

This case study aims to explore how 23 CSU campuses engage their employees internally to co-create a community that embraces diversity, equity, and inclusion. Specifically, strategic plans, DE&I statements, diversity officers' job responsibilities, and descriptions of diversity offices were collected from the official websites of the 23 CSU campuses, respectively. A thematic analysis method was then administered by the researcher to analyze the collected data. Six steps of thematic analysis proposed by Braun and Clarke (2006) were carried, including (1) organizing the data and becoming familiar with the dataset, (2) generating initial codes in association with research topics, (3) searching for broader themes based on the codes, (4) reviewing themes, (5) defining and naming the themes, and (6) writing up the themes with analytical narratives and data extraction.

Case Analysis Results

Roles of CDOs in DE&I on Campus

Almost all CSU campuses have appointed a CDO, except for CSU Dominguez Hills and San Luis Obispo State, which are in the hiring process of CDOs as of writing of this chapter. An examination of their job postings reveals that CDOs are strategic leaders in charge of advancing diversity, equity, and inclusion both centrally and across various divisions of the campus. They are expected to not only show leadership skills, but also demonstrate strong capabilities in communication and conflict resolution, especially when it comes to navigating politically charged situations. Common responsibilities of CDOs at CSU campuses include (a) developing plans for employee recruitment, retention, and development; (b) fostering open dialogue, interaction, and education within the university community on DE&I issues; (c) creating and developing strategic plans for diversity and inclusion in line with university strategic plan; and (d) establishing and implementing measurement and assessment around university diversity. Being a CDO means that one will need to constantly communicate with different university divisions, departments, and colleges where university employees have varying personal and professional experiences.

As the campus leaders of inclusivity and diversity initiatives, CDOs may directly report to the university president and collaborate with other vice presidents (e.g., Cal State Los Angeles, Cal State Pomona, San Jose State). At some campuses (e.g., Fresno State, Cal State Humboldt), CDOs report to the Vice President for Academic Affairs and the Provost. The administrative office CDOs lead carries various names at different CSU campuses, such as the Division of Equity, Inclusion, and Compliance (e.g., Cal State Bakersfield), the Office of Equity, Diversity, and Inclusion (e.g., Chico State), Office of Inclusive Excellence and Sustainability (Cal State Monterey Bay). These offices, under the leadership of CDOs, commonly aim to create a campus environment that is free of all forms of biases and where faculty, staff, and students can work and learn without any discrimination.

In delivering DE&I initiatives, CDOs and their offices manage relationships with employees with their interest in mind. They constantly and honestly disclose updates in relation to DE&I initiatives, whether it is positive or negative. Assessment of DE&I strategies is well and transparently communicated in university strategic plans and DE&I initiatives. For example, Cal State Los Angeles lists out example metrics to measure its DE&I programs, such as increase in support for faculty research and increase in the tenured/tenure-track faculty ratio. San Luis Obispo State also tracks frequency and number of bias incidents reported, donations received for diversity and inclusion initiatives, and graduation of students from under-represented groups. Campus climate survey is another way to capture employees' perception and attitude toward the university's DE&I efforts (e.g., Cal State Monterey Bay).

Engaging Employees into DE&I Issues

Engaging and Empowering Employees with Needed Resources and Support

University employees at the 23 CSU campuses are provided with an inventory of resources to incorporate DE&I initiatives into their teaching, research, and professional development. By doing so, CSU campuses engage and empower employees in their current job position. For example, Cal State Fullerton offers DE&I certificate programs (i.e., Inclusive Introductory Certificate and Inclusive Advanced Certificate) to help faculty understand human diversity in all forms, deepen cultural competency, and obtain knowledge across a broad range of diversity issues. Moreover, Cal State Fullerton provides DE&I intervention training and racial healing training that discuss critical topics such as white privilege, racism/bias, and professorial success among faculty of color. Similarly, Cal State Long Beach creates inclusive teaching training opportunities for faculty, such as workshops on inclusive teaching topics, and new tenure-track faculty training specific to cultural competence and inclusive teaching. To facilitate employees' understanding of multicultural ways of being, thinking, and acting, Cal State Fresno organizes teaching and learning communities made up of faculty, staff, and administrators. Various campuses have shared diverse and inclusive teaching resources and tools (e.g., syllabi examples) that faculty members can adopt to create a diverse and inclusive classroom (e.g., Chico State, Cal State East Bay).

Additionally, employees from underrepresented or marginalized groups can join DE&I affinity groups to seek for resources and support they need at the workplace, and at the same time, foster an environment that embraces mutual understanding and diversity. Most CSU campuses have organized African American Faculty & Staff Association, Asian Pacific Islander Faculty & Staff Association, Chicanx Latinx Faculty & Staff Association, LGBTQ+ Staff and Faculty Association, International Faculty & Staff Association, Native American Faculty & Staff Association, and so on. Via these associations, employees can obtain access to resources they need to get involved in planning and execution of university plans and participate in campus events that can accelerate cross-cultural engagement and mutual understanding.

Engaging Employees to Create Shared Organizational Values

Another way employees are engaged in DE&I initiatives is to participate in shared value creation of their employer university. As key stakeholders of higher education institutions, employees should be part of the value creation process and exert their influence on their employer organization as an essential member. Almost all CSU campuses place DE&I as their mission and/or values in university strategic plans. For example, DE&I and cultural competence are the core values of Cal State Fresno; Cal State LA defines their values of DE&I as cultivating diversity, expecting cultural competence, and actively seeking perspectives and engagement from all constituents in the community to develop just and equitable expectations. In describing their value of inclusive excellence, Cal State Monterey Bay points out that it is more than simply achieving numerical diversity in the makeup of university community; it also involves the creation of an environment that would thrive and unlock the potentialities of students, faculty, and staff. In explaining the value of equity, Sacramento State points out that we need to acknowledge circumstances (e.g., privilege and systemic and structural oppression) that are adversely impacting underrepresented and marginalized groups. Thus, Sacramento State also values innovation—the application of creative and critical thinking to create new processes, products, and services.

Engaging Employees through Shared Governance

In the process of creating university strategic plans, employees are engaged to join the action teams and strategy plan committees to express their interests and voices. For instance, Cal State Humboldt describes its strategic and institutional planning as an inclusive process, where faculty, staff, and community members co-led the planning and practiced shared governance and collaboration. In a similar manner, at Cal State San Bernardino, the president's DE&I Board is composed of representatives from shared governance bodies for faculty, staff, students, and affinity groups across the campus. Stanislaus State also states its campus community beliefs in shared governance and that student success and faculty success are intertwined. San Diego State, in establishing its DE&I initiative, refers to its shared governance initiatives to define and promote DE&I, as well as to facilitate conversations about DE&I issues.

Engaging Employees by Addressing DE&I Issues in Relation to Their Workplace Performance

When it comes to recruitment, retention, and performance evaluation of employees, the Cal State University system is committed to creating a diverse and inclusive working environment. As stated in the Cal State Fresno strategic plan, decisions related to personnel policies and practices should be made based on one's capacity to perform a job, regardless of their gender, age, ethnicity, (dis)ability, sexual orientation, religious or political beliefs, marital status, and so on. In search and hiring processes, many campuses require diversity statements in application packages (e.g., Sacramento State, Cal State Monterey Bay). Stanislaus State moves further by stating that the university actively recruits and hires faculty who are passionate about course materials reflective of underrepresented histories and participate in discussions related to these subject matters. Some campuses proactively offer DE&I trainings to faculty and staff search committees (e.g., Cal State Fullerton) and others organize DE&I subcommittees focusing on recruitment, retention, and development of both faculty and staff (e.g., Cal State San Bernardino). Some campuses explicitly point out DE&I initiatives in university employees are supposed to align with the diverse student population so that all students, faculty, and staff will feel welcomed, supported, and valued by the university (e.g., Cal State Long Beach, San Diego State, Cal State Northridge).

Conclusion and Implications for Practice

This chapter explores DE&I strategic plans, responsibilities, and organizational positions of CDOs among 23 Cal State campuses under the theoretical underpinning of ST and employee engagement. Theoretically speaking, this case study demonstrates the explanatory power of ST to describe how university employees' interests are incorporated in strategic planning of DE&I initiatives, and how employees are involved in organizational value creation process. ST concerns how an organization builds relationships and creates shared values for all stakeholders. The findings of this study empirically illustrate that CSU campuses provide needed resources and support to employees, especially those from the marginalized groups, in building organization-employee relationships; moreover, by involving faculty and staff in the creation of strategic plans, various CSU campuses invite employees to create shared organizational values on DE&I issues and foster shared governance in organizational culture. The two dimensions of employee engagement (i.e., job engagement and organizational engagement) (Saks, 2006) are both indicated in Cal State campuses' strategic plans and CDOs' duties. Namely, employees are not only engaged and supported to perform well in their job positions, but also are empowered and motivated to get involved in shared governance of DE&I issues. This chapter also discusses employee engagement from an organization's perspective. In other words, results reveal how CSU campuses make a list of organizational efforts to engage employees in DE&I issues at the workplace.

As for practical implications, this study provides insights and framework on how higher education institutions can engage employees in DE&I issues. Specifically, the following implications for communication professionals are suggested. First, hiring a CDO to lead DE&I initiatives is a trend in today's higher education. CDOs and their team members are expected to develop and maintain employee relationships through transparent communication, open dialogue, and constant collaboration on DE&I relevant issues, such as recruitment and retention of employees and organizing workshops and trainings. Second, a university strategic plan, to engage employees in DE&I issues, should contain several topics, including (a) professional development trainings about DE&I issues; (b) teaching and research resources to create a diverse, equitable, and inclusive university community; (c) affinity groups supporting the recruitment and retention of employees from marginalized groups; (d) DE&I related university mission and value; and (e) emphasis on shared governance among university employees. By doing so, university employees will get engaged and motivated both in their work position and as organizational members making an impact on organizational directions. Lastly, to effectively communicate DE&I initiatives internally, CDOs are expected to build a robust assessment plan to evaluate how they will monitor the consequences of the enacted DE&I programs. Such a plan is recommended to be data-based, measurable, and in line with an overarching strategic plan.

Learning Outcomes

1) Develop awareness about the roles of CDOs in higher education institutions.
2) Describe the importance of internal communication for the position of CDOs.
3) Explain how CDOs manage relationships with university employees (i.e., faculty and staff).
4) Describe how the DE&I-related topics in university strategic plans engage employees to excel at the workplace and get involved in DE&I initiatives.
5) Explicate how university employees are engaged in creation and maintenance of a diverse, equitable, and inclusive university environment.

Discussion Questions

1) What are the common duties and responsibilities of CDOs at 23 Cal State Campuses?

2) What key DE&I-related topics in university strategic plans are found to engage employees at their job positions?
3) What key DE&I-related topics in university strategic plans are found to engage employees to participate in creating and developing a diverse, equitable, and inclusive campus?
4) How did this case study demonstrate the relationship between employee engagement and DE&I issues at higher education institutions?
5) How did this case study help you understand the role of CDOs as an internal communicator and strategy leader in relations to DE&I issues?

Further Readings

Borah, N., & Barua, M. (2018). Employee engagement: A critical review of literature. *Journal of Organization & Human Behaviour, 7*(4), 22–30.

Hanaysha, J. (2016). Improving employee productivity through work engagement: Evidence from higher education sector. *Management Science Letters, 6*(1), 61–70. doi: 10.5267/j.msl.2015.11.006.

Johnston, K. A., & Taylor, M. (2018). Engagement as communication pathways, possibilities, and future directions. In K. A. Johnston & M. Taylor (Eds.), *The handbook of communication engagement* (1–15). Hoboken, NJ: Wiley-Blackwell.

Leon, R. A. (2014). The chief diversity officer: An examination of CDO models and strategies. *Journal of Diversity in Higher Education, 7*(2), 77–91.

Martinez, J. (2018). Framing inclusion and exclusion: The framing strategies of chief diversity officers in higher education. (Doctoral dissertation). Texas Tech University, Lubbock, TX.

Raul, L. (2014). The chief diversity officer: An examination of CDO models and strategies. *Journal of Diversity in Higher Education, 7*(2), 77–91. doi: 10.1037/a0035586.

Schneider, B., Yost, A. B., Kropp, A., Kind, C., & Lam, H. (2018). Workforce engagement: What it is, what drives it, and why it matters for organizational performance. *Journal of Organizational Behavior, 39*, 462–480. doi: 10.1002/job.2244.

Shen, H., & Jiang, H. (2019). Engaged at work? An employee engagement model in public relations. *Journal of Public Relations Research, 31*(1–2), 32–49. doi: 10.1080/1062726X.2019.1585855.

Stanley, C. A., Watson, K. L., Reyes, J. M., & Varela, K. S. (2019). Organizational change and the chief diversity officer: A case study of institutionalizing a diversity plan. *Journal of Diversity in Higher Education, 12*(3), 255–265. doi:10.1037/dhe0000099.

Verčič, A. T., & Vokić, N. P. (2017). Engaging employees through internal communication. *Public Relations Review, 43*(5), 885–893. doi: 10.1016/j.pubrev.2017.04.005.

References

Braun, V., & Clarke, V. (2006). Using thematic analysis in psychology. *Qualitative Research Psychology*, 3(2), 77–101. doi: 10.1191/1478088706qp063oa.

CSU Fact Book (2022). *The California State University, Fact Book 2022*. Available at: https://www.calstate.edu/csu-system/about-the-csu/facts-about-the-csu/Documents/facts2022.pdf.

Freeman, R. E., & Dmytriyev, S. (2017). Corporate social responsibility and stakeholder theory: Learning from each other. *Symphonya. Emerging Issues in Management*, *1*, 7–15. doi: 10.4468/2017.1.02freeman.dmytriyev.

Freeman, R. E., Phillips, R., & Sisodia, R. (2020). Tensions in stakeholder theory. *Business & Society*, *59*(2), 213–231. doi: 10.1177/0007650318773750.

Gardner, L. (2021, September). The truth about strategic plans: What makes one a success and another a waste of time? Available at: https://www.chronicle.com/article/the-truth-about-strategic-plans.

Hinton, K. E. (2012). *A practical guide to strategic planning in higher education*. Ann Arbor, MI: Society for College and University Planning.

Jeung, C.-W. (2011). The concept of employee engagement: A comprehensive review from a positive organizational behavior perspective. *Performance Improvement Quarterly*, *24*(2), 49–69. doi: 10.1002/piq.20110.

Laplumem, A. O., Sonpar, K., & Litz, R. a. (2008). Stakeholder theory: Reviewing a theory that moves us. *Journal of Management*, *34*(6), 1152–1189. doi: 10.1177/0149206308324322

National Association of Diversity Officers in Higher Education (NADOHE) (2020). *Standards of Professional Practice for Chief Diversity Officers* (Revised). Available at: https://nadohe.memberclicks.net/assets/2020SPPI/__NADOHE%20SPP2.0_200131_FinalFormatted.pdf.

Nixon, M. L. (2013). Women of color chief diversity officers: Their positionality and agency in higher education institutions (Doctoral dissertation). University of Washington, Seattle, WA.

Parker, E. T. III (2020). Do colleges need a chief diversity officer? Available at: https://www.insidehighered.com/views/2020/08/20/chief-diversity-officers-play-vital-role-if-appropriately-positioned-and-supported#:~:text=More%20than%20an%20advocate%2C%20the,to%20center%20the%20diversity%20narrative.

Rich, B. L., Lepine, J. A., & Crawford, E. R. (2010). Job engagement: Antecedents and effects on job performance. *Academy of Management Journal*, 53, 617–635. doi: 10.5465/AMJ.2010.51468988.

Saks, A. M. (2006). Antecedents and consequences of employee engagement. *Journal of Managerial Psychology*, *21*(7), 600–619. doi: 10.1108/02683940610690169.

Schaufeli, W. B., Salanova, M., González-romá, V., & Bakker, A. B. (2002). The measurement of engagement and burnout: A two sample confirmatory factor analysis approach. *Journal of Happiness Studies*, *3*, 71–92. doi: 10.1023/A:1015630930326.

Taylor, M., & Kent, M. L. (2014). Dialogic engagement: Clarifying foundational concepts. *Journal of Public Relations Research*, *26*(5), 384–398. doi: 10.1080/1062726X.2014.956106

Williams, D. A., & Wade-Golden, K. (2013). *The chief diversity officer: Strategy, structure and change management*. Sterling, VA: Stylus Publishing, LLC.

Worthington, R. L., Stanley, C. A., & Smith, D. G. (2020). Advancing the professionalization of diversity officers in higher education: Report of the presidential task force on the revision of the NADOHE standards of professional practice. *Journal of Diversity in Higher Education*, *13*(1), 1–22. doi: 10.1037/dhe0000175.

Section VIII

Remote Work, Flexible Work, and Work-Life Integration

Chapter Eighteen

Rethinking the Way of Working: In Search of Sustainable Engagement

Alessandra Mazzei, Luca Quaratino, Alfonsa Butera, and Sara Conti

Introduction

Over the last few years, the way of working inside organizations has been evolving at a very fast pace due to three main phenomena: (1) digital transformation with its impact on organizational processes and professional roles, which are becoming increasingly flexible and require new competencies; (2) the quest for sustainability at both an individual and organizational level, implying the adoption of policies for promoting work-life balance, diversity and inclusion, and corporate sustainability; and (3) the COVID-19 pandemic with its booster effect on organizational transformation, in particular on the adoption of remote working solutions.

This transformation resulted in an unprecedented working context mixing in-presence and remote working: a hybrid workplace. In this scenario, a key question arises: how is it possible to design a new hybrid working context capable of sustaining engagement in a prolonged spatial and time distance?

This chapter investigates the pillars around which building a hybrid workplace that is able to support sustainable engagement over time. The first one is a change in organizational culture and required competencies. The second one is the redesign of physical workspaces considering that fewer people are working in company buildings and the need for layouts facilitating knowledge sharing, creativity, and socialization. The third one is the adoption of technologies for the creation of communication arenas enhancing employee voices, horizontal communication, and knowledge sharing.

For each pillar, the chapter discusses a case to gather evidence from the field: Campari Group, Sella Group, and Unipol Group. The chapter ends with implications for practice, learning outcomes, and further questions to be investigated in the near future.

DOI: 10.4324/9781003195580-27

Rethinking the Way of Working

Rethinking the way of working was a key point on the agenda of both scholars and practitioners even before the COVID-19 pandemic breakout, for two main reasons. Firstly, the process of digital transformation is changing business models, products and services offered, and organizational processes and management practices (Reis et al., 2018; Ross et al., 2016). Digital technologies created unprecedented opportunities to develop relationships and networks among people and organizations, questioning the traditional model based on hierarchy, separation from the outside, and physical presence in the office. Secondly, the increasing attention of public opinion on environmental sustainability is challenging companies to work on their carbon footprint in terms of both production processes and labor organization. By limiting traveling and commuting of employees they reduce emissions and contribute to save the planet. At the same time, sustainability is increasingly intended in an individual perspective (Kotera & Correa Vione, 2020): alternating in-presence and remote working might help people to reach a better work-life balance, promoting a sense of autonomy and empowerment.

In this scenario the pandemic acted as an accelerator. In the last few years, remote working had been adopted as a pilot experience and the pandemic was a mass testing that accelerated its spreading. From one day to another, millions of workers faced a radical change in their way of working and this revolution challenged organizations in all sectors to adapt to a new situation where barriers in time and space were broken and the idea of the physical office itself was rapidly fading away (Wevers, 2021).

In the second half of 2021, with the pandemic slowly remitting, we are amid a worldwide debate about what will be the workplace of the future. Following the words of the CEO of Goldman Sachs, some believe that the remote work is an aberration to be corrected as soon as possible (McKeever, 2021), while others think that it has to be expanded further, given that work is something people do and not something for what employees must come to the office for, as shown by the Spotify project "Work From Anywhere" (Kelly, 2021). Probably the truth lies somewhere in between: if there is no going back to the pre-pandemic workplace, as many scholars and managers increasingly believe (e.g., Kane et al., 2021), at the same time it becomes crucial to learn from the pandemic experience, consolidating the benefits and correcting the mistakes and drawbacks individuals and organizations experienced. In this way, it will be possible to design and move toward a new hybrid workplace where the organizational performance and the employee experience might improve (Gratton, 2021).

Hybrid workplace can be defined as a new place and time of work where presence and remote connection, physical and digital experience virtuously blend with the aim of maximizing benefits of the two modalities for both the individual and the organization. We can consider as the key advantage of in-presence working the possibility to master the social and relational domain: cultivating interpersonal relations, developing a feeling of membership, promoting organizational cohesion, and generating team creativity. Remote working could improve the management of the operative and instrumental domain: gaining efficiency, limiting the waste of time, and increasing people focus (Blanchard, 2021; Fay & Kline, 2012; Soomar, 2020).

The challenge is to find the right balance in each organizational context between the two poles, given that there is no one-size-fits-all: business, culture, structural design, available technology, people do make a difference. In this scenario, a crucial question arises: how is it possible to design a new hybrid working context capable of sustaining employee engagement in a prolonged spatial and time distance?

Adopting a comprehensive conceptualization of employee engagement (Kahn, 1990; Macey & Schneider, 2008; Mazzei, 2018; Men et al., 2020; Saks, 2006; Schaufeli & Bakker, 2004), it can be defined as a *personal trait* expressing a disposition toward enthusiasm that interacting with situational factors determines a persistent *psychological state of cognitive absorption* in one's work; *emotional dedication*; and *vigor*, a physical-energetic component.

Temporal and spatial distance reduces opportunities for workers to interact with their colleagues. This produces less engagement in the organizational routines and consequently reduces connection and understanding (Fay & Kline, 2011).

There are three key pillars that an organization should consider when interested in designing a hybrid workplace conducive to sustainable engagement, based on existing literature: *competencies, leadership style, and organizational culture*; *physical spaces and working time*; and *technology and communication processes*.

The first pillar, *competencies, leadership style, and organizational culture,* requires investment in developing specific competencies for both managers and employees, making them able to effectively perform in the new organizational and relational context (Mortensen & Haas, 2021). Managers should aspire to base their leadership style on concepts such as empowerment, involvement, and autonomy of employees, making them responsible for achieving results (Gerards et al., 2018; Moon, 2020). This means abandoning the widespread habit of tight command and control on the team, which becomes increasingly difficult when physical presence is limited (Alstein & Williams, 2021). At the same time, employees are asked to grow personally and professionally, becoming fully accountable for the assigned objectives and responsible to organize and plan their work to a greater extent. From this point of view, organizational culture is key for these competencies to flourish in the light of a new paradigm of manager-employee relations. Specifically, cultures that are purpose-driven and based on inclusion and a strong sense of community have better chances to be effective in the new context (Hinds & Elliot, 2021; Raghuram, 2021): only when a relational atmosphere of mutual trust, genuine cooperation, and shared responsibility exists are people ready to take the risk of behaving differently.

The second pillar, *physical spaces and working time*, consists of the rethinking of physical spaces and working time to optimize a balance between individual and teamwork (Bloom, 2021). Every day the group of employees working in the offices will present a different composition, while some people will mainly contribute from home, opening relevant opportunities to involve talents from every single corner of the planet. Therefore, spaces are going to be conceived evaluating which tasks are best executed where (Wevers, 2021), and different office configurations could be deployed depending on whether a group is brainstorming, hosting a workshop, or conducting a daily stand-up meeting (Kane et al., 2021; Kingma, 2019). Open spaces could favor interaction, cooperation, use of agile processes, and peer learning; co-working solutions might foster inter-organizational networking and open innovation; private space work allows individual creativity and focus. Moreover, technology becomes crucial to organize access to and use of different spaces.

The third pillar, *technology and communication processes,* is represented by the adoption of adequate technologies that, going beyond the traditional vertical channels, allow the creation of new communication arenas promoting employee voice, horizontal communication, and knowledge sharing (Madsen, 2018): e.g., software for digital collaboration, inter-functional online communities, space for participatory communication and open debate on the intranet, or even quick and agile solutions as WhatsApp group and instant polls. On the one hand, it is a matter of investing in infrastructures and personal devices ensuring digital inclusion for everyone from anywhere, even when remotely connected (Microsoft, 2021). On the other hand, there is a more critical investment in soft skills making people able to cooperate, share and contribute also in the digital setting (Mortensen & Haas, 2021). In a team using at least partially virtual communication, relationships, and dynamics among members of the group change. For example, spontaneous interactions made possible by informal communication are difficult to replicate in the virtual setting and without face-to-face contact it becomes more complex to strengthen interpersonal bonds and maintain work relationships (Fay & Kline, 2011). If the communication arena is task-oriented and poor from the relational perspective, the organization could face an increase in its efficiency but a loss of awareness and informal interactions in the long run (Röcker, 2012).

Research Questions

The shift toward a hybrid workplace able to produce sustainable employee engagement and organizational success and, based on the development of the three pillars mentioned above, raises three main research questions that are going to be strategic in the forthcoming years.

RQ1: How is it possible to sustain a relational atmosphere of mutual trust, genuine cooperation, and shared responsibility in a hybrid setting?

RQ2: How can organizations adopting a hybrid model be capable of generating innovation and creativity?

RQ3: Finally, how is it possible to build new communication arenas in hybrid settings?

Evidence from the Field

In order to explore the challenges hidden in the new way of working and possible ways to face them, the Centre for Employee Relations and Communication (CERC) operating at Università IULM conducted qualitative exploratory research between April and September 2021. This chapter discusses three mini-case studies. Information has been collected through interviews with internal and corporate communications managers and document analysis. What emerged from each interview was recorded, transcribed, and analyzed in a qualitative way, without the support of any software: emergent data were parsed to find recurrent themes, concepts, and dimensions and related to the relevant literature.

The three mini-cases are related to the topical issues dealt with in this chapter: the Campari Group case explores the mutual relationship between the new way of working and organizational culture, employee engagement, and leadership; the case of Sella Group illustrates the dynamics of collaboration and creativity unleashed in the teams; the case of Unipol Group highlights the digital internal communication arenas.

Corporate Culture, Employee Engagement, and Leadership: The Campari Group Case

Campari Group is the sixth-largest player in the global spirits industry, with a portfolio of over 50 brands. Headquartered in Italy, it counts 4,000 employees and 22 plants worldwide and leverages its distribution network in 22 countries.

To explore how the company addresses the challenge of sustaining employee engagement in the hybrid work contexts, data were collected by interviewing two senior managers in the area of internal communication at Campari Group, considered as key informants. Additional data were collected through the company website, company presentations and speeches held at public events.

To meet the evolving needs of customers worldwide, Campari Group operates on four corporate values: integrity, passion, pragmatism, and together. The corporate culture was pivotal to navigate the uncertainty of the COVID-19 pandemic. In particular, in the words of one of the interviewees, "the culture of togetherness allowed to generate a high level of engagement, albeit virtual and at a distance." It was at the basis of the "Stronger Together" internal communication campaign that started from the narration around Campari Group's solidarity initiatives worldwide, with donations, hand sanitizer production, and financial and psychological aid to the hard-hit hospitality industry. The campaign continued with online activations, such as online aperitifs, and user-generated videos that employees were invited to produce and share with their colleagues through a virtual community: for example, yoga lessons, cocktail-building tutorials, social challenges.

Exiting the pandemic, Campari Group opted for a model combining both in-presence and remote work, thus giving white-collar employees the possibility to work 40% of their work time remotely. To support the decision to return to the offices although in a hybrid modality, Campari Group launched the "Better Together" communication plan, including engagement activities and an office restyling with posters and illustrated wall signs leveraging the "Better Together" concept, aimed at welcoming back employees.

To prepare the ground for the new ways of working, Campari Group listened to its employees through a survey to understand their needs and expectations for the workplace of the future. In particular, "the survey wanted to help the company to identify a series of guidelines aimed at improving the entire hybrid working model, assessing the sensitiveness of Camparistas regarding their right to disconnect, and gaining insights about how they think activities should be run when in office and when working remotely."

The design of the new ways of working has involved a re-thinking of the main activities carried out during the working day. First, the company is identifying challenges and solutions to make meetings effective in the hybrid modality. Second, it aims at sustaining sociality and networking among Camparistas (as employees at Campari Group are called) thanks to in-presence events for small groups of employees, for instance, through breakfasts and aperitifs. Third, for its upcoming Group Convention, the company is evaluating an experience combining both digital and offline.

During the pandemic, the leadership style assumed some features that were evident in the periodic videos that the CEO produced to communicate with all Camparistas and that are expected to be consolidated in the new working context: pragmatism, and a more informal and empathetic tone of voice. One of the interviewees remembered: "During the 2020 lockdown, the CEO recorded his videos with his smartphone, and the internal communication team needed to do just some little editing before releasing them: this was a revolution for the communication style of the company. Moreover, in his video messages the CEO openly mentioned people's concerns and emotional distress due to a global condition that impacted both professional and personal life: before the pandemic, this was not the habitual practice."

Every manager is used to adopting a personal leadership style; however, the human touch that emerged during the pandemic could be beneficial in the future when dealing with sensitive topics such as diversity and inclusion, and to speed up progress since a more emotional way of dealing with issues can make leaders braver in facing management challenges.

The Organizational Capability to Generate Innovation and Creativity: The Sella Group Case

Sella Group is one of the largest private and independent banking groups in Italy. It operates in several fields such as commercial, retail, corporate, and investment banking, and it has a foothold in 7 countries with more than 5,000 employees. It fosters an open innovation ecosystem focusing on sustainability as well as supporting Italian startups and businesses.

To investigate how the company faces the issue of stimulating innovation and social exchange through the physical space in hybrid work contexts, data were collected by interviewing a senior manager in the area of internal communication at Sella Group, who was individuated as a key informant. These data were complemented with information available in company documents and disseminated through speeches held at public events.

In the post-pandemic scenario, Sella forecasts a 70% increase in remote work compared to the pre-COVID era. The interviewee highlighted that "to sustain the creative process of exchange and collaboration in this new work setting, Sella placed strong focus on bolstering both organizational culture and interpersonal weak ties, which physical distance would otherwise undermine."

Sella designed a system of physical and virtual workplaces that encourages open innovation, a project titled Office On-Demand. In particular, the company focused on valuing those in-presence opportunities of spontaneous conversations and social interactions enhanced by physical proximity. Therefore, Sella increased the effort already in place before the pandemic to create open and flexible working areas and the re-design of those same areas: the aim was expressed in company documents as "reducing the office space while increasing interaction among people."

Alongside the re-design of physical spaces, Sella also adopted the principle of Hot Desking, in which employees will no longer have a fixed and assigned workstation. Sella's Hot Desking includes three categories. The first one refers to private hot desks: these are private spaces reserved for specific functions and business departments, in which employees rotate on those days when they work at the office. The second one relates to ONE Sella spaces: these are bookable by all Group employees, regardless of their department and throughout all Italian branches. The third one refers to Open Co-working spaces: these are available to Sella employees and also to all those professionals that are committed to work activities that concern the Group, to maintain partnerships and collaborative relations at different levels.

According to this new work formula envisioned by Sella, the interviewee underlined that "people will not occupy these spaces so that they can carry out the work activities that they could also perform independently and remotely. Conversely, they will populate these spaces for training, cooperation, and socialization." This approach is facilitated by the future introduction of an app that will allow the booking of workstations each time.

In conclusion, in this new scenario the physical locations will assume increasingly additional and complementary functions rather than simply being containers for workstations. They are becoming open meeting places for people and teams to stimulate their professional creativity and they are also evolving into an incentive for employee performance and experience, conveying the idea that the office should be considered an environment for collaboration above everything else and no longer a place for carrying out individual tasks.

The Digital Internal Communication Arenas: The Unipol Group Case

Unipol Group is one of the ten biggest groups in Europe and the second biggest insurance group in Italy. It counts around 12,000 employees and serves approximately 17 million customers.

To probe how the company leverages technologies to sustain the communication dynamics in hybrid work contexts, data were collected by interviewing a key informant, specifically a senior manager in the area of internal communication at Unipol Group, and complemented with information available in company documents and website.

In 2019, Unipol Group began to reflect on the evolution of working methods and ways to communicate and collaborate among employees, in order to develop a digital workplace, as defined in the triennial strategic plan. The pandemic led Unipol Group to accelerate the adoption of a digital workplace that could enable the remote way of working and harmonize the need of employees for a more fluid work experience. The interviewee recalled that "the main goal was to achieve a higher efficiency in operations, less fragmentation of tasks, and consistent platforms to collaborate and to get access to documents and information." The digital workplace model espoused by Unipol Group was therefore a single set of digital tools and new ways of working aimed at enabling communication, collaboration, and knowledge management to run more efficient activities and processes.

The development of the new digital working environment started with a pilot project involving the largest business unit within the company: the Claims Department. In a company document, this pilot digital workplace is described as "a single environment that allows the Claims Department people to inquire, communicate and collaborate in an easy and intuitive way." It ensured employees simple access from the personal page of the company's Intranet and a set of useful features and services to carry out daily work activities. Among these, firstly the "search a colleague" tool helped them easily get in touch with colleagues and therefore enhance new relationships and forms of collaboration. Secondly, a co-editing section allowed employees to work together on the same document in a cooperative way. Thirdly, the platform also included community spaces where employees can activate relationships and conversations with colleagues with similar professional roles, to accelerate and improve knowledge sharing and problem-solving.

For the development of the digital workplace, Unipol Group leveraged an inter-functional team with different skills. In particular, the interviewee highlighted that "the role played by the internal communication department in this team contributed to making internal communication itself responsible for the digital workplace within the whole company, also leading to a change in the name of the department from 'Internal Communication' to 'Internal Communication & Digital Workplace.'"

The project resulted in positive strategic impacts on the Claims Department which experienced a relevant increase in efficiency and effectiveness of employees' working actions. It also established a model that can be replicated by other departments in the new era of the organizational life of Unipol Group following the acute phase of the pandemic. The digital workplace in Unipol Group is expected to further evolve toward a more conversational and social model: in the words of the interviewee, "new features will be introduced to give employees richer possibilities to discretionarily activate new communication arenas and conversations with their colleagues and managers." These possibilities require caution as they can threaten the sense of hierarchy, but nevertheless they trigger informal interactions among people, which leads to an easier, greater, and less formal way of sharing information.

Discussion

The rising hybrid working context requires a new effort to sustain employee engagement over time. First, it is necessary to leverage an organizational culture and a leadership style able to foster cohesion and membership and to make people engaged and accountable (Mortensen & Haas, 2021), as confirmed by the Campari Group case. Second, in order to sustain the generation of innovation and creativity, there are some key ingredients, such as serendipitous connections with other members and redundancies in relations and communication, apparently not efficient but able to produce new ideas and perspectives. As the Sella Group case study shows, the new configuration of office spaces should be aimed at creating an environment for collaboration, brainstorming, and meeting, not at accomplishing individual tasks (Kane et al., 2021; Kingma, 2019). Third, innovative technologies could be used to sustain people involvement and active participation, smooth cooperation across functions and units, and an effective process of knowledge management and information sharing. As emerges from the Unipol Group case study, the digital workplace can be designed in order to create spaces for open communication avoiding the risks of poor digital communication (Fay & Kline, 2011; Röcker, 2012).

Implications for Practice

The analysis conducted highlights several implications for practice.

Need to Design the Hybrid Working Context

The massive remote working experienced worldwide during the COVID-19 pandemic will not disappear. The working context of the future will be hybrid, mixing in-presence and remote experience. This new setting should be designed and managed to maximize the benefits of both modalities while minimizing the pitfalls.

Sustain Engagement in a Context of Relational Distancing

The blend between in-presence and remote working can allow a better work-life balance and therefore sustain the level of employee engagement. Nevertheless, spatial and temporal distance brought by prolonged remote working can lower the level of engagement. To avoid this risk, companies should create opportunities for networking and socialization. The leadership style to sustain engagement should be based on mutual trust, human empathy, and inclusiveness.

Inclusion of Three Pillars

The design of the hybrid working context should include three pillars: the development of competencies, leadership style, and organizational culture enhancing mutual trust, genuine cooperation, and shared responsibility; the rethinking of physical spaces and working time to optimize the balance between individual and teamwork; and the adoption of technologies boosting open communication arenas.

Leveraging of Corporate Values

Organizational culture and corporate values represent an anchor during major change such as the case of sudden moving to forced remote working during the pandemic. A company can leverage its corporate values to lead the change while reassuring. At the same time, bolstering organizational culture is one of the aims to be pursued in the hybrid working context, where all the soft aspects of the organization are under stress.

Physical Working Spaces

Physical working spaces inside the corporate buildings and plants are not the place where employees should spend their entire working time anymore. These spaces have specific functions related to the company objectives: supporting the team group collaboration and creativity, allowing the individual need to work alone to be concentrated, and encouraging the creation of relationship networks and collective knowledge sharing.

Digital Working Spaces

Digital workplaces are an extraordinary opportunity to support the spontaneous development of relationship networks and knowledge sharing. In large companies or in companies that are geographically dispersed, technologies supporting the creation of professional communities and the activation of personal contacts across the organizational departments create new working environments.

Internal Communication for Change

Internal communication to support major changes should be planned in coherence with the moment. Traditional staged models do not work anymore. During the remote working forced by the pandemic most employees consolidated the habit of working from anywhere and very often they developed the beliefs that this condition works very well and increases productivity, creativity, and personal well-being. Companies should be able to reveal that this was an exceptional situation that allowed them to minimize the crisis damages. But, in order to gain net benefit from remote working, some changes should be implemented starting from a consistent although partial coming back to the physical workplace. This kind of situation requires indirect communication based on actions and the possibility for employees to immediately perceive the benefits of the proposed change.

Conclusion

In conclusion, a hybrid working context includes corporate buildings and physical offices, personal working spaces of the employees and the virtual working place supported by technologies. These three components should be harmonized and considered as a whole working sphere, where employees can enter and exit individually or in groups from one environment to another to meet and work. Whether this environment is physical at the employer premises or at the employee's home or virtual, all should be harmonized to create a hybrid workplace able to support sustainable engagement over time.

Learning Outcomes

1) Understand why and how the way of working is evolving into a hybrid one, with the digital and physical domains constituting a single working sphere
2) Understand how to support sustainable engagement in a context of prolonged spatial, time, and relational distancing

3) Understand the role of leadership style and organizational culture to sustain a performing hybrid workplace and the role of internal communication to support this major change
4) Become aware of the new configuration of physical spaces and working time that can sustain a balance between individual and teamwork
5) Be aware of the redesign of digital spaces that allow the creation of new communication arenas

Discussion Questions

In the hybrid working sphere:

1) How will employee engagement drivers evolve?
2) How should diversity and inclusion policies change?
3) How should the process of building, strengthening, and changing organizational culture be managed?
4) How will the process of newcomers' onboarding change?

Further Readings

Gerards, R., de Grip, A., & Baudewijns, C. (2018). Do new ways of working increase work engagement? *Personnel Review, 47*(2), 517–534. https://doi.org/10.1108/PR-02-2017-0050

Kane, G. C., Nanda, R., Phillips, A., & Copulsky, J. (2021) Redesigning the post-pandemic workplace. *MIT Sloan Management Review, 62*(3), 12–14.

Kotera, Y., & Correa Vione, K. (2020). Psychological impacts of the new ways of working (NWW): A systematic review. *International Journal of Environmental Research and Public Health, 17*(14), 5080. https://doi.org/10.3390/ijerph17145080

References

Alstein, T., & Williams, M. (2021, April 28). *Focus on digital work. Digital transformation after COVID-19.* Deloitte. https://www2.deloitte.com/au/en/blog/consulting-blog/2021/focus-digital-work.html

Blanchard, A. L. (2021). The effects of COVID-19 on virtual working within online groups. *Group Processes & Intergroup Relations, 24*(2), 290–296. https://doi.org/10.1177/1368430220983446

Bloom, N. (2021, March 21). Our research shows working from home works, in moderation. *The Guardian*. https://www.theguardian.com/commentisfree/2021/mar/21/research-working-from-home

Fay, M. J., & Kline, S. L. (2011). Coworker relationships and informal communication in high-intensity telecommuting. *Journal of Applied Communication Research, 39*(2), 144–163.

Fay, M. J., & Kline, S. L. (2012). The influence of informal communication on organizational identification and commitment in the context of high-intensity telecommuting. *Southern Communication Journal, 77*(1), 61–76. https://doi.org/10.1080/1041794x.2011.582921

Gerards, R., de Grip, A., & Baudewijns, C. (2018). Do new ways of working increase work engagement? *Personnel Review, 47*(2), 517–534. https://doi.org/10.1108/PR-02-2017-0050

Gratton, L. (2021). *How to do hybrid right. When designing flexible work arrangements, focus on individual human concerns, not just institutional ones.* Harvard Business Review. https://hbr.org/2021/05/how-to-do-hybrid-right

Hinds, P., & Elliot, B. (2021, February 1). WFH doesn't have to dilute your corporate culture. *Harvard Business Review.* https://hbr.org/2021/02/wfh-doesnt-have-to-dilute-your-corporate-culture

Kahn, W. A. (1990). Psychological conditions of personal engagement and disengagement at work. *The Academy of Management Journal, 12*(1), 692–724. https://doi.org/10.5465/256287

Kane, G. C., Nanda, R., Phillips, A., & Copulsky, J. (2021) Redesigning the post-pandemic workplace. *MIT Sloan Management Review, 62*(3), 12–14.

Kelly, J. (2021, February 12). Spotify will let employees work from anywhere they do their best "thinking and creating." *Forbes*. https://www.forbes.com/sites/jackkelly/2021/02/12/spotify

Kingma, S. (2019). New ways of working (NWW): Work space and cultural change in virtualizing organizations. *Culture and Organization, 25*(5), 383–406. https://doi.org/10.1080/14759551.2018.1427747

Macey, W. H., Schneider, B. (2008). The meaning of employee engagement. *Industrial and Organizational Psychology, 1*(1), 3–30. https://doi.org/10.1111/j.1754-9434.2007.0002.x

Madsen, V. T. (2018). Participatory communication on internal social media—A dream or reality? Findings from two exploratory studies of coworkers as communicators. *Corporate Communications: An International Journal, 23*(4), 614–628. https://doi.org/10.1108/CCIJ-04-2018-0039

Mazzei, A. (2018). Employee engagement. In R. L. Heath, & W. Johansen (Eds.), *The international encyclopedia of strategic communication* (557–562). Hoboken, NJ: Wiley-Blackwell.

McKeever, V. (2021, February 25). *Goldman Sachs CEO Solomon calls working from home an "aberration."* CNBC. https://www.cnbc.com/2021/02/25/goldman-sachs-ceo-solomon-calls-working-from-home-an-aberration-.html

Men, L. R., Neill, M., & Yue, C. A. (2020). Examining the effects of symmetrical internal communication and employee engagement on organizational change outcomes. *Public Relations Journal, 13*(4), 1–19. https://prjournal.instituteforpr.org/wp-content/uploads/Men_Neill_Yue_PRJ_Oct-2020.pdf

Microsoft. (2021, March 22). *2021 Work Trend Index: Annual report. The next great disruption is hybrid work—Are we ready?*. https://msworklab.azureedge.net

Mortensen, M., & Haas, M. (2021, February 24). *Making the hybrid workplace fair.* Harvard Business Review. https://hbr.org/2021/02/making-the-hybrid-workplace-fair

Moon, R. (2020). Leading remote teams: The COVID-19 pandemic has thrust many leaders into unexpected and unprecedented role of managing their teams remotely for the first time. *Ama Quarterly, 6*(2), 30–33.

Raghuram, S. (2021). Remote work implications for organisational culture. In P. Kumar, A. Agrawal, & P. Budhwar (Eds.), *Work from home: Multi-level perspectives on the new normal* (147–163). Emerald Publishing. https://doi.org/10.1108/978-1-80071-661-220210009

Reis, J., Amorim, M., Melao, N., & Matos, P. (2018). Digital transformation: A literature review and guidelines for future research. In A. Rocha, H. Adeli, L. P. Reis, & S. Costanzo (Eds.), *Trends and advances in information systems and technologies. WorldCIST'18 2018. Advances in intelligent systems and computing.* Vol. 745 (411–421). Springer. https://doi.org/10.1007/978-3-319-77703-0_41

Röcker, C. (2012). Informal communication and awareness in virtual teams. Why we need smart technologies to support distributed teamwork. *Communications in Information Science and Management Engineering, 2*(5), 1–15.

Ross, J. W., Sebastian, I. M., Beath, C., Scantlebury, S., Mocker, M., Fonstad, N., Kagan, M., Moloney, K., & Krussel, S. G. (2016). *Designing Digital Organizations* (Technical Research Report, CISR WP No. 46). MIT Center for IS Research.

Saks, A. M. (2006). Antecedents and consequences of employee engagement. *Journal of Managerial Psychology, 21*(7), 600–619. https://doi.org/10.1108/02683940610690169

Schaufeli, W. B., Bakker, A. B. (2004), Job demands, job resources, and their relationship with burnout and engagement: A multi-sample study. *Journal of Organizational Behavior, 25*(3), 293–315. https://doi.org/10.1002/job.248

Soomar, Z. (2020). A framework for building and maintain trust in remote and virtual teams. *F1000Research*, 9, 1187. https://doi.org/10.12688/f1000research.26626.1

Wevers, M. (2021). *The future of work is hybrid: moving to a hybrid, "phygital" workplace.* Deloitte. https://www2.deloitte.com/nl/nl/pages/enterprise-technology-and-performance/articles/the-future-of-work-is-hybrid.html

Chapter Nineteen

Boundary Communication: Smartphone Usage in Employees' Work–Family Conflicts When Working from Home

Feihong Pan

Introduction

The world is changing, as is the way people work. Working from home (WFH) has become more popular within the context of COVID-19, when people have been encouraged to stay at home but have also been asked to continue working. Observation of individuals reveals an identity "collapse" in these overlapped home and work environments. To explain this identity collapse, an individual's work–family conflicts (WFCs) should generate much attention. As an example of how WFH can impact the work environment, a door may be the distinct border that separates indoor and outdoor activities, but it cannot block the sudden sounds made by other members of the household. Consequently, job performance can be negatively affected, and workers can become distracted when they work from home. Meanwhile, role shifting has given individuals less time to react but more time being disturbed and trying to reenter a working mode. On the other hand, digital devices and the internet have played an increasingly significant role in work, becoming the fundamental and strongest bond between employees of enterprises in the WFH state. However, WFH can bring technology disconnections that can trigger feelings of emotional isolation and burnout for employees, which is related to employee engagement when they face time pressures from their jobs.

Effective internal communication plays an important role in the development of employee engagement (Welch, 2011), and it positively impacts employee engagement (Karanges et al., 2015; Lalić et al., 2020). With the Chinese government's "stay-at-home" policy during COVID-19, some positive employee engagement practices emerged. Until residential community lockdowns were terminated in China, many employees stayed and slept at the office rather than at home to ensure that employees worked and communicated constantly.

However, for employees working in either the workplace or at home, as long as they stay entirely in one place performing more than one role—voluntarily or involuntarily—the blur between work and family spaces produces conflicts between individuals' family

DOI: 10.4324/9781003195580-28

and working roles. This also blurs the lines between working and leisure time because of smartphones and technological advances, which greatly challenge internal communication. Appropriate internal communication appears particularly significant when an employee stays in one domain, executing different responsibilities and experiencing various shifts in their role. Such situations aggravate workloads for individuals to the point that they need to reevaluate and deal with the following difficulties:

1) The individual crosses the boundaries between work and family.
2) Work duties and family responsibilities need to be undertaken simultaneously.
3) There is an imbalance in terms of time and energy spent on job and family.
4) Internal communication and employee engagement become more or less adequate, which may lead to 5).
5) The individual experiences time pressure, burnout, and emotional exhaustion.

Hence, these points—including smartphone usage during WFCs, WFH role conflicts, employee engagement, and the COVID-19 situation in China (at the time of writing)—will be further examined, and an analysis of a local Puyang news broadcasting institution will be used as a case study, following researchers' suggestions.

Literature Review

Work–Family Border Theory

Clark (2000) proposed that people who are crossing in the two domains of work and home can be defined as "border-crossers," while the individuals who completely stay in one domain acting one role are "border-keepers." The core idea of the work–family border theory (Clark, 2000) is that individuals sometimes have to deal with the reality of crossing the boundary between work and family, like work brought home. These two domains are interpenetrative while being independent of each other.

The theory proposes that frequent supportive communication between border-keepers and border-crossers about other-domain activities moderates the negative impact of situations that would otherwise lead to imbalance and achieves individuals' greater satisfaction among various roles transition.

WFH is an example of border crossing. Some scholars propose that employees' engagement and organizations' internal communication may be intensified by the complexity and unfamiliarity of remote work, and two-way and internal crisis communication content during remote work contributes to positive employee engagement (Dhanesh & Picherit-Duthler, 2021). Hence, appropriate two-way communication may aid in resolving dilemmas employees encounter when they work from home.

WFCs and Employee Engagement

WFC refers to "a form of inter-role conflict in which the role pressures from the work and family domains are mutually incompatible in some respect" (Greenhaus & Beutell, 1985, p. 77). The term is used to describe the relationship between employee performance, job satisfaction (Soomro et al., 2018), time pressure (Brosch & Binneweis, 2018; De Carlo et al., 2019), and emotional exhaustion (Darouei & Pluut, 2021). On the other hand, employee engagement is regarded as an emotional and intellectual commitment to the organization, including three primary behaviors: say, stay, and strive (Baumruk, 2004).

Many scholars have concluded that highly engaged employees can experience high levels of WFC (Amah, 2016; Eckenrode & Gore, 1990; Macey & Schneider, 2008). However, few studies have explored how WFC can affect engagement.

Montgomery et al. (2003) pointed out that "work and home demands lead to work strain and decreased feelings of engagement" (p. 195). WFCs fall into three categories: time-based, strain-based (e.g., anxiety), and behavior-based conflicts, which refer to employees having to consume extra energy to adjust time schedules, strain, and behavior to meet the demands of two domains (Edwards & Rothbard, 2000). Such extra energy consumption may exacerbate individuals' feelings of strain from job demands (e.g., time pressure) and home demands (e.g., emotional issues), leading to disengagement.

Because of this, managing WFC—a demand that appears in both work and home domains—is expected to reduce feelings of disengagement. In other words, reducing WFC is significant for increasing employee engagement.

Supervisor Communication Is Important for WFC and Employee Engagement

Internal communication is significant in employee engagement (Hayase, 2009). Internal communication, including constant feedback, open channels of communication, and increased information sharing, boosts employee engagement (Lalić et al., 2020). Scholars have proposed that internal communication, especially communication support from supervisors, plays an integral role in "developing and maintaining optimal employee engagement" (Karanges et al., 2015, p. 130). Meanwhile, supervisor communication motivates employee engagement (Breckenridge, 2000; Karanges, 2014; Lee et al., 2021; Mishra et al., 2014) and is significantly important in reducing WFCs (Clark, 2000; Morganson et al., 2014). More importantly, excessive job demands result in time pressure, and role conflicts can be relieved by two-way communication, internal communication content, and appropriate communication technology during remote work, thus reducing employee exhaustion and disengagement (Dhanesh & Picherit-Duthler, 2021). Hence, communication support from supervisors about time pressure and emotional exhaustion can be hypothesized to be negatively related to WFC.

Technology Affordance for Employees' Engagement

During the COVID-19 lockdown, media affordance of visibility not only encouraged employees but also increased strains. All employees in this institution were asked to check in using their organization's app to confirm their working state and time and to stay connected to assure job efficiency. This supervision from mobile apps relied entirely on media affordance of visibility. Because of this, employees needed to pay much more attention to the organizational app in case they missed special COVID-19 working arrangement prompts.

Therefore, media not only plays a more significant role in work performance during remote work but also increases employees' emotional exhaustion and mental stress.

Time Pressure

Time pressure is a work-related stressor that refers to working at a fast pace or having insufficient time to complete tasks (Baer & Oldham, 2006). Most employees encounter this while working. Some scholars have investigated the relationship between WFC and time pressure and found that time pressure causes conflicts (Brosch & Binneweis, 2018; De Carlo et al., 2019). Furthermore, in work–family boundary theory, frequent and regular communication with members in both distinct domains can increase their awareness and understanding of border-crossers' activities in another domain. van Zoonen et al. (2020) have suggested that smartphone usage after hours is not correlated with communication about family demands with one's supervisor, but rather communication about family demands is negatively related to WFC. After-hours smartphone usage refers to employees using smartphones to work during non-compulsory working hours. De Carlo et al. (2019) concluded that time pressure positively correlates with WFC. Hence, based on theory and previous findings, communication about time pressure should negatively relate to WFC, and two hypotheses are proposed below:

H1a: Employees' smartphone use after hours is positively related to communication (content) about time pressure with one's supervisor.

H1b: Employees who communicate more about time pressure with their supervisor will experience less WFC than employees who do not.

Emotional Exhaustion

Emotional exhaustion is also focused on by scholars' regarding WFH and WFC (Boles et al., 1997; Nitzsche et al., 2013; Thompson et al., 2020). Work-related emotional exhaustion refers to work-related feelings of being overextended and depleted of one's emotional and physical resources (Maslach et al., 2001). WFC experienced at home in the evening is positively correlated to emotional exhaustion the next morning, and the higher the level of WFC, the more emotionally exhausted an individual feels (Darouei & Pluut, 2021). Therefore, based on previous studies, H2a and H2b are proposed as follows:

H2a: Employees' smartphone use after hours is positively related to communication (content) about work-related emotional exhaustion with one's supervisor.

H2b: Employees who communicate more about work-related emotional exhaustion with their supervisor will experience less WFC than employees who do not.

Considering employees who stay at home have little need to use smartphones to communicate with family members, there is no hypothesis on using smartphones to communicate with family members. Figure 19.1 is the hypothesized research model.

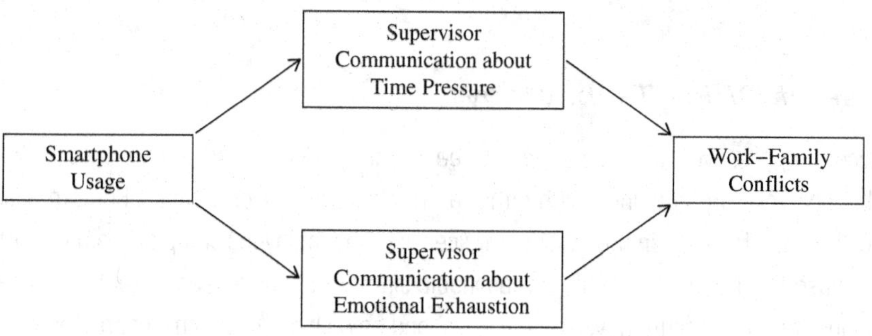

FIGURE 19.1 Hypothesized Model.

Method

This chapter follows van Zoonen et al.'s (2020) research design: Two online surveys were distributed three times within 15 days to increase the response rate (Nederhof, 1988). The first survey was a questionnaire that measured employees' work-related smartphone use after hours (van Zoonen et al., 2020) and their perceptions of WFC, while the second survey was a questionnaire that measured time pressure and emotional exhaustion. Each scale used Cronbach's α to test the reliability of each measure. The Pearson correlation was used to test H1a and H2a. In contrast, for the one-way analysis of variance, one-way (one-way ANOVA) was used to test H1b and H2b since this approach is designed to test whether there are statistically significant differences between two or more uncorrelated groups. SPSS was used to conduct data processing.

Case Study

Local Puyang News Broadcasting Institution

"I feel anxious and worry about my work performance. The asynchronous communication with my supervisor and workmates makes me feel nervous when job tasks are given to me late at night or when there is no response from them."

This was said by an employee from a local Chinese news broadcasting institution located in Puyang City in central China. It is a public institution that is half comprised of national public organization property, while the other half is of a commercial nature. Most employees have the least stable monthly income until the country goes bankrupt or the employee decides to resign. The total income is constituted of regular income and self-employment. The institution is composed of about 600 employees in seven departments.

Use of Office Technology

According to seven managers from three Puyang News Broadcasting organizations, all employees are equipped with either a private computer or a smartphone to ensure quality and efficiency in their work practices, so the employees complete tasks on internet-based digital devices. This is reasonable since most employees in news broadcasting institutions execute news-related jobs, and news has the specific characteristics of fast updates and efficient publishing. According to the managers, when they announce recruitment rules, applicants—particularly frontliners—need to keep in touch either during established working hours or after hours.

Participants and Procedure

The participants of this study consisted of employees from local Puyang news broadcasting institutions and their family members, who also work in national public organizations, to ensure the data is meaningful for institutions that have the nature of national public organizations.

Surveys were created online, and they were printed as hard copies and mailed if participants requested them. The survey was collected on the basis of voluntary completion. It was expected that more than 300 valid surveys would be collated. Surveys reached their potential participants with the help of a third-party online survey service vendor (Wenjuanxing) and managers at the institutions and were translated into Chinese and back to English for analysis. Participant recruitment criteria were established before the surveys were collected. The criteria were as follows:

1) Participants should be full-time employees at the institutions.
2) Participants should have experience with WFH, and their work location at the time of data collection should be their home.
3) Participants should have after-hours smartphone usage experience when WFH.
4) Participants should have the experience of being asked to equip themselves with at least one smartphone to keep in contact with their place of work.

In total, responses from 395 participants were obtained. Each survey was completed in more than 7 minutes by each participant.

Measures

Employees' after-hours work-related smartphone usage was measured with three items (van Zoonen et al., 2020); time pressure was measured by four items (De Carlo et al., 2019; Wood et al., 2019), emotional exhaustion was measured by five items (Maslach & Jackson, 1981), and perceptions of WFCs were measured by three items (van Zoonen et al., 2020). Employees' after-hours smartphone usage and perceptions of WFCs were self-reported. A 7-point Likert scale from 1 (weak) to 7 (strong) was provided for participants to rank their responses to the survey items. Control variables included gender, age, and education. SPSS was used for statistical purposes.

Results

Among the 395 participants, 179 were male (45.32%), and 216 were female (54.68%). All participants' mean and median age was 26–30 years old (*SD* = 1.03). The mean and median number of years employees worked for the organizations was 0.6–1 year (*SD* = 1.08). The employees in this sample have different job positions, including relatively senior managers (*n* = 9, 2%), lower-level managers (*n* = 118, 30%), and non-management (*n* = 268, 68%).

Cronbach's α was used to check the reliability of the items of the measurement tool. All α values for the variables were above 0.70 (see Table 19.1), which can be regarded as reliable measurements for the variables. The mean for each independent variable is shown in Table 19.2. A Pearson correlation analysis was conducted to test the relationship between the independent and dependent variables (see Table 19.2). The correlations between the communication of time pressure (CTP) with supervisors, the communication of emotional exhaustion (CEE) with supervisors, WFC, and after-hours smartphone usage ranged between 0.03 and 0.86, as shown in Table 19.2.

TABLE 19.1 Descriptive statistics for measurement items and test of reliability

Construct	Dimension/item	α
Smartphone after-hours usage	I use voice conversations.	0.91
	I send/receive text messages with managers.	
	I send/receive email with managers.	
CTP with supervisors	I discuss intensive work with my supervisor.	0.79
	I discuss my inability to take sufficient breaks with my supervisor.	
	I discuss the pressure to work long hours with my supervisor.	
	I discuss the unrealistic time pressures I feel with my supervisor.	
CEE with supervisors	I discuss how emotionally drained I feel from my work with my supervisor.	0.88
	I discuss how fatigued I feel when I get up in the morning to face another day on the job with my supervisor.	
	I discuss how working with people all day is a strain for me with my supervisor.	
	I discuss how burned out from my work I feel with my supervisor.	
	I discuss how I feel I am working too hard at my job with my supervisor.	
WFC	My personal life suffers because of work.	0.81
	I neglect personal needs because of work.	
	I put my personal life on hold for work.	

TABLE 19.2 Pearson correlation matrix for observed variables

Construct	Range	Mean	*SD*	1	2	3	4
1. CTP with supervisors	[1–7]	5.10	1.23	1			
2. CEE with supervisors	[1–7]	2.55	0.71	0.82**	1		
3. WFC	[1–7]	4.97	1.54	0.80**	0.86**	1	
4. Smartphone after-hours usage	[1–7]	4.66	1.11	0.03	0.03	0.05	1

Note ** Means the correlation is significant at $p < 0.01$ (2-tailed).

Notably, smartphone usage is not correlated with any of the variables. This result is consistent with van Zoonen et al.'s (2020) research, in which smartphone usage after hours had no relationship with CTP and CEE with supervisors. However, this study also found that smartphone usage after hours is not directly related to the perception of WFCs either. Therefore, H1a and H2a are rejected. Conversely, CTP with supervisors ($r = 0.80^{**}$, $p < 0.01$) is highly positively correlated to the perception of WFC, and CEE with supervisors ($r = 0.86^{**}$, $p < 0.01$) is also highly positively correlated to the perception of WFC, so, H1b and H2b are supported. One-way ANOVA was used to test H1b and H2b to evaluate whether the work–family boundary theory fits this study (i.e., will employees who communicate more about time pressure and emotional exhaustion with their supervisor when they are WFH gain more understanding from their supervisor and feel less WFC?). In one-way ANOVA, people who ranged between [1–2] (code 0), [3–5] (code 1), and [6–7] (code 2) in CTP and CEE were separated into three groups: less agree [1–2], moderately agree [3–5], and strongly agree [6–7], respectively. The perceptions of WFC were also separated into three groups using the same range.

The 395 participants were classified into three groups: slightly agree ($n = 56$), moderately agree ($n = 282$), and strongly agree ($n = 57$) in terms of CTP. Based on the test of homogeneity of variance, $p > 0.05$. This result supports that one-way ANOVA can be used for this data. Further, the effect of CTP on perceptions of WFC is significant [$F(2,392) = 460.4$, $p < 0.01$]. Therefore, a post-hoc analysis using Fisher's least significant difference (LSD) post-hoc test criterion for significance suggests that the slightly agree group ($M = 0.54$ $SD = 0.22$) is significantly different from the moderately agree group ($M = 0.96$, $SD = 0.19$), $p = 0.00$, and the strongly agree group ($M = 0.96$, $SD = 0.18$), $p = 0.00$. However, the moderately agree group is not significantly different from the strongly agree group ($p = 0.90$). This finding does not contradict what the work–family boundary theory suggests, or H1b, so H1b is supported. Similarly, the effect of CEE on perceptions of WFC is also significant, $F(2,392) = 830.50$, $p < 0.01$. And, in post-hoc analyses using the LSD post-hoc criterion for significance, the slightly agree group ($n = 66$, $M = 0.91$, $SD = 0.28$)

is significantly different from the moderately agree group ($n = 190$, $M = 0.99$, $SD = 0.10$), $p = 0.00$, and the strongly agree group ($n = 139$, $M = 0.98$, $SD = 0.15$), $p = 0.00$. However, H2b cannot be fully supported since the test of homogeneity of variance toward CEE and WFC is $p < 0.05$, which does not support these results.

Discussion

This chapter provides guidelines for whether employees can use communication strategies to solve WFCs when they are WFH. Job resources, including communication support from supervisors, were verified as relating to WFC negatively, which is expected to increase employees' feelings of engagement. Such conclusions are consistent with previous studies (Montgomery et al., 2003). Additionally, time pressure and emotional exhaustion were correlated with WFCs, and following the work–family boundary theory, communication about these two factors when individuals have to work at home but deal with two domains should help people feel less WFC. This study explored supervisor support with communication strategies in the context of Chinese organizations and found that CTP with one's supervisor is highly positively correlated with the perception of WFC, which is consistent with previous studies (De Carlo et al., 2019; van Zoonen et al., 2020). Also, this study indicated that after-hours smartphone usage has no relationship with WFC in China, which corresponds with previous studies. This may indicate that after-hours smartphone usage does not have a relationship with WFC, regardless of the national context, but I would encourage this to be tested in more countries.

Second, this study also found that CEE with one's supervisor is also highly positively correlated with the perception of WFC, which is in line with previous studies (Darouei & Pluut, 2021). However, CTP was found to help relieve feelings of WFC, and people who agree with CTP more have less WFC than those who agree with it less. However, different agreement levels with CEE are not found to significantly affect WFC. This result is not consistent with the work–family theory, but this is understandable in Chinese culture. Grounded in Chinese culture and proverbs (e.g., "言多必失, 'one is prone to say something wrong if one speaks excessively'") (Lee, 2021, p. 641), many people from mainland China are not accustomed to openly expressing their emotions to others.

Theoretical Contributions and Practical Implications

This chapter puts the work–family boundary theory into practice, and the results supplement the theory. The work–family theory provides a general map of the relationship between border-keepers and border-crossers and suggests useful advice on relieving employees' WFCs (Clark, 2000). This chapter extends the theory's practical fields, which proves that the theory is also applicable to China. The results confirm that after-hours smartphone usage has no contribution to WFC. Practically, this study provides a way for Chinese employees to relieve WFC when they have to WFH or are going through quarantine. Also, this study proposes an insightful perspective on employee engagement: Individuals should have access to more meaningful internal supervisor communication when they encounter troubles, which helps alleviate WFC and increase their employee engagement. Communication from supervisors is significant in maintaining and developing employee engagement. This chapter uniquely extends the function of supervisory communication in a WFC context, which explores a relatively new kind of boundary communication. Meanwhile, the investigation of the negative relationship between supervisory communication and WFC also provides a baseline for employees' engagement enhancement for future studies. Finally, it is also hoped that employees can reflect on whether their job deserves their efforts if the supervisors replace them merely because they want to express their feelings about the troubles they encounter.

Learning Outcomes

1) Gain a general understanding of border-crossers and WFCs.
2) Be aware of the negative consequences WFCs bring in careers.
3) Develop appropriate supervisor communication to decrease WFCs.
4) Prepare strategies to help employees engage in their jobs in a healthier way.

Discussion Questions

1) We know that internal communication with supervisors is beneficial to our WFC reduction, but how can we communicate it in an appropriate way that will not hurt the good impression we left on supervisors? Complaints, passive-aggressive words, and black moods can be avoided.
2) Would communication about negative topics be welcomed by all direct supervisors?
3) Would employees be regarded with suspicion if they only communicate with one particular supervisor but neglect others?

Further Readings

Grunig, J. E. & Hunt, T. (1984). *Managing public relations*. Fort Worth, TX: Harcourt Brace Jovanovich.

Welch, M. (2011). The evolution of the employee engagement concept: Communication implications. *Corporate Communications, 16*(4), 328–346. https://doi.org/10.1108/13563281111186968

References

Amah, O. E. (2016). Employee engagement and the WFC relationship: The role of personal and organisational resources. *South African Journal of Labour Relations, 40*(2), 118–138.

Baer, M. & Oldham, G. (2006). The curvilinear relation between experienced creative time pressure and creativity. *Journal of Applied Psychology, 91*(4), 963–970.

Baumruk, R. (2004). The missing link: The role of employee engagement in business success. *Workspan, 47*(1), 48–52.

Boles, J. S., Johnston, M. W., & Hair, J. F. Jr. (1997). Role stress, WFC and emotional exhaustion: Inter-relationships and effects on some work-related consequences. *Journal of Personal Selling & Sales Management, 17*(1), 17–28.

Breckenridge, M. B. (2000). *An exploration of the factors that influence leadership effectiveness in a corporate environment*. Indiana University of Pennsylvania.

Brosch, E., & Binneweis, C. (2018). A diary study on predictors of the work–life interface: The role of time pressure, psychological climate and positive affective states. *Management Revue, 29*(1), 55–78.

Clark, S. C. (2000). Work/family border theory: A new theory of work/family balance. *Human Relations (New York), 53*(6), 747–770. https://doi.org/10.1177/0018726700536001

Darouei, M. & Pluut, H. (2021). Work from home today for a better tomorrow! How working from home influences work-family conflict and employees' start of the next workday. *Stress and Health, 37*(5), 986–999. https://doi.org/10.1002/smi.3053

De Carlo, A., Girardi, D., Falco, A., Dal Corso, L., & Di Sipio, A. (2019). When does work interfere with teachers' private life? An application of the job demands–resources model. *Frontiers in Psychology, 10*, 1–13.

Dhanesh, G. S. & Picherit-Duthler, G. (2021). Remote internal crisis communication (RICC)—Role of internal communication in predicting employee engagement during remote work in a crisis. *Journal of Public Relations Research, 33*(5), 292–313. https://doi.org/10.1080/1062726X.2021.2011286

Eckenrode, J., & Gore, S. (1990). *Stress between work and family*. Plenum Press.

Edwards, J. R. & Rothbard, N. P. (2000). Mechanisms linking work and family: Clarifying the relationship between work and family constructs. *The Academy of Management Review, 25*(1), 178–199. https://doi.org/10.2307/259269

Greenhaus, J. & Beutell, N. (1985). Sources of conflict between work and family roles. *The Academy of Management Review, 10*(1), 76–88.

Hayase, L. K. T. (2009). *Internal communication in organizations and employee engagement* [Master's dissertation]. University of Nevada, Las Vegas.

Karanges, E. R. (2014). *Optimising employee engagement with internal communication: a social exchange perspective* [Doctoral dissertation]. Queensland University of Technology, Brisbane.

Karanges, E., Johnston, K., Beatson, A., & Lings, I. (2015). The influence of internal communication on employee engagement: A pilot study. *Public Relations Review, 41*(1), 129–131. https://doi.org/10.1016/j.pubrev.2014.12.003

Lalić, D., Milić, B., & Stanković, J. (2020). Internal communication and employee engagement as the key prerequisites of happiness. In *Joy* (75–91). Emerald Publishing Limited. https://doi.org/10.1108/S2398-391420200000005007

Lee, Y., Tao, W., Li, J.-Y. Q., & Sun, R. (2021). Enhancing employees' knowledge sharing through diversity-oriented leadership and strategic internal communication during the covid-19 outbreak. *Journal of Knowledge Management, 25*(6), 1526–1549. https://doi.org/10.1108/JKM-06-2020-0483

Macey, W. H., & Schneider, B. (2008). The meaning of employee engagement. *Industrial and Organizational Psychology, 1*(1), 3–30.

Maslach, C., & Jackson, S. E. (1981). The measurement of experienced burnout. *Journal of Organizational Behavior, 2*(2), 99–113.

Maslach, C., Schaufeli, W. B., & Leiter, M. P. (2001). Job burnout. *Annual Review of Psychology, 52*, 397–422.

Mishra, K., Boynton, L., & Mishra, A. (2014). Driving employee engagement: The expanded role of internal communications. *International Journal of Business Communication, 51*(2), 183–202.

Montgomery, A. J., Peeters, M. C. W., Schaufeli, W. B., & Den Ouden, M. (2003). Work–home interference among newspaper managers: Its relationship with burnout and engagement. *Anxiety, Stress, and Coping, 16*(2), 195–211.

Morganson, V. J., Litano, M. L., & O'Neill, S. K. (2014). Promoting work–family balance through positive psychology: A practical review of the literature. *The Psychologist-Manager Journal, 17*(4), 221–244.

Nederhof, A. J. (1988). Effects of a final telephone reminder and questionnaire cover design in mail surveys. *Social Science Research, 17*, 353–361.

Nitzsche, A., Soz, D., Pfaff, H., Jung, J., & Driller, E. (2013). Work–life balance culture, work–home interaction, and emotional exhaustion. *Journal of Occupational and Environmental Medicine, 55*(1), 67–73.

Soomro, A. A., Breitenecker, R. J., & Shah, S. A. M. (2018). Relation of work–life balance, WFC, and family–work conflict with the employee performance-moderating role of job satisfaction. *South Asian Journal of Business Studies, 7*(1), 129–146.

Thompson, M. J., Carlson, D. S., Kacmar, K. M., & Vogel, R. M. (2020). The cost of being ignored: Emotional exhaustion in the work and family domains. *Journal of Applied Psychology, 105*(2), 186–195.

van Zoonen, W., Sivunen, A., & Rice, R. E. (2020). Boundary communication: How smartphone use after hours is associated with work–life conflict and organizational identification. *Journal of Applied Communication Research, 48*(3), 372–392.

Welch, M. (2011). The evolution of the employee engagement concept: Communication implications. *Corporate Communications, 16*(4), 328–346. https://doi.org/10.1108/13563281111186968

Wood, S., Ghezzi, V., Barbaranelli, C., Di Tecco, C., Fida, R., Farnese, M. L., Ronchetti, M., & Iavicoli, S. (2019). Assessing the risk of stress in organizations: Getting the measure of organizational-level stressors. *Frontiers in Psychology, 10*, 2776. https://doi.org/10.3389/fpsyg.201

Section IX

Internal Communication and Engagement in a Global Context

Chapter Twenty

Application of the AVID Framework in a U.K. Fire and Rescue Service

Kevin Ruck

Introduction

The case study organization explored in this chapter is a Fire and Rescue Service in the U.K. It will be referred to as AFRS throughout the chapter. The service employs around 1,400 people. It is a public sector body, responsible for promoting fire safety, extinguishing fires, and protecting life and property when fires do occur, minimizing damage to property arising from firefighting operations, and rescuing people involved in road traffic collisions. Internal communication at AFRS is reviewed using Ruck's (2020) Alignment-Voice-Identification-Dialogue (AVID) framework, which incorporates the twin principles of keeping employees informed and employee voice as a theoretical foundation for good and ethical practice.

Evolution of Contemporary Practice

As Yaxley et al. (2020) observe, the roots of internal communication lie in "industrial editing" from the 1950s or the publication of in-house newspapers for employees introduced by companies as a way to counter critical underground publications that might be likely to emerge to campaign against management in the 1970s. As practice matured and evolved at the end of the twentieth century and in the first two decades of the twenty-first century, links to employee engagement became more prominent (Welch, 2020). In the U.K., the publication of the "Engaging for Success" Report (MacLeod & Clarke, 2009) shone a new light on employee engagement, which had for some time been grounded in human resources (HR) thinking around job satisfaction and motivation. The report suggested that two of the four key enablers for employee engagement are communication-oriented: strategic narrative and employee voice. Other research distinguished job engagement from organizational engagement (Ruck et al., 2017; Saks 2006; Welch, 2020), which enabled strong associations between internal communication and engagement to be established for the first time. Although the combination of strategic narrative and employee voice provided a solid basis for effective contemporary internal communication practice, strategic narrative continues to be the priority for practitioners, with far less attention paid to employee voice (Gatehouse, 2020).

DOI: 10.4324/9781003195580-30

TABLE 20.1 Mean results for employee interest in three topics across five organizations in the U.K. (shown as A–E)

Topic	A *n* = 276	B *n* = 167	C *n* = 1,259	D *n* = 205	E *n* = 159
Plans and aims	4.33	4.14	4.29	4.22	4.04
Progress and organizational information	4.05	4.19	4.23	3.99	4.13
External environment	4.20	4.00	4.15	4.18	4.12

Note Based on a 1–5 Likert scale where 4 is "interested" and 5 is "very interested."

Strategic Narrative

In terms of keeping employees informed as part of a strategic narrative approach, Ruck (2016) found that, when asked, employees report very high levels of interest in three corporate topics, as shown in Table 20.1.

Employees are, no doubt, interested in a wide range of topics in addition to those shown in Table 20.1. However, the very high interest rates reported highlight the importance of keeping employees fully informed about the organization's aims, plans, progress, and the external environment. According to Karian and Box (2021) in the U.K., employees report that they receive too much information about culture, values, purpose, IT, products and services, and policy/operational changes and not enough information about strategy, priorities, and the market/competition. Employees' information interests should not be assumed. Keeping employees informed should be based upon research that shows which topics employees are most interested in and then how well-informed they are for those topics. The resulting communication gaps become the focus for keeping employees informed. Karian and Box (2021) report that 74 percent of employees have a clear understanding of their organization's strategy/business priorities. However, there is no large scale, general data on the full range of topics that employees say they are most interested in and then how well-informed they are about those topics. Indeed, Karian and Box (2021, p. 7) conclude that "Communicators are getting the message across, but it has yet to translate into support for the priorities businesses are pursuing," which suggests that internal communication practice remains message led. Furthermore, data in the Karian and Box report reveals that "38 percent of employees feel that the tone of communications is too positive."

Transparent communication, defined by Men (2014) as "an organization's communication to make available all legally releasable information to employees whether positive or negative in nature" is a common theme from employees, especially in relation to change situations (Ruck, 2016). According to Rawlins (2009), to be perceived as transparent, the communicated information first of all needs to display certain substantial characteristics like timeliness, completeness, accuracy, and comprehensibility. Karian and Box (2021) report that U.K. employees are mostly satisfied with the clarity (64 percent) and transparency (62 percent) of communication, but just over half are happy with timeliness (56 percent).

Listening to Employees

Macnamara (2016) outlines seven canons of organizational listening: recognition, acknowledgment, attention, interpreting, understanding, consideration and responding. These highlight rational and emotional listening, taking what others say as receptively as possible, trying to understand others' perspectives and feelings, and providing a substantive response after considering what has been said. Macnamara (2020) argues that employee voice has no value without listening and proposes a turn from a focus on voice to active listening. Voice without appropriate consideration and response can lead to negative effects such as disengagement (Macnamara, 2016). Listening is reviewed by Macnamara in the context of public communication and principles are suggested to apply equally to a range of stakeholders. However, the dynamics of listening to employees are notably different to those that are used for listening to other groups such as customers. This is because of specific barriers that might exist inside organizations that can make listening to employees more problematic. These can, for example, include assumptions and expectations about the role of leaders and the lack of emphasis on listening to employees in leadership and management education. Furthermore, Edmondson (2019) argues that psychological safety is lacking in many organizations. In order to develop corporate climates where fears about psychological safety can be lessened, Krais et al. (2020, pp. 13–16) identify five core principles for listening to employees:

1) Openness—good listening requires an open mind
2) Planning—good listening is the result of thorough planning across the organization
3) Distributed leadership—listening needs to be led at multiple levels
4) Empathetic and creative feedback—good listening involves creating impactful and emotive feedback approaches
5) Human—good listening is rooted in a humanistic approach to communication and change.

In research with 551 communication managers, Krais et al. (2021) found that organizations rely too heavily on surveys and fail to invest fully in a wide range of listening methods and activities. In their research 59 percent of respondents stated that a "large-scale engagement survey" was used at least annually, and surveys were mentioned most often as the approach to delivering insights. In contrast, interviews and focus groups were rarely or never used and less than 20 percent of respondents cited focus groups as an insightful listening method. The study also found a clear difference in what respondents consider their organization to be like when it comes to general statements about listening to employees versus action-oriented statements. For example, 73 percent agreed that their organization "takes what employees say seriously" and yet only 42 percent agreed that their organization "responds promptly." This suggests that there may be a degree of complacency with regard to listening to employees.

The Alignment-Voice-Identification-Dialogue Framework

Ruck's (2020, 2021) AVID Framework incorporates the twin principles of keeping employees informed and employee voice (as discussed in the previous sections) and associates them with organizational engagement outcomes (as illustrated in Figure 20.1).

FIGURE 20.1 The Alignment-Voice-Identification-Dialogue (AVID) framework.

Alignment

According to Robinson and Hayday (2009), the top two behaviors cited by team members for an engaging line manager are firstly, making it clear what is expected from the team and secondly listening to team members. Gatenby et al. (2009) conclude that it is important for most managers to focus on doing the "simple" things well, including communicating clear work objectives that employees can understand. This emphasizes the focus on communication about team tasks. However, as Men (2014) highlights, a symmetrical communication environment is typified by managers who listen and align individual goals with organizational goals. The challenge for line manager communication is therefore to connect the micro to the macro. This is not straightforward. Indeed, Baumruk (2006) suggests that line managers may not be the best people to communicate about strategy as senior managers believe that they have problems with "complexity" and "strategic stuff." It is therefore unrealistic to expect line managers to communicate about strategy *per se*. Instead, they should be informed enough about "strategic stuff," with the support of their managers (the middle management layer in organizations), to be able to make meaningful connections that resonate with their team at a time when it is most appropriate to do so—in an unforced and authentic manner.

Voice

The term "voice" within the AVID framework is based on a broader understanding of voice that includes consideration of what is said and responding. It operates at line and senior manager levels and is underpinned by a systemic, multi-method approach to listening throughout the organization. This approach to voice and listening can be extended into a spectrum, as outlined by Krais et al. (2020), ranging from passive to deep. Listening and dialogue are now increasingly perceived as important activities, with 80 percent of internal communication manager respondents agreeing that they are involved with "two-way communication with employees" (Gatehouse, 2020, p. 7). As Macnamara (2020, p. 381) highlights, "in the era of online digital communication, natural language processing, machine learning content and textual analysis applications, voice to text (VTT) software, and other sense-making tools, expressions of voice can be listened to 24/7, compared with traditional employee engagement surveys that are usually conducted once a year." Madsen and Johansen (2019) found that employees are now making use of internal social media platforms to raise concerns that were, generally, treated seriously by managers who either accepted or rejected the issue raised. If they did not accept it, they typically supplied a long and well-supported explanation of why things were the way they were.

Identification

Identification with an organization stems from organization engagement Welch (2020). Engagement is not simply with one's work. As Kahn (2010, pp. 27–30) observes, employees also engage with leaders and aspects of the organization itself:

> Leaders needed to learn to dismantle the obstacles to engagement—structures, processes, and, for some, themselves—and create new patterns of interaction with and among employees. They had to create learning forums that were safe enough for employees to tell them the truth of their experiences.

Millward and Postmes (2010) report that the fact that identification with the superordinate grouping of "the organization" was particularly relevant to performance is important for theoretical, empirical, and pragmatic reasons. Fleck and Inceoglu (2010, p. 38) outline two separate dimensions for organizational engagement: identification—a sense of belonging, and alignment—the congruence between employees' beliefs about where the organization should be heading, what the goals and aspirations of the organization should be, and the actual direction of the organization. They argue that identification is affective and alignment is cognitive. This conceptual differentiation underpins the AVID framework, with an important distinction being made between the communication role for line managers (for alignment) and for senior managers (for identification). According to Galunic and Hermreck (2012), although local job conditions matter, senior management has a unique voice and understanding of strategy, and this may help explain the substantial influence they have on strategic embeddedness when they engage with employees.

Identification is dependent on symmetrical internal communication, which focuses on "employee-centric values and organizations' genuine care and concern for employees' interests" (Men & Bowen, 2017, p. 174). This includes meaning making and empathy which, according to Yue et al. (2020), enhances organizational identification. Men and Yue (2019) found that when the desire to be heard is satisfied and when this takes place in open and equal communication, employees can be happy, proud, appreciative, and affectionate. This is a relational perspective of leadership (Fairhurst & Uhl-Bien, 2012) where it is seen not as a trait or behavior, but as a phenomenon generated in the interactions among people acting in context.

Dialogue

In the public relations literature, Kent and Taylor (2002, pp. 24–25) set out five dimensions for dialogue:

- Mutuality—The acknowledgment that organizations and publics are inextricably linked
- Propinquity—The willingness and capacity of publics to express their demands to the organization, and the latter's ability to consult the former regarding matters of mutual interest
- Empathy—The atmosphere or environment required for fruitful dialogue
- Risk—The fact that the outcome of a dialogic process may be unpredictable
- Commitment—The parties to the dialogue must be truly committed to real conversation.

In extending these points, DeBussy and Suprawan (2015, p. 74) outline the following three attributes that apply specifically to dialogue in the workplace:

- Listening—suspending one's own frame of reference
- Positive regard—valuing people as people
- Willingness to change—participants must enter into dialogue with the intent to reach an understanding

At the core of this approach to dialogue in the workplace is the assumption that leadership is co-constructed in social interaction processes. CEOs should communicate in a "responsive, warm, friendly, empathetic, sincere, caring, and interested manner to demonstrate their concern for their employees, openness, and willingness to listen," as this is positively associated with employee-organization relationships (Men, 2015, p. 469). Furthermore, Walker and Aritz (2014, p. 13) suggest that this approach to leadership means that communication becomes "the primary concern rather than a secondary or tertiary consideration."

Methods

The case study is based on secondary data analysis of strategy documents, content analysis of internal communication delivered, and qualitative analysis of interviews and meetings with firefighters, the internal communication team, and the Chief Fire Officer.

Desk research commenced with analysis of the internal communication strategy and plan as outlined in the following documents:

- Review of structure charts
- Review of survey data collected as part of a government inspectorate report (2018/19)
- Review of Internal Communication Strategy (2020–2022)
- Review of Internal Communication Channel Spreadsheet

Content analysis of internal communication was then conducted, which included the following:

- Review of four monthly Chief Fire Officer updates (January–April 2021)
- Sample review of three Chief Fire Officer videos
- Sample review of one corporate weekly update (including a round-up of 24 intranet articles)
- Sample review of four Chief Fire Officer broadcast emails

Interviews and meetings were then conducted, which included two fire station visits, an interview with an on-call firefighter, an interview with a fire and rescue station leader, three meetings with the Chief Fire Officer, and five meetings with the internal communication team.

Findings

The analysis of strategy documents and organizational charts revealed a complex organizational structure, incorporating a complicated rota system and regularly changing working patterns for firefighters. The firefighter structure is split into three groups; east and west of county firefighters and on-call fighters (who are contracted to the organization to be on-call for duties at stations that are not permanently staffed). The organization also has a corporate service group (finance, IT and HR) and a prevention and customer engagement group which are office-based, although at the time of the research, these employees were often working from home due to COVID-19 restrictions. This structure presents numerous internal communication challenges. Many firefighters rely on face-to-face briefings from station leaders as they have limited access to corporate IT systems. Information needs also vary greatly between groups. There are more than 30 fire stations of various types and sizes (whole-time shift station, day-crew station, and on-call station), which makes it challenging for ongoing senior manager visits. Communication is also provided to firefighters on a regular basis by their union. A further notable issue that arose from the analysis of strategy documents is the importance of striking an appropriate and engaging balance between being seen as a modern employer and the critical, formal, operational systems and rules that have to be followed.

Analysis of examples of briefings and all-employee emails suggests that internal communication in AFRS relies heavily on Chief Fire Officer's monthly updates and ad-hoc emails, supported with personal ad-hoc videos and stories on the intranet, which are collated and emailed out weekly. The content in the Chief Fire Officer's monthly updates is wide ranging and during the period of the review in early 2021 focused on inclusion, diversity, and wellbeing. The updates are quite formal in tone and are lengthy documents to read. There is evidence that email open rates for the update have steadily declined over the past 18 months. The videos are engaging; the Chief Fire Officer speaks personally without notes and makes a point of thanking employees at the start of every video. The Chief Fire Officer's personal emails are used when a perceived urgent need to make things clear or to get things done arises. The weekly e-bulletin can contain a lot of pieces (for example, 24 in 1 week). At the firefighter level, briefings are also provided face to face. However, the content included is left to the discretion of the station leader/crew manager. Information also flows through various levels of management meetings, wellbeing meetings, and station visits. In general, much of the communication is reactive, formal in tone, and to some degree ad-hoc.

Analysis of an interview with a station leader and station visits (which included an unstructured and unplanned conversation with an on-call firefighter) underlined the importance of history within the buildings and the sense of public service and being part of the local community. For example, in the on-call station there were pictures of the team holding an open day, together with boards showing the names of all the firefighters who have served at the station. The on-call firefighter talked about his sense of camaraderie with the crew who all lived in the local village. This was contrasted with more modern posters that depicted the organization's aim. The on-call firefighter talked about his interest in wider AFRS news, such as other services that it was now offering and news in general about how the organization was performing.

The station leader interview highlighted issues of information overload and timing of information. He talked about the challenges of picking out the pertinent information provided in emails that needed to be briefed each week to firefighters because of the numerous emails received. He also cited an example of a Chief Fire Officer email that had been sent out about a sensitive issue before he had a chance to brief his team, which had caused some consternation. The station leader agreed that more tailored communication, with better-defined employee groupings, would be a way to improve the process together with a more clearly defined theme to communication in a particular period. He also agreed that a system to tailor and check urgent operational messages, using agreed criteria based on level of seriousness, urgency, employee group affected, and appropriate channel would be a step forward.

The interviews with the Chief Fire Officer were wide ranging. His approach to leadership and communication were discussed in an open way and he was receptive to the analysis of his updates, videos, and all-employee emails. It was clear that he understood that communication and engagement of employees should start with the senior leader of the organization and he took that responsibility very seriously. The interviews revealed some frustrations in changing attitudes about inclusion and diversity together with some issues in getting simple, day-to-day administrative tasks completed by firefighters. Much of the discussion centered around process and forward planning to ensure maximum impact of communication. Suggestions about stronger branding and a better design for update briefings were well received. The communication role of the Assistant Fire Chief was also discussed in terms of taking more responsibility for reinforcing themes and messages agreed in the plan, filtering prioritized messaging from management meetings to assistant directors and area heads for cascade to station leaders, and personally sending out urgent operational messaging. Discussions about employee voice revealed a genuine desire to listen to employees, but there were limited processes in place to do this in a systemic way, so it was conducted through an employee forum and ad-hoc station visits.

Analysis of meetings with the internal communication team highlights the frustrations of working with limited resources to keep up with a constant stream of demands for support with communication. Although the team has a well-developed and well-articulated internal communication plan and channel matrix, it struggled to move from a heavily reactive to a forward planned and themed strategic approach. Discussions with the team centered on:

- Establishing a program of ongoing employee research and communication measurement
- A process whereby the senior leadership team discuss and agree broad quarterly themes for the year ahead

- A process to support agreed themes with targeted messages for each employee group
- A monthly content and channel mix signed off by the director Prevention, Protection, Customer Engagement and Safety each month (ongoing throughout each quarter)
- A system of monthly calls with station leaders to discuss key messages to be briefed each month, discuss potential stories that can be used for future communication, and listen to feedback being generated in firefighter briefings

A summary of the situation at AFRS that emerged from the research is shown in Table 20.2.

TABLE 20.2 Summary analysis of situation at AFRS using the AVID framework

Alignment	Voice	Identification	Dialogue
Information needs vary greatly between teams—communication not tailored to specific employee groups Issues of information overload and timing of information Content in face-to-face firefighter briefings is left to the discretion of the station leader/crew manager	Genuine desire to listen to employees Largely unstructured opportunities for voice—indicative of a passive approach to listening Limited focus on voice in internal communication plans	Chief Fire Officer adopts a strong personal approach to corporate internal communication Briefings include strategic *and* operational messages and are overly formal in tone Videos are personal and include expressions of gratitude and support for employees	Internal communication is message-led Limited opportunities for firefighters to engage with topics, other than in local team meetings Some opportunities provided for wider employee voice, but these are not systemized

Discussion and Conclusion

The AVID framework was used to assess strengths and weaknesses of the current approach to internal communication at AFRS. This highlighted strong leadership communication, a belief in employee voice, and well-established firefighter briefing sessions. However, it revealed shortcomings in forward planning processes, mixed messaging, an occasionally overly formal tone of voice, a lack of systematic voice, information overload, and limited processes for employee segmentation.

In terms of alignment, corporate messaging in the form of posters promoting the organization's aim and attempts to format leadership briefings into strategic themes compete with union communication and a station leader/crew manager's understandable preference to focus on local-level issues in team briefings. This highlights a fundamental drawback in cascade team briefing systems. As Baumruk (2006) suggests, line managers may not be the best people to communicate about strategy and more responsibility should be taken by senior and middle managers to either communicate personally or support line managers more effectively. Communication based on objectives for alignment in AFRS is heavily message led, although the formal tone of voice in briefings and some issues around timeliness and comprehensibility undermine understanding and engagement. The findings from this case study therefore, to a degree, support a broader contention that "Communicators are getting the message across, but it has yet to translate into support for the priorities businesses are pursuing" (Karian and Box, 2021).

A genuine intention and willingness to listen to employees at AFRS is clear from interviews with the Chief Fire Officer, the station leader, and the internal communication team. And employees do have opportunities in various forums to express their views. However, there is no systematic process in place for listening and employee voice does not feature prominently in the internal communication plan. The formal nature of the organization, its history and the complex structure may explain a tendency to provide direction and conformity in communication, where leadership is understood as needing to "provide answers." Employee voice at AFRS is therefore representative of what Krais et al. (2020) describe as a "passive" approach and this case study supports their findings that suggest that a shift from passive to active listening requires a step-change in approach in many organizations.

Identification within the AVID framework focuses on the communication role of senior leaders in the organization. The Chief Fire Officer at AFRS takes personal responsibility for communication very seriously. The focus on issues of diversity and inclusion in the Chief Fire Officer's communication is a clear indication of the ambition to develop a stronger sense of belongingness and community. However, the tone in written communication is somewhat formal and does not convey a "responsive, warm, friendly and empathetic" approach, advocated for CEOs by Men (2015, p. 469), although this is more evident in other communication.

Three pillars of the AVID framework (alignment, voice, and identification) form the basis for dialogue in the workplace, which is defined in this chapter as incorporating listening, positive regard, and a willingness to change. By applying the framework to the case study, it becomes clear that more systemic listening processes are required before high levels of dialogue can be achieved, with the associated benefits of higher levels of engagement. To develop more dialogical communication, two conditions outlined by Taylor and Kent (2014, p. 935) need to be met: (a) public relations professionals are trained in how to facilitate dialogue and (b) management becomes convinced of its value.

In summary, this chapter has used the AVID framework to assess internal communication at a Fire and Rescue Service in the U.K. The framework itself is underpinned by robust academic research and scholarly knowledge and is associated with employee engagement. In applying concepts such as alignment, voice, and identification, it focuses attention on different aspects of internal communication in a way that informs strategic planning for good practice.

Learning Outcomes

1) Apply the AVID framework to assess and inform strategic internal communication planning.
2) Differentiate between line manager and senior leader internal communication responsibilities.
3) Embed employee voice as a core component of strategic internal communication practice.

Discussion Questions

1) How could the AVID framework be used for internal communication planning in your organization? How are line managers supported for communication with their teams in your organization?
2) To what extent do senior leaders at your organization take personal responsibility for communication about strategy?
3) To what extent is listening to employees embedded throughout your organization?

Further Reading

Ruck, K. 2020. *Exploring internal communication, towards informed employee voice. Fourth edition.* Abingdon: Routledge.

References

Baumruk, A. (2006). Why managers are crucial to increasing engagement, identifying steps managers can take to engage their workforce. *Strategic HR Review, 5*(2), 24–27. https://doi.org/10.1108/14754390680000863

DeBussy, N. M., & Suprawan, L. (2015). Employee dialogue: A framework for business success. In Ruck. K. (Ed.), *Exploring Internal Communication* (3rd ed.). Farnham: Gower Publishing Ltd.

Edmondson, A. C. (2019). *The fearless organization. Creating psychological safety in the workplace for learning, innovation and growth.* Hoboken, NJ: John Wiley and Sons Inc.

Fairhurst, G. T., & Uhl-Bien, M. (2012). Organizational discourse analysis (ODA): Examining leadership as a relational process. *The Leadership Quarterly, 23*(6), 1043–1062. https://doi.org/10.1016/j.leaqua.2012.10.005

Fleck, S., & Inceoglu, I. (2010). A comprehensive framework for understanding and predicting engagement. In A. Albrecht (Ed.), *Handbook of employee engagement, perspectives, issues, research and practice.* Cheltenham: Edward Elgar Publishing Ltd.

Galunic, C., & Hermreck, I. (December 2012). How to Help Employees "Get" Strategy. *Harvard Business Review.* Business Communication. Available at: https://hbr.org/2012/12/how-to-help-employees-get-strategy

Gatehouse. (2020). *State of the Sector 2020. Vol 12. The definitive global survey of the internal communication landscape.* Gatehouse: A Gallagher Company.

Gatenby, M., Alfes, K., Truss, K., & Soane, E. (2009). Harnessing employee engagement in UK public services. [Paper presentation]. *Public Management Research Association Conference,* Columbus, Ohio.

Kahn, W. A. (2010). The essence of engagement: Lessons from the field. In S.L. Albrecht (Ed), *Handbook of employee engagement, perspectives, issues, research and practice.* Cheltenham: Edward Elgar Publishing Ltd.

Karian and Box. (2021). *IC UK 2021. The most comprehensive study of UK employees' communication and engagement preferences.* https://www.karianandbox.com/insight/20/ic-uk-2021-the-most-comprehensive-study-of-uk-employees-communications-and-engagement-preferences

Kent, M. L., & Taylor, M. (2002). Toward a dialogic theory of public relations. *Public Relations Review, 28*(1), 21–37. https://doi.org/10.1016/S0363-8111(02)00108-X

Krais, H., Pounsford, M., & Ruck, K. (2020). *Who's listening? Update. Good listening practice.* London: PR Academy, Couravel & IABC UK.

Krais, H., Pounsford, M., & Ruck, K. (2021). *Who's listening? Update. From Measurement to Meaning.* London: PR Academy, Couravel & IABC UK.

Macnamara, J. (2016). *Organizational listening. The missing essential in public communication.* New York, NY: Peter Lang Publishing.

Macnamara, J. (2020). Corporate listening: Unlocking insights from VOC, VOE and VOS for mutual benefits. *Corporate Communications: An International Journal, 25*(3), 377–393. https://doi.org/10.1108/CCIJ-08-2019-0102

MacLeod, D., Clarke, N. (2009). Engaging for success: Enhancing performance through employee engagement, A Report to Government [Great Britain]. Department for Business, Innovation and Skills.

Madsen, V. T., & Johansen, W. (2019). A spiral of voice? When employees speak up on internal social media. *Journal of Communication Management, 23*(4), 331–347. https://doi.org/10.1108/JCOM-03-2019-0050

Men, L. R. (2015). The internal communication role of the chief executive officer: Communication channels, style, and effectiveness. *Public Relations Review, 41*(4), 461–471. https://doi.org/10.1016/j.pubrev.2015.06.021

Men, L. R. (2014). Strategic internal communication: Transformational leadership, communication channels, and employee satisfaction. *Management Communication Quarterly, 28*(2), 264–284. https://doi.org/10.1177/0893318914524536

Men, R. L., & Bowen, S. A. (2017). *Excellence in internal relations management.* New York, NY: Business Expert Press.

Men, R. L., & Yue, C. A. (2019). Creating a positive emotional culture: Effect of internal communication and impact on employee supportive behaviors. *Public Relations Review, 45*(3). https://doi.org/10.1016/j.pubrev.2019.03.001

Millward, L., & Postmes, T. (2010). Who we are affects how we do: The financial benefits of organizational identification. *British Journal of Management, 21*(2), 327–339. https://doi.org/10.1111/j.1467-8551.2009.00667.x

Rawlins, B. L. (2009). Give the emperor a mirror: Toward developing a stakeholder measurement of organizational transparency. *Journal of Public Relations Research, 21*(1), 71–99. https://doi.org/10.1080/10627260802153421

Ruck, K. (2016). Informed employee voice: the synthesis of internal corporate communication and employee voice and the associations with Organizational engagement. PhD thesis. University of Central Lancashire, UK.

Ruck, K. (2020). The AVID framework for good and ethical practice. In K. Ruck (Ed.), *Exploring internal communication, towards informed employee voice.* 4th Edition. Abingdon: Routledge.

Ruck, K. (2021). Employee voice and internal listening: Towards dialogue in the workplace. In L. R. Men & A. Tkalac Verčič (Eds.), *Current trends and issues in internal communication: Theory and practice* (93–111). Cham, Switzerland, Palgrave Macmillan.

Ruck, K., Welch, M., & Menara, B. (2017). Employee voice: An antecedent to organizational engagement? *Public Relations Review, 43*(5), 904–914. https://doi.org/10.1016/j.pubrev.2017.04.008

Saks, A. M. (2006). Antecedents and consequences of employee engagement. *Journal of Managerial Psychology, 21*(7), 600–619. https://doi.org/10.1108/02683940610690169

Taylor, M. & Kent, M. L. (2014). Dialogic engagement: Clarifying foundational concepts. *Journal of Public Relations Research, 26*(5), 384–398. https://doi.org/10.1080/1062726X.2014.956106

Walker, R., & Aritz, J. (2014). *leadership talk, a discourse approach to leader emergence.* New York, NY: Business Expert Press.

Welch, M. (2020). Dimensions of internal communication and implications for employee engagement. In Ruck, K. (Ed.), *Exploring internal communication, towards informed employee voice* (4th ed.). Abingdon: Routledge.

Yaxley, H., Pilkington, A., & Ruck, K. (2020). The evolution of practice and the changing role of the practitioner. In Ruck, K. (Ed.), *Exploring internal communication, towards informed employee voice.* 4th Edition. Abingdon: Routledge.

Yue, C. A., Men, R. L., & Ferguson, M. A. (2020). Examining the effects of internal communication and emotional culture on employees' organizational identification. *International Journal of Business Communication.* https://doi.org/10.1177/2329488420914066

Chapter Twenty-One

Revs Your Heart: How Yamaha Motors Revved Up Its Employees during Corporate Transformation

Masamichi Shimizu and Koichi Yamamura

Introduction

Globalization of business is not an easy task for many Japanese companies. Unlike Anglo-American companies, the de facto global language—English—is not their mother language. Unlike European companies, they are not used to dealing with different cultures and languages in their daily life. This case study illustrates how YMC communicated with its employees, in particular with those in its overseas operations, when the company went through a major transformation in response to the 1997 Asian currency crisis and the 2007–2008 global financial crisis. YMC's experience is not unique to Japanese companies; rather, this case can provide a reference for many non-Euro-American companies expanding their businesses globally.

Literature Review

In his discussion about global public relations, Sriramesh notes that culture determines the nature of public relations, and different cultural environments require different public relations strategies and techniques for effective communication (Sriramesh, 2020). Culture represents patterns of thinking, feeling, and acting. Culture is a collective phenomenon that is learned and derived from one's social environment (Hofstede et al, 2010). According to Hofstede Insights (*Country comparison*, n.d.), the key differences between Thai culture, one of the regions where YMC operates, and Japanese culture are in the dimensions of masculinity and long-term orientation, followed by uncertainty avoidance. These differences suggest that the Japanese have the drive for excellence and perfection in material production, maintain a high rate of investment in R&D even in economically difficult times, try to take into account all the risk factors before any project can start and managers ask for all the detailed facts and figures before making any decisions. Thai, on the other hand, are less assertive and competitive and very normative and focus on achieving quick results, do not readily accept change, and are very risk-averse.

DOI: 10.4324/9781003195580-31

Kotter (2011) notes eight steps to transforming an organization: (1) establishing a sense of urgency, (2) forming a powerful guiding coalition, (3) creating a vision, (4) communicating the vision, (5) empowering others to act on the vision, (6) planning for and creating short-term wins, (7) consolidating improvements and producing still more change, and (8) institutionalizing new approaches.

While the importance of communication during the organizational change in determining employees' perception of the change is widely acknowledged, many organizations encounter difficulties because of the one-way nature of communication strategies and the predominant focus on providing information with strategic issues rather than job-related issues. Also, the source of information may be an important factor that affects employees' attitude toward a change rather than the quality of information alone (Allen et al., 2007). During organizational change, small informal discussions and general information meetings tend to be used most frequently for disseminating information about the change (Lewis, 2007).

In communicating change, there are two implementation approaches, programmatic and participatory. The programmatic approach focuses on "telling and selling" and the participatory approach focuses on seeking input from employees on the assumption that they should be active participants in the change process. Implementers usually do not use participatory communication activities to solicit input from staff and when they do, they are informal in nature (Russ, 2008). While both mediated and interpersonal communication helps foster perceived communication transparency, interpersonal channels are efficient in fostering perceived communication transparency and uncertainty reduction (Men et al., 2022). Internal communication, openness, and assurance of legitimacy are the main drivers of employee engagement. Employee engagement is positively related to employees' contextual performance and positive messaging behaviors, and negatively related to employees' negative messaging behaviors (Shen & Jiang, 2019). Contextual performance is closely tied to Japanese management. Tanaka (2013) noted that "in Japanese workplaces up until the 1990s, the fact that employees voluntarily did what was best for their organization was taken for granted" (p. 8). Although workplace environment in Japan is gradually changing, "there are still many members of Japanese organizations who voluntarily take on jobs that were not allocated to them to some extent" (p. 8).

For non-native speakers, English is the medium and the message that conveys power but also powerlessness, privilege, prestige, and pleasure (Tananuraksakul, 2010). This implies that when dealing with non-native speakers, native English speakers enjoy advantages as they are equipped with more power, and non-native speakers are willing to communicate in English that they may not be fluent in and feel a kind of powerlessness. Companies from English-speaking countries can enjoy such an advantage when expanding their businesses globally, but it doesn't apply to companies from non-English countries. With the exception of a few business elites, communicating in English can be problematic for both expatriate managers and employees in the host country.

Methodology

For this case study, we conducted an interview with Kazuyuki Yamashita, who led YMC's internal communication reform initiatives in 2015. We also reviewed documents and materials including YMC's internal communication magazine, YMC website, business magazines, industry journals, and Yamaha's internal survey results as reported in its internal publication.

Yamaha Motor Co., Ltd.

YMC's history goes back to 1954 when Nippon Gakki (currently Yamaha Corporation, one of the largest musical instruments manufacturers in the world) started manufacturing motorcycles. In 1955, the motorcycle division spun off as YMC (Yamaha Motors Co., Ltd., 2022). The two companies set up the Yamaha Joint Brand Committee to manage the brand and logo that they share (Yamashita, 2022).

YMC was one of the last to enter the motorcycle market in Japan but was determined to provide the highest quality product with the global market in sight. YMC entered the motorcycle race in its very first year, 1955, winning the two biggest motorcycle races in Japan, and began competing overseas in 1958 (Yamaha Motors Co., Ltd., 2022).

YMC began overseas sales in Mexico in 1958 and in the U.S. in 1960. In 1963, YMC set up a joint venture with a local company in India to manufacture small motorcycles, and in 1964, in Thailand. Since then, the company established subsidiaries and joint venture companies in Europe, the Americas, Asia, and Africa.

In the process, YMC expanded its product offerings including pleasure boat and marine engines; professional-use fishing boats; automobile engines and bodies; snowmobiles; golf cars; dune buggies; industrial robots; lawn mowers; and electric wheelchairs. YMC motorcycle's global market share in 2020 was 8.5%, selling over 3.8 million units. Global market shares of other products in 2020 were: pleasure boats 32.2%; personal watercraft 62.8%; and golf carts 35%. Today, the company has manufacturing facilities in Japan, U.S., France, Indonesia, Thailand, India, the Philippines, and Vietnam. The net annual sales for 2020 were $14.281 billion.

Cross-Cultural Communication at Thai Yamaha Motor Co., Ltd.

During the 1990s, Japan's economy suffered from a prolonged recession. What supported YMC in that period was a strong demand from Asian countries. However, the Asian financial crisis in 1997 dealt a serious blow to YMC's business. To strengthen the company's ability to cope with the rapidly changing business environment, YMC decided to take control of its overseas operations by increasing its stake to be a majority shareholder. In 1964, YMC set up Siam Yamaha jointly with a local partner to manufacture and sell motorcycles in Thailand. YMC held a minority stake and supported the company under a technical assistance agreement without any expatriate Japanese on-site. Due to the Asian financial crisis, the sale of motorcycles in Thailand fell from 373,000 in 1995 to 80,000 in 1998. There were two rounds of layoffs, reducing the number of employees from 3,000 to 600.

In 2000, to better control the company and turn around its business, YMC increased its stake in Siam Yamaha from 28% to 51% and renamed it Thai Yamaha Motor. YMC sent 31 Japanese staff to install Japanese-style engineering and manufacturing technology. For Thai managers, it was like a bolt out of the blue. "Will the Japanese take over all the key positions? What will my future be?" With these worries left unsolved, the turnaround plan soon stalled. Japanese staff, knowing that the company was on the verge of bankruptcy, were desperate to improve the operation at any cost, working till late at night. They assigned tasks to local staff, but the response was not as expected. Deadlines were not met, and they would go home on time leaving the assignment undone. This was not the way Japanese staff was used to back home and they needed to do things themselves to get things done on time. As they worked harder, the Thai staff became less motivated.

Attitude Survey

To defuse the situation, the head of the Thai operation implemented an "attitude survey on distinct culture and on-the-job training" to listen to the opinions of both sides. All 31 Japanese staff and 65 Thai managers were surveyed. Questions included: what are the problems you face; what are the things you dislike about your work; what are the things

TABLE 21.1 Initial findings of the attitude survey of the Japanese and local managers

Initial survey findings (excerpts)	
Thai staff comment	**Japanese staff comment**
Japanese only give us instruction for the work and they don't teach or guide me.	When I give a job order, local staff say they understand it, but quite often it doesn't get done by the deadline. Even when they can't get it done on time, they don't tell me about it.
I want to improve my skill and be able to replace Japanese staff and manage the organization.	Local staff doesn't have the ability to understand the root cause of problems.
I want to learn the job, but they don't have the skill to give us on-the-job training.	I want to educate local staff, but I'm too busy to do so.
	I need to do almost all the work by myself; otherwise, things don't go as planned. Therefore, I don't have time to teach local staff.

you think should be improved for Thai and Japanese to work together, and; what are the values and code of conduct that need to be observed when working? The findings are shown in Table 21.1.

In the follow-up session, Japanese staff were asked why it was difficult for them to find the time to educate local staff. The findings indicated that: the same problems occur repeatedly and Japanese staff needs to redo the work themselves; some of the work is unnecessary; the job manual is missing something important and not clearly defined. From these findings, the management learned that what needed to change was the way operations were structured.

KI Program

In 2005, the company invited an outside consultancy to implement a "Knowledge Intensive Staff Innovation Plan (KI)" program. According to the head of JMAC Thailand, who advised Thai Yamaha, KI aimed to increase intellectual productivity and energize the organizational climate by transforming the work process into one that can solve problems before it becomes a problem. Japanese staff and managers in the overseas subsidiaries were stationed as part of job rotation and some of them were assigned manager roles for the first time. Some others may have played manager roles back home, surrounded by supportive subordinates who shared the same organizational culture. They did not understand that the Japanese way of management often didn't work well outside of Japan. The core concept behind KI was the sense of objectivity (Katsuta, 2012).

KI was implemented in three phases. The first was to improve the "problem-solving skills of Japanese staff." The second was for Thai and Japanese staff to jointly engage in improving their "problem-solving skills," in which each Japanese staff worked alongside their local direct subordinates to guide them to improve their skills and listen to the issues and problems they faced to seek solutions together. The aim was for Thai staff to gain problem-solving skills and Japanese staff to gain management skills. The third was to improve the management skills of both Japanese and Thai staff.

The key components of KI were the following two sessions. The first was the consultation meeting held within each work group to discuss problems and issues they faced in their daily work. Managers asked members "why" questions and dug into the problem until core issues were identified. In doing so, they used a bulletin board illustrating the entire work process and added comments and ideas for process modification as discussed. The bulletin boards were left in the office so they could come back and review the process anytime. After initial trials, they decided not to use PCs because it was difficult to grasp the entire process and the discussion failed to involve other members. Some even forgot what was discussed a week ago. The use of a bulletin board provided a reference point for team members to review and identify the root cause and think about improvements anytime. The second was the retrospective study meeting (later renamed as "learning-from-failure meeting"). This was a meeting of 30+ managers in the manufacturing department. One of the managers was assigned to talk about the issues and failures that they had experienced and how they planned to solve the problem and improve the process. Others were asked to think about what they would do in the situation and engage in the discussion afterward. Other KI activities included "bragging meetings" to showcase results from consultation meetings to install a sense of accomplishment, and "management meetings" to discuss KI activities management to nourish management skills among staff members.

The head of the Thai operation emphasized the following five points about KI. (1) Don't engage in KI for the sake of KI. KI is just a tool to learn to solve problems in daily operations. (2) When some issue arises, don't start by blaming others. Try to seek causes in your thoughts and actions. (3) KI activities are a "safe and fair haven." Talks and comments during KI don't affect one's assessment. (4) If some other section's activity seems appealing, copy and apply it to your section immediately. (5) Managers must focus on listening to their subordinates rather than telling. Don't speculate what they think. Ask and find out what they think.

KI activities were expanded from engineering to production management, procurement, quality management, and production. After the implementation of KI, between 2006 and 2011, the number of customer complaints fell 70% and the amount of cost reduction tripled. It also broke the silo as the result of sharing experiences and problems. However, the former vice president of Yamaha Thailand acknowledged that some of the staff members still didn't understand the significance of the KI and engaged in it superficially. He hoped that someday, Yamaha Thailand would be an organization that can stand on its feet with local employees alone (Hirose, 2012). Along with KI, cross-cultural training sessions were provided by an external consultant to both Japanese and local managers to help better understand each other.

Communicating Changes during the Structural Reform

The global financial crisis in 2007–2008 brought the world economy into turmoil. The amount of global trade in 2009 fell 10.6% from the previous year (Ministry of Economy, Trade, and Industry, 2014). YMC's sales in 2008 dropped 9% from the previous year and another 28% in 2009, with the largest-ever loss in the company's history. YMC's business was on the verge of collapse. In 2009, YMC launched the structural reform project and appointed then production general manager Hiroyuki Yanagi to lead the project. In 2010, Yanagi was appointed as President and CEO of YMC and continued to lead the structural reform. It required efficient and effective internal communication to maintain employee morale in times of difficulty. Yanagi thought it was important for every single member of YMC to head in the same direction and have a sense of ownership. To that end, reformation of internal communication was critical. The first major structural reform was to streamline production facilities to bring down the break-even point. Before the structural reform, in the headquarters location alone, there were 25 manufacturing units in 12 different factories. Instead of simply telling its employees which unit will be closed or merged with other units, YMC utilized visualization to show which unit is located in which factory. By visually showing the current and future placement of manufacturing units among factories, it became easier for its employees to understand why such reform was necessary and how they were expected to cope with the change. As a side effect, the use of this visualization turned out to be quite effective in communicating with media and investors as well (Yanagi, 2018).

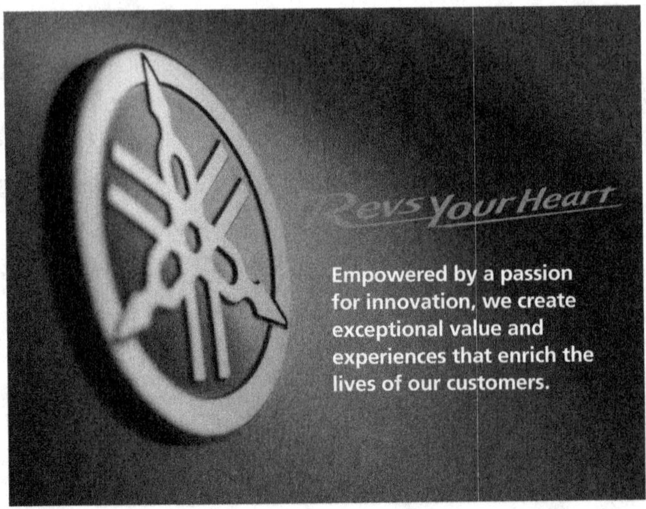

FIGURE 21.1 Revs Your Heart. Credit: Yamaha Motor Co., Ltd.

Yanagi also knew the importance of branding. In 2013, YMC set a new brand slogan, "Revs Your Heart," and a brand statement, "Empowered by a passion for innovation, we create exceptional value and experiences that enrich the lives of our customers." The brand slogan and the brand statement accompanied by the company logo is shown in Figure 21.1. The concept behind the brand statement was illustrated by five Kanji characters and corresponding English words as shown in Figure 21.2.

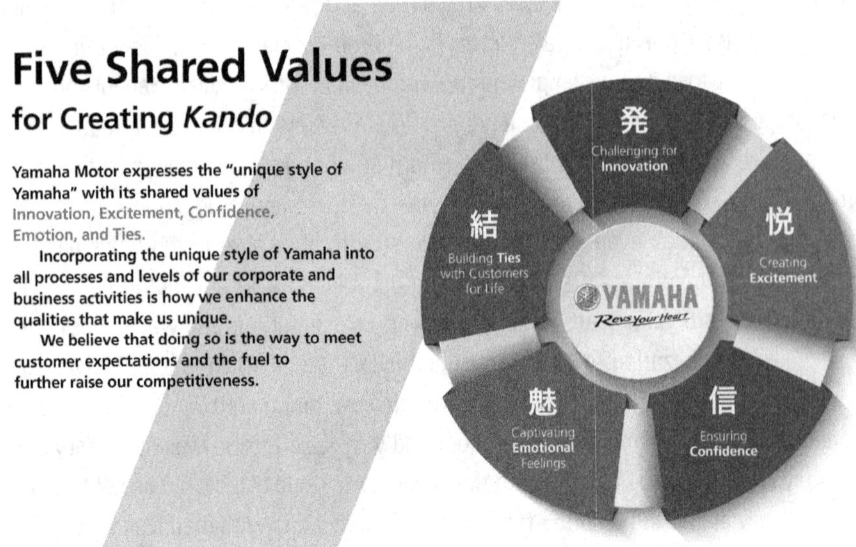

FIGURE 21.2 Five shared values for creating Kando. Credit: Yamaha Motor Co., Ltd.

Transformation of Internal Communication Tools

YMC started publishing an internal communication magazine titled *Shaho Yamaha* [Company News Yamaha] in 1956 and it became monthly in 1964. It was published in Japanese and distributed to its employees in Japan and Japanese managers stationed abroad. YMC's operations spread around the globe, but many of its factory workers didn't have English proficiency, and to publish monthly *Shaho Yamaha* in multiple languages would require far more resources than YMC could afford. Publication of local internal communication magazine/newsletter was left to the discretion of local entities.

Yanagi understood the importance of internal branding and YMC published multi-language extra editions of *Shaho Yamaha* on three occasions. In 2015, a brand book titled "Yamaha na hito no monozukuri yogoshu [Typical Yamaha people's glossary of manufacturing terms]" was published and distributed to all employees around the world. This was first published in Japanese and English, but upon request from overseas units, Thai and Vietnamese versions were published. As YMC was cautious of cultural bias and misinterpretation, the company employed back translation to make sure the nuances were properly conveyed. Although it was titled glossary of terms, the purpose of this publication was to convey the concept behind the newly set brand slogan, "Revs Your Heart," and management's view as to what the YMC brand means. In the same year, the new intermediate-term business plan was published in both English and Japanese as *Shaho Yamaha* extra edition and distributed to all employees in Japan and managers at overseas locations. In 2017, *Shaho Yamaha* extra edition commemorating MOTO GP 500th victory was published in Japanese, English, Spanish, French, Indonesian, Thai, Vietnam, and simplified Chinese. The internal communication section at YMC headquarters planned to print and distribute the publication globally, but interestingly, YMC Europe, reflecting their environmental consciousness, asked to send the data file instead of printed material. The U.S., on the other hand, was happy with the excellent quality of the print.

President Email

In 2002, YMC began sending the president's messages by email to employees in Japan. The messages were sent twice a year with additional issues on special occasions. In 2012, two years after Yanagi became the YMC president, the president's emails began reaching overseas. However, as many of the local operations were in the beginning controlled by local partners, YMC overseas operations did not have a uniform IT platform.

Because of the security concern, only fully owned subsidiaries in the U.S., Europe, South America, Australia, New Zealand, and some in China received the president email. Thanks to the gradual improvement of IT systems, today all YMC subsidiaries receive president emails.

Since its first issue in 2002, the president emails have been translated into English. Initially, the English versions were sent only to local heads, but the further distribution within the unit was left to the discretion of the local operation. In 2010, YMC began circulating some of the president emails that were particularly relevant to overseas operations in both English and Japanese. Starting 2015, every president emails were circulated in English and Japanese simultaneously, with the exception of certain region-specific issues.

Yamaha Group News WEB

In 2009, YMC launched a website in Japanese and English, catering to communicating with its employees. However, with the difficulty of maintaining website security on multiple IT platforms, YMC made it available only to 100% subsidiaries. Consequently, the usage of the website was limited. In 2016, YMC embedded the group news website in the company-wide Office 365 system, making it available to about 80% of its global workforce, but except in a few countries, most of the non-manager employees were not proficient in English. Currently, the number of overseas employees who view Yamaha Group News WEB is about 2,000, roughly the same as the number of managers outside of Japan. Of these, about 600 view it regularly (K. Yamashita, personal communication, January 21, 2022).

Global Management Committee

In 2012, YMC launched the Global Management Committee. Until then, there was no opportunity for local management to share their experiences. From each YMC overseas subsidiary, the highest-ranking local member and the highest-ranking Japanese expatriate gathered in Japan for three days biannual meeting to discuss group-wide mid-to-long term topics including branding, future technology, and human resource development.

Global Management Development Program

As of 2012, about 50% of the senior management of 77 YMC overseas operations were local employees. President Yanagi wanted to increase the share of local management

(Yamaha Motors Co., Ltd., 2012). Yamaha Global Management Development Program was launched in 2015. Every year, about 20 next-generation management candidates were selected from each region including Japan and gathered in Japan for a week to learn the company's history, corporate philosophy, and business practices at the headquarters. An unstated but important purpose of the program was to nourish personal relationships among participants and with senior management.

As part of the program, YMC selected one or two local young staff every year from overseas to work at the headquarters in Japan for two years. Those future-management staff may be able to communicate and get along in Japan, but their spouses were often reluctant to come to Japan because of language and cultural barriers. As a result, though YMC wished to pick more, some candidates declined the offer and only one or two are stationed every year.

Case Analysis

As global companies need to strike a balance between local culture and the corporate culture under which much of the decisions are made, it is critical for management and employees at overseas units to understand and respect both local and the company's home country culture (Hofstede et al., 2010). When collaboration among Japanese and Thai staff members became an issue, Thai Yamaha applied a knowledge-intensive staff innovation plan, or KI, that urges managers to evaluate their messages not by their own value but by how receivers perceive the message. KI assumed that what was important was not to just fix the problem. What was important was for the manager to change the message content of the instruction, how instructions were given, and how to manage the situation throughout the process. Otherwise, the manager would continue to face problems in various forms and circumstances (Hirose, 2012). The application of KI and attitude survey showed that Thai Yamaha management knew the importance of communication during organizational change and understanding culture in managing overseas units.

The fact that Thai Yamaha's effort started by listening to the voices of both Japanese and Thai staff, and then educating Japanese staff behavior first rather than changing local staff, shows that the company knew the importance of respecting local culture and engaging in two-way communication. It is also a good example of participatory communication during organizational change and how interpersonal channels help reduce uncertainty among employees (Men et al., 2022).

Communication initiatives led by CEO Yanagi during post-global financial crisis corporate transformation shows that YMC knew the importance of message source, but it also shows the limitation of tactics that can be applied to company-wide communication. Hence, it becomes clear that organizations need to combine programmatic approaches through mediated channels and participatory approaches through interpersonal channels at regional levels to effectively communicate during organizational transformation (Russ, 2008).

Conclusion

While none of the measures YMC implemented would be considered something advanced, this case illustrates the efforts YMC made to facilitate global internal communication under limited resources, and language and cultural barriers. However, this doesn't necessarily mean that the company is truly globalized. YMC's experience in Thailand shows that pressed with the urgency of turning around the operation, Japanese staff initially were unable to convey their knowledge and expertise to local staff. This is also a reflection of the fact that the Japanese language, unlike English, is not the universal business language. YMC learned that English is not functional when it comes to communicating with factory workers in non-English speaking countries. There is a lack of network connection with non-manager factory workers. As can be seen in the YMC's efforts in Thailand and CEO Yanagi's initiatives, YMC seems to have understood the value of employee engagement. However, the company didn't verbalize or quantify the concept. It was in February 2022 that the company officially defined employee engagement as one of the KPIs for its human resource strategy and stipulated the measurement of employee engagement in the medium-term business plan for 2022–2024 (Yamaha Motors Co., Ltd., 2022).

Of 10,000 employees in Japan, 3,000 have experience working at YMC's overseas locations. Currently, about 600 employees are stationed overseas (Yamashita, 2022). Under the Japanese culture of lifelong employee commitment, the abundance of Japanese in local operations and accumulated experience in the headquarters may result in the lack of a sense of urgency to foster local talent. President Yanagi saw the importance of implanting YMC's corporate culture in local staff and at the same time transforming Japanese staff into one that can understand local culture and work in tandem with local employees. As of 2021, YMC is aiming to increase local talent among the management of overseas subsidiaries to 60% (Yamaha Motors Co., Ltd., 2022). Despite their hard efforts, there is still a long way to go.

Learning Outcomes

1) Understand how lack of proficiency in English can affect intercultural communication in global companies
2) Realize how difficult it is for non-Anglo-American companies to expand its operations globally
3) Know how to convey and implant knowledge and expertise beyond language and cultural barriers

Discussion Questions

1) How would YMC construct its global internal communication if its mother language was English?
2) How would YMC construct its global internal communication if the host country was an English-speaking country?
3) Among language, national culture, and organizational culture, which one is the largest obstacle for YMC in communicating with its global workforce?

References

Allen, J., Jimmieson, N. L., Bordia, P., & Irmer, E. (2007). Uncertainty during organizational change: Managing perceptions through communication. *Journal of Change Management, 7,* 187–210.

Country comparison. Hofstede Insights. (n.d.) Retrieved May 24, 2022, from https://www.hofstede-.com/country-comparison/

Hirose, S. (2012, August). Frank exchange of opinions and review of thought process spirals up individual and the organization. *Kojo Kanri* [*Factory Management*], 58(8), 8–13.

Hofstede, G., Hofstede, G. J., & Minkov, M. (2010). *Cultures and organizations software of the mind; Intercultural Cooperation and its importance for survival.* New York, NY: McGraw-Hill.

Katsuta, H. (2012, August). Nihonjin wo fukumeta "Hito" no seicho nakushite genchika no seiko nashi [Without staff development including Japanese staff, there is no success in localization]. *Kojo Kanri* [*Factory Management*], 58(8), 70–77.

Kotter, J. P. (2011). Leading change: Why transformation efforts fail. In Harvard Business Review (Ed.), *HBS's 10 must reads on change management,* 1–16. Boston, MA: Harvard Business School Publishing.

Lewis, L. K. (2007). An organizational stakeholder model of change implementation communication. *Communication Theory, 17*(2), 176–204.

References

Men, L. R., Neill, M. S., Yue, C. A., & Verghese, A. K. (2022). The role of channel selection and communication transparency in enhancing employee commitment to change. *Journalism & Mass Communication Quarterly*. Advance online publication. https://doi.org/10.1177/10776990221100518

Ministry of Economy, Trade and Industry of Japan. (2014). *Trade White Paper 2014*. https://www.meti.go.jp/report/tsuhaku2014/2014honbun/index.html

Russ, T. L. (2008). Communicating change: A review and critical analysis of programmatic and participatory implementation approaches. *Journal of Chang Management, 8*(3–4), 199–211.

Shen, H. M., & Jiang, H. (2019). Engaged at work? An employee engagement model in public relations. *Journal of Public Relations Research, 31*(1–2), 32–49.

Sriramesh, K. (2020). Culture. In K. Sriramesh & D. Vercic (Eds.), *The global public relations handbook* (28–38). New York, NY: Routledge.

Tanaka, K. (2013). Organizational citizenship behavior in contemporary workplaces in Japan. *Japan Labor Review, 10*(3), 5–18.

Tananuraksakul, N. (2010). An exploration of English as the medium and the message in the "global village": A case study. *International Journal of Communication, 4*, 914–931.

Yamaha Motors Co., Ltd. (February 2012). President's message. *Shaho Yamaha* [*Yamaha News*], 3–4.

Yamaha Motors Co., Ltd. (2022). *Yamaha Motors global site*. Yamaha Motors: https://global.yamaha-motor.com/

Yanagi, H. (2018). Management is all about execution. *Diamond Harvard Business Review*, October 2018, 67–76.

Chapter Twenty-Two

Conclusion

Nance McCown, Linjuan Rita Men, Hua Jiang, and Hongmei Shen

Internal communication and employee engagement are, indeed, intertwined and complex. As such, case studies can be particularly helpful in exploring these areas because they employ a range of data sources and lenses to uncover nuances and subtleties within particular contexts (Baxter & Jack, 2008). We hope this edited scholarly volume of case studies, the first to examine these closely related, multifaceted topics in tandem, has served to provide readers with in-depth insights into real-world settings. Through the narratives and explications offered in these pages, our desire is that organizational leaders and professionals have discovered connections between theory and practice, direct applications in their particular work environments, and springboards to fresh ideas and new strategies for improved internal communication and increased employee engagement. Moreover, we hope educators and students, through their reading, thinking, and robust classroom discussions, have been prompted to new scholarly pursuits in these areas so crucial to organizational understanding and success around the globe.

Certainly, challenges in internal communication and employee engagement have plagued business leaders and managers throughout history, despite concerted efforts toward improvement in more recent years. The COVID-19 pandemic further stressed these difficulties, contributing in part to what Klotz termed "The Great Resignation" of millions from the workforce (Cohen, 2021) and to the employee-driven demand for more flexible and remote work opportunities as pandemic restrictions eased. As organizations continue to grapple with balancing requirements and processes with employee needs, the exigency for ongoing close examination of internal communication and employee engagement—along with establishing and updating best practices and exploring new strategies—will persist.

To that end, we propose a number of directions for future research, all with an eye toward better equipping organizations to create and maintain open, agile, and supportive workplaces where their employees can stay engaged, productive, and satisfied while contributing toward organizational success.

First, we propose research that continues to refine definitions and understandings of internal communication within organizational contexts. Men and Bowen's (2017) work

DOI: 10.4324/9781003195580-32

provides a comprehensive foundation, but global workforce changes and emerging technologies warrant further examination and expansion in this area. Given the broad array of existing organizational types, sizes, employee bases, and missions, continual honing of what constitutes effective internal communication is needed. In addition, scholars should continue to investigate pioneering tools (including but not limited to social media) and evolving technologies such as artificial intelligence and metaverse for internal communication and the application of emerging technologies in a variety of work environments.

Building on the crucial role effective internal communication plays in strengthening employee engagement, we also propose scholars continue refining understanding of strategies that foster employee engagement and exploring the role of employee engagement in organizations, communities, and nations. Shen and Jiang's (2019) proposed model offers an excellent catalyst for further exploration and extension of engagement theories into a wider variety of contexts and organizational settings.

Next, evolving work environments now include greater flexibility in hours, work locations, and hybrid combinations of in-person and remote work. Each of these contexts presents unique challenges in internal communication and employee engagement, thus calling for further research to test, enhance, and adjust existing theories and develop appropriate best practices. We expect a flurry of new scholarly activity to emerge even as organizations adjust to accommodate the move from pandemic to endemic status globally while recognizing employee desires and addressing obstacles to traditional, 9-to-5, in-person work environments.

In addition, societal trends, expectations, and realities demand further research linking internal communication and employee engagement with critical areas such as CSR/CSA and DE&I. As organizational leaders consider sustainable, philanthropic, ethical, and individual-respecting practices and organizations' enhanced roles in advancing social changes, they must have the foundational knowledge to develop appropriate, research-based initiatives and incentives to garner employee buy-in and support. We urge scholars specializing in many of these communication, social science, and public relations-related areas to extend their research into this realm.

In light of emerging global trends toward polarization, incivility, and increased litigation—coupled with instantaneous communication both external and internal to organizations, we also propose further investigation into the roles internal communication and employee engagement play in risk, issues, change, and crisis communication.

Fully engaged, in-the-loop employees have much to offer in precluding, mitigating, and addressing crisis and potential crisis situations, but only if equipped to do so. In today's increasingly VUCA business environment, research-based internal communication and engagement strategies will assist organizational leaders in both training employees and harnessing their full contributory potential in crisis prevention and resolution.

Finally, recalling again engagement's multifaceted nature and the numerous disciplines that influence and are influenced by it—communication, public relations, business, human resources, psychology, sociology, and more—we encourage greater cross-disciplinary collaboration in research. By leaving investigative silos behind and working together, the academic community can share diverse perspectives, discover important subtleties and nuances, and provide more detailed theories and specific case studies foundational to facilitating organizational leaders' strategic development and daily practices in internal communication and employee engagement. We look forward to a future where excellence in these two interdependent areas enables greater organizational success and on-board, fully engaged, and thriving employees.

References

Baxter, P., & Jack, S. (2008). Qualitative case study methodology: Study design and implementation for novice researchers. *The Qualitative Report, 13*, 544–559.

Cohen, A. (May 21, 2021.) How to quit your job in the great post-pandemic resignation boom. *Bloomberg Business Workplace.* https://www.bloomberg.com/news/articles/2021-05-10/quit-your-job-how-to-resign-after-covid-pandemic#xj4y7vzkg

Men, R. L., & Bowen, S. A. (2017). *Excellence in internal communication management.* New York, NY: Business Expert Press.

Shen, H., & Jiang, H. (2019). Engaged at work? An employee engagement model in public relations. *Journal of Public Relations Research, 31* (1–2), 32–49. https://doi.org/10.1080/1062726X.2019.1585855

Index

Note: Page references in *italics* denote figures and in **bold** tables.

Printed in the United States
by Baker & Taylor Publisher Services